Secret of
the Ages

ROBERT COLLIER

Table of Contents

"A fire-mist and a planet,
A crystal and a cell,
A jellyfish and a saurian,
A cave where the cave men dwell;
Then a sense of law and order,
A face upturned from the clod;
Some call it Evolution,
And others call it God."

—Reprinted from The New England Journal.

Foreword

If you had more money than time, more millions than you knew how to spend, what would be your pet philanthropy? Libraries? Hospitals? Churches? Homes for the Blind, Crippled or Aged? Mine would be "Homes"—but not for the aged or infirm. *For young married couples!*

I have often thought that, if ever I got into the "Philanthropic Billionaire" class, I'd like to start an Endowment Fund for helping young married couples over the rough spots in those first and second years of married life—especially the second year, when the real troubles come. Take a boy and a girl and a cozy little nest—add a cunning, healthy baby—and there's nothing happier on God's green footstool. But instead of a healthy babe, fill in a fretful, sickly baby—a wan, tired, worn-out little mother—a worried, dejected, heartsick father—and, there's nothing more pitiful.

A nurse for a month, a few weeks at the shore or mountains, a "lift" on that heavy doctor's bill—any one of these things would spell H-E-A-V-E-N to that tiny family. But do they get it? Not often! And the reason? Because they are not poor enough for charity. They are not rich enough to afford it themselves. They belong to that great "Middle Class" which has to bear the burdens of both the poor and the rich—and take what is left for itself.

It is to them that I should like to dedicate this book. If I cannot endow libraries or colleges for them, perhaps I can point the way to get all good gifts for them.

For men and women like them do not need "charity"—or even sympathy. What they do need is inspiration—and opportunity—the kind of inspiration that makes a man go out and create his own opportunity. And that, after all, is the greatest good one can do anyone. Few people appreciate free gifts. They are like the man whom admiring townsfolk presented with a watch. He looked it over critically for a minute. Then—"Where's the chain?" he asked.

But a way to win for themselves the full measure of success they've dreamed of but almost stopped hoping for—that is something every young couple would welcome with open arms. And it is something that, if I can do it justice, will make the "Eternal Triangle" as rare as it is today common, for it will enable husband and wife to work together—not merely for domestic happiness, but for business success as well.

ROBERT COLLIER.

VOLUME ONE

I

The World's Greatest Discovery

"You can do as much as you think you can,
But you'll never accomplish more;
If you're afraid of yourself, young man,
There's little for you in store.
For failure comes from the inside first,
It's there if we only knew it,
And you can win, though you face the worst,
If you feel that you're going to do it."

—EDGAR A. GUEST
(From "A Heap o' Livin'." The Reilly & Lee Co.)

What, in your opinion, is the most significant discovery of this modern age? The finding of dinosaur eggs on the plains of Mongolia, laid—so scientists assert—some 10,000,000 years ago? The unearthing of the Tomb of Tutankh-Amen, with its matchless specimens of a bygone civilization? The radioactive time clock by which Professor Lane of Tufts College estimates the age of the earth at 1,250,000,000 years? Wireless? The Aeroplane? Man-made thunderbolts?

No—not any of these. The really significant thing about them is that from all this vast research, from the study of all these bygone ages, men are for the first time beginning to get an understanding of that "Life Principle" which —somehow, some way—was brought to this earth thousands or millions of years ago. They are beginning to get an inkling of the infinite power it puts in their hands—to glimpse the untold possibilities it opens up.

This is the greatest discovery of modern times—that every man can call upon this "Life Principle" at will, that it is as much the servant of his mind as was ever Aladdin's fabled "genie-of-the-lamp" of old; that he has but to understand it and work in harmony with it to get from it anything he may need— health or happiness, riches or success. To realize the truth of this, you have but to go back for a moment to the beginning of things.

In the Beginning

It matters not whether you believe that mankind dates back to the primitive ape-man of 500,000 years ago, or sprang full-grown from the mind of the creator. In either event, there had to be a first cause—a creator. Some power had to bring to this earth the first germ of life, and the creation is no less wonderful if it started with the lowliest form of plant life and worked up through countless ages into the highest product of today's civilization, than if the whole were created in six days. In the beginning, this earth was just a fire mist—six thousand or a billion years ago—what does it matter which?

The one thing that does matter is that some time, some way, there came to this planet the germ of life—the life principle that animates all nature—plant, animal, and man. If we accept the scientists' version of it, the first form in which life appeared upon earth was the humble algae—a jelly-like mass that floated upon the waters. This, according to the scientists, was the beginning, the dawn of life upon the earth.

Next came the first bit of animal life—the lowly amoeba, a sort of jelly fish, consisting of a single cell, without vertebrae, and with very little else to distinguish it from the water round about. But it had *life*—the first bit of *animal* life—and from that life, according to the scientists, we could trace everything we have and are today. All the millions of forms and shapes and varieties of plants and animals that have since appeared are but different manifestations of *life*—formed to meet differing conditions. For millions of years this "Life Germ" was threatened by every kind of danger—from floods, from earthquakes, from droughts, from desert heat, from glacial cold, from volcanic eruptions—but to it each new danger was merely an incentive to finding a new resource, to putting forth Life in some new shape.

To meet one set of needs, it formed the dinosaur—to meet another, the butterfly. Long before it worked up to man, we see its unlimited resourcefulness shown in a thousand ways. To escape danger in the water, it sought land. Pursued on land, it took to the air. To breathe in the sea, it developed gills. Stranded on land, it perfected lungs. To meet one kind of danger it grew a shell; for another, a sting. To protect itself from glacial cold, it grew fur; in temperate climates, hair. Subject to alternate heat and cold, it produced feathers. But ever, from the beginning, it showed its power to meet every changing condition, to answer every creature need.

Had it been possible to kill this "Life Idea," it would have perished ages ago, when fire and flood, drought and famine followed each other in quick succession. But obstacles, misfortunes, cataclysms, were to it merely new opportunities to assert its power. In fact, it required obstacles to awaken it, to show its energy and resource.

The great reptiles, the monster beasts of antiquity passed on. But the "Life Principle" stayed, changing as each age changed, always developing, and always improving.

Whatever power it was that brought this "Life Idea" to the earth, it came endowed with unlimited resources, unlimited energy, unlimited LIFE! No other force can defeat it. No obstacle can hold it back. All through the history of life and mankind you can see its directing intelligence—call it nature, call it providence, call it what you will—rising to meet every need of life.

The Purpose of Existence

 No one can follow it down through the ages without realizing that the whole purpose of existence is GROWTH. Life is dynamic—not static. It is ever moving forward—not standing still. The one unpardonable sin of nature is to stand still, to stagnate. The Giganotosaurus, that was over a hundred feet long and as big as a house; the Tyrannosaurus, that had the strength of a locomotive and was the last word in frightfulness; the Pterodactyl or Flying Dragon—all the giant monsters of Prehistoric Ages—are gone. They ceased to serve a useful purpose. They did not know how to meet the changing conditions. They stood still—stagnated—while the life around them passed them by.

Egypt and Persia, Greece and Rome, all the great Empires of antiquity, perished when they ceased to grow. China built a wall about her and stood still for a thousand years. Today she is the football of the powers. In all nature, to cease to grow is to perish.

It is for men and women who are not ready to stand still, who refuse to cease to grow, that this book is written. It will give you a clearer understanding of your own potentialities, show you how to work with and take advantage of the infinite energy all about you.

The terror of the man at the crossways, not knowing which road to take, will be no terror to you. Your future is of your own making. For the only law of infinite energy is the law of supply. The "Life Principle" is your principle. To survive, to win through, and to triumphantly surmount all obstacles has been its everyday practice since the beginning of time. It is no less resourceful now than ever it was. You have but to supply the urge, to work in harmony with it, to get from it anything you may need.

For if this "Life Principle" is so strong in the lowest forms of animal life that it can develop a shell or a poison to meet a need; if it can teach the bird to circle and dart, to balance and fly; if it can grow a new limb on a spider to replace a lost one, how much more can it do for you—a reasoning, rational being, with a mind able to work with this "Life Principle," with an energy and an initiative to urge it on!

The evidence of this is all about you. Take up some violent form of exercise— rowing, tennis, and swimming, riding. In the beginning your muscles are weak, easily tired. But keep on for a few days. The "Life Principle" promptly strengthens them, toughens them, to meet their new need. Do rough manual labor—and what happens? The skin of your hands becomes tender, blisters, and hurts. Keep it up, and does the skin all wear off? On the contrary, the "Life Principle" provides extra thicknesses, extra toughness—calluses, we call them—to meet your need.

All through your daily life you will find this "Life Principle" steadily at work. Embrace it, work with it, take it to yourself, and there is nothing you cannot do. The mere fact that you have obstacles to overcome is in your favor, for when there is nothing to be done, when things run along too smoothly, this "Life Principle" seems to sleep. It is when you need it, when you call upon it urgently, that it is most on the job.

It differs from "Luck" in this, that fortune is a fickle jade that smiles most often on those who need her least. Stake your last penny on the turn of a card—have nothing between you and ruin but the spin of a wheel or the speed of a horse—and its a thousand to one "Luck" will desert you! But it is just the opposite with the "Life Principle." As long as things run smoothly, as long as life flows along like a song, this "Life Principle" seems to slumber, secure in the knowledge that your affairs can take care of themselves.

But let things start going wrong, let ruin and disgrace stare you in the face—*then* is the time this "Life Principle" will assert itself if you but give it a chance.

The "Open, Sesame!" of Life

There is a Napoleonic feeling of power *that insures success* in the knowledge that this invincible "Life Principle" is behind your every act. Knowing that you have working with you a force, which never yet has failed in anything it has undertaken, you can go ahead in the confident knowledge that it will not fail in your case, either. The ingenuity, which overcame every obstacle in making you what you are, is not likely to fall short when you have immediate need for it. It is the reserve strength of the athlete, the "second wind" of the runner, the power that, in moments of great stress or excitement, you unconsciously call upon to do the deeds which you ever after look upon as superhuman.

But they are in no wise superhuman. They are merely beyond the capacity of your conscious self. Ally your conscious self with that sleeping giant within you, rouse him daily to the task, and those "superhuman" deeds will become your ordinary, everyday accomplishments.

W. L. Cain, of Oakland, Oregon, writes: "I know that there is such a power, for I once saw two boys, 16 and 18 years of age, lift a great log off their brother, who had been caught under it. The next day, the same two boys, with another man and me, tried to lift the end of the log, but could not even budge it."

How was it that the two boys could do at need what the four were unable to do later on, when the need had passed? Because they never stopped to question whether or not it *could* be done. They saw only the urgent need. They concentrated all their thought, all their energy on that one thing—never doubting, never fearing—and the genie which is in all of us waiting only for such a call, answered their summons and gave them the strength—not of two men, but of ten!

It matters not whether you are banker or lawyer, businessman or clerk. Whether you are the custodian of millions, or have to struggle for your daily bread. This "Life Principle" makes no distinction between rich and poor, high and low. The greater your need, the more readily will it respond to your call. Wherever there is an unusual task, wherever there is poverty or hardship or sickness or despair, there is this servant of your mind, ready and willing to help, asking only that you call upon him.

And not only is it ready and willing, but it is always ABLE to help. Its ingenuity and resource are without limit. It is Mind. It is thought. It is the Telepathy that carries messages without the spoken or written word. It is the Sixth Sense that warns you of unseen dangers. No matter how stupendous and complicated, nor how simple your problem may be—the solution of it is somewhere in Mind, in Thought. And since the solution does exist, this Mental Giant can find it for you. It can KNOW, and it can DO, every right thing. Whatever it is necessary for you to know, whatever it is necessary for you to do, you can know and you can do if you will but seek the help of this genie-of-your-mind and work with it in the right way.

II
The Genie-of-Your-Mind

"It matters not how strait the gate,
How charged with punishment the scroll,
I am the Master of my Fate;
I am the Captain of my Soul."

—HENLEY.

First came the Stone Age, when life was for the strong of arm or the fleet of foot. Then there was the Iron Age—and while life was more precious, still the strong lorded it over the weak. Later came the Golden Age, and riches took the place of strength—but the poor found little choice between the slave drivers' whips of olden days and the grim weapons of poverty and starvation.

Now we are entering a new age—the Mental Age—when every man can be his own master, when poverty and circumstance no longer hold power and the lowliest creature in the land can win a place side by side with the highest.

To those who do not know the resources of mind these will sound like rash statements; but science proves beyond question that in the wellsprings of every man's mind are unplumbed depths—undiscovered deposits of energy, wisdom and ability. Sound these depths—bring these treasures to the surface—and you gain an astounding wealth of new power.

From the rude catamaran of the savages to the giant liners of today, carrying their thousands from continent to continent is but a step in the development of Mind. From the lowly cave man, cowering in his burrow in fear of lightning or fire or water, to the engineer of today, making servants of all the forces of Nature, is but a measure of difference in mental development.

Man, without reasoning mind, would be as the monkeys are—prey of any creature fast enough and strong enough to pull him to pieces, at the mercy of wind and weather; a poor timid creature, living for the moment only, fearful of every shadow.

Through his superior mind, he learned to make fire to keep himself warm; weapons with which to defend himself from the savage creatures round about; habitations to protect himself from the elements. Through mind he conquered the forces of Nature. Through mind he has made machinery do the work of millions of horses and billions of hands. What he will do next, no man knows, for man is just beginning to awaken to his own powers. He is just getting an inkling of the unfathomed riches buried deep in his own mind. Like the gold seekers of '49, he has panned the surface gravel for the gold swept down by the streams. Now he is starting to dig deeper to the pure vein beneath.

We bemoan the loss of our forests. We worry over our dwindling resources of coal and oil. We decry the waste in our factories. But the greatest waste of all, we pay no attention to—the waste of our own potential mind power. Professor Wm. James, the world-famous Harvard psychologist, estimated that the average man uses only 10% of his mental power. He has unlimited power—yet he uses but a tithe of it. Unlimited wealth all about him—and he doesn't know how to take hold of it. With God-like powers slumbering within him, he is content to continue in his daily grind —eating, sleeping, working—plodding through an existence little more eventful than the animals, while all of Nature, all of life, calls upon him to awaken, to bestir himself.

The power to be what you want to be, to get what you desire, to accomplish whatever you are striving for, abides within you. It rests with you only to bring it forth and put it to work. Of course you must know *how* to do that, but before you can learn how to use it, you must *realize* that you *possess* this power. So our first objective is to get acquainted with this power.

For Psychologists and Metaphysicians the world over, are agreed in this—that Mind is all that counts. You can be whatever you make up your mind to be. You need not be sick. You need not be unhappy. You need not be poor. You need not be unsuccessful. You are not a mere clod. You are not a beast of burden, doomed to spend your days in unremitting labor in return for food and housing. You are one of the Lords of the Earth, with unlimited potentialities. Within you is a power, which, properly grasped and directed, can lift you out of the rut of mediocrity and place you among the Elect of the earth—the lawyers, the writers, the statesmen, the big business men—the DOERS and the THINKERS. It rests with you only to learn to use this power, which is yours—this Mind that can do all things.

Your body is for all practical purposes merely a machine, which the mind uses. This mind is usually thought of as consciousness; but the *conscious part* of your mind is in fact the *very smallest part of it*. Ninety per cent of your mental life is subconscious, so when you make active use of only the conscious part of your mind you are using but a fraction of your real ability; you are running on low gear. And the reason why more people do not achieve success in life is because so many of them are content to run on low gear all their lives—on SURFACE ENERGY. If these same people would only throw into the fight the resistless force of their subconscious minds they would be amazed at their undreamed of capacity for winning success.

Conscious and subconscious are, of course, integral parts of the one mind. But for convenience sake let us divide your mind into three parts—the conscious mind, the subconscious mind, and the Infinite, Subliminal or Universal Mind.

The Conscious Mind

When you say, "I see—I hear—I smell—I touch," it is your conscious mind that is saying this, for it is the force governing the five physical senses. It is the phase of mind with which you feel and reason—the phase of mind with which everyone is familiar. It is the mind with which you do business. It controls, to a great extent, all your voluntary muscles. It discriminates between right and wrong, wise and foolish. It is the generalissimo, in charge of all your mental forces. It can plan ahead—and get things done as it plans. Or it can drift along haphazardly, a creature of impulse, at the mercy of events—a mere bit of flotsam in the current of life.

For it is only through your conscious mind that you can reach the subconscious and the Universal Mind. Your conscious mind is the porter at the door, the watchman at the gate. It is to the conscious mind that the subconscious looks for all its impressions. It is on it that the subconscious mind must depend for the teamwork necessary to get successful results. You wouldn't expect much from an army, no matter how fine its soldiers, whose general never planned ahead, who distrusted his own ability and that of his men, and who spent all his time worrying about the enemy instead of planning how he might conquer them. You wouldn't look for good scores from a ball team whose pitcher was at odds with the catcher. In the same way, you can't expect results from the subconscious when your conscious mind is full of fear or worry, or when it does not know what it wants.

The one most important province of your conscious mind is to center your thoughts on the thing you want, and to shut the door on every suggestion of fear or worry or disease.

If you once gain the ability to do that, nothing else is impossible to you.

For the subconscious mind does not reason inductively. It takes the thoughts you send in to it and works them out to their logical conclusion. Send to it thoughts of health and strength, and it will work out health and strength in your body. Let suggestions of disease, fear of sickness or accident penetrate to it, either through your own thoughts or the talk of those around you, and you are very likely to see the manifestation of disease working out in yourself.

Your mind is master of your body. It directs and controls every function of your body. Your body is in effect a little universe in itself, and mind is its radiating center—the sun that gives light and life to all your system, and around which the whole revolves. And your *conscious thought* is master of this sun center. As Emile Coué puts it —"The conscious can put the subconscious mind over the hurdles."

The Subconscious Mind

Can you tell me how much water, how much salt, how much of each different element there should be in your blood to maintain its proper specific gravity if you are leading an ordinary sedentary life? How much and how quickly these proportions must be changed if you play a fast game of tennis, or run for your car, or chop wood, or indulge in any other violent exercise? Do you know how much water you should drink to neutralize the excess salt in salt fish? How much you lose through perspiration? Do you know how much water, how much salt, how much of each different element in your food should be absorbed into your blood each day to maintain perfect health?

13

No? Well, it need not worry you. Neither does any one else. Not even the greatest physicists and chemists and mathematicians. But your subconscious mind knows.

And it doesn't have to stop to figure it out. It does it almost automatically. It is one of those "Lightning Calculators." And this is but one of thousands of such jobs it performs every hour of the day. The greatest mathematicians in the land, the most renowned chemists, could never do in a year's time the abstruse problems which your subconscious mind solves every minute.

And it doesn't matter whether you've ever studied mathematics or chemistry or any other of the sciences. From the moment of your birth your subconscious mind solves all these problems for you. While you are struggling along with the three R's, it is doing problems that would leave your teachers aghast. It supervises all the intricate processes of digestion, of assimilation, of elimination, and all the glandular secretions that would tax the knowledge of all the chemists and all the laboratories in the land. It planned and built your body from infancy on up. It repairs it. It operates it. It has almost unlimited power, not merely for putting you and keeping you in perfect health but for acquiring all the good things of life. Ignorance of this power is the sole reason for all the failures in this world. If you would intelligently turn over to this wonderful power all your business and personal affairs in the same way that you turn over to it the mechanism of your body, no goal would be too great for you to strive for.

Dr. Geo. C. Pitzer sums up the power of the subconscious mind very well in the following:

"The subconscious mind is a distinct entity. It occupies the whole human body, and, when not opposed in any way, it has absolute control over all the functions, conditions, and sensations of the body. While the objective (conscious) mind has control over all of our voluntary functions and motions, the subconscious mind controls all of the silent, involuntary, and vegetative functions. Nutrition, waste, all secretions and excretions, the action of the heart in the circulation of the blood, the lungs in respiration or breathing, and all cell life, cell changes and development, are positively under the complete control of the subconscious mind. This was the only mind animal had before the evolution of the brain; and it could not, nor can it yet, reason inductively, but its power of deductive reasoning is perfect. And more, it can see without the use of physical eyes. It perceives by intuition. It has the power to communicate with others without the aid of ordinary physical means. It can read the thoughts of others. It receives intelligence and transmits it to people at a distance. Distance offers no resistance against the successful missions of the subconscious mind. It never dies. We call this the 'soul mind.' It is the living soul."

In "*Practical Psychology and Sex Life*," by David Bush, Dr. Winbigler is quoted as going even further. To quote him:

"It is this mind that carries on the work of assimilation and upbuilding whilst we sleep . . .

It reveals to us things that the conscious mind has no conception of until the consummations have occurred.

It can communicate with other minds without the ordinary physical means.

It gets glimpses of things that ordinary sight does not behold.

It makes God's presence an actual, realizable fact, and keeps the personality in peace and quietness.

It warns of approaching danger.

It approves or disapproves of a course of conduct and conversation.

It carries out all the best things, which are given to it, providing the conscious mind does not intercept and change the course of its manifestation.

It heals the body and keeps it in health, if it is at all encouraged."

It is, in short, the most powerful force in life, and when properly directed, the most beneficent. But, like a live electric wire, its destructive force is equally great. It can be either your servant or your master. It can bring to you evil or good.

The Rev. William T. Walsh, in a new book just published, explains the idea very clearly:

"The subconscious part in us is called the subjective mind, because it does not decide and command. It is a subject rather than a ruler. Its nature is to do what it is told, *or what really in your heart of hearts you desire.*

"The subconscious mind directs all the vital processes of your body. You do not think consciously about breathing. Every time you take a breath you do not have to reason, decide, command. The subconscious mind sees to that. You have not been at all conscious that you have been breathing while you have been reading this page. So it is with the mind and the circulation of blood. The heart is a muscle like the muscle of your arm. It has no power to move itself or to direct its action. Only mind, only something that can think, can direct our muscles, including the heart. You are not conscious that you are commanding your heart to beat. The subconscious mind attends to that. And so it is with the assimilation of food, the building and repairing of the body. In fact, all the vital processes are looked after by the subconscious mind."

"Man lives and moves and has his being" in this great subconscious mind. It supplies the "intuition" that so often carries a woman straight to a point that may require hours of cumbersome reasoning for a man to reach. Even in ordinary, every-day affairs, you often draw upon its wonderful wisdom.

But you do it in an accidental sort of way without realizing what you are doing.

Consider the case of "Blind Tom." Probably you've heard or read of him. You know that he could listen to a piece of music for the first time and go immediately to a piano and reproduce it. People call that abnormal. But as a matter of fact he was in this respect more normal than any of us. We are abnormal because we cannot do it.

Or consider the case of these "lightning calculators" of whom one reads now and then. It may be a boy seven or eight years old; but you can ask him to divide 7,649.437 by 326.2568 and he'll give you the result in less time than it would take you to put the numbers down on a piece of paper. You call him phenomenal. Yet you ought to be able to do the same yourself. Your subconscious mind can.

Dr. Hudson, in his book "*The Law of Psychic Phenomena,*" tells of numerous such prodigies. Here are just a few instances:

"Of mathematical prodigies there has been upwards of a score whose calculations have surpassed, in rapidity and accuracy, those of the greatest educated mathematicians. These prodigies have done their greatest feats while but children from three to ten years old. In no case had these boys any idea how they performed their calculations, and some of them would converse upon other subjects while doing the sum. Two of these boys became men of eminence, while some of them showed but a low degree of objective intelligence."

Whateley spoke of his own gift in the following terms:

"There was certainly something peculiar in my calculating faculty. It began to show itself at between five and six, and lasted about three years. I soon got to do the most difficult sums, always in my head, for I knew nothing of figures beyond numeration. I did these sums much quicker than anyone could upon paper, and I never remember committing the smallest error. When I went to school, at which time the passion wore off, I was a perfect dunce at ciphering, and have continued so ever since."

"Professor Safford became an astronomer. At the age of ten he worked correctly a multiplication sum whose answer consisted of thirty-six figures. Later in life he could perform no such feats."

"Benjamin Hall Blyth, at the age of six, asked his father at what hour he was born. He was told that he was born at four o'clock. Looking at the clock to see the present time, he informed his father of the number of seconds he had lived. His father made the calculation and said to Benjamin, 'You are wrong; 172,000 seconds.' The boy answered, 'Oh, papa, you have left out two days for the leap years 1820 and 1824,' which was the case."

"Then there is the celebrated case of Zerah Colburn, of whom Dr. Schofield writes:

"'Zerah Colburn could instantaneously tell the square root of 106,929 as 327, and the cube root of 268,336,125 as 645. Before the question of the number of minutes in forty-eight years could be written he said 25,228,810. He immediately gave the factors of 247,483 as 941 and 263, which are the only two; and being asked then for those of 36,083, answered none; it is a prime number. He could not tell how the answer came into his mind. He could not, on paper, do simple multiplication or division.'"

The time will come when, as H. G. Wells envisioned in his "*Men Like Gods*," schools and teachers will no longer be necessary except to show us how to get in touch with the infinite knowledge our subconscious minds possess from infancy.

"The smartest man in the world," says Dr. Frank Crane in a recent article in *Liberty* "is the Man Inside. By the Man Inside I mean that Other Man within each one of us that does most of the things we give ourselves credit for doing. You may refer to him as Nature or the Subconscious Self or think of him merely as a Force or a Natural Law, or, if you are religiously inclined, you may use the term God.

"I say he is the smartest man in the world. I know he is infinitely more clever and resourceful than I am or than any other man is that I ever heard of. When I cut my finger it is he that calls up the little phagocytes to come and kill the septic germs that might get into the wound and cause blood poisoning. It is he that coagulates the blood, stops the gash, and weaves the new skin.

"I could not do that. I do not even know how he does it. He even does it for babies that know nothing at all; in fact, does it better for them than for me.

"No living man knows enough to make toenails grow, but the Man Inside thinks nothing of growing nails and teeth and thousands of hairs all over my body; long hairs on my head and little fuzzy ones over the rest of the surface of the skin.

"When I practice on the piano I am simply getting the business of piano playing over from my conscious mind to my subconscious mind: in other words, I am handing the business over to the Man Inside.

"Most of our happiness, as well as our struggles and misery, come from this Man Inside. If we train him in ways of contentment, adjustment, and decision he will go ahead of us like a well trained servant and do for us easily most of the difficult tasks we have to perform."

Dr. Jung, celebrated Viennese specialist, claims that the subconscious mind contains not only all the knowledge that it has gathered during the life of the individual, but that in addition it contains all the wisdom of past ages. That by drawing upon its wisdom and power the individual may possess any good thing of life, from health and happiness to riches and success.

You see, the subconscious mind is the connecting link between the Creator and us, between Universal Mind and our conscious mind. It is the means by which we can appropriate to ourselves all the good gifts, all the riches and abundance that Universal Mind has created in such profusion.

Berthelot, the great French founder of modern synthetic chemistry, once stated in a letter to a close friend that the final experiments which led to his most wonderful discoveries had never been the result of carefully followed and reasoned trains of thought, but that, on the contrary, "they came of themselves, so to speak, from the clear sky."

Charles M. Barrows, in "*Suggestion Instead of Medicine*," tells us that:

"If man requires another than his ordinary consciousness to take care of him while asleep, not less useful is this same psychical provision when he is awake. Many persons are able to obtain knowledge, which does not come to them through their senses in the usual way, but arrives in the mind by direct communication from another conscious intelligence, which apparently knows more of what concerns their welfare than their ordinary reason does. I have known a number of persons who, like myself, could tell the contents of letters in their mail before opening them. Several years ago a friend of mine came to Boston for the first time, arriving at what was then the Providence railroad station in Park Square. He wished to walk to the Lowell station on the opposite side of the city. Being utterly ignorant of the streets as well as the general direction to take, he confidently set forth without asking the way, and reached his destination by the most direct path. In doing this he trusted solely to 'instinctive guidance,' as he called it, and not to any hints or clews obtained through the senses."

The geniuses of literature, of art, commerce, government, politics and invention are, according to the scientists, but ordinary men like you and me who have learned somehow, some way, to draw upon their subconscious minds.

Sir Isaac Newton is reported to have acquired his marvelous knowledge of mathematics and physics with no conscious effort. Mozart said of his beautiful symphonies "they just came to him." Descartes had no ordinary regular education.

To quote Dr. Hudson:

"This is a power which transcends reason, and is independent of induction. Instances of its development might be multiplied indefinitely. Enough is known to warrant the conclusion that when the soul is released from its objective environment it will be enabled to perceive all the laws of its being, to 'see God as He is,' by the perception of the laws which He has instituted. It is the knowledge of this power which demonstrates our true relationship to God and confirms our inheritance of our rightful share of his attributes and powers…"

Our subconscious minds are vast magnets, with the power to draw from Universal Mind unlimited knowledge, unlimited power, unlimited riches.

"Considered from the standpoint of its activities," says Warren Hilton in "*Applied Psychology*," "the subconscious is that department of mind, which on the one hand directs the vital operations of the body, and on the other conserves, subject to the call of interest and attention, all ideas and complexes not at the moment active in consciousness.

"Observe, then, the possibility that lies before you. On the one hand, if you can control your mind in its subconscious activities, you can regulate the operation of your bodily functions, and can thus assure yourself of bodily efficiency and free yourself of functional disease. On the other hand, if you can determine just what ideas shall be brought forth from subconsciousness into consciousness, you can thus select the materials out of which will be woven your conscious judgments, your decisions and your emotional attitudes.

"To achieve control of your mind is, then, to attain (a) health, (b) success, and (c) happiness."

Few understand or appreciate, however, that the vast storehouse of knowledge and power of the subconscious mind can be drawn upon at will. Now and then through intense concentration or very active desire we do accidentally penetrate to the realm of the subconscious and register our thought upon it. Such thoughts are almost invariably realized. The trouble is that as often as not it is our negative thoughts—our fears—that penetrate. And these are realized just as surely as the positive thoughts.

What you must manage to do is learn to communicate only such thoughts as you wish to see realized to your subconscious mind, for it is exceedingly amenable to suggestion. You have heard of the man who was always bragging of his fine health and upon whom some of his friends decided to play a trick. The first one he met one morning commented upon how badly he looked and asked if he weren't feeling well. Then all the others as they saw him made similar remarks. By noontime the man had come to believe them, and before the end of the day he was really ill.

That was a rather glaring example. But similar things are going on every day with all of us. We eat something that someone else tells us isn't good for us and in a little while we think we feel a pain. Before we know it we have indigestion, when the chances are that if we knew nothing about the supposed indigestible properties of the food we could eat it the rest of our days and never feel any ill effects.

Let some new disease be discovered and the symptoms described in the daily paper. Hundreds will come down with it at once. They are like the man who read a medical encyclopedia and ended up by concluding he had everything but "housemaid's knee." Patent medicine advertisers realize this power of suggestion and cash in upon it. Read one of their ads. If you don't think you have everything the matter with you that their nostrums are supposed to cure, you are the exception and not the rule.

That is the negative side of it. Emile Coué based his system on the positive side—which you suggest to your subconscious mind that whatever ills it thinks you have are getting better. And it is good psychology at that. Properly carried out it will work wonders. But there arc better methods. And I hope to be able to show them to you before we reach the end of this book.

Suffice it now to say that your subconscious mind is exceedingly wise and powerful; that it knows many things that are not in books. When properly used it has infallible judgment, unfailing power. It never sleeps and it never tires.

Your conscious mind may slumber. It may be rendered impotent by anesthetics or a sudden blow. But your

subconscious mind works on, keeping your heart and lungs, your arteries and glands ever on the job.
Under ordinary conditions, it attends faithfully to its duties, and leaves your conscious mind to direct the outer life of the body. But let the conscious mind meet some situation with which it is unable to cope, and, if it will only call upon the subconscious, that powerful Genie will respond immediately to its need.

You have heard of people who had been through great danger tell how, when death stared them in the face and there seemed nothing they could do, things went black before them and, when they came to, the danger was past. In the moment of need, their subconscious mind pushed the conscious out of the way, the while it met and overcame the danger. Impelled by the subconscious mind, their bodies could do things absolutely impossible to their ordinary conscious selves.

For the power of the subconscious mind is unlimited. Whatever it is necessary for you to do in any right cause, it can give you the strength and the ability to do.

Whatever of good you may desire, it can bring to you. "The Kingdom of Heaven is within you."

The Universal Mind

Have you ever dug up a potato vine and seen the potatoes clustering underneath? How much of intelligence do you suppose one of these potatoes has? Do you think it knows anything about chemistry or geology? Can it figure out how to gather carbon gas from the atmosphere, water and all the necessary kinds of nutriment from the earth round about to manufacture into sugar and starch and alcohol? No chemist can do it. How do you suppose the potato knows? Of course it doesn't. It has no sense. Yet it does all these things. It builds the starch into cells, the cells into roots and vines and leaves—and into more potatoes.

"Just old Mother Nature," you'll say. But old Mother Nature must have a remarkable intelligence if she can figure out all these things that no human scientist has ever been able to figure. There must be an all-pervading Intelligence behind Mother Nature—the Intelligence that first brought life to this planet—the Intelligence that evolved every form of plant and animal—that holds the winds in its grasp—that is all-wise, all-powerful. The potato is but one small manifestation of this Intelligence. The various forms of plant life, of animals, of man—all are mere cogs in the great scheme of things.

But with this *difference*—that man is an active part of this Universal Mind. That he partakes of its creative wisdom and power and that by working in harmony with Universal Mind he can *do* anything *have* anything, *be* anything.

There is within you—within everyone—this mighty resistless force with which you can perform undertakings that will dazzle your reason, stagger your imagination. There constantly resides within you a Mind that is all-wise, all-powerful; a Mind that is entirely apart from the mind which you consciously use in your everyday affairs yet which is one with it.

Your subconscious mind partakes of this wisdom and power, and it is through your subconscious mind that you can draw upon it in the attainment of anything you may desire. When you can intelligently reach your subconscious mind, you can be in communication with the Universal Mind.

Remember this: the Universal Mind is omnipotent. And since the subconscious mind is part of the Universal Mind, there is no limit to the things which it can do when it is given the power to act. Given any desire that is in harmony with the Universal Mind and you have but to hold that desire in your thought to attract from the invisible domain the things you need to satisfy it.

For mind does its building solely by the power of thought. Its creations take form according to its thought. Its first requisite is a mental image, and your desire held with unswerving purpose will form that mental image.

An understanding of this principle explains the power of prayer. The results of prayer are not brought about by some special dispensation of Providence. God is not a finite being to be cajoled or flattered into doing as you desire. But when you pray earnestly you form a mental image of the thing that you desire and you hold it strongly in your thought. Then the Universal Intelligence, which is your intelligence—Omnipotent Mind—begins to work with and for you, and this is what brings about the manifestation that you desire.

The Universal Mind is all around you. It is as all pervading as the air you breathe. It encompasses you with as little trouble as the water in the sea encompasses the fish. Yet it is just as thoroughly conscious of you as the water would be, were it intelligent, of every creature within it.

It seems hard to believe that a Mind busied with the immensities of the universe can consider such trivial affairs as our own when we are but one of the billions of forms of life which come into existence. Yet consider again the fish in the sea. It is no trouble for the sea to encompass them. It is no more trouble for the Universal Mind to encompass us. Its power, its thought, is as much at our disposal as the sunshine and the wind and the rain. Few of us take advantage to the full of these great forces. Fewer still take advantage of the power of the Universal Mind. If you have any lack, if you are prey to poverty or disease, it is because you do not believe or do not understand the power that is yours. It is not a question of the Universal giving to you. It offers everything to everyone— there is no partiality. You have only to take.

"With all thy getting, get understanding," said Solomon. And if you will but get understanding, everything else will be added unto you.

To bring you to a realization of your indwelling and unused power, to teach you simple, direct methods of drawing upon it, is the beginning and the end of this course.

VOLUME TWO

III
The Primal Cause

This city, with all its houses, palaces, steam engines, cathedrals and huge, immeasurable traffic and tumult, what is it but millions of Thoughts made into one—a huge immeasurable Spirit of a Thought, embodied in brick, in iron, smoke, dust, Palaces, Parliaments, coaches, docks and the rest of it! Not a brick was made but some man had to think of the making of that brick.

-CARLYLE.

For thousands of years the riddle of the universe has been the question of causation. Did the egg come first, or the chicken? "The globe," says an Eastern proverb, "rests upon the howdah of an elephant. The elephant stands upon a tortoise, swimming in a sea of milk." But then what?

And what is life? As the Persian poet puts it—

"What without asking, hither hurried whence,
And without asking whither hurried hence?"

It has been said that every man, consciously or unconsciously, is either a materialist or an idealist. Certainly throughout the ages the schools of philosophy as well as individuals have argued and quarreled, but always, human thought through one or the other of these channels "has rolled down the hill of speculation into the ocean of doubt."

The materialist, roughly speaking, declares that nothing exists but matter and the forces inherent therein.

The idealist declares that all is mind or energy, and that matter is necessarily unreal.

The time has come when people have become dissatisfied with these unceasing theories, which get them nowhere. And today, as the appreciation of a Primal Cause becomes more clearly defined, the spiritual instinct asserts itself determinedly.

"Give me a base of support," said Archimedes, "and with a lever I will move the world."

And the base of support is that all started with *mind.* In the beginning was nothing—a fire mist. Before anything could come of it there had to be an idea, a model on which to build. *Universal Mind* supplied that idea, that

21

model. Therefore the primal cause is mind. Everything must start with an idea. Every event, every condition, every thing is first an idea in the mind of someone.

Before you start to build a house, you draw up a plan of it. You make an exact blueprint of that plan, and your house takes shape in accordance with your blueprint. Every material object takes form in the same way. Mind draws the plan. Thought forms the blueprint, well drawn or badly done, as your thoughts are clear or vague. It all goes back to the one cause. The creative principle of the universe is mind, and thought is the eternal energy.

But just as the effect you get from electricity depends upon the mechanism to which the power is attached, so the effects you get from mind depend upon the way you use it. We are all of us dynamos. The power is there— unlimited power. But we've got to connect it up to something—set it some task— give it work to do—else are we no better off than the animals.

The "Seven Wonders of the World" was built by men with few of the opportunities or facilities that are available to you. They conceived these gigantic projects first in their own minds, pictured them so vividly that their subconscious minds came to their aid and enabled them to overcome obstacles that most of us would regard as insurmountable. Imagine building the Pyramids of Gizeh, enormous stone upon enormous stone, with nothing but bare hands. Imagine the labor, the sweat, the heartbreaking toil of erecting the Colossus of Rhodes, between whose legs a ship could pass! Yet men built these wonders, in a day when tools were of the crudest and machinery was undreamed of, by using the unlimited power of Mind.

Mind is creative, but it must have a model on which to work. It must have thoughts to supply the power.

There are in Universal Mind ideas for millions of wonders far greater than the "Seven Wonders of the World." And those ideas are just as available to you as they were to the artisans of old, as they were to Michael Angelo when he built St. Peter's in Rome, as they were to the architect who conceived the Woolworth Building, or the engineer who planned the Hell Gate Bridge.

Every condition, every experience of life is the result of our mental attitude. We can *do* only what we think we can do. We can *be* only what we think we can be. We can *have* only what we think we can have. What we do, what we are, what we have, all depend upon what we think. We can never express anything that we do not first have in mind. The secret of all power, all success, all riches, is in first thinking powerful thoughts, successful thoughts, and thoughts of wealth, of supply. We must build them in our own mind first.

William James, the famous psychologist, said that the greatest discovery in a hundred years was the discovery of the power of the subconscious mind. It is the greatest discovery of all time. It is the discovery that man has within himself the power to control his surroundings; that he is not at the mercy of chance or luck; that he is the arbiter of his own fortunes; that he can carve out his own destiny. He is the master of all the forces round about him. As James Allen puts it:

"Dream lofty dreams, and as you dream, so shall you become. Your vision is the promise of what you shall one day be; your Ideal is the prophecy of what you shall at last unveil."

For matter is in the ultimate but a product of thought. Even the most material scientists admit that matter is not what it appears to be. According to physics, matter (be it the human body or a log of wood—it makes no difference which) is made up of an aggregation of distinct minute particles called atoms. Considered individually, these atoms are so small that they can be seen only with the aid of a powerful microscope, if at all.

MATTER — Dream or Reality?

Until recently these atoms were supposed to be the ultimate theory regarding matter. We ourselves—and all the material world around us—were supposed to consist of these infinitesimal particles of matter, so small that they could not be seen or weighed or smelled or touched individually—but still particles of matter *and indestructible.*

Now, however, these atoms have been further analyzed, and physics tells us that they are not indestructible at all —that they are mere positive and negative buttons of force or energy called protons and electrons, without hardness, without density, without solidity, without even positive actuality. In short, they are vortices in the ether —whirling bits of energy—dynamic, never static, pulsating with life, but the life is *spiritual!* As one eminent British scientist put it—"Science now explains matter by *explaining it away!"*

And that, mind you, is what the solid table in front of you is made of, is what your house, your body, the whole world is made of—*whirling bits of energy!*

To quote the New York *Herald-Tribune* of March 11, 1926: "We used to believe that the universe was composed of an unknown number of different kinds of matter, one kind for each chemical element. The discovery of a new element had all the interest of the unexpected. It might turn out to be anything, to have any imaginable set of properties.

"That romantic prospect no longer exists. We know now that instead of many ultimate kinds of matter there are only two kinds. Both of these are really kinds of electricity. One is negative electricity, being, in fact, the tiny particle called the electron, familiar to radio fans as one of the particles vast swarms of which operate radio vacuum tubes. The other kind of electricity is positive electricity. Its ultimate particles are called protons. From these protons and electrons all of the chemical elements are built up. Iron and lead and oxygen and gold and all the others differ from one another merely in the number and arrangement of the electrons and protons, which they contain. That is the modern idea of the nature of matter. *Matter is really nothing but electricity."*

Can you wonder then that scientists believe the time will come when mankind *through mind* can control all this energy, can be absolute master of the winds and the waves? For Modern Science is coming more and more to the belief that what we call *matter is a force subject wholly to the control of mind.*

How tenuous matter really is, is perhaps best illustrated by the fact that a single violin string, tuned to the proper pitch, could start a vibration that would shake down the Brooklyn Bridge! Oceans and mountains, rocks and iron, all can be reduced to a point little short of the purely spiritual. Your body is *85* per cent water, 15 per cent ash and phosphorus! And they in turn can be dissipated into gas and vapor. Where do we go from there?

Is not the answer that, to a great degree at least, and perhaps altogether, this world round about us is one of our mind's own creating? And that we can put into it, and get from it, pretty much what we wish? You see this illustrated every day. A panorama is spread before you. To you it is a beautiful picture; to another it appears a mere collection of rocks and trees. A girl comes out to meet you. To you she is the embodiment of loveliness, while to another all that grace and beauty may look drab and homely. A moonlit garden, with its fragrant odors and dew-drenched grass may mean all that is charming to you, while to another it brings only thoughts of asthma or fever or rheumatism. A color may be green to you that to another is red. A prospect may be inviting for you that to another is rugged and hard.

To quote *"Applied Psychology,"* by Warren Hilton:

"The same stimulus acting on different organs of sense will produce different sensations. A blow upon the eye will cause you to 'see stars'; a similar blow upon the ear will cause you to hear an explosive sound. In other words, the vibratory effect of a touch on eye or ear is the same as that of light or sound vibrations.

"The notion you may form of any object in the outer world depends solely upon what part of your brain happens to be connected with that particular nerve-end that receives an impression from the object.

"You see the sun without being able to hear it because the only nerve-ends tuned to vibrate in harmony with the ether-waves set in action by the sun are nerve-ends that are connected with the brain center devoted to sight. 'If,' says Professor James, 'we could splice the outer extremities of our optic nerves to our ears, and those of our auditory nerves to our eyes, we should hear the lightning and see the thunder, see the symphony and hear the conductor's movements.'

"In other words, the kind of impressions we receive from the world about us, the sort of mental pictures we form concerning it; in fact, the character of the outer world, the nature of the environment in which our lives are cast— all these things depend for each one of us simply upon how he happens to be put together, upon his individual mental make-up."

In short, it all comes back to the old fable of the three blind men and the elephant. To the one who caught hold of his leg, the elephant was like a tree. To the one who felt of his side, the elephant was like a wall. To the one who seized his tail, the elephant was like a rope. The world is to each one of us the world of *his individual perceptions.*

You are like a radio receiving station. Every moment thousands of impressions are reaching you. You can tune in on whatever ones you like—on joy or sorrow, on success or failure, on optimism or fear. You can select the particular impressions that will best serve you, you can hear only what you want to hear, you can shut out all disagreeable thoughts and sounds and experiences, or you can tune in on discouragement and failure and despair.

Yours is the choice. You have within you a force against which the whole world is powerless. By using it, you can make what you will of life and of your surroundings.

"But," you will say, "objects themselves do not change. It is merely the difference in the way you look at them." Perhaps. But to a great extent, at least, we find what we look for, just as, when we turn the dial on the radio, we tune in on whatever kind of entertainment or instruction we may wish to hear. And who can say that it is not our thoughts that put it there? Who, for the matter of that, can prove that our surroundings in waking hours are not as much the creature of our minds as are our dreams? You've had dreams many a time where every object seemed just as real as when you were awake. You've felt of the objects, you've pinched yourself, yet still you were convinced that you were actually *living* those dreams. May not your waking existence be largely the creation of your own mind, just as your dream pictures are?

Many scientists believe that it is, and that in proportion as you try to put into your surroundings the good things you desire, rather than the evil ones you fear, *you will find those good things.* Certain it is that you can do this with your own body. Just as certain that many people are doing it with the good things of life. They have risen above the conception of life in which matter is the master.

Just as the most powerful forces in nature are the invisible ones—heat, light, air, electricity—so the most powerful forces of man are his invisible forces, his thought forces. And just as electricity can fuse stone and iron, so can your thought forces control your body, and so can they make or mar your destiny.

The Philosopher's Charm

There was once a shrewd necromancer who told a king that he had discovered a way to make gold out of sand. Naturally the king was interested and offered him great rewards for his secret. The necromancer explained his process. It seemed quite easy, except for one thing. Not once during the operation must the king think of the word Abracadabra. If he did, the charm was broken and the gold would not come. The king tried and tried to follow the directions, but he could not keep that word Abracadabra out of his mind. And he never made the gold.

Dr. Winbigler puts the same idea in another way: "Inspiration, genius, power, are often interfered with by the conscious mind's interposing, by man's failing to recognize his power, afraid to assist himself, lacking the faith in himself necessary to stimulate the subconscious so as to arouse the genius asleep in each."

From childhood on we are assured on every hand—by scientists, by philosophers, by our religious teachers—that "ours is the earth and the fullness thereof." Beginning with the first chapter of Genesis, we are told that "God said, Let us make man in our image, after our likeness; and let them have dominion over the fish of the sea, and over the fowl of the air, and over the cattle, and over all the earth—and over every living thing that moveth upon the earth." All through the Bible, we are repeatedly adjured to use these God-given powers.

"The kingdom of God is within you." We hear all this; perhaps we even think we believe, but always, when the time comes to use these God-given talents, there is the "doubt in our heart."

Baudouin expressed it clearly: "To be ambitious for wealth and yet always expecting to be poor; to be always doubting your ability to get what you long for, is like trying to reach east by traveling west. There is no philosophy which will help a man to succeed when he always doubts his ability to do so, thus attracting failure.

"You will go in the direction in which you face . . .

"There is a saying that every time the sheep bleats, it loses a mouthful of hay. Every time you allow yourself to complain of your lot, to say, 'I am poor; I can never do what others do; I shall never be rich; I have not the ability that others have; I am a failure; luck is against me;' you are laying up so much trouble for yourself.

"No matter how hard you may work for success, if your thought is saturated with the fear of failure, it will kill your efforts, neutralize your endeavors, and make success impossible."

And that is responsible for all our failures. We are like the old lady who decided she wanted the hill behind her house removed. So she got down on her knees and prayed the good Lord to remove it. The next morning she got up and hurried to the window. The hill was still in its same old place. "I knew it!" she snapped. "I gave Him his chance. But I knew all the time there was nothing to this prayer business."

Neither is there, as it is ordinarily done. Prayer is not a mere asking of favors. Prayer is not a paean of praise. Rather prayer is a realization of the God-power within you—of your right of dominion over your own body, your environment, your business, your health, your prosperity. And that as such, no evil has power over you, whereas you have all power for good. And "good" means not merely holiness. Good means happiness—the happiness of everyday people. Good means everything that is good in this world of ours—comforts and pleasures and prosperity for us, health and happiness for those dependent upon us. There are no limits to "Good" except those we put upon it ourselves.

What was it made Napoleon the greatest conqueror of his day? Primarily his magnificent faith in Napoleon. He had a sublime belief in his destiny, an absolute confidence that the obstacle was not made which Napoleon could not find a way through, or over, or around. It was only when he lost that confidence, when he hesitated and vacillated for weeks between retreat and advance, that winter caught him in Moscow and ended his dreams of world empire. Fate gave him every chance first. The winter snows were a full month late in coming. But Napoleon hesitated—and was lost. It was not the snows that defeated him. It was not the Russians. It was his loss of faith in himself.

The Kingdom of Heaven

"The Kingdom of Heaven is within you." Heaven is not some far-away state—the reward of years of tribulation here. Heaven is right here—here and now! Heaven is within us means that the power for happiness, for good, for everything we need of life, is within each one of us.

That most of us fail to realize this Heaven is the reason why so many are sickly and suffering, why more are ground down by poverty and worry. We were given the power to overcome these evils; if we fail to find the way, the fault is ours. To enjoy the Heaven that is within us, to begin here and now to live the life eternal, takes only a fuller understanding of the Power-that- is-within-us.

Even now, with the limited knowledge at our command, we can control circumstances to the point of making the world without an expression of our own world within, where the real thoughts, the real power, resides. Through this world within you can find the solution of every problem, the cause for every effect. Discover it—and all power, all possession is within your control.

For the world without is but a reflection of that world within. Your thought *creates* the conditions your mind images. Keep before your mind's eye the image of all you want to be and you will see it reflected in the world without. Think abundance, feel abundance, BELIEVE abundance, and you will find that as you think and feel and believe, abundance will manifest itself in your daily life. But let fear and worry be your mental companions, thoughts of poverty and limitation dwell in your mind, and worry and fear, limitation and poverty will be your constant companions day and night.

Your mental concept is all that matters. Its relation to matter is that of idea and form. There has got to be an idea before it can take form. As Dr. Terry Walter says:

"The impressions that enter the subconscious form indelible pictures, which are never forgotten, and whose power can change the body, mind, manner, and morals; can, in fact, revolutionize a personality.

"All during our waking hours the conscious mind, through the five senses, acts as constant feeder to the subconscious; the senses are the temporal source of supply for the content of the soul mind; therefore it is most important that we know and realize definitely and explicitly that every time we think a thought or feel an emotion, we are adding to the content of this powerful mind, good or bad, as the case may be. Life will be richer or poorer for the thoughts and deeds of today."

Your thoughts supply you with limitless energy, which will take whatever form your mind demands. The thoughts are the mold, which crystallizes this energy into good or ill, according to the form you impress upon it. You are free to choose which. But whichever you choose, the result is sure. Thoughts of wealth, of power, of success, can bring only results commensurate with your idea of them. Thoughts of poverty and lack can bring only limitation and trouble.

"A radical doctrine," you'll say, and think me wildly optimistic. Because the world has been taught for so long to think that some must be rich and some poor, that trials and tribulations are our lot. That this is at best a vale of tears.

The history of the race shows that what is considered to be the learning of one age is ignorance to the next age.

Dr. Edwin E. Slosson, Editor of *Science Service,* speaking of the popular tendency to fight against new ideas merely because they were *new,* said: "All through the history of science, we find that new ideas have to force their way into the common mind in disguise, as though they were burglars instead of benefactors of the race."

And Emerson wrote: "The virtue in most request is conformity. Self-reliance is its aversion. It loves not realities and creators, but names and customs."

In the ages to come man will look back upon the poverty and wretchedness of so many millions today, and think how foolish we were not to take advantage of the abundance all about us. Look at Nature; how profuse she is in everything. Do you suppose the Mind that imaged that profuseness ever intended you to be limited, to have to scrimp and save in order to eke out a bare existence?

There are hundreds of millions of stars in the heavens. Do you suppose the Mind, which could bring into being worlds without number in such prodigality intended to stint you of the few things necessary to your happiness?

What is money but a mere idea of mind, a token of exchange? The paper money you have in your pockets is supposed to represent so much gold or silver currency. There are billions upon billions of this paper money in circulation, yet all the gold in the world amounts to only about $8,000,000,000. Wealth is in ideas, not in money or property. You can control those ideas through mind.

Reduced to the ultimate—to the atom or to the electron—everything in this world is an idea of mind. All of it has been brought together through mind. If we can change the things we want back into mental images, we can multiply them as often as we like, possessing all that we like.

"To Him That Hath"

Take as an example the science of numbers. Suppose all numbers were of metal—that it was against the law to write figures for ourselves. Every time you wanted to do a sum in arithmetic you'd have to provide yourself with a supply of numbers, arrange them in their proper order, work out your problems with them. If your problems were too abstruse you might run out of numbers, have to borrow some from your neighbor or from the bank.

"How ridiculous," you say. "Figures are not things; they are mere ideas, and we can add them or divide them or multiply them or subtract them as often as we like. Anybody can have all the figures he wants."

To be sure he can. And when you get to look upon money in the same way, you will have all the money you want.

"To him that hath shall be given, and from him that hath not shall be taken away even that which he hath." To him that hath the right idea everything shall be given, and from him who hath not that right idea shall be taken away everything he hath.

Thought externalizes itself. What we are depends entirely upon the images we hold before our mind's eye. Every time we think, we start a chain of causes, which will create conditions similar to the thoughts, which originated it. Every thought we hold in our consciousness for any length of time becomes impressed upon our subconscious mind and creates a pattern, which the mind weaves into our life or environment.

All power is from within and is therefore under our own control. When you can direct your thought processes, you can consciously apply them to any condition, for all that comes to us from the world without is what we've already imaged in the world within.

Do you want more money? Sit you down now quietly and realize that money is merely an idea; that your mind is possessed of unlimited ideas; that being part of Universal Mind, there is no such thing as limitation or lack. That somewhere, somehow, the ideas that shall bring you all the money you need for any right purpose are available for you. That you have but to put it up to your subconscious mind to find these ideas.

Realize that—*believe* it—and your need will be met. "What things so ever ye desire, when ye pray, believe that ye receive it and ye shall have it." Don't forget: *"believe that ye receive it."* This it is that images the thing you want on your subconscious mind. And this it is that brings it to you. Once you can image the belief clearly on your subconscious mind, "whatsoever it is that ye ask for . . . ye shall have it."

For the source of all good, of everything you wish for, is the Universal Mind, and you can reach it only through the subconscious.

And Universal Mind will be to you whatever you believe it to be. When a man realizes that his mind is part of Universal Mind, when he realizes that he has only to take any right aspiration to this Universal Mind to see it realized, he loses all sense of worry and fear. He learns to dominate instead of to cringe. He rises to meet every situation, secure in the knowledge that everything necessary to the solution of any problem is in Mind, and that he has but to take his problem to Universal Mind to have it correctly answered.

For if you take a drop of water from the ocean, you know that it has the same properties as all the rest of the water in the ocean, the same percentage of sodium chloride. The only difference between it and the ocean is in volume. If you take a spark of electricity, you know that it has the same properties as the thunderbolt, the same power that moves trains or runs giant machines in factories. Again the only difference is in volume. It is the same with your mind and Universal Mind. The only difference between them is in volume. Your mind has the same properties as the Universal Mind, the same creative genius, the same power over all the earth, the same access to all knowledge. Know this, believe it, use it, and "yours is the earth and the fullness thereof." In the exact proportion that you believe yourself to be part of Universal Mind, sharing in its all-power, in that proportion can you demonstrate the mastery over your own body and over the world about you.

All growth, all supply is from the world-within. If you would have power, if you would have wealth, you have but to image it on this world within, on your subconscious mind, through belief and understanding.

If you would remove discord, you have but to remove the wrong images—images of ill health, of worry and trouble from within. The trouble with most of us is that we live entirely in the world without. We have no knowledge of that inner world which is responsible for all the conditions we meet and all the experiences we have.

The inner world promises us life and health, prosperity and happiness—dominion over all the earth. It promises peace and perfection for its entire offspring. It gives you the right way and the adequate way to accomplish any normal purpose. Business, labor, professions, exist primarily in thought. And the outcome of your labors in them is regulated by thought. Consider the difference, then, in this outcome if you have at your command only the limited capacity of your conscious mind, compared with the boundless energy of the subconscious and the Universal Mind. "Thought, not money, is the real business capital," says Harvey S. Firestone, "and if you know absolutely that what you are doing is right, then you are bound to accomplish it in due season.

Thought is a dynamic energy with the power to bring its object out from the invisible substance all about us. Matter is inert, unintelligent. Thought can shape and control. Every form in which matter is today is but the expression of some thought, some desire, and some idea.

You have a mind. You can originate thought. And thoughts are creative. Therefore you can create for yourself that which you desire. Once you realize this you are taking a long step toward success in whatever undertaking you have in mind.

More than half the prophecies in the Scriptures refer to the time when man shall possess the earth, when tears and sorrow shall be unknown, and peace and plenty shall be everywhere. That time will come. It is nearer than most people think possible. You are helping it along. Every man who is honestly trying to use the power of mind in the right way is doing his part in the great cause. For it is only through Mind that peace and plenty can be gained. The earth is laden with treasures as yet undiscovered. But they are every one of them known to Universal Mind, for it was Universal Mind that first imaged them there. And as part of Universal Mind, they can be known to you.

"To the Manner Born"

Few of us have any idea of our mental powers. The old idea was that man must take this world as he found it. He'd been born into a certain position in life, and to try to rise above his fellows was not only the height of bad taste, but sacrilegious as well. An all-wise Providence had decreed by birth the position a child should occupy in the web of organized society. For him to be discontented with his lot, for him to attempt to raise himself to a higher level, was tantamount to tempting Providence. The gates of Hell yawned wide for such scatterbrains, who were lucky if in this life they incurred nothing worse than the ribald scorn of their associates.

That is the system that produced aristocracy and feudalism. That is the system that feudalism and aristocracy strove to perpetuate.

The new idea—the basis of all democracies—is that man is not bound by any system, that he need not accept the world as he finds it. He can remake the world to his own ideas. It is merely the raw material. He can make what he wills of it.

It is this new idea that is responsible for all our inventions, all our progress. Man is satisfied with nothing. He is constantly remaking his world. And now more than ever will this be true, for psychology teaches us that each one has within himself the power to become what he wills.

Learn to control your thought. Learn to image upon your mind only the things you want to see reflected there.

You will never improve yourself by dwelling upon the drawbacks of your neighbors. You will never attain perfect health and strength by thinking of weakness or disease. No man ever made a perfect score by watching his rival's target. You have got to think strength, think health, think riches. To paraphrase Pascal—"Our achievements today are but the sum of our thoughts of yesterday."

For thought is energy. Mental images are concentrated energy. And energy concentrated on any definite purpose becomes power. To those who perceive the nature and transcendency of force, all physical power sinks into insignificance.

What is imagination but a form of thought? Yet it is the instrument by which all the inventors and discoverers have opened the way to new worlds. Those who grasp this force, be their state ever so humble, their natural gifts ever so insignificant, becomes our leading men. They are our governors and supreme lawgivers, the guides of the drifting host, which follows them as by an irrevocable decree. To quote Glenn Clark in the *Atlantic Monthly,* "Whatever we have of civilization is their work, theirs alone. If progress was made they made it. If spiritual facts were discerned, they discerned them. If justice and order were put in place of insolence and chaos, they wrought the change. Never is progress achieved by the masses. Creation ever remains the task of the individual."

Our railroads, our telephones, our automobiles, our libraries, our newspapers, our thousands of other conveniences, comforts and necessities are due to the creative genius of but two per cent of our population.

And the same two per cent own a great percentage of the wealth of the country. The question arises, who are they? What are they? The sons of the rich? College men? No—few of them had any early advantages. Many of them have never seen the inside of a college. It was grim necessity that drove them, and somehow, some way, they found a method of drawing upon their Genie-of-the-Mind, and through that inner force they have reached success.

You don't need to stumble and grope. You can call upon your inner forces at will.

There are three steps necessary:

First, to realize that you have the power.
Second, to know what you want.
Third, to center your thought upon it with singleness of purpose.

To accomplish these steps takes only a fuller understanding of the Power-that-is-within-you.

But what is this power? Where should you go to locate it? Is it a thing, a place, an object? Has it bounds, form or material shape? No! Then how shall you go about finding it?

If you have begun to *realize* that there is a power within you, if you have begun to arouse in your conscious mind the ambition and desire to use this power— you have started in the pathway of wisdom. If you are willing to go forward, to endure the mental discipline of mastering this method, nothing in the world can hinder you or keep you from overcoming every obstacle.

Begin at once, today, to use what you have learned. All growth comes from practice. All the forces of life are active—peace—joy—power; the unused talent decays.

So let us make use of this dynamo, which is *you.* What is going to start it working? Your *Faith*—the faith that is begotten of understanding. Faith is the impulsion, the propulsion of this power within. Faith is the confidence, the assurance, the enforcing truth, the knowing that the right idea of life will bring you into the reality of existence and the manifestation of the All power.

All cause is in Mind—and Mind is everywhere. All the knowledge there is, all the wisdom there is, all the power there is, is all about you—no matter where you may be. Your Mind is part of it. You have access to it. If you fail to avail yourself of it, you have no one to blame but yourself. For, as the drop of water in the ocean shares in all the properties of the rest of the ocean water so you share in that all-power, all-wisdom of Mind. If you have been sick and ailing, if poverty and hardship have been your lot, don't blame it on "fate." Blame yourself. "Yours is the earth and everything that's in it." But you've got to *take* it. The power is there—but *you* must *use* it. It is round about you like the air you breathe. You don't expect others to do your breathing for you. Neither can you expect them to use your Mind for you. Universal Intelligence is not only the mind of the Creator of the universe, but it is also the mind of MAN, *your* intelligence, *your* mind.

So start today by KNOWING that you can do anything you wish to do, have anything you wish to have, be anything you wish to be. The rest will follow.

IV

Desire—The First Law of Gain

> "Ah, Love! Could Thou and I with Fate conspire
> To grasp this sorry Scheme of Things entire,
>   Would we not shatter it to bits—and then
>   Re-mold it nearer to the Heart's Desire!"
>
> —The Rubaiyat of Omar Khayyam.

If YOU had a fairy-wishing ring, what one thing would you wish for? Wealth? Honor? Fame? Love? What one thing do you desire above everything else in life? Whatever it is, you can have it.

Whatever you desire wholeheartedly, with singleness of purpose—you can have. But the first and all-important essential is to know what this one thing is. Before you can win your heart's desire, you've got to get clearly fixed in your mind's eye what it is that you want.

It may sound paradoxical, but few people do know what they want. Most of them struggle along in a vague sort of way, hoping—like Micawber—for something to turn up. They are so taken up with the struggle that they have forgotten—if they ever knew— what it is they are struggling for. They are like a drowning man—they use up many times the energy it would take to get them somewhere, but they fritter it away in aimless struggles— without thought, without direction, exhausting themselves, while getting nowhere.

You've got to know what you want before you stand much chance of getting it. You have an unfailing "Messenger to Garcia" in that Genie-of-your Mind—but YOU have got to formulate the message. Aladdin would have stood a poor chance of getting anything from his Genie if he had not had clearly in mind the things he wanted the Genie to get.

In the realm of mind, the realm in which is all practical power, you can possess what you want at once. You have but to claim it, to visualize it, to bring it into actuality—and it is yours for the taking. For the Genie-of-your-Mind can give you power over circumstances. Health, happiness and prosperity. And all you need to put it to work is an earnest, intense desire.

Sounds too good to be true? Well, let us go back for a moment to the start. You are infected with that "divine dissatisfaction with things as they are" which has been responsible for all the great accomplishments of this world

31

— else you would not have gotten thus far in this book. Your heart is hungering for something better. "Blessed are they which do hunger and thirst after righteousness (right-wiseness) for they shall be filled." You are tired of the worry and grind, tired of the deadly dull routine and daily tasks that lead nowhere. Tired of all the petty little ills and ailments that have come to seem the lot of man here on earth.

Always there is something within you urging you on to bigger things, giving you no peace, no rest, no chance to be lazy. It is the same "something" that drove Columbus across the ocean; that drove Hannibal across the Alps; that drove Edison onward and upward from a train boy to the inventive wizard of the century; that drove Henry Ford from a poor mechanic at forty to probably the richest man in the world at sixty.

This "something" within you keeps telling you that you can do anything you want to do, be anything you want to be, have anything you want to have—and you have a sneaking suspicion that it may be right.

That "something" within you is your subconscious self, your part of Universal Mind, your Genie-of-the-brain. Men call it ambition, and "Lucky is the man," says Arthur Brisbane, "whom the Demon of Ambition harnesses and drives through life. This wonderful little coachman is the champion driver of the entire world and of all history.

"Lucky you, if he is *your* driver. "He will keep you going until you do something worthwhile—working, running and moving ahead.

 "And that is how a real man ought to be driven.

"This is the little Demon that works in men's brains, that makes the blood tingle at the thought of achievement and that makes the face flush and grow white at the thought of failure.

"Every one of us has this Demon for a driver, IN YOUTH AT LEAST.

"Unfortunately the majority of us he gives up as very poor, hopeless things, not worth driving, by the time we reach twenty-five or thirty.

"How many men look back to their teens, when they were harnessed to the wagon of life with Ambition for a driver? When they could not wait for the years to pass and for opportunity to come?

"It is the duty of ambition to drive, and it is your duty to *keep Ambition alive and driving.*

"If you are doing nothing, if there is no driving, no hurrying, no working, *you may count upon it that there will be no results; nothing much worthwhile in the years* to *come.*

"Those that are destined to be the big men twenty years from now, when the majority of us will be nobodies *are those whom this demon is driving relentlessly, remorselessly, through the hot weather and the cold weather, through early hours and late hours.*

"Lucky YOU if you are in harness and driven by the Demon of Ambition."
Suppose you *have* had disappointments, disillusionments along the way. Suppose the fine point of your ambition has become blunted. Remember, there is no obstacle that there is not some way around, or over, or through—and if you will depend less upon the 10 per cent of your abilities that reside in your conscious mind, and leave more to the 90 per cent that constitutes your subconscious, you can overcome all obstacles. Remember this—there is no

condition so hopeless, no life so far gone, that mind cannot redeem it.

Every untoward condition is merely *a lack* of something. Darkness, you know, is not real. It is merely a lack of light. Turn on the light and the darkness will be seen to be nothing. It vanishes instantly. In the same way poverty is simply a lack of necessary supply. Find the avenue of supply and your poverty vanishes. Sickness is merely the absence of health. If you are in perfect health, sickness cannot hurt you. Doctors and nurses go about at will among the sick without fear—and suffer as a rule far less from sickness than does the average man or woman.

So there is nothing you have to *overcome.* You merely have to *acquire* something. And always Mind can show you the way. You can obtain from Mind anything you want, if you will learn how to do it. "I think we can rest assured that one can do and be practically what he desires to be," says Farnsworth in "*Practical Psychology.*" And psychologists all over the world have put the same thought in a thousand different ways.

"It is not will, but desire," says Charles W. Mears, "that rules the world." "But," you will say, "I have had plenty of desires all my life. I've always wanted to be rich. How do you account for the difference between my wealth and position and power and that of the rich men all around me?"

The Magic Secret

The answer is simply that you have never focused your desires into one great dominating desire. You have a host of mild desires. You mildly wish you were rich, you wish you had a position of responsibility and influence; you wish you could travel at will. The wishes are so many and varied that they conflict with each other and you get nowhere in particular. You lack one *intense* desire, to the accomplishment of which you are willing to subordinate everything else.

Do you know how Napoleon so frequently won battles in the face of a numerically superior foe? By concentrating his men at the actual *point of contact!* His artillery was often greatly outnumbered, but it accomplished far more than the enemy's because instead of scattering his fire, he *concentrated it all on the point of attack!*

The time you put in aimlessly dreaming and wishing would accomplish marvels if it were concentrated on one definite object. If you have ever taken a magnifying glass and let the sun's rays play through it on some object, you know that as long as the rays were scattered they accomplished nothing. But focus them on one tiny spot and see how quickly they start something.

It is the same way with your mind. You've got to concentrate *on one idea at a time.*
"But how can I learn to concentrate?" many people write me. Concentration is not a thing to be learned. It is merely a thing to do. You concentrate whenever you become sufficiently interested in anything. Get so interested in a ball game that you jump up and down on your hat, slap a man you have never seen before on the back, embrace your nearest neighbor—*that* is concentration. Become so absorbed in a thrilling play or movie that you no longer realize the orchestra is playing or there are people around you—*that* is concentration.

And that is all concentration ever is—getting so interested in some one thing that you pay no attention to anything else that is going on around you.

If you want a thing badly enough, you need have no worry about your ability to concentrate on it. Your thoughts will just naturally center on it like bees on honey.

Hold in your mind the thing you most desire. Affirm it. Believe it to be an existing fact. Your subconscious mind is exceedingly amenable to suggestion. If you can truly believe that you have received something, can impress that belief upon your subconscious mind, depend upon it, it will see that you have it. For being a part of Universal Mind, it shares that Universal Mind's all power.

The people who live in beautiful homes, who have plenty to spend, who travel about in yachts and fine cars, are for the most part people who started out to accomplish *some one definite thing*. They had one clear goal in mind, and everything they did centered on that goal.

Most men just jog along in a rut, going through the same old routine day after day, eking out a bare livelihood, with no definite desire other than the vague hope that fortune will some day drop in their lap. Fortune doesn't often play such pranks. And a rut, you know, differs from a grave only in depth. A life such as that is no better than the animals live. Work all day for money to buy bread, to give you strength to work all the next day to buy more bread. There is nothing to it but the daily search for food and sustenance. No time for aught but worry and struggle. No hope of anything but the surcease of sorrow in death.

You can have anything you want—if you want it badly enough. You can be anything you want to be, have anything you desire, accomplish anything you set out to accomplish—if you will hold to that desire with singleness of purpose; if you will understand and BELIEVE in your own powers to accomplish.

What is it that you wish in life? Is it health? In the chapter on health I will show you that you can be radiantly well—without drugs, without tedious exercises. It matters not if you are crippled or bedridden or infirm. Your body rebuilds itself entirely every eleven months. You can start now rebuilding along perfect lines.

Is it wealth you wish? In the chapter on success I will show you how you can increase your income, how you can forge rapidly ahead in your chosen business or profession.

Is it happiness you ask for? Follow the rules herein laid down and you will change your whole outlook on life. Doubts and uncertainty will vanish, to be followed by calm assurance and abiding peace. You will possess the things your heart desires. You will have love and companionship. You will win to contentment and happiness.

But desire must be impressed upon the subconscious before it can be accomplished. Merely conscious desire seldom gets you anything. It is like the daydreams that pass through your mind. Your desire must be visualized, must be persisted in, must be concentrated upon, and must be impressed upon your subconscious mind. Don't bother about the means for accomplishing your desire—you can safely leave that to your subconscious mind. It knows how to do a great many things besides building and repairing your body. If you can visualize the thing you want, if you can impress upon your subconscious mind the *belief that you have it,* you can safely leave to it the finding of the means of getting it. Trust the Universal Mind to show the way. The mind that provided everything in such profusion must joy in seeing us take advantage of that profusion.

You do not have to wait until tomorrow, or next year, or the next world, for happiness. You do not have to die to be saved. "The Kingdom of Heaven is within you." That does not mean that it is up in the heavens or on some star or in the next world. It means *here* and *now!* All the possibilities of happiness are always here and always available. At the open door of every man's life there lies this pearl of great price—the understanding of man's dominion over the earth. With that understanding and conviction you can do everything, which lies before you to do, and you can do it to the satisfaction of everyone and the well being of yourself. God and good are synonymous. And God-good-is absent only to those who believe He is absent.

Find your desire, impress it upon your thought, and you have opened the door for opportunity. And remember, in this new heaven and new earth, which I am trying to show you, *the door of opportunity is never closed.* As a matter of fact, you constantly have *all that you will take.* So keep yourself in a state of receptivity. It is your business to receive abundantly and perpetually. The law of opportunity enforces its continuance and availability.

Believe that you share in that goodness and bounty. Act the part you wish to play in this life. Act healthy, act prosperous, and act happy. Make such a showing with what you have that you will carry the conviction to your subconscious mind that all good and perfect gifts ARE yours. Register health, prosperity and happiness on your inner mind and some fine morning soon you will wake to find that *you are* healthy, prosperous and happy, that you *have* your dearest wish in life.

The Soul's Sincere Desire

Do you know what prayer is? Just an earnest desire that we take to God—to Universal Mind—for fulfillment. As Montgomery puts it—"Prayer is the soul's *sincere desire,* uttered or unexpressed." It is our Heart's Desire. At least, the only prayer that is worth anything is the prayer that asks for our real desires. That kind of prayer is heard. That kind of prayer is answered.

Mere lip prayers get you nowhere. It doesn't matter what your lips may say. The thing that counts is what your heart desires, what your mind images on your subconscious thought, and through it on Universal Mind.

But even sincere desire is not enough by itself. There must be BELIEF, too. "What things so ever ye desire, when ye pray, believe that ye receive them and ye shall have them." You must realize God's ability to give you every good thing. You must believe in his readiness to do it. Model your thoughts after the Psalmists of old. They first asked for that which they wanted, then killed all doubts and fears by affirming God's power and His willingness to grant their prayers. Read any of the Psalms and you will see what I mean. So when you pray, ask for the things that you want. Then affirm God's readiness and His Power to grant your prayer. Glenn Clark, in "The Soul's Sincere Desire," gives some wonderfully helpful suggestions along these lines. To quote him:

"For money troubles, realize: There is no want in Heaven, and affirm:

"Our Heavenly Father, we know that thy Love is as infinite as the sky is infinite, and Thy Ways of manifesting that love are as unaccountable as the stars of the heavens.

"Thy Power is greater than man's horizon, and Thy Ways of manifesting that Power are more numerous than the sands of the sea.

"As Thou keepest the stars in their courses, so shalt Thou guide our steps in perfect harmony, without clash or discord of any kind, if we keep our trust in Thee. For we know Thou wilt keep him in perfect peace whose mind is stayed on Thee, because he trusteth in Thee. We know that, if we acknowledge Thee in all our ways, Thou wilt direct our paths. For Thou art the God of Love, Giver of every good and perfect gift, and there is none beside Thee. Thou art omnipotent, omniscient, and omnipresent, in all, through all, and over all, the only God. And Thine is the Kingdom, and the Power, and the Glory, forever, Amen.

"For aid in thinking or writing, realize: There is no lack of ideas, and affirm:

"Thy wisdom is greater than all hidden treasures, and yet as instantly available for our needs as the very ground beneath our feet."

"For happiness: There is no unhappiness in Heaven, so affirm:

"Thy joy is brighter than the sun at noonday and Thy Ways of expressing that Joy as countless as the sunbeams that shine upon our path."

This is the kind of prayer the Psalmists of old had recourse to in their hours of trouble—this is the kind of prayer that will bring you every good and perfect gift.

Make no mistake about this—*prayer is effective.* It *can* do anything. It doesn't matter how trivial your desires may be—if it is RIGHT for you to have them, it is RIGHT for you to pray for them.

According to a United Press dispatch of May 3, 1926:

"Prayer belongs to the football field as much as to the pulpit, and a praying team stands a good chance of getting there," Tim Lowry, Northwestern University football star, told a large church audience here.

"Just before the Indiana-Northwestern game last year," Tim said. 'We worried a great deal about the outcome. Then we saw that bunch of big husky Indiana players coming toward us and we knew something had to be done quickly.

"'Fellows,' I said, 'I believe in prayer and we better pray.' We did and won a great victory.

"When the next game came, every fellow prayed again.

"You don't need to think that churches have a copyright on prayer."

In "*Prayer as a Force*," A. Maude Royden compares the man who trusts his desires to prayer with the swimmer who trusts himself to the water:

"Let me give you a very simple figure which I think may perhaps convey my meaning. If you are trying to swim you must believe that the sea is going to keep you afloat. You must give yourself to the sea. There is the ocean and there are you in it, and I say to you, 'According to your faith you will be able to swim!' I know perfectly well that it is literally according to your faith. A person who has just enough confidence in the sea and in himself to give one little hop from the ground will certainly find that the water will lift him but not very much; he will come down again. Persons who have enough confidence really to start swimming but no more, will not swim very far, because their confidence is so very small and they swim with such rapid strokes, and they hold their breath to such an extent, that by and by they collapse; they swim five or six, or twelve or fourteen strokes, but they do not get very far, through lack of confidence.

"Persons who know with assurance that the sea will carry them if they do certain things, will swim quite calmly, serenely, happily, and will not mind if the water goes right over them. 'Oh,' you say, 'that person is doing the whole thing!' *He can't do it without the sea!* You might hypnotize people into faith; you might say, 'You are now in the ocean; swim off the edge of this precipice' (which is really a cliff). You might make them do it, they might have implicit faith in you, you might hypnotize them into thinking they were swimming; but if they swam off the edge of the cliff they would fall. You can't swim without the sea! I might say to you, 'It lies with you whether you swim or not, according to your faith be it unto you'; but if the sea is not there you can't swim. That is exactly what I feel about God. 'According to your faith be it unto you.' Yes, certainly, if you try to swim in that ocean which is the love of God your faith will be rewarded, and according to your faith it will be to you. In exact proportion to your faith you will find the answer, like a scientific law. There is not one atom of faith you put in God that will not receive its answer."

But remember: you would not plant a valuable seed in your garden, and then, a day or a week later, go out and dig it up to see if it were sprouting. On the contrary, you would nourish it each morning with water. It is the same with your prayers. Don't plant the seed of your desire in your subconscious mind and then go out the next morning and tear it up with doubts and fears. Nourish it by holding in thought the thing you desire, by believing in it, visualizing it, SEEING it as an accomplished fact.

If you ask for my own formula for successful prayer, I would say—

1st. Center your thoughts on the thing that you want. Visualize it. Make a mental image of it. You are planting the seed of Desire. But don't be content with that. Planting alone will not make a seed of corn grow. It has to be warmed by sunshine, nurtured by rain. So with the seed of your Desire. It must be warmed by Faith, nurtured by constant Belief. So—

2nd. Read the 91st and the 23rd Psalms, just as a reminder of God's power and His readiness to help you in all your needs.

3rd. Don't forget to be thankful, not merely for past favors, *but for the granting of this favor you are now asking!* To be able to thank God for it sincerely, in advance of its actual material manifestation, is the finest evidence of belief.

4th. BELIEVE! Picture the thing that you want so clearly, see it in your imagination so vividly, that for the moment, at least, you will actually BELIEVE THAT YOU HAVE IT!

It is this sincere conviction, registered upon your subconscious mind, and through it upon Universal Mind that brings the answer to your prayers. Once convince your subconscious mind that you HAVE the thing you want, and you can forget it and go on to your next problem. Mind will attend to the bringing of it into being.

VOLUME THREE

V

Aladdin & Company

> "But the feeble hands and helpless,
> Groping blindly in the darkness,
> Touch God's right hand in that darkness,
> And are lifted up and strengthened."
>
> —LONGFELLOW.

It is not always the man who struggles hardest who gets on in the world. It is the direction as well as the energy of struggle that counts in making progress. To get ahead—you must swim with the tide. Men prosper and succeed who work in accord with natural forces. A given amount of effort with these forces carries a man faster and farther than much more effort used against the current. Those who work blindly, regardless of these forces, make life difficult for themselves and rarely prosper.

It has been estimated by wise observers that on the average something like 90 per cent of the factors producing success or failure lie outside a man's conscious efforts—separate from his daily round of details. To the extent that he cooperates with the wisdom and power of Universal Mind he is successful, well and happy. To the extent that he fails to cooperate, he is unsuccessful, sick and miserable.

All down the ages some have been enabled to "taste and see that the Lord is good." Prophets being blessed with the loving kindness of God have proclaimed a God of universal goodnes. Now we know that this Infinite Good is not more available to one than it is to all. We know that the only limit to it is in our capacity to receive. If you had a problem in mathematics to work out, you would hardly gather together the necessary figures and leave them to arrange themselves in their proper sequence. You would know that while the method for solving every problem has been figured out, *you* have got to *work* it. The principles are there, but *you* have got to *apply* them.

The first essential is to understand the principle—to learn how it works—how to use it. The second—and even more important part—is to APPLY that understanding to the problem in hand.

In the same way, the Principle of Infinite Energy, Infinite Supply, is ever available. But that Energy, that Supply, is static. You've got to make it dynamic. You've got to understand the law. You've got to apply your understanding in order to solve your problems of poverty, discord, and disease.

Science shows that it is possible to accomplish any good thing. But distrust of your ability to reach the goal desired often holds you back and failure is the inevitable result.

Only by understanding that there is but one power—and that this power is Mind, not circumstances or environment—is it possible to bring your real abilities to the surface and put them to work.

Few deny that intelligence governs the universe. It matters not whether you call this intelligence Universal Mind or Providence or God or merely Nature. All admit Its directing power. All admit that It is a force for good, for progress. But few realize that our own minds are a part of this Universal Mind in just the same way that the rays of the sun are part of the sun.

If we will work in harmony with It, we can draw upon Universal Mind for all power, all intelligence, in the same way that the sun's rays draw upon their source for the heat and light they bring the earth.

It is not enough to know that you have this power. You must put it into practice—not once, or twice, but every hour and every day. Don't be discouraged if at first it doesn't always work. When you first studied arithmetic, your problems did not always work out correctly, did they? Yet you did not on that account doubt the principle of mathematics. You knew that the fault was with your methods, not with the principle. It is the same in this. The power is there. Correctly used, it can do anything.

All will agree that the Mind, which first brought the Life Principle to this earth—which imaged the earth, itself and the trees and the plants and the animals—is all-powerful. All will agree that to solve any problem, to meet any need, Mind has but to realize the need and it will be met. What most of us do not understand or realize is that we ourselves, being part of Universal Mind, have this same power, just as the drop of water from the ocean has all the properties of the great bulk of the water in the ocean; just as the spark of electricity has all the properties of the thunderbolt. And having the power, we have only to realize it and use it to get from life any good we may desire.

In the beginning all was void—space—nothingness. How did Universal Mind construct the planets, the firmaments, the earth and all things on and in it from this formless void? *By first making a mental image on which to build.*

That is what you, too, must do. You control your destiny, your fortune, your happiness to the exact extent to which you can think them out, VIZUALIZE them, SEE them, and allow no vagrant thought of fear or worry to mar their completion and beauty. The quality of your thought is the measure of your power. Clear, forceful thought has the power of attracting to itself everything it may need for the fruition of those thoughts. As W. D. Wattles puts it in his "*Science of Getting Rich*":

"There is a thinking stuff from which all things are made and which, in its original state, permeates, penetrates, and fills the interspaces of the universe. A thought in this substance produces the thing that is imagined by the thought. Man can form things in his thought, and, by impressing his thought upon formless substance, can cause the thing he thinks about to be created."

The connecting link between your conscious mind and the Universal is thought, and every thought that is in harmony with progress and good, every thought that is freighted with the right idea, can penetrate to Universal Mind. And penetrating to it, it comes back with the power of Universal Mind to accomplish it. You don't need to originate the ways and means. The Universal Mind knows how to bring about any necessary results. There is but one right way to solve any given problem. When your human judgment is unable to decide what that one right way is, turn to Universal Mind for guidance. You need never fear the outcome, for if you heed its advice you cannot go wrong.

Always remember—your mind is but a conductor—good or poor as you make it—for the power of Universal Mind. And thought is the connecting energy. Use that conductor, and you will improve its conductivity. Demand much, and you will receive the more.

That is the law of life. And the destiny of man lies not in poverty and hardship, but in living up to his high estate in unity with Universal Mind, with the power that governs the universe.

To look upon poverty and sickness as sent by God and therefore inevitable, is the way of the weakling. God never sent us anything but good. What is more, He has never yet failed to give to those who would use them the means to overcome any condition not of His making. Sickness and poverty are not of His making. They are not evidences of virtue, but of weakness. God gave us everything in abundance, and he expects us to manifest that abundance. If you had a son you loved very much, and you surrounded him with good things which he had only to exert himself in order to reach, you wouldn't like it if he showed himself to the world half-starved, ill-kempt and clothed in rags, merely because he was unwilling to exert himself enough to reach for the good things you had provided. No more, in my humble opinion, does God.

Man's principal business in life, as I see it, is to establish a contact with Universal Mind. It is to acquire an understanding of this power that is in him. "With all thy getting, get understanding," said Solomon.

> "Happy is the man that findeth wisdom, And the man that getteth understanding.
> For the gaining of it is better than the gaining of silver.
> And the profit thereof than fine gold.
> She is more precious than rubies: And none of the things thou canst desire are to be compared unto her.
> Length of days is in her right hand: In her left hand are riches and honor.
> Her ways are ways of pleasantness, And all her paths are peace.
> She is a tree of life to them that lay hold upon her.
> And happy is every one that retaineth her."
>
> —Proverbs.

When you become conscious, even to a limited degree, of your oneness with Universal Mind, your ability to call upon It at will for anything you may need, it makes a different man of you. Gone are the fears gone are the worries. You know that your success, your health, your happiness will be measured only by the degree to which you can impress the fruition of your desires upon mind.

The toil and worry, the wearisome grind and the backbreaking work, will go in the future as in the past to those who will not use their minds. The less they use them, the more they will sweat. And the more they work only from the neck down, the less they will be paid and the more hopeless their lot will become. It is Mind that rules the world.

But to use your mind to the best advantage doesn't mean to toil along with the mere conscious part of it. It means hitching up your conscious mind with the Man Inside You, with the little "Mental Brownies," as Robert Louis Stevenson called them, and then working together for a definite end.

"My Brownies! God bless them!" said Stevenson, "Who do one-half of my work for me when I am fast asleep, and in all human likelihood do the rest for me as well when I am wide awake and foolishly suppose that I do it myself. I had long been wanting to write a book on man's double being. For two days I went about racking my brains for a plot of any sort, and on the second night I dreamt the scene in Dr. Jekyll and Mr. Hyde at the window; and a scene, afterward split in two, in which Hyde, pursued, took the powder and underwent the change in the presence of his pursuer."

Many another famous writers have spoken in similar strain, and every man who has problems to solve has had like experiences. You know how, after you have studied a problem from all angles, it sometimes seems worse jumbled than when you started on it. Leave it then for a while—forget it—and when you go back to it, you find your thoughts clarified, the line of reasoning worked out, your problem solved for you. It is your little "Mental Brownies" who have done the work for you!

The flash of genius does not originate in your own brain. Through intense concentration you've established a circuit through your subconscious mind with the Universal, and it is from It that the inspiration comes. All genius, all progress, is from the same source. It lies with you merely to learn how to establish this circuit at will so that you can call upon It at need. It can be done.

"In the Inner Consciousness of each of us," quotes Dumont in "*The Master Mind*," "there are forces which act much the same as would countless tiny mental brownies or helpers who are anxious and willing to assist us in our mental work, if we will but have confidence and trust in them. This is a psychological truth expressed in the terms of the old fairy tales. The process of calling into service these Inner Consciousness helpers is similar to that which we constantly employ to recall some forgotten fact or name. We find that we cannot recollect some desired fact, date, or name, and instead of racking our brains with an increased effort, we (if we have learned the secret) pass on the matter to the Inner Consciousness with a silent command, 'Recollect this name for me,' and then go on with our ordinary work. After a few minutes—or it may be hours—all of a sudden, pop! will come the missing name or fact before us—flashed from the planes of the Inner Consciousness, by the help of the kindly workers or 'brownies' of those planes. The experience is so common that we have ceased to wonder at it, and yet it is a wonderful manifestation of the Inner Consciousness' workings of the mind. Stop and think a moment, and you will see that the missing word does not present itself accidentally, or 'just because.' There are mental processes at work for your benefit, and when they have worked out the problem for you they gleefully push it up from their plane on to the plane of the outer consciousness where you may use it.

"We know of no better way of illustrating the matter than by this fanciful figure of the 'mental brownies,' in connection with the illustration of the 'subconscious storehouse.' If you would learn to take advantage of the work of these Subconscious Brownies, we advise you to form a mental picture of the Subconscious Storehouse in which is stored all sorts of knowledge that you have placed there during your lifetime, as well as the impressions that you have acquired by race inheritance—racial memory, in fact. The information stored away has often been placed in the storage rooms without any regard for systematic storing, or arrangement, and when you wish to find something that has been stored away there a long time ago, the exact place being forgotten, you are compelled to call to your assistance the little brownies of the mind, which perform faithfully your mental command, 'Recollect this for me!' These brownies are the same little chaps that you charge with the task of waking you at four o'clock tomorrow morning when you wish to catch an early train—and they obey you well in this work of the mental alarmclock. These same little chaps will also flash into your consciousness the report, 'I have an engagement at two o'clock with Jones'—when looking at your watch you will see that it is just a quarter before the hour of two, the time of your engagement.

"Well then, if you will examine carefully into a subject which you wish to master, and will pass along the results of your observations to these Subconscious Brownies, you will find that they will work the raw materials of thought into shape for you in a comparatively short time. They will analyze, systematize, collate, and arrange in consecutive order the various details of information which you have passed on to them, and will add thereto the articles of similar information that they will find stored away in the recesses of your memory. In this way they will group together various scattered bits of knowledge that you have forgotten. And, right here, let us say to you that you never absolutely forget anything that you have placed in your mind. You may be unable to recollect certain things, but they are not lost—sometime later some associative connection will be made with some other fact, and lo! the missing idea will be found fitted nicely into its place in the larger idea—the work of our little brownies. Remember Thompson's statement: 'In view of having to wait for the results of these unconscious processes, I 'have proved the habit of getting together material in advance, and then leaving the mass to digest itself until I am ready to write about it.' This subconscious 'digestion' is really the work of our little mental brownies.

"There are many ways of setting the brownies to work. Nearly everyone has had some experience, more or less, in the matter, although often it is produced almost unconsciously, and without purpose and intent. Perhaps the best way for the average person—or rather the majority of persons—to get the desired results is for one to get as clear an idea of what one really wants to know—as clear an idea or mental image of the question you wish answered. Then after rolling it around in your mind—mentally chewing it, as it were—giving it a high degree of voluntary attention, you can pass it on to your Subconscious Mentality with the mental command: '*Attend to this for me—work out the answer!*' or some similar order. This command may be given silently, or else spoken aloud —either will do. Speak to the Subconscious Mentality—or its little workers—just as you would speak to persons in your employ, kindly but firmly. Talk to the little workers, and firmly command them to do your work. And then forget all about the matter—throw it off your conscious mind, and attend to your other tasks. Then in due time will come your answer—flashed into your consciousness—perhaps not until the very minute that you must decide upon the matter, or need the information. You may give your brownies orders to report at such and such a time—just as you do when you tell them to awaken you at a certain time in the morning so as to catch the early train, or just as they remind you of the hour of your appointment, if you have them all well trained."

Have you ever read the story by Richard Harding Davis of "*The Man Who Could Not Lose*"? In it the hero is intensely interested in racing. He has studied records and "dope" sheets until he knows the history of every horse backward and forward.

The day before the big race he is reclining in an easy chair, thinking of the morrow's race, and he drops off to sleep with that thought on his mind. Naturally, his subconscious mind takes it up, with the result that he dreams the exact outcome of the race.

That was mere fiction, of course, but if races were run solely on the speed and stamina of the horses, it would be entirely possible to work out the results in just that way. Unfortunately, other factors frequently enter into every betting game.

But the idea behind Davis' story is entirely right. The way to contact with your subconscious mind, the way to get the help of the "Man Inside You" in working out any problem is:

First, fill your mind with every bit of information regarding that problem that you can lay your hands on.

Second, pick out a chair or lounge or bed where you can recline in perfect comfort, where you can forget your body entirely.

Third, let your mind dwell upon the problem for a moment, not worrying, not fretting, but placidly, and then turn it over to the "Man Inside You." Say to him—"This is your problem. You can do anything. You know the answer to everything. Work this out for me!" And utterly relax. Drop off to sleep, if you can. At least, drop into one of those half-sleepy, half-wakeful reveries that keep other thoughts from obtruding upon your consciousness, Do as Aladdin did—summon your Genii, give him your orders, then forget the matter, secure in the knowledge that he will attend to it for you. When you waken, *you will have the answer!*

For whatever thought, whatever problem you can get across to your subconscious mind at the moment of dropping off to sleep, that "Man Inside You," that Genie-of-your-Mind, will work out for you.

Of course, not everyone can succeed in getting the right thought across to the subconscious at the first or the second attempt. It requires understanding and faith, just as the working out of problems in mathematics requires an understanding of and faith in the principles of mathematics. But keep on trying, and you WILL do it. And when you do, *the results are sure.*

If it is something that you want, VISUALIZE it first in your mind's eye; see it in every possible detail; see yourself going through every move it will be necessary for you to go through when your wish comes into being. Build up a complete story, step by step, just as though you were acting it all out. Get from it every ounce of pleasure and satisfaction that you can. Be *thankful* for this gift that has come to you. Then relax; go on to sleep if you can; give the "Man Inside You" a chance to work out the consummation of your wish without interference.

When you waken, hold it all pleasurably in thought again for a few moments. Don't let doubts and fears creep in, but go ahead, confidently, knowing that your wish is working itself out. Know this, believe it—and if there is nothing harmful in it, IT WILL WORK OUT!

For somewhere in Universal Mind there exists the correct solution of every problem. It matters not how stupendous and complicated, nor how simple a problem may appear to be. There always exists the right solution in Universal Mind. And because this solution does exist, there also exists the ability to ascertain and to prove what that solution is. You can know, and you can do, every right thing. Whatever it is necessary for you to know, whatever it is necessary for you to do, you can know and you can do, if you will but seek the help of Universal Mind and be governed by its suggestions.

Try this method every night for a little while, and the problem does not exist that you cannot solve.

VI

See Yourself Doing It

You say big corporations scheme To keep a fellow down;
They drive him, shame him, starve him, too, if he so much as frown.
God knows I hold no brief for them; Still, come with me today and watch those fat directors meet,
For this is what they say: "In all our force not one to take the new work that we plan! In all the thousand men we've hired Where shall we find a man?"

—ST. CLAIR ADAMS.
(From "It Can Be Done." Copyright 1921 George Sully)

You've often heard it said that a man is worth $2 a day from the neck down. How much he's worth from the neck up depends upon how much he is able to SEE.

It was the eyes of the mind that counted in days of old just as they do today. Without them you are just so much power "on the hoof," to be driven as a horse or an ox is driven. And you are worth only a little more than they.

But given vision—imagination—the ability to visualize conditions and things a month or a year ahead; given the eyes of the mind—there's no limit to your value or to your capabilities.

The locomotive, the steamboat, the automobile, the aeroplane—all existed complete in the imagination of some man before ever they became facts. The wealthy men, the big men, the successful men, envisioned their successes in their minds' eyes before ever they won them from the world. From the beginning of time, nothing has ever taken on material shape without first being visualized in mind. The only difference between the sculptor and the mason is in the mental image behind their work. Rodin employed masons to hew his blocks of marble into the general shape of the figure he was about to form. *That was mere mechanical labor.* Then Rodin took it in hand and from that rough-hewn piece of stone there sprang the wondrous figure of "The Company. "

That was art!

The difference was all in the imagination behind the hands that wielded mallet and chisel. After Rodin had formed his masterpiece, ordinary workmen copied it by the thousands. Rodin's work brought fabulous sums. The copies brought day wages. Conceiving ideas—*creating something*—is what pays, in sculpture as in all else. Mere handwork is worth only hand wages.

"The imagination," says Glenn Clark in "*The Soul's Sincere Desire,*" "is of all qualities in man the most God-like —that which associates him most closely with God. The first mention we read of man in the Bible is where he is spoken of as an 'image.' 'Let us make man in our image, after our likeness.' The only place where an image can be conceived is in the imagination. Thus man, the highest creation of God, was a creation of God's imagination.

"The source and center of all man's creative power—the power that above all others lifts him above the level of brute creation, and that gives him dominion, is his power of making images, or the power of the imagination. There are some who have always thought that the imagination was something, which makes-believe that which is not. This is fancy—not imagination. Fancy would convert that which is real into pretense and sham; imagination enables one to see through the appearance of a thing to what it really is."

There is a very real law of cause and effect, which makes the dream of the dreamer come true. It is the law of visualization—the law that calls into being in this outer material world everything that is real in the inner world. Imagination pictures the thing you desire. VISION idealizes it. It reaches beyond the thing that is, into the conception of what can be. Imagination gives you the picture. Vision gives you the impulse to make the picture your own.

Make your mental image clear enough, picture it vividly in every detail, and the Genie-of-your-Mind will speedily bring it into being as an everyday reality.

That law holds true of everything in life. There is nothing you can rightfully desire that cannot be brought into being through visualization. Suppose there's a position you want—the general managership of your company. See yourself—just as you are now—sitting in the general manager's chair. See your name on his door. See yourself handling his affairs as you would handle them. Get that picture impressed upon your subconscious mind. See it! *Believe* it! The Genie-of-your-Mind will find the way to make it come true.

The keynote of successful visualization is this: See things, as you would have them be instead of as they are. Close your eyes and make clear mental pictures. Make them look and act just as they would in real life. In short, daydream— but daydream with a purpose. Concentrate on the one idea to the exclusion of all others, and continue to concentrate on that one idea until it has been accomplished.

Do you want an automobile? A home? A factory? They can all be won in the same way. They are in their essence all of them ideas of mind, and if you will but build them up in your own mind first, stone by stone, complete in every detail, you will find that the Genie-of-your-Mind can build them up similarly in the material world.

"The building of a transcontinental railroad from a mental picture," says C. W. Chamberlain in "*The Uncommon Sense of Applied Psychology*," "gives the average individual an idea that it is a big job. The fact of the matter is, the achievement, as well as the perfect mental picture, is made up of millions of little jobs, each fitting in its proper place and helping to make up the whole.

"A skyscraper is built from individual bricks, the laying of each brick being a single job which must be completed before the next brick can be laid."

It is the same with any work, any study. To quote Professor James:

"As we become permanent drunkards by so many separate drinks, so we become saints in the moral, and authorities and experts in the practical and scientific spheres, by so many separate acts and hours of working. Let no youth have any anxiety about the upshot of his education whatever the line of it may be. If he keeps faithfully busy each hour of the working day he may safely leave the final result to itself. He can with perfect certainty count on waking some fine morning, to find himself one of the competent ones of his generation, in whatever pursuit he may have singled out…Young people should know this truth in advance. The ignorance of it has probably engendered more discouragement and faintheartedness in youths embarking on arduous careers than all other causes taken together."

Remember that the only limit to your capabilities is the one you place upon them. There is no law of limitation. The only law is of supply. Through your subconscious mind you can draw upon universal supply for anything you wish. The ideas of Universal Mind are as countless as the sands on the seashore. Use them. And use them lavishly, just as they are given.

There is a little poem by Jessie B. Rittenhouse that so well describes the limitations that most of us put upon ourselves that I quote it here (From "The Door of Dreams," Houghton, Muffin & C0., Boston):

"I bargained with Life for a penny, And Life would pay no more, however I begged at evening when I counted my scanty store.

"For Life is a just employer; He gives you what you ask, but once you have set the wages, why, you must bear the task.

"I worked for a menial's hire, Only to learn, dismayed, That any wage I had asked of Life, Life would have paid."

Aim high! If you miss the moon, you may hit a star. Everyone admits that this world and all the vast firmament must have been thought into shape from the formless void by some Universal Mind. That same Universal Mind rules today, and it has given to each form of life power to attract to itself whatever it needs for its perfect growth. The tree, the plant, and the animal—each one finds its need.

You are an intelligent, reasoning creature. Your mind is part of Universal Mind. And you have power to say what you require for perfect growth. Don't sell yourself for a penny. Whatever price you set upon yourself, life will give. So aim high. Demand much! Make a clear, distinct mental image of what it is you want. Hold it in your thought. Visualize it, see it, and believe it! The ways and means of satisfying that desire will follow. For supply always comes on the heels of demand.

It is by doing this that you take your fate out of the hands of chance. It is in this way that you control the experiences you are to have in life. But be sure to visualize only what you want. The law works both ways. If you visualize your worries and your fears, you will make them real. Control your thought and you will control circumstances. Conditions will be what you make them.

Most of us are like factories where two-thirds of the machines are idle, where the workmen move around in a listless, dispirited sort of way, doing only the tenth part of what they could do if the head of the plant were watching and directing them. Instead of that, he is off idly dreaming or waiting for something to turn up. What he needs is someone to point out to him his listless workmen and idle machines, and show him how to put each one to working full time and overtime.

And that is what YOU need, too. You are working at only a tenth of your capacity. You are doing only a tenth of what you are capable of. The time you spend idly wishing or worrying can be used in so directing your subconscious mind that it will bring you anything of good you may desire.

Philip of Macedon, Alexander's father, perfected the "phalanx"—a triangular formation which enabled him to center the whole weight of his attack on one point in the opposing line. It drove through everything opposed to it. In that day and age it was invincible. And the idea is just as invincible today.

Keep the one thought in mind, SEE it being carried out step by step, and you can knit any group of workers into one homogeneous whole, all centered on the one idea. You can accomplish any one thing. You can put across any definite idea. Keep that mental picture ever in mind and you will make it as invincible as was Alexander's phalanx of old.

"It is not the guns or armament or the money they can pay, it's the close cooperation that makes them win the day.
It is not the individual or the army as a whole but the everlasting team work of every bloomin' soul."

- J. MASON KNOX.

VII
"As A Man Thinketh"

"Our remedies in ourselves do lie which we ascribe to heaven."

—SHAKESPEARE.

In our great-grandfather's day, when witches flew around by night and cast their spell upon all unlucky enough to cross them, men thought that the power of sickness or health, of good fortune or ill, resided outside himself or herself.

We laugh today at such benighted superstition. But even in this day and age there are few who realize that the things they *see* are but *effects*. Fewer still who have any idea of the *causes* by which those effects are brought about.

Every human experience is an effect. You laugh, you weep, you joy, you sorrow, you suffer or you are happy. Each of these is an effect, the cause of which can be easily traced.

But all the experiences of life are not so easily traceable to their primary causes. We save money for our old age. We put it into a bank or into safe bonds—and the bank breaks or the railroad or corporation goes into a receivership. We stay at home on a holiday to avoid risk of accident, and fall off a stepladder or down the stairs and break a limb. We drive slowly for fear of danger, and a speeding car comes from behind and knocks us into a ditch. A man goes over Niagara Falls in a barrel without harm, and then slips on a banana peel, breaks his leg, and dies of it.

What is the cause back of it all? If we can find it and control it, we can control the effect. We shall no longer then be the football of fate. We shall be able to rise above the conception of life in which matter is our master. There is but one answer. The world without is a reflection of the world within. We image thoughts of disaster upon our subconscious minds and the Genie-of-our Mind finds ways of bringing them into effect—even though we stay at home, even though we take every possible precaution. The mental image is what counts, be it for good or ill. It is a devastating or a beneficent force, just as we choose to make it. To paraphrase Thackeray—"The world is a looking-glass, and gives back to every man the reflection of his own thought."

For matter is not *real* substance. Material science today shows that matter has no natural eternal existence. Dr. Willis R. Whitney, in an address before the American Chemical Society on August 8th, 1925, discussing "Matter —Is There Anything In It?" stated, "The most we know about matter is that it is almost entirely *space*. It is as empty as the sky. It is almost as empty as a perfect vacuum, although it usually contains a lot of energy." Thought is the only force. Just as polarity controls the electron, gravitation the planets, tropism the plants and lower animals—just so thought controls the action and the environment of man. And thought is subject wholly to the control of mind. Its direction rests with us.

Walt Whitman had the right of it when he said—"Nothing external to me has any power over me."

The happenings that occur in the material world are in themselves neither cheerful nor sorrowful, just as outside of the eye that observes them, colors are neither green nor red. It is our thoughts that make them so. And we can color those thoughts according to our own fancy. We can make the world without but a reflection of the world within. We can make matter a force subject entirely to the control of our mind. For matter is merely our wrong view of what Universal Mind sees rightly.

We cannot change the past experience, but we can determine what the new ones shall be like. We can make the coming day just what we want it to be. We can be tomorrow what we think today. For the thoughts are causes and the conditions are the effects.

What is the reason for most people's failures in life? The fact that they first thought failure; they allowed competition, hard times, fear and worry to undermine their confidence. Instead of working aggressively ahead, spending money to make more money, they stopped every possible outlay, tried to "play safe," but expected others to continue spending with them. War is not the only place where "The best defensive is a strong offensive."

The law of compensation is always at work. Man is not at the caprice of fate. He is his own fate. "As a man thinketh in his heart, so is he." We are our own past thoughts, with the things that these thoughts have attracted to us added on.

The successful man has no time to think of failure. He is too busy thinking up new ways to succeed. You can't pour water into a vessel already full.

All about you is energy—electronic energy, exactly like that which makes up the solid objects you possess. The only difference is that the loose energy round about is unappropriated. It is still virgin gold—undiscovered, unclaimed. You can think it into anything you wish—into gold or dross, into health or sickness, into strength or weakness, into success or failure. Which shall it be? "There is nothing either good or bad," said Shakespeare, "but thinking makes it so." The understanding of that law will enable you to control every other law that exists. In it is to be found the panacea for all ills, the satisfaction of all want, all desire. It is Creative Mind's own provision for man's freedom.

Mortals are healthy or unhealthy, happy or unhappy, strong or weak, alive or dead, in the proportion that they think thoughts of health or illness, strength or weakness. Your body, like all other material things, manifests only what your mind entertains in belief. In a general way you have often noticed this yourself. A man with an ugly disposition (which is a mental state) will have harsh, unlovely features. One with a gentle disposition will have a smiling and serene countenance. All the other organs of the human body are equally responsive to thought. Who has not seen the face become red with rage or white with fear? Who has not known of people who became desperately ill following an outburst of temper? Physicians declare that just as fear, irritability and hate distort the features; they likewise distort the heart, stomach and liver.

Experiments conducted on a cat shortly after a meal showed that when it was purring contentedly, its digestive organs functioned perfectly. But when a dog was brought into the room and the cat drew back in fear and anger, the X-ray showed that its digestive organs were so contorted as to be almost tied up in a knot!

Each of us makes his own world—and he makes it through mind. It is a commonplace fact that no two people see the same thing alike. "A primrose by a river's brim, a yellow primrose was to him, and it was nothing more."

Thoughts are the causes. Conditions are merely effects. We can mould our surroundings and ourselves by resolutely directing our thoughts towards the goal we have in mind.

Ordinary animal life is very definitely controlled by temperature, by climate, by seasonal conditions. Man alone can adjust himself to any reasonable temperature or condition. Man alone has been able to free himself to a great extent from the control of natural forces through his understanding of the relation of cause and effect. And now man is beginning to get a glimpse of the final freedom that shall be his from all material causes when he shall acquire the complete understanding that mind is the only cause and that effects are what he sees.

"We moderns are unaccustomed," says one talented writer, "to the mastery over our own inner thoughts and feelings. That a man should be a prey to any thought that chances to take possession of his mind, is commonly among us assumed as unavoidable. It may be a matter of regret that he should be kept awake all night from anxiety as to the issue of a lawsuit on the morrow, but that he should have the power of determining whether he be kept awake or not seems an extravagant demand. The image of an impending calamity is no doubt odious, but its very odiousness (we say) makes it haunt the mind all the more pertinaciously, and it is useless to expel it. Yet this is an absurd position for man, the heir of all the ages, to be in. If a pebble in our boot torments us, we expel it. We take off the boot and shake it out. And once the matter is fairly understood, it is just as easy to expel an intruding and obnoxious thought from the mind. About this there ought to be no mistake, no two opinions. The thing is obvious, clear and unmistakable. It should be as easy to expel an obnoxious thought from the mind as to shake a stone out of your shoe; and until a man can do that, it is just nonsense to talk about his ascendancy over nature, and all the rest of it. He is a mere slave, and a prey to the bat-winged phantoms that flit through the corridors of his own brain. Yet the weary and careworn faces that we meet by thousands, even among the affluent classes of civilization, testify only too clearly how seldom this mastery is obtained. How rare indeed to find a *man*! How common rather to discover a creature hounded on by tyrant thoughts (or cares, or desires), cowering, wincing under the lash.

"It is one of the prominent doctrines of some of the oriental schools of practical psychology that the power of expelling thoughts, or if need be, killing them dead on the spot, *must be* attained. Naturally the art requires practice, but like other arts, when once acquired there is no mystery or difficulty about it. It is worth practice. It may be fairly said that life only begins when this art has been acquired. For obviously when, instead of being ruled by individual thoughts, the whole flock of them in their immense multitude and variety and capacity is ours to direct and dispatch and employ where we list, life becomes a thing so vast and grand, compared to what it was before, that its former condition may well appear almost ante-natal. If you can kill a thought dead, for the time being, you can do anything else with it that you please. And therefore it is that this power is so valuable. And it not only frees a man from mental torment (which is nine-tenths at least of the torment of life), but it gives him a concentrated power of handling mental work absolutely unknown to him before. The two are co-relative to each other."

There is no intelligence in matter—whether that matter be electronic energy made up in the form of stone, or iron, or wood, or flesh. It all consists of Energy, the universal substance from which Mind forms all material things. Mind is the only intelligence. It alone is eternal. It alone is supreme in the universe.

When we reach that understanding, we will no longer have cause for fear, because we will realize that Universal Mind is the creator of *life* only; that death is not an actuality—it is merely the *absence* of life—and life will be ever-present. Remember the old fairy story of how the Sun was listening to a lot of earthly creatures talking of a very dark place they had found? A place of Stygian blackness. Each told how terrifically dark it had seemed. The Sun went and looked for it. He went to the exact spot they had described. He searched everywhere. But he could find not even a tiny dark spot. And he came back and told the earth-creatures he did not believe there was any dark place.

When the sun of understanding shines on all the dark spots in our lives, we will realize that there is no cause, no creator, no power, except good; evil is not an entity—it is merely the *absence of good*. And there can be no ill effects without an evil cause. Since there is no evil cause, only good can have reality or power. There is no beginning or end to good. From it there can be nothing but blessing for the whole race. In it is found no trouble. If God (or Good—the two are synonymous) is the only cause, then the only effect must be like the cause. "All things were made by Him; and without Him was not anything made that was made."

Don't be content with passively reading this. Use it! Practice it! Exercise is far more necessary to mental development that it is to physical. Practice the "daily dozen" of right thinking. Stretch your mind to realize how infinitely far it can reach out, what boundless vision it can have. Breathe out all the old thoughts of sickness, discouragement, failure, worry and fear. Breathe in deep, long breaths (thoughts) of unlimited health and strength, unlimited happiness and success. Practice looking forward—always looking forward to something better —better health, finer physique, greater happiness, bigger success. Take these mental breathing exercises every day. See how easily you will control your thoughts. How quickly you will see the good effects. You've got to think all the time. Your mind will do that anyway. And the thoughts are constantly building—for good or ill. So be sure to exhale all the thoughts of fear and worry and disease and lack that have been troubling you, and inhale only those you want to see realized.

VIII

The Law of Supply

"They do me wrong who say I come no more when once I knock and fail to find you in; For every day I stand outside your door, and bid you wake, and rise to fight and win.
 "Wail not for precious chances passed away, Weep not for golden ages on the wane! Each night I burn the records of the day— At sunrise every soul is born again!"

—WALTER MALONE.
(Courtesy of Mrs. Ella Malone Watson)

Have you ever run a race, or worked at utmost capacity for a protracted period, or swum a great distance? Remember how, soon after starting, you began to feel tired? Remember how, before you had gone any great distance, you thought you had reached your limit? But remember, too, how, when you kept on going, you got your second wind, your tiredness vanished, your muscles throbbed with energy, you felt literally charged with speed and endurance?

Stored in every human being are great reserves of energy of which the average individual knows nothing. Most people are like a man who drives a car in low gear, not knowing that by the simple shift of a lever he can set it in high and not merely speed up the car, but do it with far less expenditure of power.

The law of the universe is the law of supply. You see it on every hand. Nature is lavish in everything she does.

Look at the heavens at night. There are millions of stars there—millions of worlds—millions of suns among them. Surely there is no lack of wealth or profusion in the Mind that could image all of these; no place for limitation there! Look at the vegetation in the country round about you. Nature supplies all that the shrubs or trees may need for their growth and sustenance! Look at the lower forms of animal life—the birds and the wild animals, the reptiles and the insects, the fish in the sea.

Nature supplies them bountifully with everything they need. They have but to help themselves to what she holds out to them with such lavish hand. Look at all the natural resources of the world—coal and iron and oil and all metals. There is plenty for everyone. We hear a lot about the exhaustion of our resources of coal and oil, but there is available coal enough to last mankind for thousands of years. There are vast oil fields practically untouched, probably others bigger still yet to be discovered, and when all these are exhausted, the extraction of oil from shale will keep the world supplied for countless more years.

There is abundance for everyone. But just as you must strain and labor to reach the resources of your "second wind," just so you must strive before you can make manifest the law of supply in nature.

The World Belongs to You

It is your estate. It owes you not merely a living, but everything of good you may desire. You've got to *demand* these things of it, though. You've got to fear naught, dread naught, and stop at naught. You've got to have the faith of a Columbus, crossing an unknown sea, holding a mutinous crew to the task long after they had ceased to believe in themselves or in him—*and giving to the world a new hemisphere.* You've got to have the faith of a Washington—defeated, discredited, almost wholly deserted by his followers, yet holding steadfast in spite of all —*and giving to America a new liberty.* You've got to *dominate*—not to cringe. *You've* got to make the application of the law of supply.

"Consider the lilies how they grow." The flowers, the birds, all of creation, are incessantly active. The trees and flowers in their growth, the birds and wild creatures in building their nests and finding sustenance, are always working—*but never worrying.*

If all would agree to give up worrying—to be industrious, but never anxious about the outcome, it would mean the beginning of a new era in human progress, an age of liberty, of freedom from bondage.

All riches have their origin in Mind. Wealth is in ideas—not money. Money is merely the material medium of exchange for ideas. The paper money in your pockets is in itself worth no more than so many Russian rubles. It is the idea behind it that gives it value. Factory buildings, machinery, materials, are in themselves worthless without a manufacturing or a selling idea behind them. How often you see a factory fall to pieces, the machinery rusts away, after the idea behind them gave out. Factories, machines, are simply the tools of trade. It is the idea behind them that makes them go.

So don't go out a-seeking of wealth. Look within you for ideas! "The Kingdom of God is within you." Use it— *purposefully*! Use it to THINK constructively. Don't say you are *thinking* when all you are doing is exercising your faculty of memory. As Dumont says in *"The Master Mind"*—"They are simply allowing the stream of memory to flow through their field of consciousness, while the Ego stands on the banks and idly watches the passing waters of memory flow by. They call this 'thinking', while in reality there is no process of thought under way."

They are like the old mountaineer sitting in the shade alongside his cabin. Asked what he did to pass the long hours away, he said—"Waal, sometimes I set and think; and sometimes I just set."

Dumont goes on to say, in quoting another writer: "When I use the word 'thinking,' I mean *thinking with a purpose, with an end in view, thinking to solve a problem.* I mean the kind of thinking that is forced on us when we are deciding on a course to pursue, on a life work to take up perhaps; the kind of thinking that was forced upon us in our younger days when we had to find a solution to a problem in mathematics; or when we tackled psychology in college. I do not mean 'thinking' in snatches, or holding petty opinions on this subject and on that. I mean thought on significant questions, which lie outside the bounds of your narrow personal welfare. This is the kind of thinking which is now so rare—so sadly needed!"

The Kingdom of God is the Kingdom of Thought, of Achievement, of Health, of Happiness and Prosperity. But you have got to *seek* it. You have got to do more than ponder. You have got to *think*—to think constructively—to seek how you may discover new worlds, new methods, new needs. The greatest discoveries, you know, have arisen out of things, which everybody had *seen*, but only one man had NOTICED. The biggest fortunes have been made out of the opportunities, which many men had, but only one man GRASPED.

Why is it that so many millions of men and women go through life in poverty and misery, in sickness and despair? Why? Primarily because they make a reality of poverty through their fear of it. They visualize poverty, misery and disease, and thus bring them into being. And secondly, they cannot demonstrate the law of supply for the same reason that so many millions cannot solve the first problem in algebra. The solution is simple—but they have never been shown the method. They do not understand the law.

The essence of this law is that you must *think* abundance; *see* abundance, *feel* abundance, *believe* abundance. Let no thought of limitation enter your mind. There is no lawful desire of yours for which, as far as mind is concerned, there is not abundant satisfaction. And if you can visualize it in mind, you can realize it in your daily world.

"Blessed is the man whose delight is in the *law* of the Lord: And he shall be like a tree planted by the rivers of water, that bringeth forth his fruit in his season: his leaf also shall not wither; and whatsoever he doeth shall prosper."

Don't worry. Don't doubt. Don't dig up the seeds of prosperity and success to see whether they have sprouted. Have faith! Nourish your seeds with renewed desire. Keep before your mind's eye the picture of the thing you want. BELIEVE IN IT! No matter if you seem to be in the clutch of misfortune, no matter if the future looks black and dreary—FORGET YOUR FEARS! Realize that the future is of your own making. There is no power that can keep you down but yourself. Set your goal. Forget the obstacles between. Forget the difficulties in the way. Keep only the goal before your mind's eye—*and you'll win it*!

Judge Troward, in his Edinburgh Lectures on *Mental Science*, shows the way:

The initial step, then, consists in determining to picture the Universal Mind as the ideal of all we could wish it to be, both to ourselves and to others, together with the endeavor to reproduce this ideal, however imperfectly, in our own life; and this step having been taken, we can then cheerfully look upon it as our ever-present Friend, providing all good, guarding from all danger, and guiding us with all counsel. Similarly if we think of it as a great power devoted to supplying all our needs, we shall impress this character also upon it, and by the law of subjective mind, it will proceed to enact the part of that special providence which we have credited it with being; and if, beyond general care of our concerns, we would draw to ourselves some particular benefit, the same rule holds good of impressing our desire upon the universal subjective mind. And thus the deepest problems of philosophy bring us back to the old statement of the law: 'Ask and ye shall receive; seek and ye shall find; knock and it shall be opened unto you.' This is the summing-up of the natural law of the relation between the Divine Mind and us. It is thus no vain boast that mental science can enable us to makes our lives what we will. And to this law there is no limit. What it can do for us today it can do tomorrow, and through all that procession of tomorrows that loses itself in the dim vistas of eternity. *Belief in limitation is the one and only thing that causes limitation*, because we thus impress limitation upon the creative principle; and in proportion as we lay that belief aside, our boundaries will expand, and increasing life and more abundant blessing will be ours."

You are not working for some firm merely for the pittance they pay you. You are part of the great scheme of things. And what you do has its bearing on the ultimate result. That being the case, you are working for Universal Mind, and Universal Mind is the most generous paymaster there is. Just remember that you can look to it for all good things. Supply is *where* you are and *what* you need.

Do you want a situation? Close your eyes and realize that somewhere is the position for which you of all people are best fitted, and which is best fitted to your ability; the position where you can do the utmost of good, and where life, in turn, offers the most to you. Realize that Universal Mind knows exactly where this position is, and that through your subconscious mind you, too, can know it. Realize that this is YOUR position, that it NEEDS you, that it belongs to you, that it is right for you to have it, that you are entitled to it. Hold this thought in mind every night for just a moment, then go to sleep knowing that your subconscious mind HAS the necessary information as to where this position is and how to get in touch with it. Mind you—not WILL have, but HAS. The earnest realization of this will bring that position to you, and you to it, as surely as the morrow will bring the sun. Make the law of supply operative and you find that the things you seek are seeking you.

Get firmly fixed in your own mind the definite conviction that you can do anything you greatly want to do. There is no such thing as lack of opportunity. There is no such thing as only one opportunity. You are subject to a law of boundless and perpetual opportunity, and you can enforce that law in your behalf just as widely as you need. Opportunity is infinite and ever present.

Berton Braley has it well expressed in his poem on "Opportunity":
(From "A Banjo at Armageddon." Copyright 1917, George H. Doran Company)

"For the best verse hasn't been rhymed yet, the best house hasn't been planned, the highest peak hasn't been climbed yet, the mightiest rivers aren't spanned;
Don't worry and fret, faint hearted, the chances have just begun, for the Best jobs haven't been started, the Best work hasn't been done."

Nothing stands in the way of a will, which wants—an intelligence, which knows. The great thing is to start. "Begin your work," says Ausonius. "To begin is to complete the first half. The second half remains. Begin again and the work is done." It matters not how small or unimportant your task may seem to be. It may loom bigger in Universal Mind than that of your neighbor, whose position is so much greater in the eyes of the world. Do it well —and Universal Mind will work with you.

But don't feel limited to any one job or any one line of work. Man was given dominion over all the earth. "And God said, Let us make man in our image, after our likeness: and let them have dominion over the fish of the sea, and over the fowl of the air, and over the cattle, and over all the earth, and over every creeping thing that creepeth upon the earth."

All of energy, all of power, all that can exercise any influence over your life, is in your hands through the power of thought. God—good—is the only power there is. Your mind is part of His mind. So don't put any limit upon His power by trying to limit your capabilities. You are not in bondage to anything. All your hopes and dreams can come true. Were you not given dominion over all the earth? And can anyone else take this dominion from you?

All the mysterious psychic powers about which you hear so much today are perfectly natural. I have them. You have them. They only await the time when they shall be allowed to assert their vigor and prove themselves your faithful servitors.

"Be not afraid!" Claim your inheritance. The Universal Mind that supplies all wisdom and power is your mind. And to the extent that you are governed by your understanding of its infinite law of supply you will be able to demonstrate plenty.

"According to your faith, be it unto you."

"Analyze most of the great American fortunes of the past generation," says *Advertising and Selling Fortnightly*, "and you will find that they were founded on great faiths. One man's faith was in oil, another's in land, and another's in minerals.

"The fortunes that are being built today are just as surely being built on great faiths, but there is this difference:

the emphasis of the faith has been shifted. Today it takes faith in a product or an opportunity, as it always did, but it takes faith in the public, in addition. Those who have the greatest faith in the public—the kind of faith possessed by Henry Ford and H. J. Heinz—*and make that faith articulate*—build the biggest fortunes."

"Wanted"

There is one question that bothers many a man. Should he stick to the job he has, or cast about at once for a better one? The answer depends entirely upon what you are striving for. The first thing is to set your goal. What is it you want? A profession? A political appointment? An important executive position? A business of your own?

Every position should yield you three things:

1. Reasonable pay for the present.
2. Knowledge, training, or experience that will be worth money to you in the future.
3. Prestige or acquaintances that will be of assistance to you in attaining your goal.

Judge every opening by those three standards. But don't overlook chances for valuable training, merely because the pay is small. Though it is a pretty safe rule that the concern with up-to-the-minute methods that it would profit you to learn, also pays up-to-the-minute salaries.

Hold each job long enough to get from it every speck of information there is in it. Hold it long enough to learn the job ahead. Then if there seems no likelihood of a vacancy soon in that job ahead, find one that corresponds to it somewhere else.

Progress! Keep going ahead! Don't be satisfied merely because your salary is being boosted occasionally. Learn something every day. When you reach the point in your work that you are no longer adding to your store of knowledge or abilities, you are going backward, and it's time for you to move. Move upward in the organization you are with if you can—but MOVE!

Your actual salary is of slight importance compared with the knowledge and ability you add to your mind. Given a full storehouse there, the salary or the riches will speedily follow. But the biggest salary won't do you much good for long unless you've got the knowledge inside you to back it up.

It's like a girl picking her husband. She can pick one with a lot of money and no brains, or she can pick one with no money but a lot of ability. In the former case, she'll have a high time for a little while, ending in a divorce court or in her having a worthless young "rounder" on her hands and no money to pay the bills. In the other, the start will be hard, but she is likely to end up with a happy home she has helped to build, an earnest, hard working husband who has "arrived"—*and happiness.*

Money ought to be a consideration in marriage—but never *the* consideration. Of course it's an easy matter to pick a man with neither money nor brains. But when it's a choice of money or brains—take the brains every time. Possessions are of slight importance compared to mind.

Given the inquiring, alert type of mind—you can get any amount of possessions. But the possessions without the mind are nothing. Nine times out of ten the best thing that can happen to any young couple is to have to start out with little or nothing and work out their salvation together.

What is it *you* want most from life? Is it riches?

Picture yourself with all the riches you could use, with all the abundance that Nature holds out with such lavish hand everywhere. What would you do with it?

Daydream for a while. Believe that you *have* that abundance *now*. Practice being rich in your own mind. See yourself driving that expensive car you have always longed for, living in the sort of house you have often pictured, well-dressed, surrounded by everything to make life worth while. Picture yourself spending this money that is yours, lavishly, without a worry as to where more is coming from, knowing that there is no limit to the riches of Mind. Picture yourself doing all those things you would like to do, living the life you would like to live, providing for your loved ones as you would like to see them provided for. *See* all this in your mind's eye. *Believe* it to be true for the moment. *Know* that it will all be true in the not-very-distant future. Get from it all the pleasure and enjoyment you can.

It is the *first step* in making your dreams come true. You are creating the model in mind. And if you don't allow fear or worry to tear it down, Mind will re-create that model for you in your everyday life.

A single glance at the heavens and the earth will show you that God has all riches in abundance. Reach out mentally and appropriate to yourself some of these good gifts. You've got to do it mentally before you can enjoy it physically. "'Tis mind that makes the body rich," as Shakespeare tells us.

See the things that you want as *already yours*. Know that they will come to you at need. Then LET them come. Don't fret and worry about them. Don't think about your LACK of them. Think of them as YOURS, as *belonging* to you, as already in your possession.

Look upon money as water that runs the mill of your mind. You are constantly grinding out ideas that the world needs. Your thoughts, your plans, are necessary to the great scheme of things. Money provides the power. But it needs YOU; it needs your ideas, before it can be of any use to the world. The Falls of Niagara would be of no use without the power plants that line the banks. The Falls need these plants to turn their power to account. In the same way, money needs your ideas to become of use to the world.

So instead of thinking that you need money, realize that money needs YOU. Money is just so much wasted energy without work to do. Your ideas provide the outlet for it, the means by which money can do things. Develop your ideas; secure in the knowledge that money is always looking for such an outlet. When the ideas are perfected, money will gravitate your way without conscious effort on your part, if only you don't dam up the channels with doubts and fears.

"First have something good—then advertise!" said Horace Greeley. First have something that the world needs, even if it be only faithful, interested service—then open up your channels of desire, and dollars will flow to you.

And remember that the more you have to offer—the more of riches will flow to you. Dollars are of no value except as they are used.

You have seen the rich attacked time and again in newspapers and magazines. You have read numberless articles and editorials against them. You have heard agitators declaim against them by the hour. But have you ever heard one of them say a single word against the richest man of them all—Henry Ford? I haven't. And why? Because Henry Ford's idea of money is that it is something to be *used*—something to provide more jobs, something to bring more comfort, more enjoyment, into an increasingly greater number of lives.

That is why money flows to him so freely. That is why he gets so much out of life.

And that is how you, too, can get in touch with Infinite Supply. Realize that it is not money you have to seek, but a way to use money for the world's advantage. *Find the need*! Look at everything with the question—How could that be improved? To what new uses could this be put? Then set about supplying that need, in the absolute confidence that when you have found the way, money will flow freely to and through you. Do your part—and you can confidently look to Universal Mind to provide the means.

Get firmly in mind the definite conviction that YOU CAN DO ANYTHING RIGHT THAT YOU MAY WISH TO DO. Then set your goal and let everything you do, all your work, all your study, and all your associations, be a step towards that goal. To quote Berton Braley*—

"If you want a thing bad enough to go out and fight for it, work day and night for it, give up your time and your peace and your sleep for it, if only desire of it makes you quite mad enough never to tire of it, makes you hold all other things tawdry and cheap for it, if life seems all empty and useless without it and all that you scheme and you dream is about it, if gladly you'll sweat for it, fret for it, plan for it, lose all your terror of God or man for it, if you'll simply go after that thing that you want, with all your capacity, strength and sagacity, faith, hope and confidence, stern pertinacity, if neither cold poverty, famished and gaunt, nor sickness nor pain of body or brain can turn you away from the thing that you want, if dogged and grim you besiege and beset it, you'll get it!"

* From "Things As They Are." Copyright 1916, George H. Doran Company, New York.

VOLUME FOUR

IX
The Formula of Success

"One ship drives east, and another drives west, with the self-same winds that blow.
'Tis the set of the sails, and not the gales which tells us the way they go.
"Like the waves of the sea are the ways of fate as we voyage along thru life.
'Tis the set of the soul which decides its goal and not the calm or the strife."

—ELLA WHEELER WILCOX.

What is the eternal question, which stands up and looks you and every sincere man squarely in the eye every morning?

"How can I better my condition?" That is the real life question, which confronts you, and I will haunt you every day till you solve it.

Read this chapter carefully and I think you will find the answer to this important life question which you and every man must solve if he expects ever to have more each Monday morning, after pay day, than he had the week before.

To begin with, all wealth depends upon a clear understanding of the fact that mind—thought—is the only creator. The great business of life is thinking. Control your thoughts and you control circumstance.

Just as the first law of gain is desire, so the formula of success is BELIEF. Believe that you have it—see it as an existent fact—and anything you can rightly wish for is yours. Belief is "the substance of things hoped for, the evidence of things not seen."

You have seen men, inwardly no more capable than yourself accomplish the seemingly impossible. You have seen others, after years of hopeless struggle; suddenly win their most cherished dreams. And you've often wondered, "What is the power that gives new life to their dying ambitions, that supplies new impetus to their jaded desires, that gives them a new start on the road to success?"

That power is belief—faith. Someone, something, gave them a new belief in themselves and a new faith in their power to win—and they leaped ahead and wrested success from seemingly certain defeat.

Do you remember the picture Harold Lloyd was in two or three years ago, showing a country boy who was afraid of his shadow? Every boy in the countryside bedeviled him. Until one day his grandmother gave him a talisman that she assured him his grandfather had carried through the Civil War and which, so she said, had the property of making its owner invincible. Nothing could hurt him, she told him, while he wore this talisman. Nothing could stand up against him. He believed her. And the next time the bully of the town started to cuff him around, he wiped up the earth with him. And that was only the start. Before the year was out he had made a reputation as the most daring soul in the community.

Then, when his grandmother felt that he was thoroughly cured, she told him the truth—that the "talisman" was merely a piece of old junk she'd picked up by the roadside—that she knew all he needed was *faith in himself,* belief that he could do these things.

The Talisman of Napoleon

Stories like that are common. It is such a well-established truth that you can do only what you think you can, that the theme is a favorite one with authors. I remember reading a story years ago of an artist—a mediocre sort of artist—who was visiting the field of Waterloo and happened upon a curious lump of metal half buried in the dirt, which so attracted him that he picked it up and put it in his pocket. Soon thereafter he noticed a sudden increase in confidence, an absolute faith in himself, not only as to his own chosen line of work, but in his ability to handle any situation that might present itself. He painted a great picture—just to show that he *could* do it. Not content with that, he envisioned an empire with Mexico as its basis, actually led a revolt that carried all before it—until one day he lost his talisman. *And immediately his bubble burst.*

I instance this just to illustrate the point that it is *your own belief in yourself* that counts. It is the consciousness of dominant power within you that makes all things attainable. *You can do anything you think you can.* This knowledge is literally the gift of the gods, for through it you can solve every human problem. It should make of you an incurable optimist. It is the open door to welfare. *Keep it open*—by expecting to gain everything that is right.

You are entitled to every good thing. Therefore expect nothing but good. Defeat does not *need* to follow victory. You don't have to "knock wood" every time you congratulate yourself that things have been going well with you. Victory should follow victory—and it will if you let this Mind work. It is the mind that means health and life and boundless opportunity and recompense. No limitation rests upon you. So don't let any enter your life. Remember that Mind will do every good thing for you. It will remove mountains for you.

Bring all your thoughts, your desires, your aims, your talents, into the Storehouse—the Consciousness of Good, the Law of Infinite supply—and prove these blessings. There is every reason to know that you are entitled to adequate provision. Everything that is involved in supply is a thing of thought. Now reach out, stretch your mind, and try to comprehend *unlimited thought, unlimited supply.*

Do not think that supply must come through one or two channels. It is not for you to dictate to Universal Mind the means through which It shall send Its gifts to you. There are millions of channels through which It can reach you. Your part is to impress upon Mind your need, your earnest desire, your boundless belief in the resources and the willingness of Universal Mind to help you. Plant the seed of desire. Nourish it with a clear visualization of the ripened fruit. Water it with sincere faith. But leave the means to Universal Mind.

Open up your mind. Clear out the channels of thought. Keep yourself in a state of receptivity. Gain a mental attitude in which you are constantly *expecting good.* You have the fundamental right to all good, you know. "According to your faith, be it unto you."

The trouble with most of us is that we are mentally lazy. It is much easier to go along with the crowd than to break trail for ourselves. But the great discoverers, the great inventors, the great geniuses in all lines have been men who dared to break with tradition, who defied precedent, who believed that there is no limit to what Mind can do—and who stuck to that belief until their goal was won, in spite of all the sneers and ridicule of the wiseacres and the "It-can't-be-done'rs."

Not only that, but they were never satisfied with achieving just one success. They knew that the first success is like the first olive out of the bottle. All the others come out the more easily for it. They realized that they were a part of the Creative Intelligence of the Universe, and that the part shares all the properties of the whole. And that realization gave them the faith to strive for any right thing, the knowledge that the only limit upon their capabilities was the limit of their desires. Knowing that, they couldn't be satisfied with any ordinary success. They had to keep on and on and on.

Edison didn't sit down and fold his hands when he gave us the talking machine or the electric light. These great achievements merely opened the way to new fields of accomplishment.

Open up the channels between your mind and Universal Mind, and there is no limit to the riches that will come pouring in. Concentrate your thoughts on the particular thing you are most interested in, and ideas in abundance will come flooding down, opening up a dozen ways of winning the goal you are striving for.

But don't let one success—no matter how great—satisfy you. The Law of Creation, you know, is the Law of Growth. You can't stand still. You must go forward—or be passed by. Complacency—self-satisfaction—is the greatest enemy of achievement. You must keep looking forward. Like Alexander, you must be constantly seeking new worlds to conquer. Depend upon it; the power will come to meet the need. There is no such thing as failing powers, if we look to Mind for our source of supply. The only failure of mind comes from worry and fear—or from disuse.

William James, the famous psychologist, taught that "The more mind does, the more it can do." For ideas release energy. You can *do* more and better work than you have ever done. You can *know* more than you know now. You know from your own experience that under proper mental conditions of joy or enthusiasm, you can do three or four times the work without fatigue that you can ordinarily. Tiredness is more boredom than actual physical fatigue. You can work almost indefinitely when the work is a pleasure.
You've seen sickly persons, frail persons, who couldn't do an hour's light work without exhaustion, suddenly buckle down when heavy responsibilities were thrown upon them, and grow strong and rugged under the load. Crises not only draw upon the reserve power you have, but they help to create new power.

"It Couldn't Be Done"

It may be that you have been deluded by the thought of incompetence. It may be that you have been told so often that you cannot do certain things that you've come to believe you can't. Remember that success or failure is merely a state of mind. Believe you cannot do a thing—and you can't. Know that you *can* do it—and you *will*. You must *see yourself doing it.*

"If you think you are beaten, you are; If you think you dare not, you don't; If you'd like to win, but you think you can't, it's almost a cinch you won't; If you think you'll lose, you've lost, for out in the world you'll find success begins with a fellow's will— it's all in the state of mind.

"Full many a race is lost ere even a race is run, and many a coward fails ere even his work's begun.
Think big, and your deeds will grow, think small and you fall behind, think that you can, and you will; It's all in the state of mind.

"If you think you are outclassed, you are; You've got to think high to rise; You've got to be sure of yourself before you can ever win a prize.
Life's battle doesn't always go to the stronger or faster man; But sooner or later, the man who wins is the fellow who thinks he can."

There's a vast difference between a proper understanding of one's own ability and a determination to make the best of it—and offensive egotism. It is absolutely necessary for every man to believe in himself, before he can make the most of himself. All of us have something to sell. It may be our goods, it may be our abilities, it may be our services. You've got to believe in yourself to make your buyer take stock in you at par and accrued interest. You've got to feel the same personal solicitude over a customer lost, as a revivalist over a backslider, and hold special services to bring him back into the fold. You've got to get up every morning with determination, if you're going to go to bed that night with satisfaction.

There's mighty sound sense in the saying that the entire world loves a booster. The one and only thing you have to win success with is MIND. For your mind to function at its highest capacity, you've got to be charged with good cheer and optimism. No one ever did a good piece of work while in a negative frame of mind. Your best work is always done when you are feeling, happy and optimistic.

And a happy disposition is the *result*—not the *cause*—of happy, cheery thinking. Health and prosperity are the *results* primarily of optimistic thoughts. *You* make the pattern. If the impress you have left on the world about you seems faint and weak, don't blame fate—blame your pattern! You will never cultivate a brave, courageous demeanor by thinking cowardly thoughts. You cannot gather figs from thistles. You will never make your dreams come true by choking them with doubts and fears. You've got to put foundations under your air castles, foundations of UNDERSTANDING and BELIEF. Your chances of success in any undertaking can always be measured by your BELIEF in yourself.

Are your surroundings discouraging? Do you feel that if you were in another's place success would be easier? Just bear in mind that your real environment is within you. All the factors of success or failure are in your inner world. *You* make that own inner world—and through it your outer world. You can choose the material from which to build it. If you've not chosen wisely in the past, you can choose again now the material you want to rebuild it. The richness of life is within you. No one has failed so long as he can begin again.

Start right in and *do* all those things you feel you have it in you to do. Ask permission of no man. Concentrating your thought upon any proper undertaking will make its achievement possible. Your belief that you *can* do the thing gives your thought forces their power. Fortune waits upon you. Seize her boldly, hold her—and she is yours. She belongs rightfully to you. But if you cringe to her, if you go up to her doubtfully, timidly, she will pass you by in scorn. For she is a fickle jade who must be mastered, who loves boldness, who admires confidence.

A Roman boasted that it was sufficient for him to strike the ground with his foot and legions would spring up. And his very boldness cowed his opponents. It is the same with your mind. Take the first step, and your mind will mobilize all its forces to your aid. But the first essential is that you *begin*. Once the battle is started, all that is within and without you will come to your assistance, if you attack in earnest and meet each obstacle with resolution. But *you* have got to start things.

"The Lord helps them that help themselves" is a truth as old as man.

It is, in fact, plain common sense. Your subconscious mind has all power, but your conscious mind is the watchman at the gate. *It* has got to open the door. *It* has got to press the spring that releases the infinite energy. No failure is possible in the accomplishment of any right object you may have in life, if you but understand your power and will perseveringly try to use it in the proper way.

The men who have made their mark in this world all had one trait in common—*they believed in themselves!* "But," you may say, "how can I believe in myself when I have never yet done anything worth while, when everything I put my hand to seems to fail?" You can't, of course. That is, you couldn't if you had to depend upon your conscious mind alone. But certainly the Mind that imaged the heavens and the earth and all that they contain has all wisdom, all power, and all abundance. With this Mind to call upon, you know there is no problem too difficult for you to undertake. The *knowing* of this is the first step. *Faith.* But faith without work is dead. So go on to the next step. Decide on the one thing you want most from life, no matter what it may be. There is no limit, you know, to Mind. Visualize this thing that you want. See it, feel it, BELIEVE in it. Make your mental blueprint, and *begin to build!*

Suppose some people DO laugh at your idea. Suppose Reason does say—"It can't be done!" People laughed at Galileo. They laughed at Henry Ford. Reason contended for countless ages that the earth was flat. Reason said— or so numerous automotive engineers argued—that the Ford motor wouldn't run. But the earth is round—and the twelfth or fifteenth million Ford is on the road.

Let us start right now putting into practice some of these truths that you have learned. What do you want most of life right now? Take that one desire, concentrate on it, and impress it upon your subconscious mind.

Psychologists have discovered that the best time to make suggestions to your subconscious mind is just before going to sleep, when the senses are quiet and the attention is lax. So let us take your desire and suggest it to your subconscious mind tonight. The two prerequisites are the earnest DESIRE, and an intelligent, understanding BELIEF. Someone has said, you know, that education is three-fourths encouragement, and the encouragement is the suggestion that the thing can be done.

You know that you can have what you want—if you want it badly enough and can believe in it earnestly enough. So tonight, just before you drop off to sleep, concentrate your thought on this thing that you most desire from life. BELIEVE that you have it. SEE YOURSELF possessing it. FEEL yourself using it.

Do that every night until you ACTUALLY DO BELIEVE that you have the thing you want. When you reach that point, YOU *WILL HAVE IT!*

X

"This Freedom"

> "Ye shall know the truth
> And the Truth shall make you free."

I have heard that quotation ever since I was a little child. Most of us have. But to me it was never anything much but a quotation—until a few years ago. It is only in the past several years that I have begun to get an inkling of the real meaning of it—an understanding of the comfort back of it. Perhaps to you, too, it has been no more than a sonorous phrase. If so, you will be interested in what I have since gotten from it.

To begin with, what is the "truth" that is so often referred to in all our religious teaching? The truth about what? And what is it going to free us from?

The truth as I see it now is the underlying reality in everything we meet in life.

There is, for instance, one right way to solve any given problem in mathematics. That one right way is the truth as far as that problem is concerned. To know it is to free yourself from all doubt and vain imagining and error. It is to free yourself from any trouble that might arise through solving the problem incorrectly.

In the same way, there is but one BEST way of solving every situation that confronts you. That BEST way is the truth. To know it is to make you free from all worry or trouble in connection with that situation. For if it is met in the RIGHT way, only good can come of it.

Then there is your body. There is only one RIGHT idea of every organism in your body. One CORRECT method of functioning for each of them. And Universal Mind holds that RIGHT idea, that CORRECT method. The functioning of your body, the rebuilding of each cell and tissue, is the work of your subconscious mind. If you will constantly hold before it the thought that its model is perfection, that weakness or sickness or deformity is merely ABSENCE of perfection—not a reality in itself—in short, if you will realize the *Truth* concerning your body, your subconscious mind will speedily make you free and keep you free from every ill.

It matters not what is troubling you today. If you will KNOW that whatever it may seem to be is merely the absence of the true idea, if you will realize that the only thing that counts is the truth that Universal Mind knows about your body, you can make that truth manifest.

Affirm the good, the true—and the evil will vanish. It is like turning on the light—the darkness immediately disappears. For there is no actual substance in darkness—it is merely absence of light. Nor is there any substance in sickness or evil—it is merely the absence of health or good.

All sickness, all poverty, all sorrow, is the result of the incorrect use of some gift of God, which in itself is inherently good. It is just as though we took the numbers that were given us to work out a problem, and put them in the wrong places. The result would be incorrect, inharmonious. We would not be expressing the truth. The moment we rearrange those numbers properly, we get the correct answer—harmony—the *truth*! There was nothing wrong with the principle of mathematics before—the fault was all with us, with our incorrect arrangement of the figures.

What is true of the principle of mathematics is true of every principle. The principle is changeless, undying. It is only our expression of the principle that changes as our understanding of it becomes more thorough. Lightning held only terror for man until he made of electricity his servant. Steam was only so much waste until man learned to harness it. Fire and water are the most destructive forces known—until properly used, and then they are man's greatest helpers. There is nothing wrong with any gift of God—once we find the way to use it. The truth is always there if we can find the principle behind it. The figures in mathematics are never bad. It is merely our incorrect arrangement of them.

The great need is an open mind and the desire for understanding. How far in the science of mathematics would you get if you approached the study of it with the preconceived notion that two plus two makes five, and nothing you heard to the contrary was going to change that belief?

You must drop all your preconceived ideas, all your prejudices. You must never say—"Oh, that sounds like so-and-so. I don't want any of it." Just remember that any great movement must have at least a grain of truth back of it, else it could never grow to any size. Seek that grain of truth. Be open-minded. Keep your eyes and ears open for the truth. If you can do this, you will find that new wordings, different interpretations, are but the outer shell. You can still see the Truth beneath.

The Only Power

He who is looking for wisdom, power, or permanent success, will find it only within. Mind is the only cause. Your body is healthy or sick according to the images of thought you impress upon your subconscious mind. If you will hold thoughts of health instead of sickness, if you will banish all thoughts of disease and decay, you can build up a perfect body. Dr. William S. Patten of New York says, "To know and to understand the organization of mind and to recognize the action of mind is the first and the only requisite of a sound body." For all disease starts in the mind. It may be in your own conscious mind, from reading of an epidemic or from meeting with circumstances which education has taught you will bring about disease. It may be suggested to your subconscious mind, as so frequently happens with young children, by the fears and worries and thoughts of contagion of those around you.

But whichever it is, it is FEAR that starts it. You visualize, consciously or unconsciously, the disease that you fear, and because that is the image held before your thought, your body proceeds to build in accordance with that model. You believe that disease is necessary, that you have got to expect a certain amount of it. You hear of it every day, and subconsciously at least you are constantly in fear of it. And through that very fear you create it, when if you would spend that same amount of time thinking and believing in the necessity of HEALTH, you would never need to know disease.

God does not send disease. It is not a visitation of Providence. If it were, what would be the use of doctoring it? You couldn't fight against the power of God!

God never sent us anything but good. He never gave us disease. When we allow disease to take hold of us, it is because we have lost touch with God—lost the perfect model of us that He holds in mind. And what we have got to strive for is to get back the belief in that perfect model—to forget the diseased image we are holding in our thought.

Remember the story of Alexander and his famous horse, Bucephalus? No one could ride the horse because it was afraid of its shadow. But Alexander faced it towards the sun—and rode it without trouble. Face towards the sun and the shadows will fall behind you, too. Face towards the perfect image of every organ, and the shadows of disease will never touch you.

There is no germ in a draft capable of giving you a cold. There are no bacteria in exposure to the weather that can give you a fever or pneumonia. It is you that gives them to yourself. The draft doesn't reason this out. Neither does your body. They are both of them merely phases of matter. They are not intelligent. It is your conscious mind that has been educated to think that a cold must follow exposure to a draft. This it is that suggests it to your subconscious mind and brings the cold into being.

Before you decide again that you have a cold, ask yourself, who is it that is taking this cold? It cannot be my nose, for it has no intelligence. It does only what my subconscious mind directs. And anyway, how could my nose know that a draft of air has been playing on the back of my neck? If it wasn't my nose that decided it, what was it? The only thing it can have been is my mind. Well, if mind can tell me to have a cold, surely it can stop that cold, too. So let's reverse the process, and instead of holding before the subconscious mind images of colds and fevers, think only of health and life and strength. Instead of trying to think back to discover how we "caught" cold, and thus strengthening the conviction that we have one, let us deny its existence and so knock the props out from under the creative faculties that are originating the cold. Let us hold before our subconscious mind only the perfect idea of nose and head and throat that is in Universal Mind. Let us make it use the Truth for its pattern, instead of the illusory ideas of conscious mind.

Every form of disease or sickness is solely the result of wrong thinking. The primary law of being is the law of health and life. When you recognize this, when you hold before your mind's eye only a perfect body, perfect organisms functioning perfectly, you will "realize the truth that makes you free."

Farnsworth in his "Practical Psychology" tells of a physician who has lived on a very restricted diet for years while at home. But about once a year he comes to New York for a week. While here, he eats anything and everything that his fancy dictates, and never suffers the least inconvenience. As soon as he gets home he has to return to his diet. Unless he sticks to his diet, he expects to be ill—*and he is ill*. "As a man thinketh, so is he." What one expects to get he is apt to get, especially where health is concerned. For matter has no sensation of its own. The conscious mind is what produces pain, is what feels, acts or impedes action.

Functional disorders are caused by certain suggestions getting into the subconsciousness and remaining there. They are not due to physical, but to mental causes—due to wrong thinking. The basis of all functional disorders is in the mind, though the manifestation is dyspepsia, melancholia, palpitation of the heart, or any one of a hundred others. There is nothing organically wrong with the body. It is your mental image that is out of adjustment. Change the one and you cure the other.

In this day of the gymnasium and the daily dozen, it may sound impractical to suggest that it is the mind, not the body, which needs the care. But I am far from being the first to suggest it.

There is a very successful physician in London whose teaching is that gymnastic exercise does more harm than good. He contends that the only exercise necessary for the perfect development of the body is yawning and stretching.

I would go farther than that. I would say that no physical exercise is *essential* to the perfect development of the body. That since the only cause is mind, the principal good of exercise is that when we go through the motions we impress upon our subconscious mind the picture of the perfect figure that we would have. And that mental visualization is what brings the results.

You can get the same results without the physical exercise by visualizing in your mind's eye the figure of the man you want to be, by intensely desiring it, by BELIEVING that you have it.

You can win to perfect health by knowing that there is but one right idea in Universal Mind for every organism in your body—that this right idea is perfect and undying—that you have only to hold it before your subconscious mind to see it realized in your body. *This is the truth that makes you free.*

XI
The Law of Attraction

For life is the mirror of king and slave.
'Tis just what you are and do; then give to the world the best you have, and the best will come back to you.

—MADELINE BRIDGES.

The old adage that "He profits most who serves best" is no mere altruism.

Look around you. What businesses are going ahead? What men are making the big successes? Are they the ones who grab the passing dollar, careless of what they offer in return? Or are they those who are striving always to give a little greater value, a little more work than they are paid for?

When scales are balanced evenly, a trifle of extra weight thrown into either side overbalances the other as effectively as a ton.

In the same way, a little better value, a little extra effort, makes the man or the business stand out from the great mass of mediocrity like a tall man among pigmies, and brings results out of all proportion to the additional effort involved.

It pays—not merely altruistically, but in good, hard, round dollars—to give a little more value than seems necessary, to work a bit harder than you are paid for. It's that extra ounce of value that counts.

For the law of attraction is service. We receive in proportion as we give out. In fact, we usually receive in far greater proportion. "Cast thy bread upon the waters and it will return to you an hundred-fold."

Back of everything is the immutable law of the Universe—that what you are but the effect. Your thoughts are the causes. The only way you can change the effect is by first changing the cause.

People live in poverty and want because they are so wrapped up in their sufferings that they give out thoughts only of lack and sorrow. They expect want. They open the door of their mind only to hardship and sickness and poverty. True—they hope for something better—but their hopes are so drowned by their fears that they never have a chance.

You cannot receive good while expecting evil. You cannot demonstrate plenty while looking for poverty. "Blessed is he that expecteth much, for verily his soul shall be filled." Solomon outlined the law when he said:

"There is that scattereth, and increaseth yet more; And there is that withholdeth more than is meet, but it tendeth only to want.
The liberal soul shall be made fat; And he that watereth shall be watered also himself."

The Universal Mind expresses itself largely through the individual. It is continually seeking an outlet. It is like a vast reservoir of water, constantly replenished by mountain springs. Cut a channel to it and the water will flow in ever-increasing volume. In the same way, if you once open up a channel of service by which the Universal Mind can express itself through you, its gifts will flow in ever increasing volume and YOU will be enriched in the process.

This is the idea through which great bankers are made. A foreign country needs millions for development. Its people are hard working, but lack the necessary implements to make their work productive. How are they to find the money?

They go to a banker—put their problem up to him. He has not the money himself, but he knows how and where to raise it. He sells the promise to pay of the foreign country (their bonds, in other words) to people who have money to invest. His is merely a service. But it is such an invaluable service that both sides are glad to pay him liberally for it.

In the same way, by opening up a channel between universal supply and human needs—by doing your neighbors or your friends or your customer's service—you are bound to profit yourself. And the wider you open your channel— the greater service you give or the better values you offer—the more things are bound to flow through your channel, the more you are going to profit thereby.

But you've got to *use* your talent if you want to profit from it. It matters not how small your service—using it will make it greater. You don't have to retire to a cell and pray. That is a selfish method—selfish concern for your own soul to the exclusion of all others. Mere self-denial or asceticism as such does no one good. You've got to DO something, to USE the talents God has given you to make the world better for your having been in it.

Remember the parable of the talents. You know what happened to the man who went off and hid his talent, whereas those who made use of theirs were given charge over many things.

That parable, it has always seemed to me, expresses the whole law of life. The only right is to use all the forces of good. The only wrong is to neglect or to abuse them.

"Thou shalt love the Lord thy God. This is the first and the greatest Commandment." Thou shalt show thy love by using to the best possible advantage the good things (the "talents" of the parable) that He has placed in your hands. "And the second is like unto it. Thou shalt love thy neighbor as thyself." Thou shalt not abuse the good things that have been provided you in such prodigality, by using them against your neighbor. Instead, thou shalt treat him (love him) as he would treat you. Thou shalt use the good about you for the advantage of all.

If you are a banker, you've got to use the money you have in order to make more money. If you are a merchant, you've got to sell the goods you have in order to buy more goods. If you are a doctor, you must help the patient you have in order to get more practice. If you are a clerk, you must do your work a little better than those around you if you want to earn more money than they. And if you want more of the universal supply, you must use that which you have in such a way as to make yourself of greater service to those around you.

In other words, if you would be great, you must serve. And he who serves most shall be greatest of all. If you want to make more money, instead of seeking it for yourself, see how you can make more for others. In the process you will inevitably make more for yourself, too. We get as we give—but we must give first.

It matters not where you start—you may be a day laborer. But still you can give—give a bit more of energy, of work, of thought, than you are paid for. Try to put a little extra skill into your work. Use your mind to find some better way of doing whatever task may be set for you. It won't be long before you are out of the common labor class.

There is no kind of work than cannot be bettered by thought. There is no method that cannot be improved by thought. So give generously of your thought to your work. Think every minute you are at it—"Isn't there some way in which this could be done easier, quicker, better?" Read in your spare time everything that relates to your own work or to the job ahead of you. In these days of magazines and books and libraries, few are the occupations that are not thoroughly covered in some good work.

Remember in Lorimer's "*Letters of a Self-Made Merchant to His Son,*" the young fellow that old Gorgan Graham hired against his better judgment and put in the "barrel gang" just to get rid of him quickly? Before the month was out the young fellow had thought himself out of that job by persuading the boss to get a machine that did the work at half the cost and with a third of the gang. Graham just had to raise his pay and put him higher up. But he wouldn't stay put. No matter what the job, he always found some way it could be done better and with fewer people, until he reached the top of the ladder.

There are plenty of men like that in actual life. They won't stay down. They are as full of bounce as a cat with a small boy and a dog after it. Thrown to the dog from an upper window, it is using the time of falling to get set for the next jump. By the time the dog leaps for where it hit, the cat is up the tree across the street.

The true spirit of business is the spirit of that plucky old Danish sea captain, Peter Tordenskjold. Attacked by a Swedish frigate, after all his crew but one had been killed and his supply of cannon balls was exhausted, Peter boldly kept up the fight, firing pewter dinner-plates and mugs from his one remaining gun.

One of the pewter mugs hit the Swedish captain and killed him, and Peter sailed off triumphant!

Look around YOU now. How can YOU give greater value for what you get? How can you SERVE better? How can you make more money for your employers or save more for your customers? Keep that thought ever in the forefront of your mind and *you'll never need to worry about making more for yourself!*

A Blank Check

There was an article by Gardner Hunting in a recent issue of "*Christian Business,*" that was so good that I reprint it here entire:

"All my life I have known in a vague way that getting money is the result of earning it; but I have never had a perfect vision of that truth till recently. Summed up now, the result of all my experience, pleasant and unpleasant, is that a man gets back exactly what he gives out, only multiplied.

"If I give to anybody service of a kind that he wants I shall get back the benefit myself. If I give more service I shall get more benefit. If I give a great deal more, I shall get a great deal more. But I shall get back more than I give. Exactly as when I plant a bushel of potatoes, I get back thirty or forty bushels, and more in proportion to the attention I give the growing crop. If I give more to my employer than he expects of me, he will give me a raise— and on no other condition. What is more, his giving me a raise does not depend on his fair-mindedness— he has to give it to me or lose me, because if he does not appreciate me somebody else will.

"But this is only part of it. If I give help to the man whose desk is next to mine, it will come back to me multiplied, even if he apparently is a rival. What I give to him, I give to the firm, and the firm will value it, because it is teamwork in the organization that the firm primarily wants, not brilliant individual performance. If I have an enemy in the organization, the same rule holds; if I give him, with the purpose of helping him, something that will genuinely help him, I am giving service to the organization. Great corporations appreciate the peacemaker, for a prime requisite in their success is harmony among employees. If my boss is unappreciative, the same rule holds; if I give him more, in advance of appreciation, he cannot withhold his appreciation and keep his own job.

"The more you think about this law, the deeper you will see it goes. It literally hands you a blank check, signed by the Maker of Universal Law, and leaves you to fill in the amount—and the kind—of payment you want! Mediocre successes are those that obey this law a little way—that fill in the check with a small amount—but that stop short of big vision in it. If every employee would only get the idea of this law firmly fixed in him as a principle, not subject to wavering with fluctuating moods, the success of the organization would be miraculous. One of my fears is apt to be that, by promoting the other fellow's success, I am sidetracking my own; but the exact opposite is the truth.

"Suppose every employee would look at his own case as an exact parallel to that of his firm. What does his firm give for the money it gets from the public? Service! Service in advance! The better the service that is given out, the more money comes back. What does the firm do to bring public attention to its service? It advertises; that is part of the service. Now, suppose that I, as an employee, begin giving my service to the firm in advance of all hoped for payment. Suppose I advertise my service. How do I do either? I cannot do anything constructive in that firm's office or store or plant or premises that is not service, from filing a letter correctly to mending the fence or pleasing a customer; from looking up a word for the stenographer, to encouraging her to look it up herself; demonstrating a machine to a customer or encouraging him to demonstrate it himself; from helping my immediate apparent rival to get a raise, to selling the whole season's output. As for advertising myself, I begin advertising myself the moment I walk into the office or the store or the shop in the morning; I cannot help it. Everybody who looks at me sees my advertisement. Everybody around me has my advertisement before his eyes all day long. So has the boss—my immediate chief and the head of the firm, no matter where they are. And if I live up to my advertising, nobody can stop me from selling my goods— my services! The more a man knocks me, the more he advertises me; because he calls attention to me; and if I am delivering something better than he says I am, the interested parties—my employers—will see it, and will not be otherwise influenced by what he says.

"More than that, I must give to every human being I come in contact with, from my wife to the bootblack who shines my shoes; from my brother to my sworn foe. Sometimes people will tell you to smile; but the smile I give has got to be a real smile that lives up to its advertising. If I go around grinning like a Cheshire cat, the Cheshire-cat grin will be what I get back—multiplied! If I give the real thing, I'll get back the real thing—multiplied! If anybody objects that this is a selfish view to take, I answer him that any law of salvation from anything by anybody that has ever been offered for any purpose, is a selfish view to take. The only unselfishness that has ever been truly taught is that of giving a lesser thing in hope of receiving a greater.

"Now, why am I so sure of this law? How can you be sure? I have watched it work; it works everywhere. You have only to try it, and keep on trying it and it will prove true for you. It is not true because I say so, nor because anybody else says so; it is just true. Theosophists call it the law of Karma; humanitarians call it the law of Service; businessmen call it the law of common sense; some call it the law of Love. It rules whether I know it or not, whether I believe it or not, whether I defy it or not. I *can't* break it! And this because it is the Truth, which we all, whether we admit it or not, worship *as* God. No man can honestly say that he does not put the truth supreme.

"It is the truth—the principle of giving and receiving—only there are few men who go the limit on it. But going the limit is the way to unlimited returns!

"What shall I give? What I have, of course. Suppose you believe in this idea—and suppose you should start giving it out, the idea itself, tactfully, wisely, and living it yourself in your organization.

How long do you think it will be before you are a power in that organization, recognized as such and getting pay as such? It is more valuable than all the cleverness and special information you can possibly possess without it. What you have, give—to everybody. If you have an idea, do not save it for your own use only; give it. It is the best thing you have to give and therefore the thing best to give—and therefore the thing that will bring the best back to you. I believe that if a man would follow this principle, even to his trade secrets, he would profit steadily more and more; and more certainly than he will by holding on to anything for himself. He would never have to worry about his own affairs because he would be working on fundamental law. Law never fails—and it will be easy for you to discover what is or is not law. And if law is worth using part of the time, it is worth using all the time.

"Look around you first, with an eye to seeing the truth, and then put the thing to the test. Through both methods of investigation you will find a blank check waiting for you to fill in with 'whatsoever you desire,' and a new way to pray and to get what you pray for."

VOLUME FOUR - A Blank Check

XII
The Three Requisites

"Waste no tears upon the blotted record of lost years, but turn the leaf, and smile, oh smile, to see the fair white pages that remain for thee.
Prate not of thy repentance. But believe the spark divine dwells in thee: let it grow.
That which the up-reaching spirit can achieve the grand and all creative forces know; They will assist and strengthen as the light lifts up the acorn to the oak-tree's height.
Thou hast but to resolve, and lo! God's whole great universe shall fortify thy soul."

—ELLA WHEELER WILCOX.

Sometime today or tomorrow or next month, in practically every commercial office and manufacturing plant in the United States, an important executive will sit back in his chair and study a list of names on a sheet of white paper before him.

Your name may be on it.
A position of responsibility is open and he is face to face with the old, old problem—
"Where can I find the man?"

The faces, the words, the work, the impressions of various men will pass through his mind in quick review. What is the first question he will ask concerning each?

"Which man is strongest on initiative, which one can best assume responsibility?"

Other things being equal, THAT is the man who will get the job. For the first requisite in business as in social life is confidence in yourself—*knowledge of your power*. Given that, the second is easy—initiative or *the courage to start things*. Lots of men have ideas, but few have the confidence in themselves or the courage to start anything.

With belief and initiative, the third requisite follows almost as a matter of course—*the faith to go ahead* and do things in the face of all obstacles.

"Oh, God," said Leonardo da Vinci, "you sell us everything for the price of an effort."
Certainly no one had a better chance to know than he. An illegitimate son, brought up in the family of his father, the misfortune of his birth made him the source of constant derision. He had to do something to lift himself far above the crowd. And he did. "For the price of an effort" he became the greatest artist in Italy—probably the greatest in the world—in a day when Italy was famous for her artists. Kings and princes felt honored at being associated with this illegitimate boy. He made the name he had no right to famous for his work alone.
"Every man of us has all the centuries in him."—Morley. All the ages behind you have bequeathed you stores of abilities, which you are allowing to lie latent. Those abilities are stored up in your subconscious mind. Call upon them. Use them. As Whittier put it—

"All the good the past has had
Remains to make our own time glad."

Are you an artist? The cunning of a da Vinci, the skill of a Rembrandt, the vision of a Reynolds, is behind those fingers of yours. Use the Genie-of-your-mind to call upon them.

70

Are you a surgeon, a lawyer, a minister, and an engineer, a businessman? Keep before your mind's eye the biggest men who have ever done the things you now are doing. Use them as your model and not as your model simply, but as your inspiration. Start in where they left off. Call upon the innermost recesses of your subconscious mind, for their skill, their judgment, their initiative. Realize that you have it in you to be as great as they. Realize that all that they did, all that they learned, all the skill they acquired is stored safely away in Universal Mind and that through your subconscious mind *you have ready access to it.*

The mind in you is the same mind that animated all the great conquerors of the past, all the great inventors, all the great artists, statesmen, leaders, business men. What they have done is but a tithe of what still remains to do—of what men in your day and your children's day will do. You can have a part in it. Stored away within you is every power that any man or woman ever possessed. It awaits only your call.

In *"Thoughts on Business,"* we read: "It is a great day in a man's life when he truly begins to discover himself. The latent capacities of every man are greater than he realizes, and he may find them if he diligently seeks for them. A man may own a tract of land for many years without knowing its value. He may think of it as merely a pasture. But one day he discovers evidences of coal and finds a rich vein beneath his land. While mining and prospecting for coal he discovers deposits of granite. In boring for water he strikes oil. Later he discovers a vein of copper ore, and after that silver and gold. These things were there all the time—even when he thought of his land merely as a pasture. But they have a value only when they are discovered and utilized.

"Not every pasture contains deposits of silver and gold, neither oil nor granite, nor even coal. But beneath the surface of every man there must be, in the nature of things, a latent capacity greater than has yet been discovered. And one discovery must lead to another until the man finds the deep wealth of his own possibilities. History is full of the acts of men who discovered somewhat of their own capacity; but history has yet to record the man who fully discovered all that be might have been."

Everything that has been done, thought, gained, or been is in Universal Mind. And you are a part of Universal Mind. You have access to it. You can call upon it for all you need in the same way you can go to your files or to a library for information. If you can realize this fact, you will find in it the key to the control of every circumstance, the solution of every problem, the satisfaction of every right desire.

But to use that key, you've got to bear in mind the three requisites of faith in your powers, initiative, and courage to start. "Who would stand before a blackboard," says *"Science and Health,"* "and pray the principle of mathematics to solve the problem? The rule is already established, and it is our task to work out the solution." In the same way, all knowledge you can need is in Universal Mind, but it is up to *you* to tap that mind.

And without the three requisites you will never do it.

Never let discouragement hold you back. Discouragement is the most dangerous feeling there is, because it is the most insidious. Generally it is looked upon as harmless, and for that very reason it is the more sinister. For failure and success are oftentimes separated by only the distance of that one word—Discouragement.

There is an old-time fable that the devil once held a sale and offered all the tools of his trade to anyone who would pay their price. They were spread out on the table, each one labeled—hatred, and malice, and envy, and despair, and sickness, and sensuality—all the weapons that everyone knows so well.

But off on one side, apart from the rest, lay a harmless looking, wedge-shaped instrument marked "Discouragement." It was old and worn looking, but it was priced far above all the rest. When asked the reason why, the devil replied:

"Because I can use this one so much more easily than the others. No one knows that it belongs to me, so with it I can open doors that are tight bolted against the others. Once I get inside I can use any tool that suits me best."

No one ever knows how small is the margin between failure and success. Frequently the two are separated only by the width of that one word—*discouragement*. Ask Ford, ask Edison, ask any successful man and he will tell you how narrow is the chasm that separates failure from success, how surely it can be bridged by perseverance and faith.

Cultivate confidence in yourself. Cultivate the feeling that you ARE succeeding. Know that you have unlimited power to do every right thing. Know that with Universal Mind to draw upon, no position is too difficult, and no problem too hard. When you put limitations upon yourself, when you doubt your ability to meet any situation, you are placing a limit upon Universal Mind.

With that knowledge of your power, with that confidence in the unlimited resources of Universal Mind, it is easy enough to show initiative, it is easy enough to find the courage to start things.

You have a right to dominion over all things—over your body, your environment, your business, your health. Develop these three requisites and you will gain that dominion. Remember that you are a part of Universal Mind, and that the part shares every property of the whole. Remember that, as the spark of electricity to the thunderbolt, so is your mind to Universal Mind. Whatever of good you may desire of life, whatever qualification, whatever position, you have only to work for it whole heartedly, confidently, with singleness of purpose—*and you can get it*.

XIII
That Old Witch—Bad Luck

"How do you tackle your work each day?
Are you scared of the job you find?
Do you grapple the task that comes your way with a confident, easy mind?
Do you stand right up to the work ahead or fearfully pause to view it?
Do you start to toil with a sense of dread or feel that you're going to do it?
"What is the thought that is in your mind?
Is fear ever running through it?
If so, just tackle the next you find by thinking you're going to do it."

—EDGAR A. GUEST.
(From "A heap o' Livin'." The Reilly & Lee Co.)

Has that old witch—bad luck— ever camped on your doorstep? Have ill health, misfortune and worry ever seemed to dog your footsteps?

If so, you will be interested in knowing that YOU were the procuring cause of all that trouble. For fear is merely creative thought in negative form.

Remember back in 1920 how fine the business outlook seemed, how everything looked rosy and life flowed along like a song? We had crops worth ten billions of dollars. We had splendid utilities, great railways, almost unlimited factory capacity. Everyone was busy. The government had a billion dollars in actual money. The banks were sound. The people were well employed. Wages were good. Prosperity was general. *Then something happened.* A wave of fear swept over the country. The prosperity could not last. People wouldn't pay such high prices. There was too much inflation. What was the result?

As Job put it in the long ago, "The thing that I greatly feared has come upon me." The prosperity vanished almost over night. Failures became general. Hundreds of thousands were thrown out of work. And all because of panic—fear.
'Tis true that readjustments were necessary. 'Tis true that prices were too high, that inventories were too big, that values generally were inflated.

But it wasn't necessary to burst the balloon to let out the gas. There are orderly natural processes of readjustment that bring things to their proper level with the least harm to anyone.

But fear—panic—knows no reason. It brings into being overnight the things that it fears. It is the greatest torment of humanity. It is about all there is to Hell. *Fear is, in short, the devil*. It causes most of the sin, disaster, disease and misery of the world. It is the only thing you can put into business, which won't draw dividends in either fun or dollars. If you guess right, you don't get any satisfaction out of it.

The real cause of all sickness is fear. You image some disease in your thought, and your body proceeds to build upon this model that you hold before it. You have seen how fear makes the face pallid, how it first stops the beating of the heart, then sets it going at trip-hammer pace. Fear changes the secretions. Fear halts the digestion. Fear puts lines and wrinkles into the face. Fear turns the hair gray.
Mind controls every function of the human body. If the thought you hold before your subconscious mind is the fear of disease, of colds or catarrh, of fever or indigestion, those are the images your subconscious mind will work out in your body. For your body itself is merely so much matter—an aggregation of protons and electrons, just as the table in front of you is an aggregation of these same buttons of force, but with a different density. Take away your mind, and your body is just as inert, just as lifeless, and just as senseless, as the table. Every function of your body, from the beating of your heart to the secretions in your glands, is controlled by mind. The digestion of your food is just as much a function of your mind as the moving of your finger. So the all-important thing is not what food you put into your stomach, but what your mind decides shall be done with it. If your mind feels that certain food should make you sick, it will make you sick. If, on the other hand, your mind decides that though the food has no nutritive value, there is no reason why unintelligent matter should make you sick; mind will eliminate that food without harm or discomfort to you.

Your body is just like clay in the hands of a potter. Your mind can make of it what it will. The clay has nothing to say about what form it shall take. Neither have your head, your heart, your lungs, your digestive organs anything to say about how conditions shall affect them. They do not decide whether they shall be dizzy or diseased or lame. It is mind that makes this decision. They merely conform to it AFTER mind has decided it. Matter has undergone any and every condition without harm, when properly sustained by mind. And what it has done once, it can do again.

When you understand that your muscles, your nerves, your bones have no feeling or intelligence of their own, when you learn that they react to conditions only as mind directs that they shall react, you will never again think or speak of any organ as imperfect, as weak or ailing. You will never again complain of tired bodies, aching muscles, or frayed nerves. On the contrary, you will hold steadfast to thoughts of exhaustless strength, of super-abundant vitality, knowing that, as Shakespeare said—"There is nothing, either good or bad, but thinking makes it so."

Never fear disaster, for the fear of it is an invitation to disaster to come upon you. Fear being vivid, easily impresses itself upon the subconscious mind. And by so impressing itself, it brings into being the thing that is feared. It is the Frankenstein monster that we all create at times, and which, created, and turns to rend its creator. Fear that something you greatly prize will be lost and the fear you feel with creates the very means whereby you will lose it.

Fear is the Devil. It is the ravening lion roaming the earth seeking whom it may devour. The only safety from it is to deny it. The only refuge is in the knowledge that it has no power other than the power you give to it.

He Whom a Dream Hath Possessed

You fear debt. So your mind concentrates upon it and brings about greater debts.

You fear loss. And by visualizing that loss you bring it about.

The only remedy for fear is to know that evil has no power—that it is a non-entity—merely a lack of something. You fear ill health, when if you would concentrate that same amount of thought upon good health you would insure the very condition you fear to lose. Functional disturbances are caused solely by the mind through wrong thinking. The remedy for them is a not drug, but right thinking, for the trouble is not in the organs but in the mind.

Farnsworth in his "*Practical Psychology*" tells of a man who had conceived the idea when a boy that the eating of cherries and milk together had made him sick. He was very fond of both, but always had to be careful not to eat them together, for whenever he did he had been ill. Mr. Farnsworth explained to him that there was no reason for such illness, because all milk sours anyway just as soon as it reaches the stomach. As a matter of fact it cannot be digested until it does sour. He then treated the man mentally for this wrong association of ideas, and after the one treatment the man was never troubled in this way again, though he had been suffering from it for forty-five years.

If you had delirium tremens, and thought you saw pink elephants and green alligators and yellow snakes all about you, it would be a foolish physician that would try to cure you of snakes. Or that would prescribe glasses to improve your eyesight, when he knew that the animals round about you were merely distorted visions of your mind.

The indigestion that you suffer from, the colds that bother you—in short, each and every one of your ailments—is just as much a distorted idea of your mind as would be the snakes of delirium tremens. Banish the idea and you banish the manifestation.

The Bible contains one continuous entreaty to cast out fear. From beginning to end, the admonition "Fear not" is insistent. Fear is the primary cause of all bodily impairment.

Struggle there is. And struggle there will always be. But struggle is merely wrestling with trial. We need difficulties to overcome. But there is nothing to be afraid of. Everything is an effect of mind. Your thought forces, concentrated upon anything, will bring that thing into manifestation. Therefore concentrate them only upon good things, only upon those conditions you wish to see manifested. *Think* health, power, abundance, and happiness. Drive all thoughts of poverty and disease, of fear and worry, as far from your mind as you drive filth from your homes. For fear and worry is the filth of the mind that causes all trouble, that brings about all disease.

Banish it! Banish from among your associates any man with a negative outlook on life. Shun him as you would the plague. Can you imagine a knocker winning anything? He is doomed before he starts. Don't let him pull you down with him. For there is no surer way of doing the wrong thing in business or in social life than to fret yourself, to worry, to fume, to want action of some kind, regardless of what it may be. Remember the Lord's admonition to the Israelites, "*Be still*—and know that I am God."

Have you ever stood on the shore of a calm, peaceful lake and watched the reflections in it? The trees, the mountains, the clouds, the sky, all were mirrored there—just as perfectly, as beautifully, as the objects themselves. But try to get such a reflection from the ocean! It cannot be done, because the ocean is always restless, always stirred up by winds or waves or tides.

So it is with your mind. You cannot reflect the richness and plenty of Universal Mind, you cannot mirror peace and health and happiness, if you are constantly worried, continually stirred by waves of fear, winds of anger, tides of toil and striving. You must relax at times. You must give mind a chance. You must realize that, when you have done your best, you can confidently lean back and leave the outcome to Universal Mind.

Just as wrong thinking produces discord in the body, so it also brings on a diseased condition in the realm of commerce. Experience teaches that we need to be protected more from our fears and wrong thoughts, than from so-called evil influences external to ourselves. We need not suffer for another man's wrong, for another's greed, dishonesty, avarice or selfish ambition. But if we hug to ourselves the fear that we do have to so suffer, take it into our thought, allow it to disturb us, then we sentence ourselves. We are free to reject every suggestion of discord, and to be governed harmoniously, in spite of what anything or anybody may try to do to us.

Do you know why old army men would rather have soldiers of 18 or 20 than mature men of 30 or 40? Not because they can march farther. They can't! Not because they can carry more. They can't! But because when they go to sleep at night, they really sleep. *They wipe the slate clean!* When they awaken in the morning, they are ready for a new day and a new world.

But an older man carries the nervous strain of one day over to the next. He worries! With the result that at the end of a couple of month's hard campaigning, the older man is a nervous wreck.

And that is the trouble with most men in business. *They never wipe the slate clean! They worry!* And they carry each day's worries over to the next, with the result that some day the burden becomes more than they can carry.

The Bars of Fate

Fear results from a belief that there are really two powers in this world—Good and Evil. Like light and darkness. When the fact is that Evil is no more real than darkness. True, we lose contact with Good at times. We let the clouds of fear and worry come between us and the sunlight of Good and then all seems dark. But the sun is still shining on the other side of those clouds, and when we drive them away, we again see its light.

Realizing this, realizing that Good is ever available if we will but turn to it confidently in our need, what is there to fear? Everyone will admit that Universal Mind can do anything good. Everyone will admit that It can bring to a successful conclusion any undertaking It may be interested in. If Mind created your business, if It inspired your work, then It is interested in its successful conclusion.

Why not, then, call upon Mind when you have done all you know how to do and yet success seems beyond your efforts. Why not put your problem up to Mind, secure in the belief that It CAN and WILL give you any right thing you may desire? I know that many people hesitate to pray for material things, but if Universal Mind made them, they must have been made for some good purpose, and as long as you intend to use them for good, by all means ask for them.

If you can feel that your business, your work, is a good work, if you can be sure that it is advancing the great Scheme of Things by ever so little, you will never again fear debt or lack or limitation. For "The earth is the Lord's and the fullness thereof." Universal Mind is never going to lack for means to carry on Its work. Where you are, Mind is, and where Mind is, there is all the power, all the supply of the universe.

You are like the owner of a powerhouse that supplies electricity for light and heat and power to the homes and the factories around you. There is unlimited electricity everywhere about you, but you have got to set your dynamo going to draw the electricity out of the air and into your power lines, before it can be put to practical account.

Just so, there are unlimited riches all about you, but you have got to set the dynamo of your mind to work to bring them into such form as will make them of use to yourself and the world.

So don't worry about any present lack of money or other material things. Don't try to win from others what they have. Go where the money is! The material wealth that is in evidence is so small compared with the possible wealth available through the right use of mind, that it is negligible by comparison. The great rewards are for the pioneers. Look at Carnegie; at Woolworth; at Ford! Every year some new field of development is opened, some new world discovered. Steam, gas, electricity, telegraphy, wireless, the automobile, and the aeroplane—each opens up possibilities of new worlds yet to come.

A hundred years ago, people probably felt that everything had been discovered that could be discovered. That everything was already known that was likely ever to be known. Just as you may feel about things now, yet look at the tremendous strides mankind has taken in the past hundred years. And they are as nothing to what the future holds for us, once man has learned to harness the truly unlimited powers of his subconscious mind.

There are billions of dollars worth of treasure under every square mile of the earth's surface. There are millions of ways in which this old world of ours can be made a better place to live. Set your mind to work locating some of this treasure, finding some of those ways. Don't wait for someone else to blaze the trail.

No one remembers who else was on the *Santa Maria,* but Columbus' name will be known forever! Carnegie is said to have made a hundred millionaires, but he alone became almost a *billionaire*!

Have you ever read Kipling's "*Explorer?*"

"'There's no sense in going further—it's the edge of cultivation, So they said, and I believed it—broke my land and sowed my crop—Built my barns and strung my fences in the little border station Tucked away below the foothills where the trails run out and stop. "Till a voice, as bad as Conscience, rang interminable changes on one everlasting Whisper day and night repeated—so: 'something hidden. Go and find it. Go and look behind the Ranges—Something lost behind the Ranges. Lost and waiting for you. Go!'"

Your mind is part and parcel of Universal Mind. You have the wisdom of all the ages to draw upon. Use it! Use it to do your work in a way it was never done before. Use it to find new outlets for your business, new methods of reaching people, new and better ways of serving them. Use it to uncover new riches, to learn ways to make the world a better place to live in.

Concentrate your thought upon these things, knowing that back of you is the vast reservoir of Universal Mind, that all these things are *already* known to It, and that you have but to make your contact for them to be known to you.

Optimism based on such a realization is never overconfidence. It is the joyous assurance of *absolute faith*. It is the assurance that made Wilson for a time the outstanding leader of the world. It is the assurance that heartened Lincoln during the black days of the Civil War. It is the assurance that carried Hannibal and Napoleon over the Alps, that left Alexander sighing for more worlds to conquer, that enabled Cortez and his little band to conquer a nation.

Grasp this idea of the availability of Universal Mind for your daily needs, and your vision will become enlarged, your capacity increased. You will realize that the only limits upon you are those you put upon yourself. There will be no such thing then as difficulties and opposition barring your way.

Exercise

You feed and nourish the body daily. But few people give any thought to nourishing that far more important part —the Mind. So let us try, each day, to set apart a few minutes time to give the Mind a repast.

To begin with, *relax*! Stretch out comfortably on a lounge or in an easy chair and let go of every muscle, loosen every bit of tension, forget every thought of fear or worry. Relax mentally and physically.

Few people know how to relax entirely. Most of us are on a continual strain, and it is this strain that brings on physical disturbances—not any real work we may do. Here is a little exercise that will help you to thoroughly relax:

Recline comfortably on a lounge or bed. Stretch luxuriously first, then when you are settled at your ease again, lift the right leg a foot or two. Let it drop limply. Repeat slowly twice. Do the same with the left leg. With the right arm. With the left arm. You will find then that all your muscles are relaxed. You can forget them and turn your thoughts to other things.

Try to realize the unlimited power that is yours. Think back to the dawn of time, when Mind first imaged from nothingness the heavens and the earth and all that in them is. Remember that, although your mind is to Universal Mind only as a drop of water to the ocean, this drop has all the properties of the great ocean; one in quality although not in quantity; your mind has all the creative power of Universal Mind.

"And God made man in His image, after His likeness." Certainly God never manifested anything but infinite abundance, infinite supply. If you are made in His image, there is no reason why you should ever lack for anything of good. You can manifest abundance, too.

Round about you are the same electronic energy from which Universal Mind formed the heavens and the earth. What do you wish to form from it? What do you want most from life? Hold it in your thought, visualize it, and SEE it! Make your model clear-cut and distinct.

1. Remember, the first thing necessary is a sincere desire, concentrating your thought on one thing with singleness of purpose.

2. The second is visualization—SEEING YOURSELF DOING IT—imaging the object in the same way that Universal Mind imaged all of creation.

3. Next is faith; BELIEVING that you HAVE this thing that you want. Not that you are GOING to have it, mind

you—but that you HAVE it.

4. And the last is gratitude—gratitude for this thing that you have received, gratitude for the power that enabled you to create it, gratitude for all the gifts that Mind has laid at your feet.

"Trust in the Lord . . . and verily thou shalt be fed."

"Delight thyself also in the Lord, and He shall give thee the desires of thy heart."

"Commit thy way unto the Lord, and He Shall bring it to pass."

VOLUME FIVE

XIV
Your Needs Are Met

"Arise, 0 Soul, and gird thee up anew, though the black camel Death kneel at this gate; No beggar thou that thou for alms shouldst sue; Be the proud captain still of thine own fate."

—KENYON.

You've heard the story of the old man who called his children to his bedside to give them a few parting words of advice. And this was the burden of it.

"My children," he said, "I have had a great deal of trouble in my life—a great deal of trouble—*but most of it never happened."*
We are all of us like that old man. Our troubles weigh us down—in prospect—but we usually find that when the actual need arrives, Providence has devised some way of meeting it.

Dr. Jacques Loeb, a member of the Rockefeller Institute, conducted a series of tests with parasites found on plants, which show that even the lowest order of creatures have the power to call upon Universal Supply for the resources to meet any unusual need.
"In order to obtain the material," reads the report of the tests, "potted rose bushes are brought into a room and placed in front of a closed window. If the plants are allowed to dry out, the aphides (parasites), previously wingless, change to winged insects. After the metamorphosis, the animals leave the plants, fly to the window and then creep upward on the glass.

"It is evident that these tiny insects found that the plants on which they had been thriving were dead, and that they could therefore secure nothing more to eat and drink from this source. The only method by which they could save themselves from starvation was to grow temporary wings and fly, which they did."
In short, when their source of sustenance was shut off and they had to find the means of migrating or perish, Universal Supply furnished the means for migration.

If Universal Mind can thus provide for the meanest of its creatures, is it not logical to suppose that It will do even more for us—the highest product of creation—if we will but call upon It, if we will but have a little faith? Viewed in the light of Mind's response to the need of those tiny parasites, does it seem so unbelievable that a sea should roll back while a people marched across it dry-shod? That a pillar of fire should lead them through the wilderness by night? That manna should fall from heaven, or water gush forth from a rock?

In moments of great peril, in times of extremity, when the brave soul has staked its all—those are the times when miracles are wrought, if we will but have faith.
That doesn't mean that you should rest supinely at your ease and let the Lord provide. When you have done all that is in you to do—when you have given of your best—don't worry or fret as to the outcome. Know that if more is needed, your need will be met. You can sit back with the confident assurance that having done your part; you can depend upon the Genie-of-your-Mind to do the rest.

When the little state of Palestine was in danger of being overrun by Egypt on the one hand, or gobbled up by

Assyria on the other, its people were frantically trying to decide which horn of the dilemma to embrace, with which enemy they should ally themselves to stave off the other. "With neither," the Prophet Isaiah told them, "in calmly resting your safety lieth; in quiet trust shall be your strength."

So it is with most of the great calamities that afflict us. If we would only "calmly rest, quietly trust," how much better off we should be. But no—we must fret and worry, and nine times out of ten do the wrong thing. And the more we worry and fret, the more likely we are to go wrong.

All of Universal Mind that is necessary to solve any given problem, to meet any need, is wherever that need may be. Supply is always *where* you are and *what* you need. It matters not whether it be sickness or trouble, poverty or danger, the remedy is there, waiting for your call. Go at your difficulty boldly, knowing that you have infinite resources behind you, and you will find these forces closing around you and coming to your aid.

It's like an author writing a book. For a long time he works in a kind of mental fog, but let him persevere, and there flashes suddenly a light that clarifies his ideas and shows him the way to shape them logically. At the moment of despair, you feel a source of unknown energy arising in your soul.

That doesn't mean that you will never have difficulties. Difficulties are good for you. They are the exercise of your mind. You are the stronger for having overcome them. But look upon them as mere exercise. As "stunts" that are given you in order that you may the better learn how to use your mind, how to draw upon Universal Supply. Like Jacob wrestling with the Angel, don't let them go until they have blessed you—until, in other words, you have learned something from having encountered them.

Remember this: No matter how great a catastrophe may befall mankind, no matter how general the loss, you and yours can be free from it. There is always a way of safety. There is always an "ark" by which the understanding few can be saved from the flood. The name of that ark is understanding—understanding of your inner powers. When the children of Israel were being led into the Promised Land, and Joshua had given them their directions, they answered him: "All that thou commandest us we will do, and whithersoever thou sendest us, we will go... Only the Lord thy God be with thee, as He was with Moses."

They came to the river Jordan, and it seemed an insurmountable barrier in their path, but Joshua commanded them to take the Ark of the Covenant, representing God's understanding with them, before them into the Jordan. They did it, and "the waters which came down from above stood and rose up upon an heap. . . . And the priests that bare the Ark of the Covenant of the Lord stood firm on dry ground in the midst of Jordan, and all the Israelites passed over on dry ground, until all the people were passed clean over Jordan."

The Ark of the Covenant

All through the Old Testament, when war and pestilence, fire and flood, were the common lot of mankind, there is constant assurance of safety for those who have this understanding, this "Covenant" with the Lord. "Because thou hast made the Lord which is my refuge—even the Most High—thy habitation, there shall no evil befall thee, neither shall any plague come nigh thy dwelling. For He shall give His angels charge over thee to keep thee in all thy ways."

That is His agreement with us—an agreement that gives us the superiority to circumstances, which men have sought from time immemorial. All that is necessary on our side of the agreement is for us to remember the infinite powers that reside within us, to remember that our mind is part of Universal Mind and as such it can foresee, it can guard against and it can protect us from harm of any kind. We need not run away from trials or try to become stoical towards them. All we need is to bring our understanding to bear upon them—to know that no situation has ever yet arisen with which Universal Mind—and through it our own mind—was not fully competent to deal; to know that the right solution of every problem is in Universal Mind. We have but to seek that solution and our trial is overcome.

If evil threatens us, if failure, sickness or accident seems imminent, we have only to decide that these evils do not come from Universal Mind, therefore they are unreal and have no power over us. They are simply the absence of the right condition, which Universal Mind knows. Refuse, therefore, to see them, to acknowledge them—and seek through Mind for the right condition, which shall nullify them.

If you will do this, you will find that you can appropriate from Mind whatever you require for your needs, *when* you require it. The greater your need, the more surely it will be met, if you can but realize this truth.

Remember that your thought is all-powerful. That it is creative. That there is no limitation upon it of time or space. And that it is ever available.

Forget your worries. Forget your fears. In place of them, visualize the conditions you would like to see. Realize their availability. Declare to yourself that you already *have* all these things that you desire, that your needs *have* been met. Say to yourself: "How thankful I am that Mind has made all these good things available to me. I have everything that heart could desire to be grateful for."

Every time you do this, you impress the thought upon your subconscious mind. And the moment you can convince your subconscious mind of the truth of it—*that moment* your mind will proceed to *make* it true. This is the way to put into practice—"Believe that ye RECEIVE it, and ye SHALL HAVE it."

There is no condition so hopeless, no cause so far gone, that this truth will not save it. Time and again patients given over by their doctors as doomed have made miraculous recoveries through the faith of some loved one.

"I hope that everyone who reads this Book may gain as much from their first reading as I did," writes a happy subscriber from New York City. "I got such a clear understanding from that one reading that I was able to break the mental chain holding a friend to a hospital bed, and she left the hospital in three days, to the very great astonishment of the doctors handling the case."

In the same way, there are innumerable instances where threatened calamity has been warded off and good come instead. The great trouble with most of us is, we do not *believe*. We insist upon looking for trouble. We feel that the "rainy day" is bound to come, and we do our utmost to make it a surety by keeping it in our thoughts, preparing for it, fearing it. "Cowards die many times before their deaths; the valiant never taste of death but once." We cross our bridges a dozen times before we come to them. We doubt ourselves, we doubt our ability, we doubt everyone and everything around us, and our doubts sap our energy; kill our enthusiasm; rob us of success. We arc like the old lady who "enjoys poor health." We always place that little word "but" after our wishes and desires, feeling deep down that there are some things too good to be true. We think there is a power apart from Good, which can withhold blessings that should be ours. We doubt because we cannot see the way by which our desires can be fulfilled. We put a limit upon the good that can come to us.

"Prove me now herewith, saith the Lord of Hosts," cried the Prophet Malachi, "if I will not open you the windows of heaven and pour you out a blessing that there shall not be room enough to receive it…And all nations shall call you blessed, for ye shall be a delightsome land."

Your mind is part of Universal Mind. And Universal Mind has all supply. You are entitled to, and you can have, just as much of that supply as you are able to appropriate. To expect less is to get less, for it dwarfs your power of receiving.

It doesn't matter what your longings may be, provided they are right longings. If your little son has his heart set on a train and you feel perfectly able to get him a train, you are not going to hand him a picture book instead. It may be that the picture book would have greater educational value, but the love you have for your son is going to make you try to satisfy his longings as long as those longings are not harmful ones.

In the same way, Universal Mind will satisfy your longings, no matter how trivial they may seem, as long as they are not harmful ones. "Delight thyself also in the Lord, and He shall give thee the desires of thine heart."

If we would only try to realize that God is not some far-off Deity, not some stern Judge, but the beneficent force that we recognize as Nature—the life Principle that makes the flowers bud, and the plants grow, that spreads abundance about us with lavish band. If we could realize that He is the Universal Mind that holds all supply, that will give us the toy of our childhood or the needs of maturity, that all we need to obtain from Him our Heart's Desire is a right understanding of His availability—then we would lose all our fears, all our worries, all our sense of limitation.

For Universal Mind is an infinite, unlimited source of good. Not only the source of general good, but the specific good things you desire of life. To It there is no big or little problem. The removal of mountains is no more difficult than the feeding of a sparrow.

The Science of Thought

Can you stretch your mind a bit and try to comprehend this wonderful fact—that the ALL POWERFUL, ALL-KNOWING, EVERLASTING CREATOR and Governor of the infinite universe, "Who hath measured the waters in the hollow of his hand, and meted out heaven with the span, and comprehended the dust of the earth in a measure, and weighed the mountains in scales, and the hills in a balance," is your working power? In proportion as we understand this fact, and make use of it, in that same proportion are we able to perform our miracles.

Your work is inspired to the extent that you realize the presence of Universal Mind in your work. When you rely entirely on your own conscious mind, your work suffers accordingly. And mind you, this inspiration, this working of Universal Mind with you, is available for all of your undertakings. Mind could not show Itself in one part of your life and withhold Itself from another, since It is all in all. Every rightly directed task, no matter how insignificant or menial it may appear to you, carries with it the inspiration of Universal Mind, since by the very nature of omnipotence, Its love and bestowals must be universal and impartial.
Too many of us are like the maiden in the old Eastern legend. A Genii sent her into a field of grain, promising her a rare gift if she would pick for him the largest and ripest ear she could find; His gift to be in proportion to the size and perfection of the ear.

But he made this condition—she must pluck but one ear, and she must walk straight through the field without stopping, going back or wandering hither and thither.

Joyously she started. As she walked through the grain, she saw many large ears, many perfect ones. She passed them by in scorn, thinking to find an extra-large, super-perfect one farther along. Presently, however, the soil became less fertile, the ears small and sparse. She couldn't pick one of these! Would now that she had been content with an ordinary-sized ear farther back. But it was too late for that. Surely they would grow better again farther on!

She walked on—and on—and always they became worse—'till presently she found herself at the end of the field —*empty handed as when she set out!*

So it is with life. Every day has its worthwhile rewards for work well done. Every day offers its chance for happiness. But those rewards seem so small, those chances so petty, compared with the big things we see ahead. So we pass them by, never recognizing that the great position we look forward to, the shining prize we see in the distance, is just the sum of all the little tasks, the heaped up result of all the little prizes that we must win as we go along.

You are not commanded to pick out certain occupations as being more entitled to the Lord's consideration than others, but "Whatsoever ye do." Whether it be in the exalted and idealistic realms of poetry, music and art, whether in the cause of religion or philanthropy, whether in government, in business, in science, or simply in household cares, "whatsoever ye do" you are entitled to and *have* all of inspiration at your beck and call. If you seem to have less than all, it is because you do not utilize your gift.

How shall you take advantage of this Universal Supply? When next any need confronts you, when next you are in difficulties, close your eyes for a moment and realize that Universal Mind knows how that need can best be met, knows the solution of your difficulties. Your subconscious mind, being part of the Universal Mind, can know this, too. So put your problem up to your subconscious mind with the sublime confidence that it will find the solution. Then forget it for a while. When the time comes, the need will be met.

Dr. Winbigler corroborates the working out of this idea in the following:

"Suggestions lodged in the mind can effect a complete change, morally and physically, if mankind would become in spirit 'as a little child,' trusting in God implicitly, the greatest power would be utilized in the establishment of health and equilibrium, and the results would be untold in comfort, sanity, and blessing. For instance, here is one who is suffering from worry, fear, and the vexations of life. How can he get rid of these things and relieve this suffering? Let him go to a quiet room or place, twice a day, lie down and relax every muscle, assume complete indifference to those things which worry him and the functions of the body, and quietly accept what God, through this law of demand and supply, can give. In a few days he will find a great change in his feelings, and the sufferings will pass away and life will look bright and promising. Infinite wisdom has established that law; and its utilization by those who are worried and fearful will secure amazing results in a short time.

"The real reason for the change is found in the possibility of recovery by using the laws that God has placed within our reach, and thus securing the coveted health and power for all that we want and ought to do. The subliminal life is the connecting link between man and God, and by obeying His laws, one's life is put in contact with infinite resources and all that God is able and willing to give. Here is the secret of all the cures of disease, and the foundation for the possibility of a joyful existence, happiness and eternal life. Suggestion is the method of securing what God gives, and the mind is the agent through which these gifts are received. This is not a matter of theory, but a fact. If any one who is sick or who desires to he kept well will have stated periods of relaxation, open-mindedness, and faith, he can prove the beneficial and unvarying result of this method."

XV
The Master of Your Fate

"A craven hung along the battle's edge, and thought, 'Had I a sword of keener steel— that blue blade that the king's son bears,—but this blunt thing—!'

And lowering crept away and left the field.

Then came the king's son, wounded, sore bestead and weaponless, and saw the broken sword, and ran and snatched it, and with battle-shout lifted afresh he hewed his enemy down, and saved a great cause that heroic day."

—EDWARD ROWLAND SILL
(From 'Poems," Houghton, Muffin Co.)

Where will you be at 65? Five men in six at the age of 65 are living on charity. Just one in twenty is able to live without working at 65.
That is what the American Bankers Association found when it took one hundred healthy men at 25 and traced them to 65.

These hundred were healthy to start with. They all had the same chance for success. The difference lay in the way they used their MINDS. Ninety-five out of one hundred just do the tasks that are set them. They have no faith in themselves—no initiative—none of the courage that starts things. They are always directed or controlled by someone else.

At 65, where will you be? Dependent or independent? Struggling for a living—accepting charity from someone else—or at the top of the heap?

"I am the Master of my fate."

Until you have learned that, you will never attain life's full success. Your fate is in your own hands. *You* have the making of it. What you are going to be six months or a year from now depends upon what you think today.

So make your choice now:
Are you going to bow down to matter as the only power? Are you going to look upon your environment as something that has been wished upon you and for which you are in no way responsible?

Or are you going to try to realize in your daily life that matter is merely an aggregation of protons and electrons subject entirely to the control of Mind, that your environment, your success, your happiness, are all of your own making, and that if you are not satisfied with conditions as they you have but to visualize them as you would have them be in order to change them?

The former is the easier way right now—the easy way that leads to the hell of poverty and fear and old age.

But the latter is the way that brings you to your Heart's Desire.

And merely because this Power of Universal Mind is invisible, is that any reason to doubt it? The greatest powers of Nature are invisible. Love is invisible, but what greater power is there in life? Joy is invisible, happiness, peace, and contentment. The radio is invisible—yet you hear it. It is a product of the law governing sound waves. Law is invisible, yet you see the manifestation of different laws every day. To run a locomotive, you study the law of applying power, and you apply that law when you make the locomotive go.

These things are not the result of invention. The law has existed from the beginning. It merely waited for man to learn how to apply it. If man had known how to call upon Universal Mind to the right extent, he could have applied the law of sound waves, the law of steam, ages ago. Invention is merely a revelation and an unfoldment of Universal Wisdom.

That same Universal Wisdom knows millions of other laws of which man has not even a glimmering. You can call upon It. You can use that Wisdom as your own. By thinking of things as they might be instead of as they are you will eventually find some great Need. And to find a need is the first step towards finding the supply to satisfy that need. You've got to know what you are after, before you can send the Genie-of-your Mind a-seeking of it in Universal Mind.

The Acre of Diamonds

You remember the story of the poor Boer farmer who struggled for years to glean a livelihood out of his rocky soil, only to give it up in despair and go off to seek his fortune elsewhere. Years later, coming back to his old farm, he found it swarming with machinery and life—more wealth being dug out of it every day than he had ever dreamed existed. It was the great Kimberley Diamond Mine!

Most of us are like that poor Boer farmer. We struggle along under our surface power, never dreaming of the giant power that could be ours if we would but dig a little deeper—rouse that great Inner Self who can give us more even than any acre of diamonds.

As Orison Swett Marden put it:

"The majority of failures in life are simply the victims of their mental defeats. Their conviction that they cannot succeed as others do, rob them of that vigor and determination which self-confidence imparts, and they don't even half try to succeed.

"There is no philosophy by which a man can do a thing when he thinks he can't. The reason why millions of men are plodding along in mediocrity today, many of them barely making a living, when they have the ability to do something infinitely bigger, is because they lack confidence in themselves. They don't believe they can do the bigger thing that would lift them out of their rut of mediocrity and poverty; they are not winners mentally.

"The way always opens for the determined soul, the man of faith and courage.

"It is the victorious mental attitude, the consciousness of power, the sense of mastership, that does the big things in this world. If you haven't this attitude, if you lack self-confidence, begin now to cultivate it.

"A highly magnetized piece of steel will attract and lift a piece of unmagnetized steel ten times its own weight. Demagnetize that same piece of steel and it will be powerless to attract or lift even a feather's weight.

"Now, my friends, there is the same difference between the man who is highly magnetized by a sublime faith in himself, and the man who is de-magnetized by his lack of faith, his doubts, his fears, that there is between the magnetized and the de-magnetized pieces of steel. If two men of equal ability, one *magnetized by a divine self-confidence*, the other demagnetized by fear and doubt, are given similar tasks, one will succeed and the other will fail. The self-confidence of the one *multiplies his powers a hundredfold;* the lack of it subtracts a hundredfold from the power of the other."

Have you ever thought how much of your time is spent in choosing what you shall do, which task you will try, which way you shall go? Every day is a day of decision. We are constantly at crossroads, in our business dealings, our social relations, in our homes; there is always the necessity of a choice. How important, then, that we have faith in ourselves and in that Infinite intelligence within.

In this ever-changing material age, with seemingly complex forces all about us, we sometimes cry out that we are driven by force of circumstances. Yet the fact remains that we do those things, which we choose to do. For even though we may not wish to go a certain way, we allow ourselves to pursue it because it offers the least resistance.

"To every man there openeth a way, and ways, and a way.
And the high soul climbs the high way, and the low soul gropes the low: And in between, on the misty flats, the

rest drift to and fro.
But to every man there openeth a high way and a low, and every man decideth the way his soul shall go."

—JOHN OXENHAM.

Now, how about you? Are you taking active control of your own thought? Are you imaging upon your subconscious mind only such things, as you want to see realized? Are you thinking healthy thoughts, happy thoughts, and successful thoughts?

The difference between the successful man and the unsuccessful one is not so much a matter of training or equipment. It is not a question of opportunity or luck. It is just in the way they each of them look at things.

The successful man sees an opportunity, seizes upon it, and moves upward another rung on the ladder of success. It never occurs to him that he may fail. He sees only the opportunity, he visions what he can do with it, and all the forces within and without him combine to help him win.

The unsuccessful man sees the same opportunity, he wishes that he could take advantage of it, but he is fearful that his ability or his money or his credit may not be equal to the task. He is like a timid bather, putting in one foot and then drawing it swiftly back again—and while he hesitates some bolder spirit dashes in and beats him to the goal.

Nearly every man can look back—and not so far back either with most of us—and say, "If I had taken that chance, I would be much better off now."

You will never need to say it again, once you realize that the future is entirely within your own control. It is not subject to the whims of fortune or the capriciousness of luck. There is but one Universal Mind and that mind contains naught but good. In it is no images of Evil. From it comes no lack of supply. Its ideas are as numberless as the grains of sand on the seashore. And those ideas comprise all wealth, all power, and all happiness.

You have only to image vividly enough on your subconscious mind the thing you wish, to draw from Universal Mind, the necessary ideas to bring it into being. You have only to keep in mind the experiences you wish to meet, in order to control your own future.

When Frank A. Vanderlip, former President of the National City Bank, was a struggling youngster, he asked a successful friend what one thing he would urge a young man to do who was anxious to make his way in the world. "Look as though you have already succeeded," his friend told him. Shakespeare expresses the same thought in another way—"Assume a virtue if you have it not." Look the part. Dress the part. Act the part. Be successful in your own thought first. It won't be long before you will be successful before the world as well.

David V. Bush, in his book "*Applied Psychology and Scientific Living*," says:

"Man is like the wireless operator. Man is subject to miscellaneous wrong thought currents if his mind is not in tune with the Infinite, or if he is not keyed up to higher vibrations than those of negation.

"A man who thinks courageous thoughts sends these courageous thought waves through the universal ether until they lodge in the consciousness of someone who is tuned to the same courageous key. Think a strong thought, a courageous thought, a prosperity thought, and these thoughts will be received by someone who is strong, courageous and prosperous.

"It is just as easy to think in terms of abundance as to think in terms of poverty. If we think poverty thoughts we become the sending and receiving stations for poverty thoughts. We send out a 'poverty' mental wireless and it reaches the consciousness of some poverty-stricken 'receiver.' We get what we think.

"It is just as easy to think in terms of abundance, opulence and prosperity as it is to think in terms of lack, limitation and poverty.

"If a man will raise his rate of vibration by faith currents or hope currents, these vibrations go through the Universal Mind and lodge in the consciousness of people who are keyed to the same tune. Whatever you think is sometime, somewhere, received by a person who is tuned to your thought key.

"If a man is out of work and he thinks thoughts of success, prosperity, harmony, position and growth, just as surely as his thoughts are things—as Shakespeare says—someone will receive his vibrations of success, prosperity, harmony, position and growth.

"If we are going to be timid, selfish, penurious and picayunish in our thinking, these thought waves which we have started in the universal ether will go forth until they come to a mental receiving station of the same caliber. 'Birds of a feather flock together,' and minds of like thinking are attracted one to the other.

"If you need money, all you have to do is to send up your vibrations to a strong, courageous receiving station, and someone who can meet your needs will be attracted to you or you to him."

When you learn that you are entitled to win—in any right undertaking in which you may be engaged—*you will win*. When you learn that you have a right to a legitimate dominion over your own affairs, *you will have dominion over them.*

Universal Mind plays no favorites. No one human being has any more power than any other. It is simply that few of us use the power that is in our hands. The great men of the world are in no wise SUPER Beings. They are ordinary creatures like you and me, who have stumbled upon the way of drawing upon their subconscious mind —and through it upon the Universal Mind. Speaking of Henry Ford's phenomenal success, his friend Thomas A. Edison said of him—"He draws upon his subconscious mind."

The secret of being what you have it in you to be is simply this: Decide now what it is you want of life, exactly what you wish your future to be. Plan it out in detail. Vision it from start to finish. See yourself as you are now, doing those things you have always wanted to do. Make them REAL in your mind's eye—feel them, live them, believe them, especially at the moment of going to sleep, when it is easiest to reach your subconscious mind— and you will soon be seeing them in real life.

It matters not whether you are young or old, rich or poor. The time to begin is NOW. It is never too late. Remember those lines of Appleton's:

"I knew his face the moment that he passed triumphant in the thoughtless, cruel throng— i gently touched his arm —he smiled at me— he was the Man that Once I Meant to Be!

"Where I had failed, he'd won from life, Success; where I had stumbled, with sure feet he stood;

Alike—yet unalike—we faced the world, and through the stress he found that life was good.
And I? The bitter wormwood in the glass, the shadowed way along which failures pass!
Yet as I saw him thus, joy came to me— he was the Man that Once I Meant to Be!

"We did not speak. But in his sapient eyes i saw the spirit that had urged him on,
The courage that had held him through the fight had once been mine. I thought, 'Can it be gone?' h
He felt that unasked question—felt it so his pale lips formed the one-word answer, 'No!'

.   .   .   .

"Too late to win? No! Not too late for me—
He is the Man that Still I Mean to Be!"

(From "The Quiet Courage." D. Appleton & Co., New York.)

XVI
Unappropriated Millions

"Somebody said that it couldn't be done, but he with a chuckle replied that 'maybe it couldn't,' but he would be one who wouldn't say so till he'd tried.
So he buckled right in with the trace of a grin on his face. If he worried he hid it.
He started to sing as he tackled the thing that couldn't be done, and he did it."

—EDGAR A. GUEST.
(From "The Path to Home." The Reilly & Lee Co.)

The main difference between the mind of today and that of our great-great-grandfathers was that in their day conditions were comparatively static, whereas today they are dynamic. Civilization ran along for centuries with comparatively little change. Most people lived and died in the places where they were born. They followed their fathers' avocations. Seldom, indeed, did one of them break out of the class into which he had been born. Almost as seldom did they even *think* of trying to. No wonder, then, that civilization made little progress.

Today we are in the presence of continual change. Men are imbued with that divine unrest which is never satisfied with conditions as they are, which is always striving for improvement. And *thought* is the vital force behind all this change.

Your ability to think is your connecting link with Universal Mind, that enables you to draw upon It for inspiration, for energy, for power. Mind is the energy in *static* form. Thought is the energy in *dynamic* form.

And because life is dynamic—not static; because it is ever moving forward—not standing still; your success or failure depends entirely upon the *quality* of your thought.

For thought is creative energy. It brings into being the things that you think. Think the things you would see manifested, see them, *believe* them, and you can leave it to your subconscious mind to bring them into being.

Your mind is a marvelous storage battery of power on which you can draw for whatever things you need to make your life what you would have it be. It has within it all power, all resource, all energy—but YOU are the one that must use it. All that power is static unless you make it dynamic. In the moment of creative thinking your conscious mind becomes a Creator—it partakes of the power of Universal Mind. And there is nothing static about one who shares that All-power. The resistless Life Energy within him pushes him on to new growth, new aspirations. Just as the sap flowing through the branches of the trees pushes off the old dead leaves to make way for the new life, just so you must push away the old dead thoughts of poverty and lack and disease, before you can bring on the new life of health and happiness and unlimited supply.

This life is in all of us, constantly struggling for an outlet. Repress it—and you die. Doctors will tell you that the only reason people grow old is because their systems get clogged. The tiny pores in your arteries get stopped up. You don't throw off the old. You don't struggle hard enough, and the result is you fall an easy victim to failure and sickness and death.

Remember the story of Sinbad the Sailor, and the Old Man of the Sea? The Old Man's weight was as nothing when Sinbad first took him on his shoulders, but he clung there and clung there, slowly but surely sapping Sinbad's strength, and he would finally have killed him as he had killed so many others if Sinbad, by calling to his aid all his mental as well as his physical resources, had not succeeded in shaking him off.

Most of us have some Old Man of the Sea riding us, and because he clings tightly and refuses to be easily shaken off, we let him stay there, sapping our energies, using up our vitality, when to rid us of him it is only necessary to call to our aid ALL our resources, mental as well as physical, for one supreme effort.

When a storm arises, the hardy mariner doesn't turn off steam and drift helplessly before the wind. That might be the easy way, but that way danger lies. He turns on more steam and fights against the gale. And so should you. There is a something within you that thrives on difficulties. You prize that more which costs an effort to win. You need to blaze new trails, to encounter unusual hardships, in order to reach your hidden mental resources, just as the athlete needs to exert himself to the utmost to reach his "second wind."

Have you ever seen a turtle thrown on its back? For a while it threshes around wildly, reaching for something outside to take hold of that shall put it on its feet. Just as we humans always look for help outside ourselves first, but presently he draws all his forces within his shell, rests a bit to regain his strength, and then throws his whole force to one side—legs, head, tail, and all—*and over he goes!*

So it is with us. When we realize that the power to meet any emergency is within ourselves, when we stop looking outside for help and intelligently call upon Mind in our need, we shall find that we are tapping Infinite Resource. We shall find that we have but to center all those resources on the one thing we want most—to get anything from life that it has.

XVII
The Secret of Power

"The great were once as you.
They whom men magnify today once groped and blundered on life's way
Were fearful of themselves, and thought by magic was men's greatness wrought.
They feared to try what they could do; yet Fame hath crowned with her success the selfsame gifts that you
possess.

—EDGAR A. GUEST.

(Published by permission of The International Magazine Co. (Cosmopolitan Magazine) Copyright, 1921.)

There is a woman in one of the big Eastern cities whose husband died a year or two ago and left her nearly $100,000,000. She has unlimited power in her hands—yet she uses none of it. She has unlimited wealth   yet she gets no more from it than if it were in the thousands instead of millions. She knows nothing of her power, of her wealth. She is insane.

You have just as great power in your hands—without this poor woman's excuse for not using it.

You have access to unlimited ideas, unlimited energy, and unlimited wealth. The "Open, Sesame!" is through your subconscious mind. So long as you limit yourself to superficial conditions, so long as you are a mere "hewer of wood or carrier of water" for those around you who *do* use their minds, you are in no better position than the beasts of burden.

The secret of power is in understanding the infinite resources of your own mind. When you begin to realize that the power to do anything, to be anything, to have anything, is within yourself, then *and then only* will you take your proper place in the world.

Don't judge your ability by what you have done in the past. Your work heretofore has been done with the help of your conscious mind alone. Add to that the infinite knowledge at the disposal of your subconscious mind, and what you have done is as nothing to what you will do in the future.

For knowledge does not apply itself. It is merely so much static energy. You must convert it into dynamic energy by the power of your thought. The difference between the $25-a-week clerk and the $25,000-a-year executive is solely one of thought. The clerk may have more brains than the executive—frequently *has* in actual weight of gray matter. He may even have a far better education. But he doesn't know how to apply his thought to get the greatest good from it.

If you have brains, *use* them. If you have skill, *apply* it. The world must profit by it, and therefore you.

We all have inspired moments when we see clearly how we may do great things, how we may accomplish wonderful undertakings. But we do not believe in them enough to make them come true. An imagination, which begins and ends in daydreaming, is weakening to character.

Make the daydreams come true. Make them so clear and distinct that they impress themselves upon your subconscious mind. There's nothing wrong with daydreaming, except that most of us stop there. We don't try to make the dreams come true. The great inventor, Tesla, "dreams" every new machine complete and perfect in every particular before ever he begins his model for it. Mozart "dreamed" each of his wonderful symphonies complete before ever he put a note on paper. But they didn't stop with the dreaming. They visualized those dreams, *and then brought them into actuality.*

We lose our capacity to have visions if we do not take steps to realize them.

Power implies service, so concentrate all your thoughts on making your visions of great deeds come true. Thinking is the current that runs the dynamo of power. To connect up this current so that you can draw upon universal supply through your subconscious mind is to become a Super-man. Do this, and you will have found the key to the solution of every problem of life.

XVIII
This One Thing I Do

"How do you tackle your work each day?
Do you grapple the task that comes your way with a confident, easy mind?
Do you start to toil with a sense of dread or feel that you're going to do it?

"You can do as much as you think you can, but you'll never accomplish more; If you're afraid of yourself, young man, there's little for you in store.
For failure comes from the inside first, it's there, if we only knew it, and you can win, though you face the worst, if you feel that you're going to do it."

—EDGAR A. GUEST.
(From "A Heap o' Livin'." The Reilly & Lee Co.)

How did the Salvation Army get so much favorable publicity out of the War? They were a comparatively small part of the "Services" that catered to the boys "over there," yet they carried off the lion's share of the glory. Do you know how they did it?

By concentrating on just one thing— DOUGHNUTS!

They served doughnuts to the boys— and they did it well. And that is the basis of all success in business—to focus on one thing and do that thing well. Better far to do one thing pre-eminently well than to dabble in forty.

Two thousand years ago, Porcius Marcus Cato became convinced, from a visit to the rich and flourishing city of Carthage, that Rome had in her a rival who must be destroyed. His countrymen laughed at him. He was practically alone in his belief. But he persisted. He concentrated all his thought, all his faculties, to that one end. At the end of every speech, at the end of every talk, he centered his hearers' thought on what he was trying to put over by epitomizing his whole idea in a single sentence—"Carthage must be destroyed!" *And Carthage was destroyed.*

If one man's concentration on a single idea could destroy a great nation, what can you not do when you apply that same principle to the *building* of a business?

I remember when I was first learning horsemanship, my instructor impressed this fact upon me: "Remember that a horse is an animal of one idea. You can teach him only one thing at a time."
Looking back, I'd say the only thing wrong with his instruction was that he took in too little territory. He need not have confined himself to the horse. Most humans are the same way.

In fact, you can put ALL humans into that class if you want a thing done well. For you cannot divide your thought and do justice to any one of the different subjects you are thinking of. You've got to do one thing at a time. The greatest success rule I know in business—the one that should be printed over every man's desk, is —"This One Thing I Do." Take one piece of work at a time. Concentrate on it to the exclusion of all else. *Then finish it!* Don't half-do it, and leave it around to clutter up your desk and interfere with the next job. Dispose of it completely. Pass it along wherever it is to go. Be through with it *and forget it!* Then your mind will be clear to consider the next matter.

"The man who is Perpetually hesitating which of two things he will do first," says William Wirt, "will do neither. The man who resolves, but suffers his resolution to be changed by the first counter-suggestion of a friend—who fluctuates from plan to plan and veers like a weather-cock to every point of the compass with every breath of caprice that blows—can never accomplish anything real or useful. It is only the man who first consults wisely, then resolves firmly, and then executes his purpose with inflexible perseverance, undismayed by those petty difficulties that daunt a weaker spirit, that can advance to eminence in any line."

Everything in the world, even a great business, can be resolved into atoms. And the basic principles behind the biggest business will be found to be the same as those behind the successful running of the corner newsstand. The whole practice of commerce is founded upon them. Any man can learn them, but only the alert and energetic can apply them. The trouble with most men is that they think they have done all that is required of them when they have earned their salary.

Why, that's only the beginning. Up to that point, you are working for someone else. From then on, you begin to work for yourself. Remember, you must *give to get* and it is when you give that *extra* bit of time and attention and thought to your work that you begin to stand out above the crowd around you.

Norval Hawkins, for many years General Manager of Sales for the Ford Motor Company, wrote, "The greatest hunt in the Ford business right now is the MAN hunt." And big men in every industrial line echo his words. 'When it comes to a job that needs real ability, they are not looking for relatives or friends or men with "pull." They want a MAN—and they will pay any price for the right man.

Not only that, but they always have a weather eye open for promising material. And the thing they value most of all is INITIATIVE.

But don't try to improve the whole works at once. Concentrate on one thing at a time. Pick some one department or some one process or some one thing and focus all your thoughts upon it. Bring to bear upon it the limitless resources of your subconscious mind. Then prepare a definite plan for the development of that department or the improvement of that process. Verify your facts carefully to make sure they are workable. *Then*—and not till then —present your plan.

In "*Thoughts on Business*," you read: "Men often think of a position as being just about so big and no bigger, when, as a matter of fact, a position is often what one makes it. A man was making about $1,500 a year out of a certain position and thought he was doing all that could be done to advance the business. The employer thought otherwise, and gave the place to another man who soon made the position worth $8,000 a year— at exactly the same commission.

"The difference was in the man—in other words, in what the two men thought about the work. One had a little conception of what the work should be, and the other had a big conception of it. One thought little thoughts, and the other thought big thoughts.

"The standards of two men may differ, not especially because one is naturally more capable than the other, but because one is familiar with big things and the other is not. The time was when the former worked in a smaller scope himself, but when he saw a wider view of what his work might be he rose to the occasion and became a bigger man. It is just as easy to think of a mountain as to think of a hill—when you turn your mind to contemplate it. The mind is like a rubber band—you can stretch it to fit almost anything, but it draws in to a smaller scope when you let go.

"Make it your business to know what is the best that might be in your line of work, and stretch your mind to conceive it, and then devise some way to attain it.

"Big things are only little things put together. I was greatly impressed with this fact one morning as I stood watching the workmen erecting the steel framework for a tall office building. A shrill whistle rang out as a signal, a man over at the engine pulled a lever, a chain from the derrick was lowered, and the whistle rang out again. A man stooped down and fastened the chain around the center of a steel beam, stepped back and blew the whistle once more. Again the lever was moved at the engine, and the steel beam soared into the air up to the sixteenth story, where it was made fast by little bolts.

"The entire structure, great as it was, towering far above all the neighboring buildings, was made up of pieces of steel and stone and wood, put together according to a plan. The plan was first imagined, then penciled, then carefully drawn, and then followed by the workmen. It was all a combination of little things.

"It is encouraging to think of this when you are confronted by a big task. *Remember that it is only a group of little tasks, any of which you can easily do*. It is ignorance of this fact that makes men afraid to try."

One of the most essential requisites in the accomplishment of any important work is patience. Not the patience that sits and folds its hands and waits—Micawber like—for something to turn up. But the patience that never jeopardizes or upsets a plan by forcing it too soon. The man who possesses that kind of patience can always find plenty to do in the meantime.

Make your plan—then wait for the opportune moment to submit it. You'd be surprised to know how carefully big men go over suggestions from subordinates, which show the least promise. One of the signs of a really big man, you know, is his eagerness to learn from everyone and anything. There is none of that "know it all" about him that characterized the German general who was given a book containing the strategy by which Napoleon had for fifteen years kept all the armies of Europe at bay. "I've no time to read about bygone battles," he growled, thrusting the book away, "I have my own campaign to plan."

There is priceless wisdom to be found in books. As Carlyle put it—"All that mankind has done, thought, gained or been—it is lying in matchless preservation in the pages of books."

The truths which mankind has been laboriously learning through countless ages, at who knows what price of sweat and toil and starvation and blood—all are yours for the effort of reading them.

And in business, knowledge was never so priceless or so easily acquired. Books and magazines are filled with the hows and whys, the rights and wrongs of buying and selling, of manufacturing and shipping, of finance and management. They are within the reach of anyone with the desire to KNOW.

Nothing pays better interest than judicious reading. The man who invests in more knowledge of his business than he needs to hold his job, is acquiring capital with which to get a better job.

As old Gorgon Graham puts it in *"The Letters of a Self-Made Merchant To His Son"*—

"I ain't one of those who believe that a half knowledge of a subject is useless, but it has been my experience that when a fellow has that half knowledge, he finds it's the other half which would really come in handy.

"What you know is a club for yourself, and what you don't know is a meat-ax for the other fellow. That is why you want to be on the look-out all the time for information about the business and to nail a fact just as a sensible man nails a mosquito—the first time it settles near him."

The demands made upon men in business today are far greater than in any previous generation. To meet them, you've got to use your talents to the utmost. You've got to find in every situation that confronts you, the best, the easiest and the quickest way of working it out. And the first essential in doing this is to plan your work ahead.

You'd be surprised at how much more work you can get through by carefully planning it, and then taking each bit in order and disposing of it before starting on the next.

Another thing—once started at work, don't let down. Keep on going until it is time to quit. You know how much power it takes to start an auto that is standing motionless. But when you get it going, you can run along in high at a fraction of the expenditure of gas. It is the same way with your mind. We are all mentally lazy. We hate to start using our minds. Once started, though, it is easy to keep along on high, if only we won't let down. For the moment we let down, we have that starting to do all over again. You can accomplish ten times as much, with far less effort or fatigue, if you will keep right on steadily instead of starting and stopping, and starting and stopping again.

Volumes have been written about personal efficiency, and general efficiency, and every other kind of efficiency in business. But boiled down, it all comes to this:

1—Know what you want.
2—Analyze the thing you've got to do to get it.
3—Plan your work ahead.
4—Do one thing at a time.
5—Finish that one thing and send it on its way before starting the next.
6—Once started, KEEP GOING!

And when you come to some problem that "stumps" you, give your subconscious mind a chance.

Frederick Pierce, in "*Our Unconscious Mind*," gives an excellent method for solving business problems through the aid of the subconscious:

"Several years ago, I heard a successful executive tell a group of young men how he did his work, and included in the talk was the advice to prepare at the close of each day's business a list of the ten most important things for the next day. To this I would add: Run them over in the mind just before going to sleep, not thoughtfully, or with elaboration of detail, but with the sure knowledge that the deeper centers of the mind are capable of viewing them constructively even though conscious attention is surrendered in sleep.

"Then, if there is a particular problem which seems difficult of solution, review its features lightly as a last game for the imaginative unconscious to play at during the night. Do not be discouraged if no immediate results are apparent. Remember that fiction, poetry, musical composition, inventions, innumerable ideas, spring from the unconscious, often in forms that give evidence of the highest constructive elaboration.
"Give your unconscious a chance. Give it the material, and stimulate it with keenly dwelt-on wishes along frank Ego Maximation lines. It is a habit which, if persisted in, will sooner or later present you with some very valuable ideas when you least expect them."
I remember reading of another man—a genius at certain kinds of work—who, whenever an especially difficult problem confronted him, "slept on it." He had learned the trick as a child. Unable to learn his lessons one

evening, he had kept repeating the words to himself until he dozed in his chair, the book still in his hands. What was his surprise, on being awakened by his father a few minutes later to find that he knew them perfectly! He tried it again and again on succeeding evenings, and almost invariably it worked. Now, whenever a problem comes up that he cannot solve, he simply stretches out on a lounge in his office, thoroughly relaxes, *and lets his subconscious mind solve the problem!*

VOLUME SIX

XIX
The Master Mind

"One who never turned his back but marched breast forward, never doubted clouds would break, never dreamed though right were worsted wrong would triumph, held we fall to rise, are baffled to fight better, sleep to wake."

—BROWNING.

Among your friends there is one of those men who doesn't have much use for the word "can't."

You marvel at his capacity for work.

You'll admire him the more the longer you know him.

You'll always respect him.

For he not only has made good, but he always will make good. He has found and appropriated to himself the "Talisman of Napoleon"—*absolute confidence in himself.*

The world loves a leader. All over the world, in every walk of life, people are eagerly seeking for some one to follow. They want some one else to do their thinking for them; they need some one to hearten them to action; they like to have some one else on whom to lay the blame when things go wrong; they want some one big enough to share the glory with them when success crowns his efforts.

But to instill confidence in them, that leader must have utter confidence in himself. A Roosevelt or a Mussolini who did not believe in himself would be inconceivable. It is that which makes men invincible—the Consciousness of their own Power. They put no limit upon their own capacities—therefore they have no limit. For Universal Mind sees all, knows all, and can do all, and we share in this absolute power to the exact extent to which we permit ourselves. Our mental attitude is the magnet that attracts from Universal Mind everything we may need to bring our desires into being. We make that magnet strong or weak as we have confidence in or doubt of our abilities. We draw to ourselves unlimited power or limit ourselves to humble positions according to our own beliefs.

A long time ago Emerson wrote: "There is one mind common to all individual men. Every man is an inlet to the same *and to all* of the same. He that is once admitted to the right of reason is made a freeman of the whole estate. What Plato has thought, he may think; what a saint has felt, he may feel; what at any time has befallen any man, he can understand. Who hath access to this Universal Mind, *is a party to all that is or can be done*, for this is the only and sovereign agent."

The great German physicist, Nernst, found that the longer an electric current was made to flow through a filament of oxide of magnesium, the greater became the conductivity of the filament.

In the same way, the more you call upon and use your subconscious mind, the greater becomes its conductivity in passing along to you the infinite resources of Universal Mind. The wisdom of a Solomon, the skill of a Michael Angelo, the genius of an Edison, the daring of a Napoleon, all may be yours. It rests with you only to form the contact with Universal Mind in order to draw from it what you will.

Think of this power as something that you can connect with any time. It has the answer to all of your problems. It offers you freedom from fear, from worry, from sickness, from accident. No man and no thing can interfere with your use of this power or diminish your share of it. No one, that is, but yourself.

Don Carlos Musser expresses it well in "*You Are*": "Because of the law of gravitation the apple falls to the ground. Because of the law of growth the acorn becomes a mighty oak. Because of the law of causation, a man is 'as he thinketh in his heart.' Nothing can happen without its adequate cause."

Success does not come to you by accident. It comes as the logical result of the operation of law. Mind, working through your brain and your body, makes your world. That it is not a better world and a bigger one is due to your limited thoughts and beliefs. They dam back the flood of ideas that Mind is constantly striving to manifest through you. God never made a failure or a nobody. He offers to the highest and the lowest alike, all that is necessary to happiness and success. The difference is entirely in the extent to which each of us AVAILS himself of that generosity.

There is no reason why you should hesitate to aspire to any position, any honor, any goal, for the Mind within you is fully able to meet any need. It is no more difficult for it to handle a great problem than a small one. Mind is just as much present in your little everyday affairs as in those of a big business or a great nation. Don't set it doing trifling sums in arithmetic when it might just as well be solving problems of moment to yourself and the world.

Start something! Use your initiative. Give your mind something to work upon. The greatest of all success secrets is initiative. It is the one quality which more than any other has put men in high places.

Conceive something. Conceive it first in your own mind. Make the pattern there and your subconscious mind will draw upon the plastic substance or energy all about you to make that model real.

Drive yourself. Force yourself. It is the dreamer, the man with imagination, who has made the world move. Without him, we would still be in the Stone Age.

Galileo looked at the moon and dreamed of how he might reach it. The telescope was the fruition of that dream. Watt dreamed of what might be done with steam—and our great locomotives and engines of today are the result. Franklin dreamed of harnessing the lightning—and today we have man-made thunderbolts.

Initiative, plus imagination, will take you anywhere. Imagination opens the eyes of the mind, and there is nothing good you can imagine there that is not possible of fulfillment in your daily life.

Imagination is the connecting link between the human and the Divine, between the formed universe and formless energy. It is, of all things human, the most God-like. It is our part of Divinity. Through it we share in the creative power of Universal Mind. Through it we can turn the drabbest existence into a thing of life and beauty. It is the means by which we avail ourselves of all the good, which Universal Mind is constantly offering to us in such profusion. It is the means by which we can reach any goal; win any prize.

What was it gave us the submarine, the aeroplane, wireless, electricity? Imagination. What was it that enabled man to build the Simplon Tunnel, the Panama Canal, the Hell Gate span? Imagination. What is it that makes us successful and happy, or poor and friendless? Imagination—or the lack of it.

It was imagination that sent Spanish and English and French adventurers to this new world. It was imagination that urged the early settlers westward—ever westward. It was imagination that built our railroads, our towns, and our great cities.

Parents foolishly try to discourage imagination in their children, when all it needs is proper guidance. For imagination forms the world from which their future will take its shape. Restrain the one and you constrict the other. Develop the one in the right way, and there is no limit to the other. Uncontrolled, the imagination is like a rudderless ship. Or even, at times, like the lightning. But properly controlled, it is like the ship that carries riches from port to port. Or like the electric current, carrying unlimited power for industry and progress.

Do you want happiness? Do you want success? Do you want position, power, and riches? *Image them!* How did God first make man? "In his image created He him." He "imaged" man in His Mind.

And that is the way everything has been made since time began. It was first imaged in Mind. That is the way everything you want must start—with a mental image.

So use your imagination! Picture in it your Heart's Desire. Imagine it—daydream it so vividly, so clearly, that you will actually BELIEVE you HAVE it. In the moment that you carry this conviction to your subconscious mind—in that moment your dream will become a reality. It may be a while before you realize it, but the important part is done. You have created the model. You can safely leave it to your subconscious mind to do the rest.

Every man wants to get out of the rut, to grow, to develop into something better. Here is the open road—open to you whether you have schooling, training, position, wealth, or not. Remember this: Your subconscious mind knew more from the time you were a baby than is in all the books in all the colleges and libraries of the world.

So don't let lack of training, lack of education, hold you back. Your mind can meet every need—and will do so if you give it the chance. The Apostles were almost all poor men, uneducated men, yet they did a work that is unequalled in historical annals. Joan of Arc was a poor peasant girl, unable to read or write—*yet she saved France!* The pages of history are dotted with poor men, uneducated men, who thought great thoughts, who used their imaginations to master circumstances and became rulers of men. Most great dynasties started with some poor, obscure man. Napoleon came of a poor, humble family. He got his appointment to the Military Academy only through very hard work and the pulling of many political strings. Even as a Captain of Artillery he was so poverty-stricken that he was unable to buy his equipment when offered an appointment to India. Business today is full of successful men who have scarcely the rudiments of ordinary education. It was only after he had made his millions that Andrew Carnegie hired a tutor to give him the essentials of an education.

So it isn't training and it isn't education that makes you successful. These help, but the thing that really counts is that gift of the Gods—*Creative Imagination!*

You have that gift. Use *it*! Make every thought, every fact, that comes into your mind *pay you a profit.* Make it work and produce for you. Think of things—not as they are but as they MIGHT be. Make them real, live and interesting. Don't merely dream—but *CREATE*! Then use your imagination to make that CREATION of advantage to mankind—and, incidentally, yourself.

XX
What Do You Lack?

"I read the papers every day, and oft encounter tales which show there's hope for every jay who in life's battle fails. I've just been reading of a gent who joined the has-been ranks, at fifty years without a cent, or credit at the banks. But undismayed he buckled down, refusing to be beat, and captured fortune and renown; he's now on Easy Street. Men say that fellows down and out ne'er leave the rocky track, but facts will show, beyond a doubt, that has-beens do come back. I know, for I who write this rhyme, when forty-odd years old, was down and out, without a dime, my whiskers full of mold. By black disaster I was trounced until it jarred my spine; I was a failure so pronounced I didn't need a sign. And after I had soaked my coat, I said (at forty-three), 'I'll see if I can catch the goat that has escaped from me.' I labored hard; I strained my dome, to do my daily grind, until in triumph I came home, my billy goat behind. And any man who still has health may with the winners stack, and have a chance at fame and wealth—for has-beens do come back."

—WALT MASON.
(From "Walt Mason—His Book." Barse & Hopkins, Newark, N. J.)

The Cumaean Sibyl is said to have offered Tarquin the Proud nine books for what he thought an exorbitant sum. So he refused. She burned three of the books, and placed the same price on the six as on the original nine. Again he refused. She burned three more books, and offered the remainder for the sum she had first asked. This time

Tarquin accepted. The books were found to contain prophecies and invaluable directions regarding Roman policy, but alas, they were no longer complete.

So it is with happiness. If you take it as you go along, you get it in its entirety. But if you keep putting off the day when you shall enjoy it—if you keep taking promissory notes for happiness—every day will mean one day less of it that you will have. Yet the cost is just the same.

The purpose of existence is GROWTH. You can't grow spiritually or mentally without happiness. And by Happiness I don't mean a timid resignation to the "Will of God." That so-called "Will of God" is more often than not either pure laziness on the part of the resigned one or pure cussedness on the part of the one that is "putting something over" on him. It is the most sanctimonious expression yet devised to excuse some condition that no one has the energy or the ability to rectify.

No—by Happiness I mean the everyday enjoyment of everyday people. I mean love and laughter and honest amusement. Every one of us is entitled to it. Every one of us can have it—if he has the WILL and the ENERGY to get out and get it for himself.

Joyless work, small pay, no future, nothing to look forward to—God never planned such an existence. It is man-made—and you can be man enough to unmake it as far as you and yours are concerned.

God never made any man poor any more than He made any man sick. Look around you. All of Nature is bountiful. On every hand you see profusion—in the trees, in the flowers, in everything that He planned. The only Law of Nature is the law of Supply. Poverty is unnatural. It is man-made, through the limits man puts upon himself. God never put them there any more than He showed partiality by giving to some of His children gifts and blessings, which He withheld from others. His gifts are just as available to you as to any man on earth. The difference is all in your understanding of how to avail yourself of the infinite supply all about you.

Take the worry clamps off your mentality and you will make the poverty clamps loosen up from your finances. Your affairs are so closely related to your consciousness that they too will relax into peace, order, and plenty. Divine ideas in your spiritual consciousness will become active in your business, and will work out as your abundant prosperity.

As David V. Bush says in *"Applied Psychology and Scientific Living"*—"Thoughts are things; thoughts are energy; thoughts are magnets which attract to us the very things which we think. Therefore, if a man is in debt, he will, by continually thinking about debt, bring more debts to him. For thoughts are causes, and he fastens more debts on to himself and actually creates more obligations by thinking about debts.

"Concentrate and think upon things that you want; not on things which you ought not to have. Think of abundance, of opulence, of plenty, of position, harmony and growth, and if you do not see them manifested today, they will be realized tomorrow. If you must pass through straits of life where you do not outwardly see abundance, know that you have it within, and that in time it will manifest itself.

"I say, if you concentrate on debt, debt is what you will have; if you think about poverty, poverty is what you will receive. It is just as easy, when once the mind becomes trained, to think prosperity and abundance and plenty, as it is to think lack, limitation and poverty."

Prosperity is not limited to time or to place. It manifests when and where there is consciousness to establish it. It is attracted to the consciousness that is free from worry, strain, and tension.

So never allow yourself to worry about poverty. Be careful; take ordinary business precautions of course. But don't center your thought on your *troubles*. The more you think of them, the more tightly you fasten them upon yourself. Think of the *results* you are after—not of the difficulties in the way. Mind will find the way. It is merely up to you to choose the goal, and then keep your thought steadfast until that goal is won.

The greatest short cut to prosperity is to *LIVE IT!* Prosperity attracts. Poverty repels. To quote Orison Swett Marden—"To be ambitious for wealth and yet always expecting to be poor, to be always doubting your ability to get what you long for, is like trying to reach East by traveling West. There is no philosophy which will help a man to succeed when he is always doubting his ability to do so, and thus attracting failure."

Again: "No matter how hard you may work for success, if your thought is saturated with the fear of failure it will kill your efforts, neutralize your endeavors, and make success impossible."

The secret of Prosperity lies in so vividly imaging it in your own mind that you literally exude prosperity. You feel prosperous, you look prosperous, and the result is that before long you ARE prosperous.

I remember seeing a play a number of years ago that was based on this thought. A young fellow—a chronic failure—was persuaded by a friend to carry a roll of $1000 counterfeit bills in his pocket, and to show them, unostentatiously, when the occasion offered. Of course, everyone thought he had come into some legacy. The natural inference was that anyone who carried fifty or a hundred thousand dollar bills in his pockets must have a lot more in the bank. Opportunities flocked to him: Opportunities to make good; Opportunities to make money. He made good! Without having to spend any of this spurious money of his. For most business today is done on credit. I know many wealthy men who seldom carry anything but a little change in their pockets for tips. Everything they do, everything they buy, is "Charged." And big deals are put through in the same way. If a man is believed to have plenty of money, if he has a reputation for honesty and fair dealing, he may put through a transaction running into six or seven figures without paying one cent down. The thing that counts is not the amount of your balance at the Bank, but what others THINK of you, the IMAGE you have created in your own and in others minds.

What do you lack? What thing do you want most? Realize that before it or any other thing can be, it must first be imaged in Mind. Realize, too, that when you can close your eyes and actually SEE that thing, *you have brought it into being*—you have drawn upon that invisible substance all about you—you have *created something*. Hold it in your thought, focus your mind upon it, "BELIEVE THAT YOU HAVE IT"— and you can safely leave its material manifestation to the Genie-of-your-Mind.

God is but another name for the invisible, everywhere present, and Source-of-things. Out of the air the seed gathers the essences which are necessary to its bountiful growth; out of the invisible ether our minds gather the rich ideas that stimulate us to undertake and to carry out enterprises that bring prosperity to us. Let us see with the eye of the mind a bountiful harvest; then our minds will be quickened with ideas of abundance, and plenty will appear, not only in our world, but also everywhere.

"As the rain cometh down and the snow from heaven, and returneth not thither, but watereth the earth, and maketh it bring forth and bud, and giveth seed to the sower and bread to the eater; so shall my word be that goeth forth out of my mouth: it shall not return unto me void, but it shall accomplish that which I please, and it shall prosper in the thing whereto I sent it."—Isaiah.

XX
The Sculptor and the Clay

"Eternal mind the Potter is, and thought the eternal clay.
The hand that fashions is divine; His works pass not away.
God could not make imperfect man his model Infinite, Unhallowed thought he could not plan—love's work and
love must fit."

—ALICE DAYTON.

When you step into your office on Monday morning, no doubt you have dreams of wonderful achievement. Your step is firm, your brain is clear and you have carefully thought out just WHAT you will do and HOW you will accomplish big things in your business. Perhaps the very plans you have in mind will influence your whole business career, and you have visions of the dollars that will be yours rolling into your bank account.

But do these dreams come true?

Are you always able to put through what you had planned to do—does your day's work have the snap and power you imagined it would have? Are you ever forced to admit that your dreams of big accomplishment are often shattered because of "fagged nerves" and lack of energy, because you have not the "pep"?

How easy it is to think back and see how success was in your grasp if only you had felt equal to that extra bit of effort, if only you had had the "pep," the energy to reach out and take it? The great men of the world have been well men, strong men. Sickness and hesitancy go hand in hand. Sickness means weakness, querulous ness, lack of faith, and lack of confidence in oneself and in others.

But there is no real reason for sickness or weakness, and there is no reason why you should remain weak or sick if you are so afflicted now.

Remember the story of the sculptor Pygmalion? How he made a statue of marble so beautiful that every woman who saw it envied it? So perfect was it that he fell in love with it himself, hung it with flowers and jewels, spent day after day in rapt admiration of it, until finally the gods took pity upon him and breathed into it the breath of life.

There is more than Pagan mythology to that story. There is this much truth in it—that any man can set before his mind's eye the image of the figure he himself would like to be, and then breathe the breath of life into it merely by keeping that image before his subconscious mind as the model on which to do its daily building.

For health and strength are natural. It is ill health and weakness that are unnatural. Your body was meant to be lithe, supple, muscular, and full of red-blooded energy and vitality. A clear brain, a powerful heart, a massive chest, wrists and arms of steel—all these were meant for you—all these you can have if you will but *know*, and *feel*, and *think aright*.

Just take stock of yourself for a moment. Are your muscles tough, springy and full of vim? Do they do all you ask of them—and then beg for more? Can you eat a good meal—and forget it?

If you can't, it's your own fault. You can have a body alive with vitality, a skin smooth and fine of texture, muscles supple and virile. You can be the man you have always dreamed of being, without arduous dieting, without tiresome series of exercises, merely by following the simple rules herein laid down.

For what is it that builds up the muscles, puts energy and vitality into your system, gives you the pep and vigor of youth? *Is it exercise?* Then why is it that so many day laborers are poor, weak, anemic creatures, forced to lay off from one to three months every year on account of sickness? They get plenty of exercise and fresh air. Why is it that so many athletes die of tuberculosis or of weak hearts? They get the most scientific exercise year in and year out.

Just the other day I read of the sudden death of Martin A. Delaney, the famous trainer, known all over the country as a physical director. He taught thousands how to be strong, but "Athletic Heart" killed him at 55. Passersby saw him running for a car, then suddenly topple over dead.

"Exercise as a panacea for all human ills is dangerously overrated," Dr. Charles M. Wharton, in charge of health and physical education at the University of Pennsylvania, said today (March 20, 1926), according to an Associated Press dispatch.

Dr. Wharton, who has been a trainer of men for thirty years and was an all-American guard on the Pennsylvania football team in 1895 and 1896, declared the search for the fountain of youth by exercise and diet has been commercialized to a point of hysteria.

"Some one should cry a halt against this wild scramble for health by Unnatural means," said Dr. Wharton. "This indiscriminate adoption of severe physical training destroys the health of more people than it improves."

Dr. Wharton said he was appalled by the amount of physical defects and weaknesses developed by overindulgence in athletics by students in preparatory schools.

"I know I am presenting an unpopular viewpoint, and it may sound strange coming from a physical director.

"In gymnasium work at the University of Pennsylvania we try to place our young men in sports *which they will enjoy*, and thus get a physical stimulation from *relaxed play.*"

Is it diet? Then why is it that so many people you know, who have been dieting for years, are still such poor, flabby creatures? Doesn't it always work, or is it merely a matter of guess-work-and those were the cases where no one happened to guess right? Why is it that doctors disagree so on what is the correct diet? For years we have been taught to forswear too much meat. For years we have been told that it causes rheumatism and gout and hardening of the arteries—and a dozen or more other ailments.

Now comes Dr. Woods Hutchinson—a noted authority, quoted the world over—and says: "All the silly old prejudice against meat, that it heated the blood (whatever that means) and produced uric acid to excess, hardened the arteries, inflamed the kidneys, caused rheumatism, etc., has now been proved to be pure fairy tales, utterly without foundation in scientific fact.

"Red meats have nothing whatever to do with causing gout and rheumatism, because neither of these diseases is due to foods or drinks of any sort, but solely to what we call local infections. Little pockets of pus (matter) full of robber germs—mostly streptococci—around the roots of our teeth, in the pouches of our tonsils, in the nasal passages and sinuses of our foreheads and faces opening into them; . . . Our belief now is: 'No pockets of pus, no

102

rheumatism or gout.' Food of any kind has absolutely nothing to do with the case.

"On the other hand, the very worst cases on record in all medical history of hardening and turning to lime (calcification) of the arteries all over the body, and in the kidneys and intestines particularly, have been found in Trappist and certain orders of Oriental monks who live almost exclusively upon starch and—that is, peas, beans, and lentils, and abstain from meat entirely."

Then what is right? *Is it the combination of diet and exercise?* But surely the patients in sanitariums and similar institutions would have every chance to get just the right combination, yet how often you see them come out little, if any, better off than when they went in.

No. None of these is the answer. As a matter of fact, the principal good of either diet or exercise is that it keeps before the patient's mind the RESULT he is working for, and in that way tends to impress it upon his subconscious mind. That is why physical culturists always urge you to exercise in front of a mirror. If results are achieved, it is MIND that achieves them—not the movements you go through or the particular kind of food you eat.

Understand, I don't ask you to stop exercising. A reasonable amount of light, pleasant exercise is good for you mentally and physically. It develops your will power. It helps to impress upon your subconscious mind the image you want to see realized in your body. And it takes your mind off your troubles and worries, centering your thoughts instead upon your desires; just where your thoughts should always be.

Outdoor exercise, tennis, horseback, swimming—any sort of active *game*—is the best rest there is for a tired mind. For mental tiredness comes from a too steady contemplation of one's problems. And anything that will take ones mind completely off them, and give the subconscious time to work out the solution, is good. That is why it so often happens that you go back to your work after a day of play—not merely refreshed, but with so clear a mind that the problems, which before seemed insurmountable are but as child's play to you.

You who envy the rosy cheek and sparkling eye of youth, who awake in the morning weary and unrefreshed, who go to your daily tasks with fagged brain and heavy tread—just remember that Perfect Youth or Perfect Health is merely a state of mind.

There is only one thing that puts muscles on your bones. There is only one thing that keeps your organs functioning with precision and regularity. There is only one thing that builds for you a perfect body. That one thing is your subconscious mind.

Every cell and tissue, every bone and sinew, every organ and muscle in your entire body is subject to the control of your subconscious mind. As it directs, so they build or function.

True, that subconscious mind accepts suggestions from your conscious mind. Hold before it the thought that the exercise you are taking is building muscle upon your arms or shoulders, and your subconscious mind will fall in readily with the suggestion and strengthen those muscles. Hold before it the thought that some particular food gives you unusual energy and "pep," and the subconscious mind will be entirely agreeable to producing the added vigor.

But have you ever noticed how some sudden joy (which is entirely a mental state) energizes and revitalizes you—*more than all the exercise or all the tonics you can take?* Have you ever noticed how martial music will relieve the fatigue of marching men? Have you ever noticed how sorrow (which is entirely a mental state) will depress and devitalize you, *regardless of any amount of exercise or health foods you may take?*

Each of us has within him all the essentials that go to the making of a Super-Man. But so has every acorn the essentials for making a great oak tree, yet the Japanese show us that even an oak may be stunted by continual pruning of its shoots. Negative and weak thoughts, thoughts of self-doubt, of mistrust, continually prune back the vigorous life ever seeking so valiantly to show forth the, splendor and strength of the radiant inner self.

Choose what you will be! Your responsibility is to think, speak, act the true inner self. Your privilege is to show forth in this self, the fullness of peace and plenty. Keep steadfastly in mind the idea of yourself that you want to see realized. Your daily, hourly, and continual idea of yourself, your life, your affairs, your world, and your associates, determines the harvest, the showing forth. Look steadfastly to your highest ideal of self, and your steadfast and lofty ideal will draw forth blessing and prosperity not only upon you, but also upon all who know you.

For mind is the only creator, and thought is the only energy. All that counts is the image of your body that you are holding in your thought. If heretofore that image has been one of weakness, of ill health, change it *now*— TODAY. Repeat to yourself, the first thing upon awakening in the morning and the last thing before going to sleep at night—"My body was made in the image and likeness of God. God first imagined it in its entirety, therefore every cell and bone and tissue is perfect, every organ and muscle performing its proper function. That is the only model of me in Universal Mind. That is the only model of me that my Subconscious Mind knows. Therefore, since Mind—God—is the only creator, that is the only model of me that I can have!"

XXII
Why Grow Old?

"And Moses was an hundred and twenty years old when he died: his eye was not dim, nor his natural force abated."

Remember how you used to plough through great masses of work day after day and month after month, cheerily, enthusiastically, with never a sign of tiring or nervous strain? Remember how you used to enjoy those evenings, starting out as fresh from your office or shop as if you hadn't just put a hard day's work behind you?

No doubt you've often wondered why you can't work and enjoy yourself like that now, but solaced yourself with the moth-eaten fallacy that "As a man grows older he shouldn't expect to get the same fun out of life that he did in his earlier years."

Poor old exploded idea!

Youth is not a matter of time. It is a mental state. You can be just as brisk, just as active, just as light-hearted now as you were ten or twenty years ago. Genuine youth is just a perfect state of health. You can have that health, and the boundless energy and capacity for work or enjoyment that go with it. You can cheat time of ten, twenty or fifty years—not by taking thought of what you shall eat or what you shall drink, not by diet or exercise, but solely through a right understanding of what you should expect of your body.

"If only I had my life to live over again!" How often you have heard it said. How often you have thought it. But the fact is that you CAN have it. You can start right now and live again as many years as you have already experienced. Health, physical freedom and full vigor need not end for you at 35 or 40—nor at 60 or 70. Age is not a matter of years. It is a state of mind.

In an address before the American Sociological Society a few months ago Dr. Hornell Hart of Bryn Mawr predicted that—"Babies born in the year 2000 will have something like 200 years of life ahead of them, and men and women of 100 years will be quite the normal thing. But instead of being wrinkled and crippled, these centenarians will be in their vigorous prime."

Thomas Parr, an Englishman, lived to be 152 years old, and was sufficiently hale and hearty at the age of 120 to take unto himself a second wife. Even at 152, his death was not due to old age, but to a sudden and drastic change in his manner of life. All his days he had lived upon simple fare, but his fame reaching the King, he was invited to London and there feasted so lavishly that he died of it.

In a dispatch to the New York Times on February 14th last, I read of an Arab now in Palestine, one Salah Mustapha Salah Abu Musa, who at the age of 105 *is growing his third set of teeth!*
There is an ancient city in Italy, which can be approached by sea only through a long stretch of shallow water full of rocks and cross currents. There is one safe channel, and it is marked by posts. In the days of the Sea Rovers the city used to protect itself by pulling up the posts whenever a rover hove in sight.

Mankind has taken to planting posts along its way to mark the flight of time. Every year we put in a new one, heedless of the fact that we are thus marking a clear channel for our Archenemy, Age, to enter in from the sea of human belief.

But the fact is that there is no natural reason for man to grow old as soon as he does; *no biological reason for him to grow old at all!*

Why is it that the animals live eight to ten times their maturity, when man lives only about twice his? Why? Because man hastens decrepitude and decay by holding the thought of old age always before him.

Dr. Alexis Carrel, Noble Prize winner and member of the Rockefeller Institute, has demonstrated that living cells taken from a body, properly protected and fed, can be kept alive indefinitely. Not only that, but they grow! In 1912 he took Sonic tissue from the heart of an embryo chick and placed it in a Culture medium. It is living and growing yet.

Recently Dr. Carrel showed a moving picture of these living cells before the American Institute of Electrical Engineers. They grow so fast that they double in size every twenty-four hours, and have to be trimmed daily!

The cells of your being can be made to live indefinitely when placed outside your body. Single-celled animals never die a natural death. They live on and on until something kills them. Now scientists are beginning to wonder if multi-cellular animals like man really need to die.

Under the title, "*Immortality and Rejuvenation in Modern Biology,*" M. Metalnikov, of the Pasteur Institute, has just published a volume that should be read by all those who have decided that it is necessary to grow old and die.

Here is the first sentence of the concluding chapter of the book: "What we have just written forces us to maintain our conviction that immortality is the fundamental property of living organisms."

And further on:

"Old age and death are not a stage of earthly existence…"

And that, mind you, is set forth under the aegis of a scientific establishment that has no equal in the world, and of a scholar universally respected.

As the *Journal of Paris* says in reviewing the article:

"Most religious and philosophic systems assert the immortality of the soul. But the positive sciences have shown themselves more skeptical on this point. This idea seems to them quite contradictory to all that we know, or think we know, of animal life. Animal life originates as a tiny germ, which becomes an embryo, developing into an adult organism, which grows old and finally dies. This means the disappearance of all the faculties of life that so clearly distinguish it from an inanimate object. There is no scientific evidence to show that at this moment the 'soul' does not disappear with the body, and that it continues its existence separately. Biologists cannot even conceive the possibility of separation of soul and body, so strong and indissoluble are the bonds that unite all our psychic manifestations with our bodily life. For them an immortal soul only can exist in an immortal body. What if it were so? What if our organism is really indestructible? It is this that M. Metalnikoy attempts scientifically to prove.

"Death is a permanent and tangible phenomenon only in the case of man and the higher animals. It is not so for plants and for the simpler forms of animal life, the protozoans. These last, composed often of a single cell, just observable under the microscope, are however without the chief faculties that characterizes the higher animals. They move about by means of vibratory hair-like processes, sustain themselves, seek their food, hunt animals still smaller than themselves, react to irritations of different kinds, and multiply. But this multiplication is not effected by means of special organs, as among the higher animals, but by the division of the whole organism into two equal parts. The common infusorians, which abound in fresh water, thus divide once or twice every twenty-four hours. Each daughter cell continues to live like the mother cell, of which it is the issue; it feeds, grows, and divides in its turn. And never, in this constantly renewed cycle in their lives, do we find the phenomenon of natural death, so characteristic and so universal in the higher animals. The infusorium is subject only to accidental death, such as we can cause by the addition of some poisonous element to the water in which it lives, or by heat.

"Experiments along this line were made long ago. The first were by de Saussure, in 1679. Having put an infusorium in a drop of water, he saw it divide under his eye. Four days later it was impossible to count the number of creatures. However, some authors thought that this reproductive facility was not unlimited. Maupas himself, who made a minute study of it forty years ago and succeeded in observing 700 successive generations of a single species, thought that it was finally subject to old age and to death.

"But the more recent works of Joukovsky at Heidelberg, of Koulaghine at Petrograd, of Calkins in England, of Weissmann, and still others, lead to an opposite opinion. The degeneration observed by these workers was due to autointoxication, caused by not renewing the culture medium.

"Decisive experiments were made in Russia, dating from 1907, by Woodruff and by M. Metalnikoy himself. Begun at Tsarskoe Selo, they continued until the tragic hours of the 1917 revolution, and were renewed at the University of Crimea. These investigators took an infusorium found in an aquarium, the Paramoecium caudatum, whose characteristics are well determined, and in thirteen years, in 1920, they had obtained 5,000 successive generations…
"Thus we are bound to say that a unicellular body possesses within itself the power of immortality.

"And we ourselves are made up only by the juxtaposition of simple cells."

The Fountain of Youth

Four hundred years ago Ponce de Leon set sail into the mysteries of an unknown world in search of the Fountain of Youth, when all the time the secret of that fountain was right within himself.

For the fact is, that no matter how many years have passed since you were born, *you are only eleven months old today!* Your body is constantly renewing itself. The one thing about it you can be surest of is CHANGE. Every one of the millions of cells of which it is composed is constantly being renewed. Even your bones are daily renewing themselves in this way.

These cells are building—building—building. Every day they tear down old tissue and rebuild it with new. There is not a cell in your body, not a muscle or tissue, not a bone, that is more than eleven months old! Why then should you feel age? Why should you be any less spry, any less cheerful, than these youngsters around you that you have been envying?

The answer is that you *need not*—if you will but realize your YOUTHFULNESS. Every organ, every muscle, tissue and cell of your body is subject to your subconscious mind. They rebuild exactly as that mind directs them. What is the model you are holding before your mind's eye? Is it one of age, of decrepitude? That is the model that most men use, because they know no better. That is the result that you see imaged upon their bodies.

But you need not follow their outworn models. You can hold before your mind's eye only the vision of youth, of manly vigor, of energy and strength and beauty *and that is the model that your cells will use to build upon.*

Do you know what is responsible for the whole difference between Youth and Age? Just one thing. Youth looks *forward* always to something better. Age looks backward and sighs over its "lost" youth.

In youth we are constantly growing. We KNOW we have not yet reached our prime. We know we can expect to continually IMPROVE. We look forward to ever-increasing physical powers. We look forward to a finer, more perfect physique. We look forward to greater mental alertness. We have been educated to expect these things. Therefore we BELIEVE we shall get them—and we GET them!

But what happens after we get to be thirty or forty years of age? We think we have reached our prime. We have been taught that we can no longer look forward to greater growth—that all we can hope for is to "hold our own" for a little while, and then start swiftly downward to old age and decay. History shows that no nation, no institution and no individual can continue for any length of time to merely "hold his own." You must go forward —or back. You must move—or life will pass you by. Yours is the choice if you will realize that there is never any end to GROWTH— that your body is constantly being rebuilt—that perfection is still so far ahead of you that you can continue GROWING towards it indefinitely—you need never know age. You can keep on growing more perfect, mentally and physically, every day. Every minute you live is a minute of Conception and rebirth.

You may be weak and anemic. You may be crippled or bent. No matter! You can start today to rebuild along new lines. In eleven months at the most, every one of those weak and devitalized cells, every one of those bent and crippled bones, will be replaced by new, strong, vigorous tissue.

Look at Annette Kellerman—crippled and deformed as a child—yet she grew up into the world's most perfectly formed woman. Look at Roosevelt—weak and anemic as a young man—yet he made himself the envy of the world for boundless vigor and energy. And they are but two cases out of thousands I could quote. Many of the world's strongest men were weaklings in their childhood. It matters not what your age, what your condition—you can start now renewing your youth, growing daily nearer the model of YOU that is imaged in Universal Mind.

Arthur Brisbane says that at the age of 85 George F. Baker is doing the work of ten men.

That is what every man of 85 ought to be doing, for he should have not only the physical vigor and strength and enthusiasm of 21, but combined with them he should have the skill and experience, the ripened judgment of 85.

There is no more despairing pronouncement than the belief of the average man that he matures only to begin at once to deteriorate and decay. When the actual fact is, as stated in a recent utterance by the eminent Dr. Hammond, *there is no physiological reason* why a man should die. He asserted—and the statement is corroborated by scientists and physiologists—that the human body possesses inherent capacity to renew and continue itself and its functions, indefinitely!

Your body wears out? Of course it does—just as all material things do. But with this difference your body is being renewed just as fast as it wears out! Have you damaged some part of it? Don't worry. Down inside you is a chemical laboratory, which can make new parts just as good or better than the old. Up in your subconscious mind is a Master Chemist with all the formulas of Universal Mind to draw upon, who can keep that chemical laboratory of yours making new parts just as fast as you can wear out the old.

But that Master Chemist is like all of us—like you. He is inclined to lazy a bit on the job—if you let him. Try to relieve him of some of his functions—and he won't bother about them further. Take to the regular use of drugs or other methods of eliminating the waste matter from the body, and your Master Chemist will figure that your conscious mind has taken over this duty from him—and he will leave it thereafter to your conscious mind. Lead him to believe that you no longer expect him to rebuild your body along such perfect lines as in youth—and he will slow down in his work of removing the old, worn-out tissues, and of replacing them with new, better material. The result? Arteries clogged with worn-out cells. Tissues dried and shrunken. Joints stiff and creaky. In short—Old Age.

The fault is not with the Master Chemist. It is with you. You didn't hold him to the job. When a business or an enterprise or an expedition fails, it is not the rank and file who are to blame—it is the directing head. He didn't give his men the right plans to work on. He didn't supply the proper leadership. He didn't keep them keyed up to their best work.

What would you think of an engineer who, with the best plans in the world, the best material with which to build, threw away his plans when he was half through with the job and let his men do as they pleased, ruining all his early work and all his fine material by putting the rest of it together any which way?

Yet that is what you do when you stop LOOKING FORWARD at 30 or 40, and decide thereafter to just grow old any which way. You throw away the wonderful model on which you have been building, you take the finest material in the world, and let your workmen put it together any way they like. In fact, you do worse than that. You tell them you don't expect much from them any more. That any sort of a patched up job they put together after that will be about as good as you can look for.

Man alive! What would you expect from ordinary workmen to whom you talked like that? Your inner workmen are no different. You will get from them just what you look for—no more, no less.

"Your time of life" should be the best time you have yet known. The engineer who has built forty bridges should be far more proficient than the one who has built only a few. The model you are passing on to your Master

Chemist now ought to be a vastly more perfect model than the one you gave to him at twenty. Instead of feeling that your heart is giving out and your stomach weak, you ought to be boasting of how much better a heart you are now making than a few years ago, how much more perfectly your stomach is functioning than before you learned that you were its boss.

Of one thing you can be sure. God never decreed a law of decay and death. If there is any such law, it is man-made—and man can unmake it. The Life Principle that came to this planet thousands or millions of years ago brought no Death Principle with it. For death is like darkness—it is nothing in itself. Death is merely the absence of life, just as darkness is merely the absence of light. Keep that life surging—strongly.

Universal Mind knows no imperfection—no decay—no death. It does not produce sickness and death. It is your conscious mind that has decreed these evils. Banish the thought—and you can banish the effect. Life was never meant to be measured by years.

I remember reading a story of a traveler who had journeyed to a land of perpetual sun. Since there was no sunrise and no sunset, no moons or changing seasons, there was no means of measuring time. Therefore to the inhabitants of that land, time did not exist. And having no time, they never thought to measure ages and consequently never grew old. Like organisms with a single cell, they did not die except by violence.

There is more truth than fiction to that idea. The measurement of life by the calendar robs youth of its vigor and hastens old age. It reminds me of the days of our grandparents, when a woman was supposed to doff her hat and don a bonnet at 40. And donning a bonnet was like taking the veil. She was supposed to retire to her chimney corner and make way for the younger generation.

Men and women ought to *grow* with years into greater health, broader judgment, and mature wisdom. Instead of becoming atrophied, and dead to all new ideas, their minds should through practice hold ever-stronger images before them of youthful vigor and freshness.

No one need retire to the chimney corner, no matter how many years have passed over his head. Years should bring wisdom and greater health—not decrepitude. Many of the world's famous men did their greatest work long after the age when most men are in their graves. Tennyson composed the immortal lines of "*Crossing the Bar*" at the age of 80. Plato still had pen in hand at 81. Cato learned Greek at the same age. Humboldt completed his "*Cosmos*" in his ninetieth year, while John Wesley at 82 said—"It is twelve years now since I have felt any such sensation as fatigue."

You are only as old as your mind. Every function, every activity of your body, is controlled by your mind. Your vital organs, your blood that sends the material for rebuilding to every cell and tissue, the processes of elimination that remove all the broken down and waste material, all are dependent for their functioning upon the energy derived from your mind.

The human body can be compared to an electric transportation system. When the dynamo runs at full power every car speeds along, and everything is handled with precision. But let the dynamo slow down and the whole system lags.

That dynamo is your mind, and your thoughts provide the energy that runs it. Feed it thoughts of health and vigor and your whole system will reflect energy and vitality. Feed it thoughts of decrepitude and age, and you will find it slowing down to the halting pace you set for it.

VOLUME SIX - The Fountain of Youth

You can grow old at 30. You can be young at 90. It is up to you. Which do you choose?

If you choose youth, then start this minute renewing your youth. Find a picture—or, better still, a statuette—of the man you would like to be, the form you would like to have. Keep it in your room. When you go to bed at night, *visualize* it in your mind's eye—hold it in your thought as *YOU*—as the man *YOU ARE GOING TO BE!* *The Journal of Education* had the idea in their story of "The Prince and the Statue" in a recent issue:

"There was once a prince who had a crooked back. He could never stand straight up like even the lowest of his subjects. Because he was a very proud prince his crooked back caused him a great deal of mental suffering.

"One day he called before him the most skilful sculptor in his kingdom and said to him: 'Make me a noble statue of myself, true to my likeness in every detail with this exception—make this statue with a straight back. I wish to see myself as I might have been.

"For long months the sculptor worked hewing the marble carefully into the likeness of the prince, and at last the work was done, and the sculptor went before the prince and said: 'The statue is finished; where shall I set it up?' One of the courtiers called out: 'Set it before the castle gate where all can see it,' but the prince smiled sadly, and shook his head. 'Rather,' said he, 'place it in a secret nook in the palace garden where only I shall see it.' The statue was placed as the prince ordered, and promptly forgotten by the world, but every morning, and every noon, and every evening the prince stole quietly away to where it stood and looked long upon it, noting the straight back and the unlifted head, and the noble brow. And each time he gazed, something seemed to go out of the statue and into him, tingling in his blood and throbbing in his heart.

"The days passed into months and the months into years; then strange rumors began to spread throughout the land. Said one: 'The prince's back is no longer crooked or my eyes deceive me.' Said another: 'The prince is more noble-looking or my eyes deceive me.' Said another: 'Our prince has the high look of a mighty man,' and these rumors came to the prince, and he listened with a queer smile. Then went he out into the garden to where the statue stood and, behold, it was just as the people said, his back had become as straight as the statue's, his head had the same noble bearing; he was, in fact, the noble man his statue proclaimed him to be."

A novel idea? Not at all! 2,500 years ago, in the Golden Age of Athens, when its culture led the world, Grecian mothers surrounded themselves with beautiful statues that they might bring forth perfect children and that the children in turn might develop into perfect men and women.

Eleven months from now *you* will have an entirely new body, inside and out. Not a single cell, not a single bit of tissue that is now in you will be there then. What changes do you want made in that new body? What improvements?

Get your new model clearly in your mind's eye. Picture it. VISUALIZE it! Look FORWARD daily to a better physique, to greater mental power.

Give that model to your Subconscious Mind to build upon—and before eleven months are out, that model *WILL BE YOU!*

VOLUME SEVEN
XXIII
The Medicine Delusion

"I find the medicine worse than the malady."

—SHAKESPEARE.

We are getting rid of the drug illusion," declared Dr. Woods Hutchinson, the noted medical writer of America, at a luncheon given on June 6, 1925, by the English- Speaking Union to 700 American and Canadian doctors assembled in London, England.

"We are willing even to subscribe to the dictum of Oliver Wendell Holmes," the doctor added, "that if 99 per cent of all drugs we possess were thrown into the sea it would be a good thing for the human race, but rather hard on the fishes."

Sir Arbuthnot Lane, Surgeon to King George, seconded Dr. Hutchinson's remarks. "They might say," he went on, "that he was trying to establish a 'suicide club' for doctors. It practically came to that, because as the public became educated in matters of health the medical profession might disappear. It was in fact an anomaly that a medical profession should exist. If people were healthy, there was no reason to have doctors at all."

Twenty-five years ago, the charms of the Patent Medicine fakir and the incantations of the Indian Medicine Man were in the heyday of their popularity. So long as you talked about their aches and pains, their diseases and ailments, people would buy any kind of a nostrum that an unscrupulous fakir chose to palm off upon them. Patent medicine manufacturers made fabulous fortunes selling cheap whisky adulterated with burnt sugar and water, under a hundred different names for $1.00 the bottle. You could hardly pick up a magazine or newspaper without seeing a dozen of their lurid ads.

The day of the Indian Medicine Man and street-corner fakir has passed. And for a time, thanks to the crusade against them led by *Collier's*, and backed by a number of other reputable magazines, patent medicine manufacturers suffered an eclipse.
But they are back again today in a more respectable guise. Pick up almost any small town paper and you will find a dozen "sovereign remedies" for tired women or fretful children or run-down men. Concoctions, most of them, containing just enough alcohol to give you a pleasant sense of stimulation, enough burnt sugar to color them—and a whole lot of water.

But if that were all, no great harm would be done. If the peddling of drugs depended entirely—or even mostly—on Patent Medicine advertisers, the end of it would soon be in sight. But it doesn't. The worst offenders of all are the ones who, of all people, should know better—some of the doctors.
Understand, I don't mean all of them. And I don't mean the best of them. There are thousands of them like Dr. Woods Hutchinson who have the courage to get up and say that medicine itself cannot cure disease. That it never has cured disease. That Nature is the only Healer. Drugs can give you temporary relief from pain—yes. They can cleanse—yes. But as for *curing* anything, the drug is not made that can do it.

The principal good that the administering of a drug has is in its effect upon the mind of the patient. Men have

111

been taught for so many years that drugging is the only way to cure disease, that when you give them something, they BELIEVE they are going to be cured, and to the extent that they believe, they ARE CURED.

The best proof of that is to let two patients suffering from the same complaint go to two different physicians—the one a doctor of the regular school, the other a homeopath. The regular doctor will administer a dose containing ten thousand times as much of the mother drug as the homeopath. In fact, there is so slight a trace of any drug in the homeopath's prescription that it might be called none at all. Yet it frequently happens that his patient will respond just as readily to his denatured dose as the other will to his drug.

Dr. Gour, in a recent issue of *Pearson's Magazine*, said: "A few years ago there appeared an article in the *Atlantic Monthly* written by a young woman physician who was with the Red Cross in Russia. Immediately following the Kerensky revolution, the Russian peasants who, for the first time in their lives, found that they could keep what they earned, began to think of going to doctors for ailments which had afflicted them for years, but which they could never before afford to have treated. Within two weeks' time this young physician exhausted her supply of medicine. But the rush of peasant patients continued and she was reduced to the placebo idea of administering colored waters with a slight amount of a single drug-quinine, if I recall correctly. For several weeks she obtained such wonderful results in every conceivable form of affliction that she said her faith in specific medication was completely lost."

In a dispatch from Rome to the New York *Herald-Tribune*, under date of June 15, 1926, I read:

"Under the skeptical eyes of local doctors Don Luigi Garofalo, a priest in the Quarto sector of Naples, alleges that he is curing all the ills that flesh is heir to, from pneumonia to broken bones, by a practical application of the theory derived from the text, 'Man is of dust and to dust he shall return.' Don Luigi argues that from a homeopathic view point dust should be a curative element. So from dust taken from the reddish earth near Pozznoli, which contains traces of sulphur and copper, he makes pills for the afflicted, but he contends that any other earth will do.

"The cures, most of which have been effected by means of the red earth, include the healing of broken limbs, tubercular cases, toothache, internal lesions, heart diseases, mumps, paralysis and fevers."

Of course, it is not to be inferred from this that reliance can be placed upon red earth—or any other kind of earth —to cure you of any ill. But it shows that even so common, ordinary a thing as a bit of dirt can be used to arouse people from the lethargic condition in which sickness so frequently leaves them, and gives them the power to help themselves.

Take another case. Your doctor prescribes regular doses of some drug. You take it once. It has the desired effect. You take it again. The effect is not quite so pronounced. You keep it up—and in a short time *the drug seems to have lost its efficacy.*

Why? The same chemical elements are there. And if you mix the same chemical elements in a retort, you will get the same results whether you do it once or a thousand times. Why doesn't it work the same way with drugs and your body?

Because the strongest factor in bringing about the desired effect in the beginning was your BELIEF—yours and that of your doctor. But as you kept on and on, your belief began to falter, until presently it died away altogether. You may have *hoped*, but the active belief suggestions to your subconscious mind had stopped carrying conviction.

Dr. Richard C. Cabot, Professor of Medicine at Harvard University, in a recent address, declared, "Three-quarters of all illnesses are cured without the victims even knowing they have had them.

"Proof of this contention is to be found in post-mortem examinations, which time after time reveal indelible and unmistakable traces of disease which the subject has conquered all unknowingly. Ninety per cent of all typhoid cures itself, as does 75 per cent of all pneumonia. In fact, out of a total of 215 diseases known to medical science, there are only about eight or nine which doctors conquer—the rest conquer themselves."

He went on to say that—"If nature, assisted by the proper mental and emotional moods, is capable of curing an ulcer in three or four weeks, why isn't it possible for the same force to heal a similar ulcer in a few minutes, when the curative processes have been speeded up abnormally?"

Great physicians have, on numerous occasions, maintained that there is no science in *medicating* people. In Preventive Medicine—yes. In Surgery. In Obstetrics. In a score of different lines that fall under the heading of the medical profession.

But the art of drugging is little ahead of where it was in the Middle Ages, when Egyptian mummies were in great demand among druggists and "powdered Pharaoh" was considered the greatest remedy for any ill that flesh was heir to.

Every day brings the discovery of some new drug, and the consequent dictum that the remedy previously prescribed was all a mistake—that it had little or no real value whatever.

One doctor says: "A medicine that will not kill you if you take an overdose is no good." Another: "The most prominent doctors now claim that there is not a single drug that will do what it has been prescribed for in the past."

Dr. Douglas White, writing in *The Churchman*, sums it up thus:

"All cure of every disease is spiritual. Healing can never be imposed from without by either the surgeon or physician; it is the living organism which, helped by the skill of the one or the other, is enabled to work its way back to health. The whole principle of healing in all cases is the *vis medicatrix naturae*. And when we speak of nature, we are only personifying the principle of life which Christians call God."

In the *Medical Record* of September 25, 1920, Dr. Joseph Byrne, Professor of Neurology at Fordham University Medical School, said:

"At a conservative estimate it may be admitted that of all the ailments for which relief is sought, 90% or over are self limited and tend to get well. It may also be admitted that in over 90% of all human ailments, the *psychic* is the dominating factor."

In other words, Mind is the Healer. Drugs can sometimes make its work easier by removing obstructions, by killing off parasites. But the regular use of drugs is far more likely to harm than to heal. We might well quote to the druggists the old Hindoo proverb:

"God gives the mango; The farmer plants the seed.
God cures the patient; The doctor takes the fees."

In the Great War, the one drug that most proved its worth was Iodine. And what is Iodine? A *cleanser*. It killed germs. It cleansed wounds. But it has no healing power. And no healing was expected of it. It did all that was asked. It cauterized—cleansed so that Nature (Mind) could do its own healing, unobstructed.

That would seem to be the most that should be expected of any drug—kill the germs of sickness or disease, cleanse so that Nature can then more easily do its rebuilding. And that is where the use of drugs should stop. Mind works best when it is interfered with least—when we throw ourselves entirely upon it for Support, rather than share the responsibility with some outside agency.

Dr. Burnett Rae, a well-known English specialist, addressing a large audience on the subject of "Spiritual Healing and Medical Science," said the term "spiritual healing" was sometimes used in a manner which seemed to imply that there was a form of healing which was of a non-spiritual character, and that spiritual healing was incompatible with, or opposed to, medical practice. Healing could never be regarded as a purely physical process. He would go so far as to say that healing was always effected through the control of the mind, and medicinal remedies only set the machinery of the mind in motion. We are too apt to think of medical science as concerned with drugs or appliances and operations. *These might completely pass away during the next twenty or fifty years.*

It is not through drugs that the medical profession has done so much of good for the world. It is not through drugs that they have improved the general health, cleaned up plague spots, cut down infant mortality, and lengthened the average life expectancy of mankind by fifteen years.

It is by scotching disease at its very source. It is by getting rid of artificially created *unwholesome* conditions, getting back to *natural wholesome* conditions.

What is it causes typhus? Filth—an entirely unwholesome condition, man-made.

And how do doctors prevent the spread of typhus? By cleaning up—by getting back to natural wholesome conditions.

What is it causes typhoid? Impure water. And its prevention is simply the purifying of the water—getting back to natural wholesome supply.

Yellow fever has been practically stamped out of existence. Typhus is almost a forgotten plague, except in such backward places as parts of Russia and Asia.

Malaria has been conquered. And doctors predict that in another generation tuberculosis will be an almost forgotten malady.

How were these wonderful results brought about? Not through drugs—but by cleaning up! Cleaning out swamps and filth. Purifying water. Building drainage systems. Making everything round about as clean and wholesome as Nature herself.
Cleanliness—Purity—Sunshine!

God gave us in abundance all that is necessary for perfect health—clean air, pure water, clear sunshine. All we need to do is to keep these pure and clean, and to use all we possibly can of them. The greatest good the medical profession has done mankind is in discovering the value of these gifts of God and showing us how to use them.

The Chinese have long had the right idea—they pay their physicians to keep them well, not to cure them of sickness. And the thing that made the reputation of such men as Gorgas, Reed, Flexner, Carrel, was not their *cure* of disease—but their *prevention* of it.

That way lies the future of medicine—bringing our surroundings back to the natural wholesome conditions for which we were created. That way lies health and happiness for all—cleanliness inside and out, clean air, pure water, plenty of sunshine—*and right thinking!*

In the next Chapter, I shall try to show you how you can apply the illimitable power of Mind hopefully towards the successful treatment of disease.

XXIV

The Gift of the Magi

> "Sweep up the debris of decaying faiths;
> Sweep down the cobwebs of worn-out beliefs,
> And throw your soul wide open to the light
> Of Reason and of Knowledge. Be not afraid
> To thrust aside half-truths and grasp the whole."
>
> —ELLA WHEELER WILCOX.

All over the world, sick, weak and devitalized men and women are searching for health and strength. By the hundreds of thousands, they drag their weary and aching bones around, or languish on sick beds, waiting for someone to bring health to them corked up in a bottle.
But real, lasting health was never found in pillboxes or medicine bottles. There is one method—and only one— by which it can be gained and kept. That method is by using the power of the Subconscious Mind.

For a long time the doctors pooh-poohed any such idea. Then as the evidence piled up, they grudgingly admitted that nervous troubles and even functional disorders might be cured by mind.

Even now there are some who, as Bernard Shaw put it, "Had rather bury a whole hillside ethically than see a single patient cured unethically. They will give credit to no method of healing outside the tenets of their own school."
Yet, as Warren Hilton has it in "*Applied Psychology*":

"All the literature of medicine, whether of ancient or modern times, abounds in illustrations of the power of the mind over the body in health and in disease. And medical Science has always based much of its practice on this principle. No reputable school of medicine ever failed to instruct its students in practical applications of the principle of mental influence at the bedside of their patients. A brisk and cheery manner, a hopeful countenance, a supremely assured and confident demeanor—these things have always been regarded by the medical profession as but second in importance to sanitation and material remedies; *while the value of the sugar-coated bread pill when the diagnosis was uncertain, has long been recognized.*

"The properly trained nurse has always been expected to supplement the efforts of the attending physician by summoning the mental forces of the patient to his aid. She, therefore, surrounds the patient with an atmosphere of comfortable assurance. And by constantly advising him of his satisfactory progress toward speedy recovery she seeks to instill hope, confidence and mental effort.

"To quote Dr. Didama: 'The ideal physician irradiates the sick chamber with the light of his cheerful presence. He may not be hilarious—he is not indifferent—but he has an irrepressible good-nature which lifts the patient out of the slough of despond and places his feet on the firm land of health. In desperate cases, even a little harmless levity may be beneficial. A well-timed jest may break up a congestion; a pun may add pungency to the sharpest stimulant.' Dr. Oliver Wendell Holmes reduced this principle to its cash equivalent when he said that a cheerful smile might be worth five thousand dollars a year to a physician.

"Today, psychotherapy, or the healing of bodily disease by mental influence, has the unqualified endorsement of the American Therapeutic Society, the only national organization in America devoted exclusively to therapeutics. It has the enthusiastic support of men of such recognized international leadership in the scientific world and in the medical profession as Freud, Jung, Bleuler, Breuer, Prince, Janet, Babinski, Putnam, Gerrish, Sidis, Dubois, Munsterberg, Jones, Brill, Donley, Waterman and Taylor.

"The present attitude of reputable science toward the principle that the mind controls all bodily operations is, then, one of positive conviction. The world's foremost thinkers accept its truth. The interest of enlightened men and women everywhere is directed toward the mind as a powerful curative force and as a regenerative influence of hitherto undreamed-of resource."

The more progressive physicians everywhere now admit that there is practically no limit to how far mind can go in the cure of disease. As Dr. Walsh of Fordham University puts it: "Analysis of the statistics of diseases cured by mental influence shows that its results have been more strikingly manifest in organic than in the so-called nervous or functional diseases."

Everyone admits that the mind influences the body somewhat; for everyone has seen others grow pale with fear, or red with anger. Everyone has felt the stopping of the heartbeats at some sudden fright, the quickened breathing and the thumping of the heart caused by excitement. These and a hundred other evidences of the influence of mind over matter are common to all of us, and everyone will admit them.

But everyone does not know that our whole bodies seem to be nothing more or less than the outward expression of our thought. We sit in a draught, and education teaches us we should have a cold or fever. So we *have* a cold or fever. We eat something which we have been told is indigestible, and immediately we are assailed with pains. We see another yawn, and our impulse is to follow suit. In the same way, when we hear of sickness round about us, the fear of it visualizes it in our own minds and we, too, have it. The *fear* of these things seems to bring them about, the mental suggestion sent through to our subconscious minds. We have been educated in a medical age to think that most diseases are infectious or contagious. So the mere sight of a diseased person makes most of us withdraw into ourselves like a turtle within his shell. We fear we shall catch it—when one of the great dangers of disease is that very fear of it.

For years it has been accepted as an acknowledged fact that anyone trapped in a mine or other air-tight compartment would presently die of carbon dioxide poisoning—lack of oxygen. Now comes Houdini to prove that death for lack of oxygen is not necessary at all!

"Fear, and not poisoning by carbon dioxide, causes the death of miners and others trapped in air-tight compartments," in the opinion of Houdini, according to an Associated Press dispatch of August 6, 1926.

Houdini had himself sunk in a sealed coffin in a swimming pool, without chance for a breath of outside air to reach him, and stayed there for an hour and a half, although, according to all previous scientific belief, he should have been dead at the end of four minutes. Yet Dr. W. J. McConnell of the United States Department of Mines, who examined Houdini before and after the experiment, reported no marked physical reactions from the test, and Houdini himself said he felt only a slight dizziness when he was released from the coffin!

"Anyone can do it," said Houdini. "The important thing is to *believe that you are safe.*"

The Chinese have a saying that when the plague comes, 5,000 people may die of the plague, but 50,000 will ﹍ of the fear of it.

Did you ever hurt a limb, or a finger, so that you thought you couldn't move it? And then, under the stress of some sudden emotion, forget all about the hurt and presently wake to find yourself using the finger or the limb just as readily and as painlessly as though there had never been anything wrong with it?

I have before me a clipping from the New York *Times* of March 29, 1925, telling of a cripple who had been paralyzed for six years, but under the spur of sudden fear, he ran up a stairway unaided, without crutch or cane. He had been treated in a number of hospitals, but because of an injury to his spine received in an auto accident, had been unable to walk without crutches or canes for six years. The patient in the bed next his own suddenly went crazy and attacked him, and in his fear this paralytic leaped from his bed and ran up a flight of stairs. According to the report, *the sudden fright cured him!*

Take the miracles of Lourdes, or of St. Anne of Beaupre, or of any of the dozens of shrines that dot the world. What is it that affects the cures? Two things—*Desire* and *Faith*. You remember the story of the famous Saint of Italy, who traveled from town to town healing the lame, the halt, and the blind. A pilgrim hastening to a town where the Saint was expected met two lame beggars hurrying away. He asked them the reason for their haste, to be told, to his astonishment, it was because the Saint was coming to town. As they put it—"He will surely heal us, and where will our livelihood be then?"

So it is with many people today—not beggars, mind you—but people in every walk of life. They have become so wedded to their ailments; they "enjoy poor health" so thoroughly, that they are secretly a bit proud of it. Take away their complaints and they would be lost without them.

You must have the *sincere desire first.* That is prayer. Then the faith—not "believe ye are *going* to receive it." "Believe that ye *receive* it"—*now*—this very minute. Know that the REAL you, the image of you held in Universal Mind—in short, the *Truth* concerning every organ in your body—is perfect. *"Know the Truth."* Believe that you HAVE this perfect image. On the day that you can truly believe this—carry this sincere conviction to your subconscious mind—on that day you WILL BE perfect.

This is the faith that is responsible for the miracles of Lourdes, for miraculous healings everywhere. It matters not whether you be Catholic or Protestant, Jew or Gentile. Desire and faith such as these will heal you.

A month or two ago I read in the newspapers of a farmer, blind for two years, who went out in the field and prayed, "that he should receive his sight." At the end of the second day, his sight was completely restored. He went to no shrine—just out under the sky and prayed to God.

Today I have before me a clipping from the New York *Sun* of February 23, 1926, telling of Patrolman Dennis O'Brien of the Jersey City police force, who at the end of a Novena to Our Lady of Help at the Monastery of St. Michael's in Union City, recovered the use of his legs, which had been paralyzed since the time, two years before, when a bullet had entered the base of his spine, severing the cord of motor and sensory nerves.

Then here is one from the New York *Sun* of June 26, 1926, telling how Miss Elsie Meyer of the Bronx, New York, was healed *overnight* of a tumorous growth that had troubled her for months:

"I realized last fall that there was an unusual growth on my body," she said. "It might have resulted from the strain of lifting a trunk. I wanted to know what it was, and I first went to a doctor, who informed me it was a tumorous growth and likely to become serious.

"But I would not be frightened and refused to receive any medical remedies in the way of cure. I have been a believer in faith healing and member of the Unity Society, a branch of the New Thought organization, for a number of years, so I went to a New Thought practioner. While this seemed to help me, the tumorous growth s my faith wasn't strong enough at the time. That was last fall.

congress with the same growth, apparently unaffected by any attempts to cure it. But after ealing meeting at the congress yesterday I left with firm faith that I would get the healing I had ien I retired I noticed the tumor was still on my body, but when I awoke this morning it had disappeai.

The chronicles of every religion are full of just such miracles. And the reason for them is the same in every case —*prayer* and *faith*. Given these, no healing is impossible.

Suppose we go back for a moment to the lowly Amoeba, the first bit of animal life upon the earth. I know not whether you are Fundamentalist or Evolutionist. The facts are a bit harder to prove from the Evolution side of it, so let us argue from that angle.

The Amoeba, as you will recall from Chapter I, is the lowest form of animal life known to scientists, a sort of jelly-fish with but a single cell—without brains, without intelligence, possessing only LIFE. No one would ever contend that this jellyfish could improve itself. No one would argue that it developed the next form of life out of its own mind or ideas.

Yet, according to science, the next form of life did develop from this jelly-like mass. The Amoeba certainly was not responsible for doing it. And it couldn't develop itself. So the conclusion is forced upon us that some outside Intelligence must have done it.

But there were no other living creatures. The Amoeba was alone of all animal life upon the planet. The condition of the water and atmosphere was such that few if any other forms of animals could have sustained life at that time. So the Intelligence, which developed the next form of animal life, must have been the same that created the Amoeba—that first brought LIFE to this Planet. That Intelligence is variously called God, Providence, Nature, the Life Principle, Mind, etc. For our purposes here let us call it Universal Mind.

Having formed life here on earth, Universal Mind proceeded to develop it. Starting with a single cell, It built cell upon cell, changing each form of life to meet the different conditions of atmosphere and environment that the cooling of the earth crust brought about. When the multi-cellular structure became complicated, It gave a brain to it to direct the different functions, just as you put a "governor" on a steam engine. When land appeared and the receding tides left certain animals high and dry for periods of hours, It gave these both lungs and gills—the one for the air, the other for the water.

When the creatures began to prey upon one another, It gave one speed, another a shell, a third an ink-like fluid, that each in its own way might escape and survive.

But always It progressed. Each new stage of life was an improvement over the previous one. And always It showed Its resourcefulness, Its ability to meet ANY need.

Finally, as the culmination of all Its efforts, It made MAN—a creature endowed not only with a brain like that of the lower animals, but with the power of reason—"made in His image and likeness," sharing Infinite Intelligence — himself a Creator and a part of Universal Mind.

All through the creation—from the time of the one-celled Amoeba right up to Man—every scientist will admit that the directing intelligence of Universal Mind was on the job every minute, that It formed the models on which each new and different kind of animal was made, that each of these models was perfect—the one model best fitted to cope with the conditions it had to confront.

Certainly when It came to Man, It is not likely to have been any less successful in forming a perfect model than it was in making the tiger or the elephant. So we can take it, I assume, that all will admit that Man as formed by Universal Mind is perfect—that the idea of Man as it exists in Universal Mind is perfect in every particular.

And Universal Mind, from the very beginning, has never taken a step backward, has never stood still. Always it has PROGRESSED. So it would seem safe to assume that man is not going backward now—that he is a more perfect creature than he was 5,000, 10,000 or 100,000 years ago—that he is constantly drawing nearer and nearer the likeness of his Creator.

The next step seems just as logical. If there was inherent in even the earliest and lowest forms of life the power to develop whatever means was requisite to meet each new emergency, such as a shell or lungs or legs or wings—if this power is still inherent in the lower forms of life such as the Plant Parasites referred to in a previous chapter, does it not seem a certainty that we have the same power within ourselves, if only we knew how to call it forth? After the third century of the Christian era, that power was allowed to lapse through disuse, but of late years thousands have been taking advantage of it for themselves and for others through psychology or religion. And the basis of all these cures is that there is nothing miraculous about the cure of disease at all. That it is "Divinely Natural." That it requires merely understanding. That Mind is the only Creator. And that the only image Universal Mind holds of your body is a perfect image, neither young nor old, but full of health, of vigor, of beauty and vitality. That all you have to do when assailed by disease is to go back to Universal Mind for a new conception of its perfect image—for the Truth concerning your body, just as you would go back to the principle of mathematics for the Truth concerning any problem that worked out incorrectly. When you can make your subconscious mind copy after this Universal image— the *Truth*—instead of the diseased image you are holding in your thoughts, your sickness will vanish like the mere dream it is.

Does that sound too deep? Then look at it this way:

When you think an organ is diseased, it is your conscious mind that thinks this. Inevitably it sends this thought through to your subconscious mind, and the latter proceeds to build the cells of that organ along this imperfect, diseased model. Change the model—in other words, change your belief—and your subconscious mind will go back again to building along right lines.

Your body, you know, is simply an aggregation of millions upon millions of protons and electrons, held together by mind. They are the universal substance all about us, the plastic clay from which the sculptor Mind shapes the forms you see.

To quote the New York *Sun*: "Man's body is made up of trillions of miniature solar systems, each with whirling planets and a central sun. These tiny systems are the atoms of modern Science. The atoms of all elements are made up of protons and electrons in varying quantities and arranged in various ways. "But what are protons and electrons?

"The masters of physics have succeeded in weighing and measuring them. We know that they carry the smallest possible charges of electricity, and we are learning much about the way they behave; but students are beginning to doubt that they have real substance that they are anything one could hit with a Lilliputian hammer. Dr. H. G. Gale of the University of Chicago, addressing the Ohio Academy of Science the other day, said there was good reason to believe; that electrons were composed entirely of electricity and that their mass or weight was only a manifestation of electrical force. According to this view, *nothing exists in the Universe except electricity*—and perhaps ether."

Your subconscious mind partakes of the creative power of Mind and because of that, it is daily, hourly, changing the particles of electrical energy, which constitute your body, to conform to the image you hold before it.

The clay cannot reply to the sculptor. No more can these tiny particles of electricity. Your body has nothing to say as to whether it shall be diseased or crippled. It is MIND that decides this. For what is sickness? An illusion, a mortal dream—merely the *absence* of health. Bring back that health image, and the sickness immediately disappear. Universal Mind never created disease. The only image it knows of man is the Truth—the perfect image. The only idea it has of your body is a perfect, healthy idea.

Then where does disease come from? Who created it? *No one did*. It is a mere illusion—just as, if you think a pin is sticking you, and you concentrate your thought on the pain, it becomes unbearable. Yet when you investigate, you find that no pin was sticking you at all—merely a hair, or bit of cinder lodged against the skin. How often have you had some fancied pain, only to have it promptly disappear when your physician assured you there was nothing wrong with you at all. It would be the same way with all sickness, all pain, if you would understand that it is merely fear or suggestion working on your conscious mind, and that if you will deny this belief of pain or sickness, your subconscious mind will speedily make that denial good. Don't render that mind impotent by thoughts of fear, doubt and anxiety. If you do, it is going to get like a working crew, which is constantly being stopped by strikes or walkouts or changes of plans. It will presently get discouraged and stop trying.

To quote Dr. George E. Pitzer again—"In proper, healthy or normal conditions of life, the objective mind and the subjective mind act in perfect harmony with each other. When this is the case, healthy and happy conditions always prevail. But these two minds are not always permitted to act in perfect harmony with each other; this brings mental disturbances; excites physical wrongs, functional and organic diseases.

"Our unconscious is a tremendous storage plant full of potential energy which can be expended for beneficial or harmful ends. Like every apparatus for storing up power, it can be man's most precious ally, if man is familiar with it and, hence, not afraid of it. Ignorance and fear, on the other hand, can transform a live electric wire into an engine of destruction and death."

Even as long ago as Napoleon's day, men had begun to get an inkling of this. "Think that you are well," said the astute Tallyrand, "instead of thinking that you are sick." And the formula of the Quakers is that an energetic soul is "master of the body which it loves."

So keep in mind the one basic fact that covers the whole ground—that *Mind is all*. There is no other cause. When you drive the belief in disease from your subconscious mind, you will drive away the pain and all the other symptoms with it.

Few sick people have any idea how much they can do for themselves. There is an old saying that every man is "a fool or his own physician at 40." When the science of Mind is more generally understood, that saying will become literally true. Every man will find within himself the Mind, which "healeth all thy diseases." For every function of your body is governed by your mind. When sickness or pain assails you, *deny it!* Cling steadfastly to the one idea that covers all—that Universal Mind made your every organ perfect; that the only image of each organ now in Universal Mind is this perfect image; and that this perfect idea is endowed with resources sufficient to meet any need.

We are all sculptors, you know, but instead of marble or clay, our material is the plastic energy—protons and electrons—of which we and everything in this world about us are made. What are you making of it? What image are you holding in mind? Images of sickness? Of poverty? Of Limitation? Then you are reproducing these in your life.

Banish them! Forget them! Never let them enter your thought, and they will never again manifest themselves in your life.

You admit that mind influences your body to some extent, but you think your physical organs hold the preponderance of power. So you depend upon them, and make yourself their slave.

By holding before yourself the thought that your organs are the masters, you make them your master, and deprive yourself of the directing intelligence of your subconscious mind. When an organ ceases to function properly, you try to doctor it, when the part that needs attention is your mind. If you are running an electric machine, and the current becomes weak or is switched off, you don't take the machine part, or oil it or tamper with it to make it run better. You go to the source of the power to find what is wrong there.

In the same way, when anything seems wrong with the functioning of your body, the place to investigate is your subconscious mind. Your stomach has no intelligence, nor your heart, nor your liver, nor any other of your organs. Your liver, for instance, could never figure out how much sugar should be turned into your blood every minute to keep your bodily temperature at 98 degrees, when you are sitting in a room that is warmed to only 65 degrees. It doesn't know how much more sugar is required to keep that temperature normal when you go out into a driving gale 10 below zero. Yet it supplies the requisite amount—neither too much nor too little. And it does it instantaneously. Where does it get the information? *You* don't know it. No mortal man could figure it out in a year's time.

It gets it from your subconscious mind. It gets both the information and the directions to use it. And every other of your bodily organs gets its information in the same place. Your muscles are not self-acting. Take away mind and those muscles are just like any other bit of matter—lifeless, inert. They have nothing to say as to what they shall do. They merely obey the behests of mind.
Have you ever seen one of those great presses at work in a newspaper plant? They seem almost human in their intelligence. At one end, great rolls of paper feed in. At the other, out comes the finished newspaper, folded, ready for delivery. Everything is automatic; everything as perfect as machinery can be made. The "fingers" that fold the papers seem almost lifelike in their deftness.

But shut off the life-giving electric current—and what happens? The machinery is powerless. Take away the directing human intelligence, and how long before that wonderful machine would be a mass of scrap—mere bits of steel and rubber? How long could it function of itself?
So it is with your body. A wonderful mechanism—the most complicated, yet the most perfect in the world. But switch off the current of your mental dynamo; take away the intelligence that directs the working of your every organ, and what is left? A bit of bone and flesh—inert and useless.

In the final analysis, your body is merely a piece of mechanism—dependent entirely upon mind. It has no power, no volition, of its own. It does as mind tells it to, insofar as mind believes itself to be the Master. Your eyes, for instance, are merely lenses, which transmit light from the outer world to the brain within. They contract or elongate, they open or close, just as mind directs. And mind, in its turn, keeps them constantly nourished with new, life-giving blood, replacing old tissue, old cells, as fast as they wear out, rebuilding ever, so that your eyes may continue to function perfectly as long as your conscious mind is dependent upon them for its impressions of outer objects. It doesn't matter how old you may be or how much you use them. Your eyes are like any other muscles of your body—they improve in strength with use. Give them but enough rest intervals for mind to repair and rebuild the used tissue, keep before your subconscious mind the perfect image of eyes on which you expect it to rebuild, and you need never fear glasses, you need never worry about "your eyes going back on you."

What is it happens when your muscles refuse to work—fail to perform their functions properly? You are what has happened. You have switched off the current from some particular part. You have been holding the belief so long and so firmly that the muscles have the preponderance of power that your subconscious mind has come to believe it, too. And when the nerve or muscle suffers an injury, the subconscious mind—at the suggestion of your conscious mind—gives up all dominion over it.
All disease, all sickness, all imperfections of the human body are due to this one cause—your belief that your body is the master, that it can act, that it can catch cold, or become diseased, without the consent of mind. This is the procuring cause of all suffering. One disease is no different from another in this. They are all due to that one erroneous belief.
If you will deny the power of your body over your mind, you can destroy all fear of disease. And when the fear goes, the foundation of the disease is gone.

The way to begin is to *refuse to believe* or to heed any complaint from your body. Have no fear of climate or atmosphere, of dampness or drafts. It is only when you believe them unhealthy that they are so to you. When your stomach sends a report of distress, when it tells you that something you have eaten is disagreeing with it, treat it as you would an unruly servant. Remind it that it is not the judge of what is or is not good for it. That it has no intelligence. That it is merely a channel through which the food you give it passes for certain treatment and selection. That if the food is not good it has but to pass it through to the eliminatory organs as speedily as may be.

Your stomach is entirely capable of doing this. Every organ you have is capable of withstanding any condition—given the right state of mind to direct it. The only reason that they succumb to sickness or disease or injury is because you tell them to. Men have fallen from great heights without injury. Men have taken the most deadly poison without harm. Men have gone through fire and flood and pestilence with not a scratch to show. And what men have done once they can do again. The fact that it *has* been done shows that your body does not need to suffer injury from these conditions. And if it does not *need* to, then it would seem that the only reason it ordinarily suffers is because your fear of injury is the thought you are holding before your subconscious mind and therefore that is the thought that it images on your body.

In a dispatch from Stockholm to the New York *Herald-Tribune* dated January 18, 1926, I read that Dr. Henry Markus and Dr. Ernest Sahigren, Stockholm scientists, have been able, through hypnotic suggestion, to offset the effect of poisons on the human system to a marked degree.

The scientists put three subjects into hypnotic sleep and then administered drugs, carefully recording the effects on blood pressure and pulse, both with and without "suggestion." When a drug, which acts to increase blood pressure, was administered without "suggestion," the blood pressure readings ranged between 109 to 130 and pulse readings from 54 to 100. But when the drug was administered with the "suggestion" to the mind of the patient that it was merely so much harmless water, the blood pressures were from 107 to 116 and pulse readings all less than 67. From which one would judge that it was the patient's *belief*, which affected him, far more than any power in the drug.

Bear this in mind when anyone tells you that certain foods are not good for you. You can eat what you like, if you do it in moderation. Just remember—no matter what you may eat—if you relish it, if you BELIEVE it to be good for you, *it will be good for you!*

The moment any symptom of illness shows in your body, vigorously deny its existence. Say to yourself: "My body has no intelligence. Neither has any germ of disease. Therefore neither my body nor the disease can tell me I am sick. Mind is the only cause. And Mind has not directed them to make me sick. The only image of my body that Mind knows is a perfect, vigorous, healthy image. And that is the only image I am going to build on." Then forget the image of disease. It is only an illusion, and can be dispelled like any other illusion. Keep in your mind's eye the image of perfect health, of vigorous, boundless vitality.

Your body cannot say it is sick. Therefore when the belief of sickness assails you, it must come either from your conscious mind or from outside suggestion. In either event, it is your job to see that no belief of sickness reaches your subconscious mind, that no fear of it, no thought of it, is imaged there.

To treat one who has already succumbed to the belief of sickness, explain to him, as I have explained to you here, that his body has no power for sickness or for health, any more than a log of wood has. That his body is merely an aggregation of millions of electrons—particles of electrical energy, really—subject wholly to his mind. That these particles of energy have neither substance nor intelligence; that they are constantly changing; and that the forms they take depend entirely upon the images he holds in his own mind.

His body is, in short, a mental concept. It is an exact reflection of the thought he is holding in mind of it. If he has been sick, it is because he has been holding sickly, weak and unhealthy thoughts in his mind. If he wishes to get well, it is first necessary for him to change his thought. Instead of doctoring the machine, he is to go direct to the powerhouse and change the current. Let him repeat to himself, night and morning, this little formula:

house can be built, there must be a plan, a blueprint from which to build. Before you were created, Universal Mind held in thought the model on which you were made. That model was perfect then—is perfect now. The only idea of you that Universal Mind knows is a perfect model, where every cell and organism is formed along perfect lines.

True, many of us have built up imperfect models in our own thoughts, but we can get rid of them just as rapidly as we get rid of the fear of them.

Your body is changing every moment. Every cell, every organism, is constantly being rebuilt. Why rebuild along the old, imperfect lines? Why not build on the lines held in the thought of Universal Mind? You CAN do it!

It matters not what your ailment may be. Suppose, as an example, that your stomach has been troubling you, that you cannot eat what you would like, that you cannot assimilate your food, that you are weak and nervous is consequence. Every morning when you awake, and every night just before you drop off to sleep say to yourself— "My stomach has neither intelligence nor feeling. It functions only as mind directs it. Therefore I need have no worry about its being weak or diseased, for the only image that Mind knows of stomach is Its perfect image. And that perfect image can assimilate or remove anything I may put into it. It is perfect, as everything that Universal Mind makes is perfect. And being perfect, it can do anything right I may ask of it without fear or anxiety."

Concentrate on the one organ at a time, and repeat this formula to yourself night and morning. Say it, feel it, BELIEVE it—and you can do what you please with that organ. "As thy faith is, so be it done unto thee."

The Suffering of Little Children

"I can believe all you say about my fears and worries being responsible for my 'own illnesses," write many people, "but how about infants and little children? They have no fear. Why do they sicken and die?" What many people do not understand is that the subconscious mind is just as amenable to suggestion from those round about you as it is from your own conscious mind. Otherwise you would be in no danger from anything you did not consciously know of. And the more ignorant you were, the safer you would be.

Suppose, for instance, you took a draught of what you believed to be pure "bootleg" whisky, but which in reality was no more than wood alcohol. Many others have done it. Your conscious mind would expect no harm from it —any more than did theirs. You would have no fear of the result. No more did they. So, you would say, you should experience no harm.

Yet you would probably die—or at least go blind—as have these others. Why? Because your subconscious mind would know the wood alcohol for what it is. Your own conscious belief, and the preponderance of opinion of those about you, has instilled the conviction in your subconscious mind that wood alcohol is dire poison. Therefore when you pour this poison into your system—even though you do not consciously recognize it as such —your subconscious mind proceeds to bring about the effects you would logically expect such a poison to produce.

It is the same with contagion, with the hundreds of diseases which most people scarcely know the names of, but to which they are constantly falling victims. They don't know they have been exposed to contagion. They don't know that their systems are in such condition that certain diseases logically follow. But their subconscious minds do know it. And they have so thoroughly educated those minds to believe in the necessity for ill health, in the inevitability of sickness under certain conditions, that the subconscious proceeds to work out the contagion or the condition to its logical conclusion.

Grown people can change these subconscious convictions by the proper counter-suggestions, consciously given. But young children cannot reason. They accept the beliefs that are held by the generality of mankind, or that are strongly suggested to them by those nearest to them.

That is why babies and young children fall such easy victims to the fears of disease and contagion of their parents and those about them. That is why worry over a seeming epidemic so often results in the children catching it, even when they have apparently been in no way exposed to the contagion.

"Man," says a famous writer, "often has fear stamped upon him before his entrance into the outer world; he is reared in fear; all his life is passed in bondage of fear of disease and death and thus his whole mentality becomes cramped, limited, and depressed, and his body follows its shrunken pattern and specification. IS IT NOT SUPRISING THAT HEALTH EXISTS AT ALL? Nothing but the boundless Divine Love, exuberance, and vitality, constantly poured in, even though unconsciously to us, could in some degrees neutralize such an ocean of morbidity."

But the remedy is just as simple. Know that your children are primarily children of God. That the image He holds of them is perfect. His perfect image has within itself every power necessary to ward off disease of any kind.

Put your children actively under His care. Throw the responsibility upon Him. Depend upon it, and when you do this in the right way, no harm can come near them. Whenever fear assails you, whenever your children are exposed to danger or contagion, realize that "He shall give His angels (his thoughts) charge over them, to lead them in all their ways."

If your children are sick or ailing, read these thoughts aloud to them just as though you were talking to a grown person. Only address yourself to their subconscious minds. Read over the past few pages. Repeat to them the little formula outlined above, adapting it to their own particular need. Above all, BELIEVE it! Your faith will work just as great wonders for your children as for yourself.

Never doubt. Never fear. Go at your problem just as you would approach a difficult problem in mathematics. In mathematics, you know that the problem does not exist for which you cannot find the solution, provided you follow the rules and work in the right way.

As long as you do your part, the principle of mathematics will do the rest. It is the same in all of life. Don't worry. Don't fret. Go at your problem in the right way, no matter how difficult it may seem; follow the rules herein laid down, and you can confidently look to the Principle of Being to bring you the answer.

The Treasure

If you have begun to realize the treasure within yourself, and use it even in a small way, the most wonderful thing that can happen to anyone on this planet has happened to you. What does it mean? It means that an ordinary human being, afflicted with all the sufferings and fears and worries and superstitions of the average man, has learned the Law of Being. It means that he has acquired a power above all that of his would-be destroyers. It means that he has put his foot upon the Rock of Life that the Doorway of Heaven is open before him, that all of Good is as free to him as the air he breathes.

The world today is so much more wonderful than it was to former generations. Mankind has begun to glimpse its illimitable powers. The whole world is plastic and sensitive to new ideas. The soul of man is finding itself, and learning its relation to the Infinite. The veil between the visible and the invisible is being drawn aside. We are becoming more assured of our own power and are beginning to assert that power, recognizing the laws of Mind as divinely natural laws—as part of God's continuous plan.

The Secret of Power

Robert Collier

CONTENTS

INTRODUCTION

WHAT IS THE strongest political trend in the world today?

After the last war, it was towards democracy. But somehow democracy failed the average man. When the depression came and he found himself unable to provide food and shelter for his loved ones, he demanded something more than equality of opportunity. He demanded SECURITY from want.

To answer that demand came "Strong Men," so-called Mussolinis and Hitlers and Antonescus and Francos and the like, and Fascism was born. Men achieved security, of a kind, but they bartered their freedom for it. And soon they learned that power feeds on power, and the only end of dictatorship is war, which destroys all.

And the reason? The same reason that has impelled man since time began—the longing for security, security for the home, security against want, security for old age.

Since time began, the search for security has been one of the strongest urges in all of nature. You see it in the animal in the way it conceals its nest and tries to make it safe from predatory creatures—man or animal. You see it in the records of early man in the caves he dug into the sides of the mountains, in the tree huts, in the cliff dwellings. You follow it down through the ages to the walled cities, the turreted castles, the inaccessible mountains in which men made their homes.

Throughout history, you see this search for security as one of the dominant characteristics of all human kind. And now that the common man has realized his power, you find him all over the world banding together to take over all property, to the end that he and his may find that security from want that he has so long worked for.

What he does not seem to realize is that the mere redistribution of property never has and never will solve his problem. It will provide him with temporary supply, yes—but supply is a continuing problem, and when his small share of the general distribution is gone, he will be worse off than he was before, because production will have either ceased or been greatly curtailed.

INTRODUCTION

Redistribution is not the answer. It has been tried repeatedly, and always failed. You must go farther back than that. You must start with the source of things. And that is what we shall try to do in the following pages.

"Know this, ye restless denizens of earth,
Know this, ye seekers after joy and mirth,
Three things there are, eternal in their worth—
LOVE, that outreaches to the humblest things;
WORK, that is glad in what it does and brings;
And FAITH, that soars upon unwearied wings.
Divine the powers that on this trio wait,
Supreme their conquest, over time and fate.
LOVE, WORK and FAITH, these three alone are great.

CHAPTER 1

THE CREATIVE FORCE

By the word of the Lord were the heavens made... (Psalm 33)

What is a word? A mental concept or image, is it not? In originating language, words were coined to represent certain images or objects. The word horse, for instance, calls to mind the image left upon the retina and the brain by what one has seen of that quadruped.

But what if there were no horses? What if one were called upon to create a horse, with no previous knowledge of such an animal? You'd have to build up a clear mental image of it first, would you not? You'd have to work out a mental picture of every part of its anatomy, every physical outline. You'd need a perfect mental concept of everything that is comprised in the word horse.

And that was what happened when God created the world. In the beginning was the "Word," the mental concept, the image in God's mind of what He planned. "And the Word was made flesh." It took on shape and substance. It grew into a habitable world. It developed creatures like the fish in the sea, the birds in the air, the beasts of the field. And finally man.

Life then, as now, was a continually developing process. Those early forms of life were threatened by every kind of danger—from floods, from earthquakes, from droughts, from desert heat, from glacial cold, from volcanic eruptions—but each new danger was merely an incentive to finding some new resource, to putting forth their Creative Force in some new shape.

To meet one set of needs, the Creative Force formed the Dinosaur; to meet another, the Butterfly. Long before it worked up to man, we see its unlimited resourcefulness in a thousand ways. To escape danger in the water, some forms of Life sought land. Pursued on land, they took to the air. To breathe in the sea, the Creative Force developed gills. Stranded on land, it perfected lungs. To meet one kind of danger, it grew a shell. For another, it developed fleetness of foot, or wings that carried it into the air. To protect itself from glacial cold, it grew fur; in

8

temperate climes, hair. Subject to alternate heat and cold, it produced feathers. But ever, from the beginning, it showed its power to meet every changing condition, *to answer every creature's need.*

Had it been possible to stamp out this Creative Force, or halt its constant upward development, it would have perished ages ago, when fire and flood, drought and famine followed each other in quick succession. But obstacles, misfortunes, cataclysms, were to it merely new opportunities to assert its power. In fact, it required difficulties or obstacles to stir it up, to make it show its energy and resourcefulness.

The great reptiles, the monster beasts of antiquity, passed on as the conditions changed that had made them possible, but the Creative Force stayed, changing as each age changed, always developing, always improving.

When God put this Creative Force into His creatures, He gave to it unlimited energy, unlimited resource. No other power can equal it. No force can defeat it. No obstacle can hold it back. All through the history of life and mankind, you can see its directing intelligence rising to meet every need of life.

No one can follow it down through the ages without realizing that the purpose of existence is GROWTH, DEVELOPMENT. Life is dynamic, not static. It is ever moving forward—not standing still. The one unpardonable sin in all of nature is to stand still, to stagnate. The Gigantosaurus, that was over a hundred feet long and as big as a house; the Tyrannosaurus, that had the strength of a locomotive and was the last word in frightfulness; the Pterodactyl or Flying Dragon—all the giant monsters of pre-historic ages—are gone. They ceased to serve a useful purpose. They stood still while the life around them passed them by.

Egypt and Persia, Greece and Rome, all the great empires of antiquity, perished when they ceased to grow. China built a wall around herself and stood still for a thousand years. In all of Nature, to cease to grow is to perish.

It is for men and women who are not ready to stand still, who refuse to cease to grow, that this hook is written. Its purpose is to give you a clearer understanding of your own potentialities, to show you how to work with and take advantage of the infinite energy and power of the Creative Force working through you.

The terror of the man at the crossways, not knowing which way to turn, should be no terror for you, for your future is of your own making. The only law of infinite energy is the law of supply. The Creative Principle is your principle. To survive, to win through, to triumphantly surmount all obstacles has been its everyday practice since the beginning of time. It is no less resourceful now than it ever was. You have but to supply the urge to work in harmony with it, to get from it anything you need. For if this Creative Force is so strong in the lowest forms of animal life that it can develop a shell or a poison to meet a need; if it can teach the bird to circle and dart, to balance and fly; if it can grow a new limb on a spider or crab to replace a lost one; how much more can it do for YOU —a reasoning, rational being, with a mind able to work with this Creative Force, with energy and purpose and initiative to urge it on!

The evidence of this is all about you. Take up some violent form of exercise, and in the beginning your muscles are weak, easily tired. But keep on a few days, and what happens? The Creative Force in you promptly strengthens them, toughens them, to meet their need.

All through your daily life, you find this Force steadily at work. Embrace it, work with it, take it to your heart, and there is nothing you cannot do. The mere fact that you have obstacles to overcome is in your favor, for when there is nothing to be done, when things run along too smoothly, the Creative Force seems to sleep. It is when you need it, when you call upon it urgently, that it is most on the job.

It differs from Luck in this, that fortune is a fickle jade who smiles most on those who need her least. Stake your last penny on the turn of a card—have nothing between you and ruin but the spin of a wheel or the speed of a horse—and the chances are a hundred to one that luck will desert you.

It is just the opposite with the Creative Force in you. As long as things run smoothly, as long as life flows along like a song, this Creative Force seems to slumber, secure in the knowledge that your affairs can take care of themselves. But let things start going wrong, let ruin or death stare you in the face—then is the time this Creative Force will assert itself if you but give it the chance.

There is a Napoleonic feeling of power that insures success in the knowledge that this invincible Creative Force is behind your every act. Knowing that you have with you a force which never yet has failed in anything it has undertaken, you can go ahead in the confident knowledge that it will not fail in your case. The ingenuity which overcame every obstacle in making you what you are, is not likely to fall short when you have immediate need for it. It is the reserve strength of the athlete, the second wind of the runner, the power that, in moments of great stress or excitement, you unconsciously call upon to do the deeds which you ever after look upon as superhuman.

But they are in no wise superhuman. They are merely beyond the capacity of your conscious self. Ally your conscious self with that sleeping giant within you, rouse him daily to the task and those superhuman deeds will become your ordinary, everyday accomplishments.

It matters not whether you are banker or lawyer, businessman or clerk, whether you are the custodian of millions or have to struggle for your daily bread. The Creative Force makes no distinction between high and low, rich and poor. The greater your need, the more readily will it respond to your call. Wherever there is an unusual task, wherever there is poverty or hardship or sickness or despair, there this Servant of your mind waits, ready and willing to help, asking only that you call upon him. And not only is it ready and willing, but it is always ABLE to help. Its ingenuity and resource are without limit. It is mind. It is thought. It is the telepathy that carries messages without the spoken or written word. It is the sixth sense that warns you of unseen dangers. No matter how stupendous and complicated, or how simple your problem may be, the solution of it is somewhere in mind, in thought. And since the solution does exist, this mental giant can find it for you. It can know, and It can do, every right thing. Whatever it is necessary for you to know, whatever it is necessary for you to do, you can know and you can do if you will but seek the help of this Genie-of-your-mind and work with It in the right way.

To every living creature, God gave enough of this Creative Force to enable it to develop whatever it felt that it needed for survival. Behind and working through every living thing was this Creative Force, and to each was given the power to draw upon it at need. With the lower forms of life, that call had to be restricted to themselves, to their own bodies. They could not change their environment.

They could develop a house of shell in which to live, like the crustaceans or the snail or the turtle. They could use the Creative Force to develop strength or fleetness or teeth and claws—anything within or pertaining to themselves. But aside from building nests or caves or other more or less secure homes, they could not alter conditions around them. To man alone was given the power to make his own environment. To him alone was given dominion over things and conditions.

That he exercises this power, even today, only to a limited extent, does not alter the fact that he has it. Man was given dominion. "And God said—Let us make man in our image, after our likeness, and let them have dominion over the fish of the sea, and over the fowl of the air, and over the cattle, and over all the earth, and over every creeping thing that creepeth upon the earth."

Of course, few believe in that dominion. Fewer still exercise it for their own good or the good of all. But everyone uses the Creative Force in them to an extent. Everyone builds their own environment.

"Don't tell me," some will say indignantly, "that I built these slums around me, that I am responsible for the wretched conditions under which I work, that I had anything to do with the squalor and poverty in which my family have to live." Yet that is exactly what we do tell you. If you were born in poverty and misery, it was because your parents imaged these as something forced upon them, something they could not help, a condition that was necessary and to be expected. Thinking so, they used the Creative Force working through them to fasten those conditions upon themselves as something they were meant to suffer and could do nothing about.

Then you in your turn accepted those conditions as what you were born to, and fastened them upon yourself by your supine acceptance of them, by failing to claim better ones, by making no great or sustained efforts to get out of them.

All history shows that the determined soul who refuses to accept poverty or lack can change these to riches and power if they have the determination and the perseverance. The great men of the world have almost all come up from poverty and obscurity. The rich men of the world have mostly started with nothing.

"Always the real leaders of men, the real kings, have come up from the common people," wrote Dr. Frank Crane. "The finest flowers in the human flora grow in the woods pasture and not in the hothouse; no privileged class, no royal house, no carefully selected stock produced a Leonardo or a Michelangelo in art, a Shakespeare or Burns in letters, a Mozart or Paderewski in music, a Socrates or Kant in philosophy, an Edison or Pasteur in science, a Wesley or a Knox in religion."

It is the NEED that calls forth such geniuses, the urgent need for development or expression, and it is because these men drew powerfully upon the Creative Force within them that they became great.

"Look within," said Marcus Aurelius. "Within is the fountain of all good. Such a fountain, where springing waters can never fail, do thou dig still deeper and deeper."

THE CREATIVE FORCE

God gave to man, and to man alone, the power to make his own environment. He can determine for himself what he needs for survival, and if he holds to that thought with determination, he can draw whatever is necessary from the Creative Force working through him to make it manifest. First the Word, the mental image, then the creation or manifestation.

Professor Michael Pupin says—"Science finds that everything is a continually developing process." In other words, creation is still going on, all around you. Use your Creative Force to create the conditions you desire rather than those you fear. The life about you is constantly in a state of flux. All you have to do is create the mental mold in which you want the Creative Force to take form, and then hold to that mold with persistence and determination until the Creative Force in it becomes manifest.

Dr. Titus Bull, the famous neurologist, says—"Matter is spirit at a lower rate of vibration. When a patient is cured, it is spirit in the cell doing the healing according to its own inherent pattern. No doctor ever cured a patient. All a doctor can do is to make it possible for the patient to heal themselves."

And if that is true of the body, it is just as true of conditions around you. Matter—physical materials—is spirit or Creative Force at a lower rate of vibration. The spirit or Creative Force is all around you. You are constantly forming it into mental molds, but more often than not these are dictated by your fears rather than your desires. Why not determinedly form only good molds? Why not insist upon the things you want? It is just as easy, and it works just as surely. Writes Emerson:

"There is no great and no small,
To the soul that maketh all;
And where it cometh, all things are;
And it cometh everywhere.

I am the owner of the sphere,
Of the seven stars and the solar year,
Of Caesar's hand, and Plato's brain,
Of Lord's heart, and Shakespeare's strain."

"Give me a base of support," said Archimedes, "and with a lever I will move the world."

And the base of support is that all started with mind. In the beginning was nothing—a fire mist. Before anything could come of it there had to be an idea, a mental model on which to build. *The God Mind* supplied that idea, that model. Therefore the primal cause is mind. Everything must start with an idea. Every event, every condition, every thing is first an idea in the mind of someone.

Before you start to build a house, you draw up a plan of it. You make an exact blueprint of that plan, and your house takes shape in accordance with your blueprint. Every material object takes form in the same way. Mind draws the plan. Thought forms the blueprint, well drawn or badly done as your thoughts are clear or vague. It all goes back to the one cause. The creative principle of the universe is mind, and thought forms the molds in which its eternal energy takes shape.

But just as the effect you get from electricity depends upon the mechanism to which the power is attached, so the effects you get from mind depend upon the way you use it. We are all of us dynamos. The power is there— unlimited power. But we've got to connect it with something—set it some task—give it work to do—else are we no better off than the animals.

The "Seven Wonders of the World" were built by men with few of the opportunities or facilities that are available to you. They conceived these gigantic projects first in their own minds, pictured them so vividly that the Creative Force working through them came to their aid and helped them to overcome obstacles that most of us would regard as insurmountable. Imagine building the Pyramid of Gizeh, enormous stone upon enormous stone, with nothing but bare hands. Imagine the labor, the sweat, the heartbreaking toll of erecting the Colossus of Rhodes, between whose legs a ship could pass! Yet men built these wonders, in a day when tools were of the crudest and machinery was undreamed of, by using the unlimited power of the Creative Force.

That Creative Force is in *you*, working through you, but it must have a model on which to work. It must have thoughts to supply the molds. There are in Universal Mind ideas for millions of wonders greater far than the "Seven Wonders of the World." And those ideas are just as available to you as they were to the artisans of old, as they were to Michelangelo when he built St. Peter's in Rome, as they were to the architect who conceived the Empire State Building, or the engineer who planned the Hell Gate Bridge.

Every condition, every experience of life is the result of our mental attitude. We can only do what we think we can do. We can be only what we think we can be.

14

THE CREATIVE FORCE

We can have only what we think we can have. What we do, what we are, what we have, all depend upon what we think. There is only one limit upon the Creative Force, and that is the limit we impose upon it.

We can never express anything that we do not first believe in. The secret of all power all success, all riches, is in first thinking powerful thoughts, successful thoughts, thoughts of wealth, of supply. We must build them in our own mind first. As Edgar A. Guest so well expressed it:

"You can do as much as you think you can, But you'll never accomplish more; If you're afraid of yourself, young man, There's little for you in store.

For failure comes from the inside first, It's there if we only knew it, And you can win, though you face the worst, If you feel that you're going to do it."

William James, the famous psychologist, said that the greatest discovery in a hundred years was the discovery of the power of the subconscious mind. It is the greatest discovery of all time. It is the discovery that man has within himself the power to control his surroundings, that he is not at the mercy of chance or luck, that he is the arbiter of his own fortunes, that he can carve out his own destiny. He is the master of the Creative Force working through him. As James Allen puts it:

"Dream lofty dreams, and as you dream, so shall you become. Your vision is the promise of what you shall one day be; your Ideal is the prophecy of what you shall at last unveil."

For matter is in the ultimate but a product of thought, the result of the mold into which you have put the Creative Force working through you. Even the most material scientists admit that matter is not what it appears to be. According to physics, matter (be it the human body or a log of wood—it makes no difference which) is made up of an aggregation of distinct minute particles called atoms. Considered individually, these atoms are so small that they can be seen only with the aid of a powerful microscope, if at all.

Until comparatively recent years, these atoms were supposed to be the ultimate theory regarding matter. We ourselves—and all the material world around us— were supposed to consist of these infinitesimal particles of matter, so small that they could not be seen or weighed or smelled or touched individually—but still particles of matter *and indestructible.*

Now, however, these atoms have been further analyzed, and physicists tell us that they are not indestructible at all—that they are mere positive and negative buttons of force or energy called protons and electrons, without hardness, without density, without solidity, without even positive actuality. In short, they are vortices in the ether—whirling bits of energy—dynamic, never static, pulsating with life, but the life is *spiritual!* As one eminent British scientist put it—"Science now explains matter by *explaining it away!*"

And that, mind you, is what the solid table in front of you is made of, is what your house, your body, the whole world is made of—*whirling bits of energy!*

To quote the *New York Herald-Tribune*: "We used to believe that the universe was composed of an unknown number of different kinds of matter, one kind for each chemical element. The discovery of a new element had all the interest of the unexpected. It might turn out to be anything, to have any imaginable set of properties.

"That romantic prospect no longer exists. We know now that instead of many ultimate kinds of matter there are only two kinds. Both of these are really kinds of electricity. One is negative electricity, being, in fact, the tiny particle called the electron, familiar to radio fans as one of the particles vast swarms of which operate radio vacuum tubes. The other kind of electricity is positive electricity. Its ultimate particles are called protons. From these protons and electrons all of the chemical elements are built up. Iron and lead and oxygen and gold and all the others differ from one another merely in the number and arrangement of the electrons and protons which they contain. That is the modern idea of the nature of matter. *Matter is really nothing but electricity.*

Can you wonder then that scientists believe the time will come when mankind *through mind* can control all this energy, can be absolute master of the winds and the waves? For Modern Science is coming more and more to the belief that what we call *matter is a force subject wholly to the control of mind.*

So it would seem that, to a great degree at least, and perhaps altogether, this world round about us is one of our mind's own creating. And we can put into it, and get from it, pretty much what we wish. "Nothing is..." said Shakespeare, "but thinking makes it so." And the psychologist of today says the same in a different way when he tells us that only those things are real to each individual that he takes into his consciousness. To one with no sense of smell, for instance, there is no such thing as fragrance. To one without a radio, there is no music on the airwaves.

THE CREATIVE FORCE

To quote from "*Applied Psychology*," by Warren Hilton:

"The same stimulus acting on different organs of sense will produce different sensations. A blow upon the eye will cause you to see stars; a similar blow upon the ear will cause you to hear an explosive sound. In other words, the vibratory effect of a touch on eye or ear is the same as that of light or sound vibrations.

"The notion you may form of any object in the outer world depends solely upon what part of your brain happens to be connected with that particular nerve-end that received an impression from the object.

"You see the sun without being able to hear it because the only nerve-ends tuned to vibrate in harmony with the ether-waves set in action by the sun are nerve-ends that are connected with the brain center devoted to sight. 'If,' says Professor James, 'we could splice the outer extremities of our optic nerves to our ears, and those of our auditory nerves to our eyes, we should hear the lightning and see the thunder, see the symphony and hear the conductor's movements.'

"In other words, the kind of impressions we receive from the world about us, the sort of mental pictures we form concerning it—in fact, the character of the outer world, the nature of the environment in which our lives are cast—all these things depend for each one of us simply upon how he happens to be put together, upon his individual mental make-up."

In short, it all comes back to the old fable of the three blind men and the elephant. To the one who caught hold of his leg, the elephant was like a tree. To the one who felt of his side, the elephant was like a wall. To the one who seized his tail, the elephant was like a rope. The world is to each one of us the world of his *individual perceptions.*

You are like a radio receiving station. Every moment thousands of impressions are reaching you. You can tune in on whatever ones you like—on joy or sorrow, on success or failure, on optimism or fear. You can select the particular impressions that will best serve you, you can hear only what you want to hear, you can shut out all disagreeable thoughts and sounds and experiences, or you can tune in on discouragement and failure and despair if these are what you want.

Yours is the choice. You have within you a force against which the whole world is powerless. By using it, you can make what you will of life and of your surroundings.

"But," you will say, "objects themselves do not change. It is merely the difference in the way you look at them." Perhaps. But to a great extent, at least, we find what we look for, just as, when we turn the dial on the radio, we tune in on whatever kind of entertainment or instruction we may wish to hear. Who can say that it is not our thoughts that put it there? And why shouldn't it be? All will agree that evil is merely the lack of good, just as darkness is the lack of light. There is infinite good all about us. There is fluid cosmic energy from which to form infinitely more. Why should we not use our thoughts to find the good, or to mold it from the Creative Force all about us? Many scientists believe that we can, and that in proportion as we try to put into our surroundings the good things we desire, rather than the evil ones we fear, *we will find those good things*. Certain it is that we can do this with our own bodies. Just as certain that many people are doing it with the good things of life. They have risen above the conception of life in which matter is the master.

Just as the most powerful forces in nature are the invisible ones—heat, light, air, electricity—so the most powerful forces of man are his invisible forces, his thought forces. And just as electricity can fuse stone and iron, so can your thought forces control your body, so can they win you honor and fortune, so can they make or mar your destiny.

From childhood on we are assured on every hand—by scientists, by philosophers, by our religious teachers—that "ours is the earth and the fullness thereof." Beginning with the first chapter of Genesis, we are told that "God said, Let us make man in Our image, after Our likeness; and let them have dominion over the fish of the sea, and over the fowl of the air, and over the cattle, and over all the earth—and over every living thing that moveth upon the earth." All through the Bible, we are repeatedly adjured to use these God-given powers: "The kingdom of God is within you." We hear all this, perhaps we even think we believe, but always, when the time comes to use these God-given talents, there is the "doubt in our heart."

Baudouin expressed it clearly: "To be ambitious for wealth and yet always expecting to be poor; to be always doubting your ability to get what you long for, is like trying to reach east by traveling west. There is no philosophy which will help a man to succeed when he is always doubting his ability to do so, and thus attracting failure. You will go in the direction in which you face...

"There is a saying that every time the sheep bleats, it loses a mouthful of hay. Every time you allow yourself to complain of your lot, to say, 'I am poor; I can never do what others do; I shall never be rich; I have not the ability that others have; I am a failure; luck is against me'; you are laying up so much trouble for yourself.

"No matter how hard you may work for success, If your thought is saturated with the fear of failure, it will kill your efforts, neutralize your endeavors and make success impossible."

What was it made Napoleon the greatest conqueror of his day? Primarily his magnificent faith in Napoleon. He had a sublime belief in his destiny, an absolute confidence that the obstacle was not made which Napoleon could not find a way through, or over, or around. It was only when he lost that confidence, when he hesitated and vacillated for weeks between retreat and advance, that winter caught him in Moscow and ended his dreams of world empire. Fate gave him every chance first. The winter snows were a full month late in coming. But Napoleon hesitated—and was lost. It was not the snows that defeated him. It was not the Russians. It was his loss of faith in himself.

The Kingdom of Heaven

"The Kingdom of Heaven is within you." Heaven is not some faraway state—the reward of years of tribulation here. Heaven is right here—here and now! In the original Greek text, the word used for "Heaven" is "Ouranos." Translated literally, Ouranos means EXPANSION, in other words, a state of being where you can expand, grow, multiply, and increase.

What is the property of a seed? *It spreads*— a single seed will grow into a tree, a single tree will produce enough seeds to plant a great field. And what is the property of leaven or yeast? *It expands*—in a single night it can expand a hundred times in size. So too is the Heaven within us—the power to multiply our happiness, to increase our good, to expand everything we need in life, is within each one of us.

That most of us fail to realize this Heaven—that many are sickly and suffering, that more are ground down by poverty and worry—is no fault of God's. He gave us the power to overcome these evils; the Kingdom of Expansion is within us, the power to increase anything we have. If we fail to find the way to use it, the fault is ours. If we expand the evil instead of the good, that is our misfortune. To enjoy the Heaven that is within us, to begin here and now to live the life eternal, takes only the right understanding and use of the Creative Force working through us.

THE CREATIVE FORCE

Even now with the limited knowledge at our command, many people control circumstances to the point of making the world without an expression of their own world within where the real thoughts, the real power, resides. Through this world within, they find the solution of every problem, the cause for every effect. Discover it—and all power, all possession is within your control.

For the world without is but a reflection of that world within. Your thought *creates* the condition your mind images. Keep before your mind's eye the image of all you want to be and you will see it reflected in the world without. Think abundance, feel abundance, BELIEVE abundance, and you will find that as you think and feel and believe, abundance will manifest itself in your daily life. But let fear and worry be your mental companions, thoughts of poverty and limitation dwell in your mind, and worry and fear, limitation and poverty will be your constant companions day and night.

Your mental concept is all that matters. Its relation to matter is that of idea and form. There has got to be an idea before it can take form.

The Creative Force working through you supplies you with limitless energy which will take whatever form your mind demands. Your thoughts are the mold which crystallizes this energy into good or ill according to the form you impress upon it. You are free to choose which. But whichever you choose, the result is sure. Thoughts of wealth, of power, of success, can bring only results commensurate with your idea of them. Thoughts of poverty and lack can bring only limitation and trouble.

"A radical doctrine," you'll say, and think me wildly optimistic. Because the world has been taught for so long to think that some must be rich and some poor, that trials and tribulations are our lot. That this is at best a vale of tears.

The history of the race shows that what is considered to be the learning of one age is ignorance to the next age.

Dr. Edwin E. Slosson, editor of *Science Service,* speaking of the popular tendency to fight against new ideas merely because they are new, said: "All through the history of science, we find that new ideas have to force their way into the common mind in disguise, as though they were burglars instead of benefactors of the race."

And Emerson wrote: "The virtue in most request is conformity. Self-reliance is its aversion. It loves not realities and creators, but names and customs."

THE CREATIVE FORCE

In the ages to come, man will look back upon the poverty and wretchedness of so many millions today, and think how foolish we were not to take advantage of the abundant Creative Force all about us. Look at Nature; how profuse she is in everything. Do you suppose the Mind that imaged that profuseness ever intended you to be limited, to have to scrimp and save in order to eke out a bare existence?

There are hundreds of millions of stars in the heavens. Do you suppose the Creative Force which could bring into being worlds without number in such prodigality intended to stint you of the few things necessary to your happiness or well-being?

Nature is prodigal in all that she does. Many insects increase at such a marvelous rate that if it were not for their almost equal death rate, the world would be unable to support them. Rabbits increase so rapidly that a single pair could have 13,000,000 descendants in three years! Fish lay millions of eggs each year. Throughout Nature, everything is lavish. Why should the Creative Force working through you be less generous when it comes to your own supply?

Take as an example the science of numbers. Suppose all numbers were of metal— that it was against the law to write figures for ourselves. Every time you wanted to do a sum in arithmetic you'd have to provide yourself with a supply of numbers, arrange them in their proper order, work out your problems with them. If your problems were too abstruse you might run out of numbers, have to borrow some from your neighbor or from the bank.

"How ridiculous," you say. "Figures are not things; they are mere ideas, and we can add them or divide them or multiply them as often as we like. Anybody can have all the figures he wants."

To be sure they can. And when you learn to use the Creative Force, you will find that you can multiply your material ideas in the same way. You will EXPAND the good things in your life.

Thought externalizes itself, through the Creative Force working through us. What we are depends entirely upon the images we hold before our mind's eye. Every time we think, we start a chain of causes which will create conditions similar to the thoughts which originated it. Every thought we hold in our consciousness for any length of time becomes impressed upon our subconscious mind and creates a pattern which the Creative Force weaves into our life or environment.

THE CREATIVE FORCE

All power is from within and is therefore under our own control. When you can direct your thought processes, you can consciously apply them to any condition, for all that comes to us in the world without is what we've already imaged in the world within. The source of all good, of everything you wish for, is Mind, and you can reach it best through your subconscious. Mind will be to you whatever you believe it to be.

When a man realizes that his mind is part of the God Mind, when he knows that he has only to take any right aspiration to this Universal Mind to see it realized, he loses all sense of worry and fear. He learns to dominate instead of to cringe. He rises to meet every situation, secure in the knowledge that everything necessary to the solution of any problem is in Mind, and that he has but to take his problem to Universal Mind to have it correctly answered.

For if you take a drop of water from the ocean, you know that it has the same properties as all the rest of the water in the ocean, the same percentage of sodium chloride. The only difference between it and the ocean is in volume. If you take a spark of electricity, you know that it has the same properties as the thunderbolt, the same power that moves trains or runs giant machines in factories. Again the only difference is in volume. It is the same with your mind and the God Mind. The only difference between them is in volume. Your mind has the same properties as the God Mind, the same creative genius, the same power over all the earth, the same access to all knowledge. Know this, believe it, use it, and "yours is the earth and the fullness thereof." In the exact proportion that you believe yourself to be part of the God Mind, sharing in Its all-power, in that proportion can you demonstrate the mastery over your own body and over the world about you.

All growth, all supply is from the Creative Force working through you. If you would have power, if you would have wealth, you must first form the mold in this world within, in your subconscious mind, through belief and understanding.

If you would remove discord, you must remove the wrong images—images of ill health, of worry and trouble from within. The trouble with most of us is that we live entirely in the world without. We have no knowledge of that inner world which is responsible for all the conditions we meet and all the experiences we have. We have no conception of "the Father that is within us."

The inner world promises us life and health, prosperity and happiness—dominion over all the earth, it promises peace and perfection for all its offspring. It gives you the right way and the adequate way to accomplish any normal purpose. Business, labor, professions, exist primarily in thought. And the outcome of your labors in them is regulated by thought. Consider the difference, then, in this outcome if you have at your command only the limited capacity of your conscious mind, compared with the boundless energy of the subconscious and of the Creative Force working through it. "Thought, not money, is the real business capital," says Harvey S. Firestone, "and if you know absolutely that what you are doing is right, then you are bound to accomplish it in due season."

Thought is a dynamic energy with the power to bring its object out from the Creative Force all about us. Matter is unintelligent. Thought can shape and control. Every form in which matter is today is but the expression of some thought, some desire, some idea.

You have a mind. You can originate thought. And thoughts are creative. Therefore you can create for yourself that which you desire. Once you realize this, you are taking a long step toward success in whatever undertaking you have in mind. You are the potter. You are continually forming images—good or bad. Why not consciously form only good images?

More than half the prophecies in the scriptures refer to the time when man shall possess the earth, when tears and sorrow shall be unknown, and peace and plenty shall be everywhere. That time will come. It is nearer than most people think possible. You are helping it along. Every man or woman who is honestly trying to use the power of mind in the right way is doing their part in the great cause. For it is only through Mind that peace and plenty can be gained. The earth is laden with treasures as yet undiscovered. But they are every one of them known to the God Mind, for it was this Mind that first imaged them there. And, as part of Universal Mind, they can be known to you.

"To the Manner Born"

Few of us have any idea of our mental powers. The old idea was that man must take this world as he found it. He'd been born into a certain position in life, and to try to rise above his fellows was not only the height of bad taste, but sacrilegious as well. An All-wise Providence had decreed by birth the position a child should occupy in the web of organized society. For him to be discontented with his lot, for him to attempt to raise himself to a higher level, was tantamount to tempting Providence. The gates of Hell yawned wide for such scatterbrains, who were lucky if in this life they incurred nothing worse than the ribald scorn of their associates.

That is the system that produced aristocracy and feudalism. That is the system that feudalism and aristocracy strove to perpetuate. But the basis of all democracies is that man is not bound by any system, that he need not accept the world as he finds it. He can remake the world to his own ideas. It is merely the raw material. He can make what he will of it.

It is this idea that is responsible for all our inventions, all our progress. Man is satisfied with nothing. He is constantly remaking his world. And now more than ever will this be true, for psychology teaches us that each one has within themselves the power to use the Creative Force to become what they will.

LEARN TO CONTROL YOUR THOUGHT. Learn to image upon your mind only the things you want to see reflected there.

You will never improve yourself by dwelling upon the drawbacks of your neighbors. You will never attain perfect health and strength by thinking of weakness or disease. No man ever made a perfect score by watching his rival's target. You have to think strength, think health, think riches. To paraphrase Pascal—"Our achievements today are but the sum of our thoughts of yesterday."

For yesterday is the mold in which the Creative Force flowing through us took shape. And cosmic energy concentrated for any definite purpose becomes power. To those who perceive the nature and transcendency of this Force, all physical power sinks into insignificance.

What is imagination but a form of thought? Yet it is the instrument by which all the inventors and discoverers have opened the way to new worlds. Those who grasp this force, be their state ever so humble, their natural gifts ever so insignificant, become our leading men and women. They are our governors and supreme lawgivers, the guides of the drifting host that follows them as by an irrevocable decree. To quote Glenn Clark in the *Atlantic Monthly*, "Whatever we have of civilization is their work, theirs alone. If progress was made, they made it. If spiritual facts were discerned, they discerned them. If justice and order were put in place of insolence and chaos, they wrought the change. Never is progress achieved by the masses. Creation ever remains the task of the individual."

Our railroads, our telephones, our automobiles, our libraries, our newspapers, our thousands of other conveniences, comforts and necessities are due to the creative genius of but two percent of our population. And the same two percent own a great percentage of the wealth of the country.

The question arises, Who are they? What are they? The sons of the rich? College men? No—few of them had any early advantages. Many of them have never seen

24

the inside of a college. It was grim necessity that drove them, and somehow, some way, they found a method of drawing upon their Creative Force, and through that Force they reached success.

You don't need to stumble and grope. You can call upon the Creative Force at will. There are three steps necessary:

First, to realize that you have the power. Second, to know what you want. Third, to center your thought upon it with singleness of purpose. To accomplish these steps takes only a fuller understanding of the Power-that-is-within-you.

So let us make use of this dynamo, which is *you*. What is going to start it working? Your *Faith,* the faith that is begotten of understanding. Faith is the impulsion of this power within. Faith is the confidence, the assurance, the enforcing truth, the knowing that the right idea of life will bring you into the reality of existence and the manifestation of the All power.

All cause is in Mind—and Mind is everywhere. All the knowledge there is, all the power there is, is all about you—no matter where you may be. Your mind is part of it. You have access to it. If you fail to avail yourself of it, you have no one to blame but yourself. For as the drop of water in the ocean shares in all the properties of the rest of the ocean water, so you share in that all-power, all-wisdom of Mind. If you have been sick and ailing, if poverty and hardship have been your lot, don't blame it on "fate." Blame yourself.

"Yours is the earth and everything that's in it." But you've got to take it. The Creative Force is there—but you must use it. It is round about you like the air you breathe. You don't expect others to do your breathing for you. Neither can you expect them to use the Creative Force for you. Universal Intelligence is not only the mind of the Creator of the universe, but it is also the mind of MAN, your intelligence, your mind.

I am success, though hungry, cold, ill-clad, I wander for awhile, I smile and say, "It is but a time, I shall be glad Tomorrow, for good fortune comes my way. God is my Father, He has wealth untold, His wealth is mine, health, happiness and gold."

—ELLA WHEELER WILCOX

THE CREATIVE FORCE

So start today by knowing that you can do anything you wish to do, have anything you wish to have, be anything you wish to be. The rest will follow.

A Funny World

There is a world, a funny world, that's not a world at all;
A world that has no shape nor size, that's neither sphere nor ball;
You think at first that it exists; you think it very true;
Then, finally, you see the point: that it's just fooling you.

Perhaps, you once lived in this world with all its hates and fears;
You were a glum and saddened soul, believed in pains and tears;
You thought you had to be diseased and thought there was a hell;
When, all at once, you learned the truth. This world just went pell-mell.

And, then, this world, this shadow world, just disappeared from sight;
And in its place a world of joy, of health, of love and light
Came into view right where you were; you came to understand
That you abide in Heaven now and God is right at hand.

—FRANK BLENLARRY WHITNEY

THE CREATIVE FORCE

The Goal

If you think you can win, your battle is won! Whatever you need you can have, you'll find: It's all in the way you set your mind.

If you feel that your part in the world is small, You may never achieve your work at all; But feel that your life, of God's life is a part—Then you'll work in the way you have set your heart.

If you know you are great, you will do great things; Your thoughts will soar on eagle's wings; Your life will reach its destined goal, If you know the way to set your soul.

— KATHERINE WILDER RUGGLES

CHAPTER 2

THE URGE

WHAT IS THE STRONGEST force in life? What is the power that carries those who heed it from the bottommost pits of poverty to the top of the world—from the slums and ghettos to governorships and presidencies and the rulership of kingdoms?

 The URGE for SECURITY—for ASSURED SUBSISTENCE AND SAFETY!

When the first primitive water plants appeared, living in the saturated soil along the shores of the waters, you might think the Creative Force would have rested content for a while. It had created something that lived and grew and reproduced itself. It was the first form of life upon this earth— the thallophytes.

As with the water plants, there came next the multiple-celled creature, each dependent for life upon drawing its own nourishment from the waters about. Then a central system corresponding with the stem and roots of the fern, finally evolving into distinct organs to take care of each function of life. And so was laid the foundation for all forms of animal life that have developed from this simple beginning. The principle had been perfected—it remained now only to develop every possible ramification of it, until the highest form should be reached.

When means of protection were found necessary for survival, the Creative Force developed these too. For those subject to the abrasive effects of sand and rocks, it developed shells. To the weak, it gave means of escape. To the strong, teeth and claws with which to fight. It fitted each form to meet the conditions it had to cope with. When size was the paramount consideration, it made the Gigantosaurus, over a hundred feet long and as big as a house and all the other giant monsters of antiquity. When smallness was the objective, it developed the tiny insects and water creatures, so that it takes a powerful microscope to see them, yet so perfectly made as to form organisms as exact and well-regulated as the greatest.

THE URGE

Size, strength, fierceness, speed—all these it developed to the last degree. It tried every form of life, but each had its weaknesses, each was vulnerable in some way. The Creative Force might develop forms that would grow, but nothing physical could be made that would be invulnerable, that would ever attain SECURITY.

To man has been given the job of emulating his Maker — of becoming a creator, finding new and broader and better ways through which to express the Creative Force in him. His is the work of creating beauty, or bringing more of comfort, of joy and happiness into the world.

To every living thing on earth is given a measure of Creative Power. Of the lower forms of life all that is required is that they bring forth fruit according to their kind—"some thirty, some sixty, some an hundred fold."

Of you, however, much more is expected. To bring forth fruit according to your physical kind is good—but that is no more than the animals do. More is required of you. You must bring forth fruit, according to your mental kind as well! You are a son of God, a creator. Therefore creation is expected of you. You are to spread seeds not merely of human kind, but of the intellect as well.

You are to leave the world a better place than you found it, with more of joy in it, more of beauty, of comfort, of understanding, of light.

The real purpose of Life is expression, the constant urge onward and upward. Even in the smallest child, you see evidence of this. It plays with blocks. Why? To express the urge in him to build something. The growing boy makes toys, builds a hut. The girl sews dresses, cares for dolls, cooks, plays house. Why? To give vent to the inner urge in each, struggling for expression.

They reach the period of adolescence. They dance, they motor, they seek all manner of thrill. Why? Again to satisfy that constant craving of the Creative Force in them for *expression!*

True—at the moment, it is mostly a physical urge. But in some way, that urge must be translated into a mental one—*and satisfied!* It must be given an outlet for expression. It must be brought into the light of day, given useful, uplifting work to do, and it will then bring forth abundant fruit of happiness and accomplishment. Because no matter how it is repressed, no matter how deep it is buried in dark cellars, the Creative Force will still bring forth fruit—only then it may be fungus growths of sin and misery.

THE URGE

Through every man there flows this Creative Force, with infinite power to draw to itself whatever is necessary to its expression. It doesn't matter who you are, what your environment or education or advantages, the Creative Force in you has the same power for good or evil. Mind you, that Force never brings forth evil. Its life is good. But just as you can graft onto the trunk of the finest fruit tree a branch of the upas tree, and thereupon bring forth deadly fruit, so can you engraft upon the pure energy of your Creative Force any manner of fruit you desire. But if the fruit be bad, it is you who are to blame, not the perfect Force that flows through you.

"To every man there openeth

A high way and a low,

And every man decideth

The way his soul shall go."

What is it makes a poor immigrant boy like Edward Bok overcome every handicap of language and education, to become one of the greatest editors the country has ever known?

Isn't it that the more circumstances conspire to repress it, the stronger becomes the urge of the Creative Force in you for expression? The more it lacks channels through which to expand, the more inclined it is to burst its shell and flow forth in all directions.

It is the old case of the river that is dammed generating the most power. Most of us are so placed that some opportunity for expression is made easy for us. And that little opportunity serves like a safety valve to a boiler—it leaves us steam enough to do something worthwhile, yet keeps us from getting up enough power to burst the shell about us, and sweep away every barrier that holds us down.

Yet it is only such an irresistible head of steam as that which makes great successes. That is why the blow which knocks all the props from under us is often the turning point in our whole career.

You cannot stand still. You must go forward—or see the world slide past you. This was well illustrated by figures worked out by Russell Conwell years ago. Of all the thousands who are left fortunes through the deaths of relatives, *only one in seventeen dies wealthy!*

30

Why? Because the fortunes left them take away the need for initiative on their part. Their money gives to them easy means of expressing the urge in them, without effort on their part. It gives them dozens of safety valves, through which their steam continually escapes.

The result is that they not only accomplish nothing worthwhile, but they soon dissipate the fortunes that were left them. They are like kettles, the urge of life keeping the water at boiling point, but the open spout of ease letting the steam escape as fast as it forms, until presently there is not even any water left.

Why do the sons of rich men so seldom accomplish anything worthwhile? Because they don't have to. Every opportunity is given them to turn the Creative Force in them through pleasant channels, and they dissipate through these the energies that might carry them to any height. The result? They never have a strong enough "head of steam" left to carry through any real job.

You are a channel for power. There is no limit to the amount of Creative Force that will flow through you. The only limit to what you *get,* is the amount that you *use.* Like the widow's cruse, no matter how much you pour out, there is just as much still available, but unlike the cruse of oil, your channel and your power grow with use!

What are *you* doing to satisfy the urge in you? What are you doing to give expression—*and increase*—to the Creative Force working through you?

Many a man and woman has the urge to write—or paint—or sing—or do some other worthwhile thing. But does he? No, indeed. He is not well enough known, or has not the right training, or lacks education or opportunity or influence. Or else she has tried once or twice and failed.

What does that matter? It is not your responsibility if others fail in their appreciation. Your job is to express the Creative Force surging through you, to give it the best you have. Each time you do that, you are the better for it, whether others care for it or not. And each time you will give more perfect, more understanding expression to the Creative Force working through you, until sooner or later ALL appreciate it.

You don't suppose the great writers, the successful artists, were born with the ability to write or paint, do you? You don't suppose they had all the latest books or finest courses on the art of expression? On the contrary, all that many of them had was the URGE! The rest they had to acquire just as you do.

The Creative Force flowing through you is as perfect as the rose in the bud. But just as the life in the rose bush evolved through millions of less beautiful forms before it perfected the rose, so must you be satisfied to model but crudely at first, in the sure knowledge that if you keep giving of your best, eventually the product of your hands or your brain will be as perfect as the rose.

Every desire, every urge of your being, is Creative Force straining at the bonds of repression you have put upon it, straining for expression. You can't stand still. You can't stop and smugly say—"Look what I did yesterday, or last week, or last year!" It is what you are doing now that counts.

The Creative Force is dynamic. It is ever seeking expression—and when you fail to provide new and greater outlets for it, it slips away to work through some more ambitious soul who will. Genius is nothing but the irresistible urge for one particular channel of expression—an urge so strong that it is like a mountain torrent in flood, sweeping trees and bridges and dams and everything else before it.

So don't worry about whether those around you recognize your talents. Don't mind if the world seems indifferent to them. The world is too busy with its own little ways of expressing life to pay much attention to yours. To get under its skin, you must do something to appeal to its emotions.

You see, the world in the mass is like a child. Prod it, and you make it angry. Preach to it, or try to teach or uplift it, and you lose its attention. You bore it. But appeal to its emotions—make it laugh or weep—and it will love you! Love you and lavish upon you all the gifts in its power to give. That is why it pays a Crosby millions, and a great educator only hundreds. Yet the name of the educator may live for ages, while the entertainer will be remembered only until a better one displaces him.

So forget the immediate rewards the world has to offer, and give your energies to finding ways of better expressing the Creative Force in you. You are expressing it every day and hour. Try to express it better, to find ever-greater channels through which to work. If your urge is to write a story, put into it the best you have, no matter if you know you could get by with a third of the effort. Work always for perfection, knowing that thus only can you be sure of the greatest help of the Creative Force working through you.

THE URGE

That Creative Force is striving for a perfect body, perfect surroundings, perfect work. It is not its fault when you manifest less than these. Depend upon it, it is not satisfied with anything less. So don't you be! If you have the courage to refuse anything short of your ideal, if you have the dogged perseverance to keep trying, there's no power in the heavens or the earth that can keep you from success!

It's the way every great success has been won. Do you suppose if a Michelangelo or Da Vinci had an off day and painted some imperfect figures into a painting, he left them there? Do you think he explained to his friends that he was under the weather that day, and so, while he was sorry it spoiled the picture, he could not be held accountable for it?

Just imagine one of these great painters letting something less than his best go over his name! Why, he would cheerfully destroy a year's work rather than have that happen. The moment he noticed it, he would hasten to scratch out the offensive figure, lest others might see it and judge his work by it. Or even if no one was ever to see it, he would do it because it failed to express the genius that was his!

That is how you must feel about your work before ever it can attain greatness. The Creative Force working through you is perfect, all-powerful, without limit. So don't ever be satisfied with less than its best! Follow its urge. Use every atom of strength and skill and riches you have to express it, serene in the knowledge that you can do anything through the God working in you.

Andrew Carnegie said:

"Here is the prime condition of success, the great secret: Concentrate your energy, thought, and capital exclusively upon the business in which you are engaged. Having begun on one line, resolve to fight it out on that line, to lead in it, adopt every improvement, have the best machinery, and know the most about it. Finally, do not be impatient, for, as Emerson says, 'No one can cheat you out of ultimate success but yourself.' "

Have you ever climbed a high mountain? Did you notice, as you kept getting higher and higher, how your horizon rose with you? It is the same with life. The more you use the Creative Force, the more you have to use. Your skill and power and resources grow with your use of them.

From earliest infancy, the Creative Force is trying to express something through you. First it is purely physical—a perfect body, and through it the generation of other perfect bodies. But gradually it rises above the physical plane, and strives to express itself in some way that will leave the world a better place for your having been in it—a memory of noble thoughts, of splendid deeds, of obstacles conquered and ideals won.

Do your part by never falling short of your best, no matter in how small a thing you may express it. Perfection, you remember, is made up of trifles, but perfection is no trifle.

It doesn't matter how small or seemingly unimportant your job may be. You have the same chance to attain perfection in it as the greatest artist has in his work. It doesn't matter how little others may believe that any good or great thing can come from you. Who knows what good things may come from you?

"There's nothing to fear—you're as good as the best, As strong as the mightiest, too. You can win in every battle or test; For there's no one just like you. There's only one you in the world today; So nobody else, you see, Can do your work in as fine a way,

"You're the only you there'll be! So face the world, and all life is yours To conquer and love and live; And you'll find the happiness that endures In just the measure you give:

> *There's nothing too good for you to possess,*
> *Nor heights where you cannot go;*
> *Your power is more than belief or guess—*
> *It's something you have to know.*
> *There's nothing to fear—you can and you will,*
> *For you're the invincible you.*
> *So set your foot on the highest hill—*
> *There's nothing you cannot do."*

—ANONYMOUS

CHAPTER 3

THE MENTAL EQUIVALENT

"All the world's a stage, And all the men and women merely players."

WHAT PART ARE YOU acting in the theater of life? What place have you assigned to yourself on that stage? Are you one of the stars? Do you bear one of the important parts? Or are you merely one of the "mob" scene, just background for the action, or one of the "props" for moving the scenery around?

Whatever part is yours, it is you who have given it to you, for as Emerson says, and the whole Bible teaches from one end to the other, "Man surrounds himself with the true image of himself."

"Every spirit builds itself a house," writes Emerson, "and beyond its house a world, and beyond its world a heaven. Know then that the world exists for you. For you is the phenomenon perfect. What we are, that only can we see. All that Adam had, all that Caesar could, you have and can do. Adam called his house, heaven and earth, Caesar called his house, Rome; you perhaps call yours a cobbler's trade; a hundred acres of plowed land; or a scholar's garret. Yet line for line and point for point, your dominion is as great as theirs, though without fine names. Build therefore your own world. As fast as you conform your life to the pure idea in your mind, that will unfold its great proportions."

All men are created free and equal, in that all are given the only tool with which you can really build your life. That tool is your thought. All have the same material with which to build. That material is the Creative Force working through you. As your interior thought is, so will your exterior life be. The Creative Force takes shape in the mold your thoughts give it. "We think in secret and it comes to pass; environment is but our looking glass."

THE MENTAL EQUIVALENT

"In all my lectures," declared Emerson, "I have taught one doctrine—the infinitude of the private man, the ever-availability to every man of the divine presence within his own mind, from which presence he draws, at his need, inexhaustible power."

"Think big, and your deeds will grow; Think small, and you'll fall behind;

Think that you can, and you will— It's all in the state of mind."

"What sort of mental image do you hold of yourself?" Emmet Fox asks in one of his helpful books. "Whatever your real conviction of yourself is, that is what you will demonstrate.

"Whatever enters into your life is but the material expression of some belief of your own mind. The kind of body you have, the kind of home you have, the kind of job you have, the kind of people you meet with, are all conditioned by and correspond to the mental concept you are holding. The Bible teaches that from beginning to end.

"About twenty years ago, I coined the phrase 'mental equivalent.' And I am going to say that anything that you want in your life, anything that you would like to have in your life—a healthy body, a satisfactory vocation, friends, opportunities, above all the understanding of God—if you want these things to come into your life, you must furnish a mental equivalent for them. Supply yourself with a mental equivalent and the thing must come to you. Without a mental equivalent, it cannot come to you."

And what is this "Mental Equivalent"? What but your mental image of what you hope to be, plan to be. "Think and forms spring into shape, will and worlds disintegrate."

God hid the whole world in your heart, as one great writer tells us, so when any object or purpose is clearly held in thought, its manifestation in tangible and visible form is merely a question of time. Cause and effect are as absolute and undeviating in the hidden realm of thought as in the world of visible and material things. Mind is the master weaver, both of the interior garment of character and the outer garment of circumstance. Thinking for a purpose brings that purpose into being just as surely as a hen's "setting" on an egg matures and brings the chicken into being.

THE MENTAL EQUIVALENT

"Amid all the mysteries by which we are surrounded," wrote Herbert Spencer, "nothing is more certain than that we are ever in the presence of an infinite and eternal energy from which all things proceed."

That Infinite and eternal energy or Creative Force is molded by our thought. For thousands of years, men of wisdom have realized this and have molded their own lives accordingly. The Prophets of old did their best to impress this fact upon their people. "My word (my thought or mental image) shall not come back to me void, but shall accomplish that where unto it was sent," says one. And in a hundred places, you will find the same thought expressed. You are molding your tomorrows, whether you realize it or not. Make them the good you desire—not the evil you fear.

Clarence Edwin Flynn expresses something of the power of thought in his little poem:

"Whenever you cultivate a thought Remember it will trace With certain touch, its pictured form A story on your face.

"Whenever you dwell upon a thought, Remember it will roll Into your being and become A fiber of your soul.

"Whenever you send out a thought, Remember it will be A force throughout the universe, For all eternity."

Remember that this holds good in all of your affairs. In your own thoughts, you are continually dramatizing yourself, your environment, your circumstances. If you see yourself as prosperous, you will be. If you see yourself as continually hard up, that is exactly what you will be. If you are constantly looking for slights, if you seek trouble in your thoughts, you will not be long in finding them in your daily life. Whatever part you give yourself in the drama of life in your own thought, that part you will eventually act out on the stage of life.

So give yourself a good part. Make yourself the hero of the piece, rather than the downtrodden member of the mob or the overworked servant. Set your lines in pleasant places. It is just as easy as laying them in the slums. As long as you are bound to dramatize yourself and your surroundings and circumstances anyway, try this:

1) Dramatize yourself, in your mind's eye, with the people and surroundings and things you want most, doing the things you would like most to do, holding the sort of position you long for, doing the work you feel yourself best fitted to do. Some may call it daydreaming, but make it daydreaming with a purpose. Make the picture as clear in your mind's eye as though you saw it on the screen of a motion picture theater. And get all the enjoyment out of it that you can. Believe in it. Be thankful for it.

2) Prove your faith in your dream by making every logical preparation for the material manifestation of your desires. Just as the kings of old did when they prayed for water, dig your ditches to receive it.

3) Alter minor details of your drama as you like, but stick to the main goal. Make it your objective, and like Grant in his successful campaign, resolve to stick to it "though it takes all summer."

4) Be a finisher as well as a beginner. Remember that one job finished is worth a dozen half finished. The three-quarter horses never win a prize. It is only at the finish that the purse awaits you. So complete your drama mentally before you begin to act it out, and then stick to it actually until you've made it manifest for all to see.

5) Keep that mental drama to yourself. Don't tell it to others. Remember Samson. He could do anything as long as he kept his mouth shut. Most people's minds are like boilers with the safety valve wide open. They never get up enough of a head of steam to run their engines. Keep your plans to yourself. That way they'll generate such power that you won't need to tell others about them —they'll see the result for themselves.

THE MENTAL EQUIVALENT

"The imagination," says Glenn Clark in "The Soul's Sincere Desire," "is of all qualities in man the most Godlike—that which associates him most closely with God. The first mention we read of man in the Bible is where he is spoken of as an 'image.' 'Let us make man in our image, after our likeness.' The only place where an image can be conceived is in the Imagination. Thus man, the highest creation of God, was a creation of God's imagination.

"The source and center of all man's creative power—the power that above all others lifts him above the level of brute creation, and that gives him dominion, is his power of making images, or the power of the imagination. There are some who have always thought that the imagination was something which makes-believe that which is not. This is fancy—not imagination. Fancy would convert that which is real into pretense and sham; imagination enables one to see through the appearance of a thing to what it really is."

There is a very real law of cause and effect which makes the dream of the dreamer come true. It is the law of visualization—the law that calls into being in this outer material world everything that is real in the inner world by directing your Creative Force into it. Imagination pictures the thing you desire. VISION idealizes it. It reaches beyond the thing that is, into the conception of what can be. Imagination gives you the picture. Vision gives you the impulse to make the picture your own by directing your Creative Force into it.

Make your mental image clear enough, picture it vividly in every detail, then do everything you can to bring that image into being, and the Creative Force working through you will speedily provide whatever is necessary to make it an everyday reality.

The law holds true of everything in life. There is nothing you can rightfully desire that cannot be brought into being through visualization and faith.

The keynote of successful visualization is this: See things as you would have them be instead of as they are. Close your eyes and make clear mental pictures. Make them look and act just as they would in real life. In short, daydream—but daydream purposefully. Concentrate on the one idea to the exclusion of all others, and continue to concentrate on that one idea until it has been accomplished.

Do you want an automobile? A home? A factory? They can all be won in the same way. They are in their essence all of them ideas of mind, and if you will but build them up in your own mind first, complete in every detail, you will find that the

39

Creative Force working through you can build them up similarly in the material world.

"The building of a trans-continental railroad from a mental picture," says C. W. Chamberlain in "*The Uncommon Sense of Applied Psychology*," "gives the average individual an idea that it is a big job. The fact of the matter is, the achievement, as well as the perfect mental picture, is made up of millions of little jobs, each fitting in its proper place and helping to make up the whole. A skyscraper is built from individual bricks, the laying of each brick being a single job which must be completed before the next brick can be laid."

It is the same with any work, any study. To quote Professor James:

"As we become permanent drunkards by so many separate drinks, so we become saints in the moral, and authorities and experts in the practical and scientific spheres, by so many separate acts and hours of working. Let no youth have any anxiety about the upshot of his education whatever the line of it may be. If he keep faithfully busy each hour of the working day he may safely leave the final result to itself. He can with perfect certainty count on waking some fine morning, to find himself one of the competent ones of his generation, in whatever pursuit he may have singled out...Young people should know this truth in advance. The ignorance of it has probably engendered more discouragement and faintheartedness in youths embarking on arduous careers than all other causes taken together."

Remember that the only limit to your capabilities is the one you place upon them. There is no law of limitation. The only law is of supply. Through mind you can draw upon the Creative Force for anything you wish. Use it! There are no limitations upon it. Don't put any on yourself.

Aim high! If you miss the moon, you may hit a star. Everyone admits that this world and all the vast firmament must have been thought into shape from the formless void by some God-Mind. That same God-Mind rules today, and it has given to each form of life power to attract to itself as much of the Creative Force as it needs for its perfect growth. The tree, the plant, the animal—each one finds supply to meet its need.

You are an intelligent, reasoning creature. Your mind is part of the great God-Mind. And you have the power to *say* what you require for perfect growth. Don't sell yourself short; don't sell yourself for a penny. Whatever price you set upon yourself, life will give. So aim high. Demand much! Make a clear, distinct mental image of what it is you want. Hold it in your thoughts. Visualize it, see it, *believe it!* The ways and means of satisfying that desire will follow. For supply always comes on the heels of demand.

It is by doing this that you take your fate out of the hands of chance. It is in this way that you control the experiences you are to have in life. But be sure to visualize *only what you want.* The law works both ways. If you visualize your worries and your fears, you will make them real. Control your thought and you control circumstances. Conditions will be what you make them.

To paraphrase Thackeray—"The world is a looking glass, and gives back to every man the reflection of his own thought."

Philip of Macedon, Alexander's father, perfected the "phalanx"—a triangular formation which enabled him to center the whole weight of his attack on one point in the opposing line. It drove through everything opposed to it. In that day and age it was invincible. And the idea is just as invincible today.

Keep the one thought in mind, SEE it being carried out step by step, and you can knit any group of workers into one homogeneous whole, all centered on the one idea. You can accomplish any one thing. You can put across any definite idea. Keep that mental picture ever in mind and you will make it as invincible as was Alexander's phalanx of old.

"It is not the guns or armament
Or the money they can pay,
It's the close cooperation
That makes them win the day.
It is not the individual
Or the army as a whole
But the everlasting team work
Of every bloomin' soul."

—J.MASON KNOX

THE MENTAL EQUIVALENT

The error of the ages is the tendency mankind has always shown to limit the power of Mind, or its willingness to help in time of need. We may know that we are "temples of the Living God." We may even be proud of that fact. But we never take advantage of it to dwell in that temple, to proclaim dominion over things and conditions. We never avail ourselves of the power that is ours.

The great prophets of old had the forward look. Theirs was the era of hope and expectation. They looked for the time when the revelation should come that was to make men "sons of God." "They shall obtain joy and gladness, and sorrow and sighing shall flee away."

The world has turned in vain to materialistic philosophy for deliverance from its woes. In the future the only march of actual progress will be in the mental realm, and this progress will not be in the way of human speculation and theorizing, but in the actual demonstration of the power of Mind to mold the Creative Force into anything of good. The world stands today within the vestibule of the vast realm of divine Intelligence, wherein is found the transcendent, practical power of Mind over all things.

CHAPTER 4

I AM

YEARS AGO, Emlie Coué electrified the world with his cures of all manner of disease—solely through the power of SUGGESTION!

"Nobody ought to be sick!" he proclaimed, and proceeded to prove it by curing hundreds who came to him after doctors had failed to relieve them. Not only that, but he showed that the same methods could be used to cure one's affairs—to bring riches instead of debts, success instead of drudgery.

Originally, Coué was a hypnotist. In his little drug store, he found occasional patients whom he could hypnotize. He hypnotized them—put their conscious minds to sleep—and addressed himself directly to their subconscious.

To the subconscious, he declared that there was nothing wrong with whatever organ the patient had thought diseased, and the subconscious accepted the statement and molded the Creative Force within accordingly. When the patient came out from under the hypnotic influence, he was well! It remained then only to convince his conscious mind of this, so he would not send through new suggestions of disease to his subconscious, and the patient was cured!

How account for that? By the fact that the disease or imperfection is not so much in your body as in your mind. It is in your rate of motion, and this is entirely mind-controlled. Change the subconscious belief, and the physical manifestations change with it. You speed up your rate of motion, and in that way throw off the discordant elements of disease. Doctors recognize this when they give their patients harmless sugar pills, knowing that these will dispel fear, and that when the images conjured up by fear are gone, the supposed trouble will go with them.

But Coué found many patients whom he could not hypnotize. How treat them? By inducing a sort of self-hypnosis in themselves. It is a well-known fact that

43

constant repetition carries conviction—especially to the subconscious mind. So Coué had his patients continually repeat to themselves the affirmation that their trouble was passing, that they were getting better and better. "Every day in every way I am getting better and better." And this unreasoning affirmation cured thousands of ills that had been troubling them for years.

What is back of that success? A law as old as the hills, a law that has been known to psychologists for years—the law that the subconscious mind accepts as true anything that is repeated to it convincingly and often. And once it has accepted such a statement as true, it proceeds to mold the Creative Force working through it in such wise as to MAKE IT TRUE!

You see, where the conscious mind reasons inductively, the subconscious uses only deductive reasoning. Where the reasoning mind weighs each fact that is presented to it, questions the truth or falsity of each, and then forms its conclusions accordingly, the subconscious acts quite differently. IT ACCEPTS AS FACT ANY STATEMENT THAT IS PRESENTED TO IT CONVINCINGLY. Then, having accepted this as the basis of its actions, it proceeds logically to do all in its power to bring it into being.

That is why the two most important words in the English language are the words —"I AM." That is why the Ancients regarded these two words as the secret name of God.

You ask a friend how he is, and he replies carelessly—"I am sick, I am poor, I am unlucky, I am subject to this, that or the other thing,"—never stopping to think that by those very words he is fastening misfortune upon himself, declaring to the subconscious mind within him that he IS sick or poor or weak or the servant of some desire.

"Let the weak say—'I am strong!'" the Prophet Joel exhorted his people thousands of years ago. And the advice is as good today as it was then.

You have seen men, under hypnotic suggestion, perform prodigies of strength. You have seen them with their bodies stretched between two chairs, their heads on one, their feet on another, supporting the weight of several people standing on them, when they could not ordinarily hold up even their own bodies in that position. How can they do it? Because the hypnotist has assured their subconscious that they CAN do it, that they have the strength and power necessary.

"Therefore I say unto you, what things so ever ye desire when ye pray, BELIEVE THAT YE RECEIVE THEM, and ye shall HAVE them." How can you work up the necessary faith to accomplish the things you desire? By taking the advice of the wise men of old, of the Prophet Joel—by claiming it as yours, and setting your subconscious mind to work making those claims come true.

It is a sort of self-hypnosis, but so is all of prayer. Away back in 1915, the head of the Warsaw Psychological Institute conducted a series of experiments from which he concluded that the energy manifested by anyone during life is in direct ratio with his power for plunging himself into a condition of auto-hypnosis. In simple language, that means convincing yourself of the possibility of doing the things you want to do.

The subconscious in each of us HAS the knowledge, HAS the power to do any right thing we may require of it. The only need is to implant in it the confidence— the "BELIEVE THAT YOU RECEIVE".

In a case cited by Baudouin, the famous psychologist, a woman after using auto-suggestion as a means of helping herself, declared: "I can do twice as much work as before. During vacation, I have been able to go through two extensive tasks, such as a year ago I should never have attempted. This year I systematized my work and said, 'I can do it all; what I am undertaking is materially possible, and therefore must be morally possible; consequently I ought not to experience, and shall not experience, discouragement, hesitancy, annoyance, or slackness.' " As a result of these affirmations, the way to her inner powers was opened and she was able to say truly, "Nothing could stop me, nothing could prevent my doing what I had planned to do; you might almost have said that things were done by themselves, without the slightest effort on my part." Not only did she find herself working with a high degree of success heretofore unknown, but with a certainty and calmness of mind beyond her previous attainment.

Emerson, with his genius for condensing great truths into a few words, wrote —"Do the thing and you shall have the power."

The wise men of old learned thousands of years ago that life is like an echo. It always returns the call sent out. Like the echo, the response is always the same as the call, and the louder the call, the greater the response.

You say—"I am sick, I am poor," and your words are forerunners of your circumstance. "Every idle word that men shall speak, they shall give account of in the day of judgment." And that day of judgment comes sooner than most people think.

Be careful to speak only those words which you are willing to see take form in your life, for remember the words of wise old Job: "Thou shalt also decree a thing, and it shall be established unto thee." Never speak the word of lack or limitation, for—"By thy words shall thou be justified, and by thy words shalt thou be condemned."

Affirm constantly—"I have faith in the power of my word. I speak only that which I desire to see made manifest." Remember, "Behind you is Infinite Power, before you is endless possibility, around you is endless opportunity. Why should you fear?"

C. G. Tanner expresses the idea beautifully—

"If you have faith in what you want to do,
If you behold yourself a king's own son,
Then you have asked God's power to work through you,
And pledged yourself to see that it is done.
'With faith I place it in God's hands,' you say?
God's hands are yours! Your good must come through you!
God has no other hands with which He may
Give unto you your sonship's rightful due.

"Faith and persistence travel hand in hand,
The one without the other incomplete.
If you would reach success, then take the stand,
'This I will try once more,' and no defeat
Can cloud that beacon gleaming bright and clear,
Or conjure up dread failure's haunting wraith!
You rest secure with God. No thought of fear
Can dim the shining armor of your faith."

Most people seem to think that we work to live, but there is a deeper purpose in life than that. What we really work for is to call forth the talents that are within our own soul, to give expression to the Creative Force working through us. That is the one big purpose for which we were born—to express the Creative Force in us, to give God the chance to express Himself through us. And we CAN do it. As the famous English poet Shelley put it—"The Almighty has given men arms long enough to reach the stars, if they would but put them forth."

And the first step lies in using what you have. The key to power lies in using, not hoarding. Use releases still more power for ever-greater works. Hoarding builds a hard shell around the thing hoarded and prevents more from coming in. You may have what you want, if you are willing to use what you have now. You can do what you want to do if you are willing to do what there is to do right now. "The one condition coupled with the gift of truth," says Emerson, *"is its use."*

Professor William Bateson of the British Society for Scientific Research said: "We are finding now beyond doubt that the gifts and geniuses of mankind are due not so much to something added to the ordinary person, but instead are due to factors which in the normal person INHIBIT the development of these gifts. They are now without doubt to be looked upon as RELEASES of powers normally suppressed."

And why are they suppressed? Because of doubt, of fear of failure, of procrastination, of putting things off till the morrow. "Straight from a mighty bow this truth is driven: They fail, and they alone, who have not striven."

> *Tomorrow you will live, you always cry;*
> *In what far country does this morrow lie,*
> *That 'tis so mighty long ere it arrive?*
> *Beyond the Indies does this morrow live?'*
> *Tis so far fetched, this morrow, that I fear*
> *'Twill be both very old and very dear.*
> *Tomorrow I will live, the fool does say;*
> *Today itself's too late; the wise lived yesterday."*

—ABRAHAM COWLEY

47

I AM

"To begin," said Ausonms, "is to be half done." "Greatly begin!" wrote another sage. "Though thou have time for but a line, be that sublime." And the Easterners have a proverb that the road of a thousand miles begins with one step.

So make your start, and don't allow any thought of failure to stop you. Have faith —if not in yourself—then In the Creative Force working through you. Many a splendid work has been lost to mankind because the faith of its originator was not strong enough to release the Creative Force that would have enabled him to make his dream come true.

Remember that you cannot talk failure, or think failure, and reap success. You'll never reach the top of the ladder if doubt and fear and procrastination make you hesitate to put your foot on the first rung.

There is a Power working through you that can accomplish any aim you may aspire to. But to energize that power, you must harness it up with Faith. You must have the will to believe, the courage to aspire, and the profound conviction that success is possible to anyone who works for it persistently and believingly.

Three hundred and forty years ago, there sailed from Spain the mightiest fleet the world had ever known, Spanish galleasses, Portuguese caracks, Florentine caravels, huge hulks from other countries—floating fortresses, mounting tier upon tier of mighty cannon—140 great ships in all, manned to the full with sailors and soldiers and gentlemen adventurers.

The treasure of the Incas, the Plunder of the Aztec, had gone into the building and outfitting of this vast Armada. No wonder Spain looked upon it as invincible. No wonder England feared it. For this was the Armada that was to invade England and carry fire and sword through town and countryside. This was the Armada that was to punish these impudent Britons for the "piratical" raids of Sir Francis Drake, Morgan and all those hardy seamen who had dared death and slavery to pull down treasure ships on the Spanish Main.

The iron hand of Philip II of Spain rested heavily upon the Netherlands. It dominated all of Europe. Now he confidently looked forward to the time when England, too, would groan beneath its weight.

But he reckoned without one thing—faith! He put in charge of this Invincible Armada, the Duke of Medina Sidonia, a man who had no faith in himself, no faith in his ability, no faith in his men. And when he did that, he blunted the point of

48

every spike; he dulled the cutting edge of every sword; he took the mightiest naval weapon ever forged, and deliberately drew its sting.

Is that putting it too strongly? Just listen. Here is the letter the Duke wrote to the King, upon being notified of his appointment to the command:

"My health is bad and from my small experience of the water I know that I am always seasick...The expedition is on such a scale and the object is of such high importance that the person at the head of it ought to understand navigation and sea fighting, and I know nothing of either...The Adelantado of Castile would do better than I. The Lord would help him, he is a good Christian and has fought in naval battles. If you send me, depend upon it, I shall have a bad account to render of my trust."

He had everything to succeed with—everything but faith in himself. He expected failure—and disastrous failure met him at every turn.

One hundred and forty mighty ships—the greatest ever built. And England, to meet that splendid Armada, had only 30 small ships of war and a few merchantmen outfitted and manned by private gentlemen. Yet England, while alarmed, was yet courageous and hopeful. For had not England Sir Francis Drake? And Lord Charles Howard? And a dozen other mighty fighters who had met and bested the Spaniards a score of times on the Spanish Main? And could they not do the same again?

So said England, believing in her leaders. And her leaders echoed that sentiment. Are not English sailors the hardiest seamen and finest fighters afloat? they asked. And believed in their men.

The English had 30 or 40 little ships against the Spaniards' 140 mighty men-of-war. The English had scarce two days' powder aboard—so penurious was their Queen—while the Spanish were outfitted with everything a ship-of-war could ask.

But Howard and Drake were not depending upon any Queen to fight their battles. They were not worrying about the size of the enemy. They were thinking— "There are the Spaniards. Here are we. We have fought them and whipped them a dozen times before. We can do it now. So let's get at them!"

They went out expecting victory. And victory met them at every turn.

I AM

From the Lizard in Cornwall to Portland, where Don Pedro de Valdes and his mighty ship were left; from Portland to Calais, where Spain lost Hugo de Moncado with the galleys which he captured; from Calais, out of sight of England, around Scotland and Ireland, beaten and shuffled together, that mighty Armada was chased, until finally the broken remnants drifted back to Spain.

With all their vast squadron, they had not taken one ship or bark of England. With all those thousands of soldiers, they had not landed one man but those killed or taken prisoner.

Three-fourths of their number lost or captured, their mighty fleet destroyed. And why? Because one man lacked faith. Spanish soldiers were proving on a dozen fields that no braver fighters lived anywhere. The "Spanish Square" had withstood infantry, cavalry, artillery—then carried all before it. Yet these same soldiers, afloat in their huge fortresses, were utterly defeated by less than a fourth their number.

And the reason? Because they were a spear without a head—an army without a leader—riches and power without faith. Was ever a better example of the power of belief?

Men go all through life like the Duke of Medina Sidonia—looking ever for the dark side of things, expecting trouble at every turn—and usually finding it. It is really lack of courage—courage to try for great things, courage to dare disappointment and ridicule to accomplish a worthy end. Have you ever sat in a train and watched another train passing you? You can look right on through its windows to the green fields and pleasant vistas beyond. Or you can gaze at the partitions between the windows and see nothing but their dingy drabness. So it is with everything in life. You can look for the good, the joyful and happy—and not merely see only these but manifest them in your daily life. Or you can look for trouble, for sickness and sorrow—and find them awaiting you around every corner.

Pessimists call this the "Pollyanna Age" and ridicule such ideas as this. But ridicule or not, it works—in one's personal life as well as in business—and thousands can testify to its efficacy.

Perhaps one of the best examples of the difference that outlook makes is in the lives of Emerson and Thoreau. Emerson's philosophy of living can best be expressed in his own words—"Nerve us with incessant affirmatives. Don't bark against the bad, but chant the beauties of the good." And his tranquil and serene life reflected that attitude throughout.

Thoreau, on the other hand, was constantly searching out and denoun
With motives every whit as high as Emerson's, he believed in attacking the
problem from the opposite angle, with the result that he was constantly in hot
water, yet accomplished not a tenth of the good that Emerson did. Like the man in
d'Annunzio's play, LA CITTA MORTA—"Fascinated by the tombs, he forgot the
beauty of the sky."

It is necessary at times to clean up evil conditions in order to start afresh. It is
necessary to hunt out the source of pollution in order to purify a stream. But it
should be merely a means to an end. And the end should always be—not negative
like the mere destruction of evil, but the positive replacing of evil with good.

If you have ever walked across a high trestle, you know that it doesn't pay to look
down. That way dizziness and destruction lie. You have to look forward, picking
out the ties you are going to step on ten or twenty feet ahead, if you are to
progress. Life is just such a trestle. And looking downward too much is likely to
make one lose his balance, stumble and fall. You must gaze ever forward if you are
to keep your perspective.

There's a little poem by Edgar Guest that exemplifies the idea:

> *"Somebody said that it couldn't be done,*
> *But he with a chuckle replied*
> *That 'maybe it couldn't,' but he would be one*
> *Who wouldn't say so till he'd tried.*
> *So he buckled right in with the trace of a grin*
> *On his face. If he worried he hid it.*
> *He started to sing as he tackled the thing*
> *That couldn't be done, AND HE DID IT."*

Most of the world's progress has been made by just such men as that. Men like
Watt, who didn't know that steam could not be made to accomplish any useful
purpose, and so invented the steam engine. Men like Fulton, who didn't know that
it was foolish to try to propel a boat with wheels—and so invented the steamboat.
Men like Bell, Edison, Wright, who didn't know how foolish it was to attempt the
impossible—and so went ahead and did it.

"For God's sake, give me the young man who has brains enough to make a fool of himself!" cried Stevenson. And when they succeed, the whole world echoes that cry.

There is no limit upon you—except the limit you put upon yourself. You are like the birds—your thoughts can fly across all barriers, unless you tie them down or cage them or clip their wings by the limitations you put upon them.

There is nothing that can defeat you—except yourself. You are one with the Father. And the Father knows everything you will ever need to know on any subject.

Why then, try to repress any right desire, any high ambition? Why not put behind it every ounce of energy, every bit of enthusiasm, of which you are capable? Mahomet established a larger empire than that of Rome on nothing but enthusiasm.   And   Mahomet was but a poor camel-driver. What then can you not do?

Men repress their power for good, their capacity for success, by accepting suggestions of inferiority; by their timidity or self-consciousness; by fear; by conservatism. Never mind what others think of you. It is what you think that counts. Never let another's poor opinion of you influence your decisions. Rather, resolve to show him how unfounded is his opinion.

People thought so poorly of Oliver Cromwell that he could not win permission to emigrate to the Colonies. When he raised his regiment of cavalry that later won the name of "Ironsides" because of its practical invincibility, the old soldiers and the dandies of the day laughed at it. Seldom had a lot of more awkward-looking countrymen been gathered together.

Any soldier might have trained them. But the thing that made them invincible, the thing that enabled them to ride over and through all the legions of King Charles, was not their training, but their fervent belief in the justice of their cause, in their leader and in their God.

"Hymn-singing hypocrites," their enemies called them. But here were no hypocrites. Here were men who were animated by a common faith that God was with them as with the Israelites of old—and that with God on their side, nothing could withstand them. That was the faith of Cromwell. And he instilled that faith into every man in his regiment.

And while Cromwell lived to keep that faith alive, nothing *did* withstand them. They made the man who was not good enough to emigrate to America, Ruler of England!

Nothing worthwhile ever has been accomplished without faith. Nothing worthwhile ever will. Why do so many great organizations go to pieces after their founder's death? Why do they fail to outlive him by more than a few years? Because the ones who take up his work lack the forward look, the faith, to carry on. His idea was one of service—theirs is to continue paying dividends. His thought was to build ever greater and greater—theirs to hold what he won.

"The best defensive is a strong offensive." You can't just hold your own. You can't stand still. You've got to go forward—or backward. Which is it with you? If forward, then avoid the pessimist as you would the plague. Enthusiasm, optimism, may make mistakes—but it will learn from them and progress. Pessimism, conservatism, caution, will die of dry rot, if it is not sooner lost in the forward march of things.

So be an optimist. Cultivate the forward look.

> *"The Optimist and Pessimist,*
> *The difference is droll,*
> *The Optimist sees the doughnut,*
> *The Pessimist—the hole!"*

The good is always there—if you look for it hard enough. But you must look for it. You can't be content to take merely what happens to come into your line of vision. You have got to refuse to accept anything short of good. Disclaim it! Say it is not yours. Say it—*and believe it.* Then keep a-seeking—and the first thing you know, the good you have been seeking will be found to have been right under your nose all the time.

What is the backbone of all business? Credit. And what is credit but faith—faith in your fellowman—faith in his integrity—faith in his willingness and his ability to give you a square deal?

What do you base credit-faith upon? Upon hearsay—upon what your prospective customer has done for others, his promptness in paying them, his willingness to cooperate with them. In many cases you have never seen him—you can't be certain of your own personal knowledge that such a person exists—but you believe in him, you have FAITH. And having faith, your business grows and prospers.

If you can have such faith in a man you have never seen, as to trust large portions of your earthly goods in his hands, can you not put a little trust in the Father, too?

True, you have not seen Him—but you have far greater proof of His being than of that of your customer thousands of miles away. You have far greater proof of His reliability, of His regard for you, of His ability and His willingness at all times to come to your assistance in any right way you may ask. You don't need money with Him. You don't need high standing in your community. You don't need credit.

What is it makes a successful salesman? Faith in his house. Faith in the goods he is selling. Faith In the service they will render his customers. Faith In himself. Have you faith in your "house"—in your Father—in the manifold gifts He offers you so freely?

Men can sell for a little while solely on faith in their own ability, they can palm off anything that will show a profit to themselves. But they never make successful salesmen. The inevitable reaction comes. They grow cynical, lose all faith in others —and eventually lose faith in themselves as well. The successful salesman must have a fourfold faith—faith in his house, faith in his product, faith in the good it will do his customer, faith in himself. Given such a faith, he can sell anything. Given such a faith in the Father, you can do anything.

It wasn't superior courage or superior fighting ability that enabled Washington's half-trained army to beat the British. English soldiers were showing all over the world that they were second to none in fighting qualities. And the American soldiers were, for the most part, from the same sturdy stock. It was their faith in a greater Power outside themselves.

What is it differentiates the banker from the pawnbroker? Both make loans. Both require security. But where the pawn-broker must have tangible, material property that he can resell before he will lend a cent, the really great banker bases his loans on something bigger than any security that may be offered him—his faith in the borrower.

America was built on faith. Those great railroad builders who spanned the continent knew when they did it that there was not enough business immediately available to make their investment profitable for a long time to come. But they had faith—a faith that was the making of our country.

That same faith is evident on every hand today. Men erect vast factories—in the faith that the public will find need for and buy their products. They build offices, apartments, homes—in the faith that their cities will grow up to the need of them. They put up public utilities capable of serving twice the number of people in their territories—in the faith that the demand will not only grow with the population, but the availability of the supply will help to create new demands.

Faith builds cities and businesses and men. In fact, everything of good, everything constructive in this old world of ours is based on faith. So if you have it not, *grow it*—as the most important thing you can do. And if you have it, *tend it,* water it, cultivate it—for it is the most important thing in life.

"When nothing seems to help, I go and look at a stonecutter hammering away at his rock, perhaps a hundred times without as much as a crack showing in it. Yet at the hundred and first blow, it will split in two, and I know it was not that blow that did it, but all that had gone before."—J. A. RIIS. S.

CHAPTER 5

TALISMAN

"Like the waves of the sea are the ways of fate. As we voyage along through life. 'Tis the set of the soul which decides its goal and not the calm or the strife."

—ELLA WHEELER WILCOX

WHAT IS THE ETERNAL QUESTION which stands up and looks you and every sincere man squarely in the eye every morning?

"How can I better my condition?" That is the real life question which confronts you, and will haunt you every day until you solve it.

The answer to that question lies first in remembering that the great business of life is thinking. Control your thoughts and you mold circumstance.

Just as the first law of gain is desire, so the first essential to success is FAITH. Believe that you have—see the thing you want as an existent fact—and anything you can rightly wish for is yours. Belief is "the substance of things hoped for, the evidence of things not seen."

You have seen men, inwardly no more capable than yourself, accomplish the seemingly impossible. You have seen others, after years of hopeless struggle, suddenly win their most cherished dreams. And you've often wondered, "What is the power that gives new life to their dying ambitions, that supplies new impetus to their jaded desires, that gives them a new start on the road to success?"

That power is belief—*faith*. Someone, something, gave them a new belief in themselves and a new faith in their power to win—and they leaped ahead and wrested success from seemingly certain defeat.

56

TALISMAN

Do you remember the picture Harold Lloyd was in some years ago, showing a country boy who was afraid of his shadow? Every boy in the countryside bedeviled him. Until one day his grandmother gave him a talisman that she assured him his grandfather had carried through the Civil War and which, so she said, had the property of making its owner invincible. Nothing could hurt him, she told him, while he wore this talisman. Nothing could stand up against him. He believed her. And the next time the bully of the town started to cuff him around, he wiped up the earth with him. And that was only the start. Before the year was out he had made a reputation as the most daring soul in the community.

Then, when his grandmother felt that he was thoroughly cured, she told him the truth—that the "talisman" was merely a piece of old junk she'd picked up by the roadside—that she knew all he needed was *faith in himself,* belief that he could do these things.

Stories like that are common. It is such a well-established truth that you can do only what you think you can, that the theme is a favorite one with authors. I remember reading a story years ago of an artist—a mediocre sort of artist—who was visiting the field of Waterloo and happened upon a curious lump of metal half-buried in the dirt, which so attracted him that he picked it up and put it in his pocket. Soon thereafter he noticed a sudden increase in confidence, an absolute faith in himself, not only as to his own chosen line of work, but in his ability to handle any situation that might present itself. He painted a great picture—just to show that he *could* do it. Not content with that, he visioned an empire with Mexico as its basis, actually led a revolt that carried all before it— until one day he lost his talisman. Then the bubble burst.

It is your own belief in yourself that counts. It is the consciousness of dominant power within you that makes all things attainable. *You can do anything you think you can.* This knowledge is literally the gift of the gods, for through it you can solve every human problem. It should make of you an incurable optimist. It is the open door to welfare. *Keep it open*—by expecting to gain everything that is right.

You are entitled to every good thing. Therefore expect nothing but good. Defeat does not need to follow victory. You don't have to "knock wood" every time you congratulate yourself that things have been going well with you. Victory should follow victory.

Don't limit your channels of supply. Don't think that riches or success must come through some particular job or some rich uncle. It is not for you to dictate to the Creative Force the means through which it shall send Its gifts to you. There are millions of channels through which It can reach you. Your part is to impress upon Mind your need, your earnest desire, your boundless belief in the resources and the willingness of the Creative Force to help you. Plant the seed of desire. Nourish it with a clear visualization of the ripened fruit. Water it with sincere faith. But leave the means to the Creative Force.

Open up your mind. Clear out the channels of thought. Keep yourself in a state of receptivity. Gain a mental attitude in which you are constantly expecting good. You have the fundamental right to all good, you know. "According to your faith, be it unto you."

The trouble with most of us is that we are mentally lazy. It is so much easier to go along with the crowd than to break trail for ourselves. But the great discoverers, the great inventors, the great geniuses in all lines have been men who dared to break with tradition, who defied precedent, who believed that there is no limit to what Mind can do—and who stuck to that belief until their goal was won, in spite of all the sneers and ridicule of the wiseacres and the "It-can't-be-doners."

Not only that, but they were never satisfied with achieving just one success. They knew that the first success is like the first olive out of the bottle. All the others come out the more easily for it. They realized that they were a part of the Creative Force and Intelligence of the Universe, and that the part shares all the properties of the whole. And that realization gave them the faith to strive for any right thing, the knowledge that the only limit upon their capabilities was the limit of their desires. Knowing that, they couldn't be satisfied with any ordinary success. They had to keep on and on and on.

Edison didn't sit down and fold his hands when he gave us the talking machine, or the electric light. These great achievements merely opened the way to new fields of accomplishment.

Open up the channels between your mind and the Creative Force, and there is no limit to the riches that will come pouring in. Concentrate your thoughts on the particular thing you are most interested in, and ideas in abundance will come flooding down, opening up a dozen ways of winning the goal you are striving for.

But don't let one success—no matter how great—satisfy you. The Law of Life, you know, is the Law of Growth. You can't stand still. You must go forward—or be passed by.

TALISMAN

Complacency—self-satisfaction—is the greatest enemy of achievement. You must keep looking forward. Like Alexander, you must be constantly seeking new worlds to conquer. Depend upon it, the power will come to meet the need. There is no such thing as failing powers, if we look to the Creative Force for our source of supply. The only failure of mind comes from worry and fear—and disuse.

William James, the famous psychologist, taught that—"The more mind does, the more it can do." For ideas release energy. You can do more and better work than you have ever done. You can know more than you know now. You know from your own experience that under proper mental conditions of joy or enthusiasm, you can do three or four times the work without fatigue that you can ordinarily. Tiredness is more boredom than actual physical fatigue. You can work almost indefinitely when the work is a pleasure.

You've seen sickly persons, frail persons, who couldn't do an hour's light work without exhaustion, suddenly buckle down when heavy responsibilities were thrown upon them, and grow strong and rugged under the load. Crises not only draw upon the reserve power you have but they help to create new power.

It Couldn't be Done

It may be that you have been deluded by the thought of incompetence. It may be that you have been told so often that you cannot do certain things that you've come to believe you can't. Remember that success or failure is merely a state of mind. Believe you cannot do a thing—and you can't. Know that you can do it—and you will. You must *see yourself doing it.*

"If you think you are beaten, you are; If you think you dare not, you don't;
If you'd like to win, but you think you can't, It's almost a cinch you won't;

If you think you'll lose, you've lost,
For out in the world you'll find
Success begins with a fellow's will—
It's all in the state of mind.

TALISMAN

Full man a race is lost, Ere even a race is run, And many a coward fails Ere even his work's begun.

Think big, and your deeds will grow,
Think small and you fall behind,
Think that you can, and you will;
It's all in the state of mind.

If you think you are outclassed, you are; You've got to think high to rise; You've got to be sure of yourself before You can ever win a prize.

Life's battle doesn't always go To the stronger or faster man; But sooner or later, the man who wins Is the fellow who thinks he can."

There's a vast difference between a proper understanding of one's own ability and a determination to make the best of it—and offensive egotism. It is absolutely necessary for every man to believe in himself, before he can make the most of himself. All of us have something to sell. It may be our goods, it may be our abilities, it may be our services. You've got to believe in yourself to make your buyer take stock in you at par and accrued interest. You've got to feel the same personal solicitude over a customer lost, as a revivalist over a backslider, and hold special services to bring him over into the fold. You've got to get up every morning with determination, if you're going to go to bed that night with satisfaction.

There's mighty sound sense in the saying that all the world loves a booster. The one and only thing you have to win success with is MIND. For your mind to function at its highest capacity, you've got to be charged with good cheer and optimism. No one ever did a good piece of work while in a negative frame of mind. Your best work is always done when you are feeling happy and optimistic.

And a happy disposition is the *result*—not the *cause*—of happy, cheery thinking. Health and prosperity are the *results* primarily of optimistic thoughts. You make the pattern. If the impress you have left on the world about you seems faint and weak, don't blame fate—blame your pattern! You will never cultivate a brave, courageous demeanor by thinking cowardly thoughts. You cannot gather figs from thistles. You will never make your dreams come true by choking them with doubts and fears. You've got to put foundations under your air castles, foundations of UNDERSTANDING AND BELIEF. Your chances of success in any undertaking can always be measured by your BELIEF in yourself.

60

TALISMAN

Are your surroundings discouraging? Do you feel that if you were in another's place success would be easier? Just bear in mind that your real environment is within you. All the factors of success or failure are in your inner world. You make that inner world—and through it your outer world. You can choose the material from which to build it. If you've not chosen wisely in the past, you can choose again now the material you want to rebuild it. The richness of life is within you. No one has failed so long as he can begin again.

> *"For yesterday is but a dream,*
> *And tomorrow is only a vision.*
> *And today well-lived makes*
> *Every yesterday a dream of happiness,*
> *And every tomorrow a vision of hope."*

Start right in and *do* all the things you feel you have it in you to do. Ask permission of no man. Concentrating your thought upon any proper undertaking will make its achievement possible. Your belief that you can do the thing gives your thought forces their power. Fortune waits upon you. Seize her boldly, hold her—and she is yours. She belongs rightfully to you. But if you cringe to her, if you go up to her doubtfully, timidly, she will pass you by in scorn. For she is a fickle jade who must be mastered, who loves boldness, who admires confidence. Remember, you can have what you want if you will use what you have now. You can do what you want if you will do what there is to do right now. Take the first step, and your mind will mobilize all its forces to your aid. But the first essential is that you *begin*. Once the battle is started, all that is within and without you will come to your assistance, if you attack in earnest and meet each obstacle with resolution. But you have to start things. As the poet so well expresses it:

> *"Then take this honey from the bitterest cup,*
> *There is no failure save in giving up—*
> *No real fall so long as one still tries—*
> *For seeming setbacks make the strongman wise*
> *There's no defeat, in truth, save from within:*
> *Unless you're beaten there, you're sure to win."*

The men who have made their mark in this world all had one trait in common— *they believed in themselves!* "But," you may say, "how can I believe in myself when I have never yet done anything worthwhile, when everything I put my hand to seems to fail?" You can't, of course. That is, you couldn't if you had to depend upon your conscious mind alone. But just remember what One far greater than you said—"I can of mine own self do nothing. The Father that is within me—He doeth the works."

That same "FATHER" is within you, and back of Him and of you is all the Creative Force in the universe. It is by knowing that He is in you, and that through Him you can do anything that is right, that you can acquire the belief in yourself which is so necessary. Certainly the Mind that imaged the heavens and the earth and all that they contain has all wisdom, all power, all abundance. With this Mind to call upon, you know there is no problem too difficult to undertake. The *knowing* of this is the first step, *Faith,* but as Emerson expressed it in the modern manner: "He who learns and learns, and yet does not what he knows, is like the man who plows and plows, yet never sows." So go on to the next step. Decide on the one thing you want most from life, no matter what it may be. There is no limit, you know, to Mind.

Visualize this thing that you want. See it, feel it, BELIEVE in it. Make your mental blueprint, and *begin to build!* And not merely a mental blueprint, but make an actual picture of it, if you can. Cut out pictures from magazines that symbolize what you want. Paste them on a large sheet of paper and pin them up where you can see them often. You'll be surprised how such pictures help you to form the mental mold, and how quickly the Creative Force will take shape in that mold.

Suppose some people DO laugh at your idea. Suppose Reason does say—"It can't be done!" People laughed at Galileo. They laughed at Henry Ford. Reason contended for countless ages that the earth was flat. Reason said—or so numerous automotive engineers argued—that the Ford motor wouldn't run. But the earth is round—and some millions of Fords did run—and are running.

Let us start right now putting into practice some of these truths that you have learned. What do you want most of life right now? Take that one desire, concentrate on it, impress it upon your subconscious mind in every way you can, particularly with pictures. Visualizing what you want is essential, and pictures make this visualizing easier.

Psychologists have discovered that the best time to make suggestions to your subconscious mind is just before going to sleep, when the senses are quiet and the attention is lax. So let us take your desire and suggest it to your subconscious mind tonight. The two prerequisites are the earnest DESIRE, and an intelligent, understanding, BELIEF. Someone has said, you know, that education is three-fourths encouragement, and the encouragement is the suggestion that the thing can be done.

TALISMAN

You know that you can have what you want, if you want it badly enough and can believe in it earnestly enough. So tonight, just before you drop off to sleep, concentrate your thought on this thing that you most desire from life. BELIEVE that you have it. SEE it in your mind's eye, and see YOURSELF possessing it. FEEL yourself using it.

Do that every night until you ACTUALLY DO BELIEVE that you have the thing you want. When you reach that point, YOU WILL HAVE IT!

"Do you accept the Power within, Or do you say — 'Tomorrow, Or after that, I will begin,' And try from time to time to borrow Sweet, precious moments, quickly sped, On futile paths by error led?"

Our God has willed a legacy To all of those believing. So why not change your 'it might be' To just 'I am receiving A guiding hand in every task, And full returns for all I ask.'

Do you desire success to win? Humbly accept the Power within."

—JOHN GRAHAM

CHAPTER 6

THE PERFECT PATTERN

IN Chapter 4, we quoted Baudouin to show how a person can hypnotize himself into health, happiness, success.

This is not as foolish as it sounds, for self-hypnosis is nothing more nor less than deep concentration, and it is a well-known fact that we go in the direction of our thoughts. What we long for, or dread or fear—that we are headed towards.

You see, man is inseparable from the Creative Force. God has incarnated Himself in man, and God is dynamic—not static. He cannot be shut up. He must be expressed in one way or another. We put His power into all that we do—whether towards failure or success.

How then can we use this Creative Power for good? How can we put it into our efforts toward success?

First, by convincing ourselves that we ARE successful, that we are on the road to riches or health or power. We must "believe that we receive." And the quickest, easiest, surest way to do this is through repetition. It is now generally known and accepted that one comes to believe whatever one repeats to oneself sufficiently often, whether the statement be true or false. It comes to be the dominating thought in one's mind.

Such thoughts, when mixed with a strong feeling of desire or emotion, become a magnet which attracts from all about similar or related thoughts. They attract a host of their relatives, which they add to their own magnetic power until they become the dominating, motivating master of the individual.

Then the second law begins to work. All impulses of thought have a tendency to clothe themselves in their physical equivalent. In other words, if the dominating thought in your mind is riches, that thought will tend to draw to you opportunities for riches that you never dreamed of. Just as the magnet attracts iron, so will you attract money and ways of making more money. Or if health be your dominating thought, ways and means of winning new health and strength will come to you. The same is true of love, of happiness, of anything you may greatly desire of life.

On the other hand, if you fill your mind with fear, doubt and unbelief in your ability to use the forces of Infinite Intelligence, these in turn will become your dominating thought and form the pattern for your life.

You will be lifted up, or pulled down, according to the pattern of your thought. There are no limitations upon the Creative Force working through you. The limitations are all in you, and they are all self-imposed. Riches and poverty are equally the offspring of your thought.

So if you desire anything of good, the first and most important thing you must do is to develop your faith that *you can have that good*. Faith, like any other state of mind, can be induced by suggestion, by repetition. Tell yourself often enough that you HAVE faith, and you will have it, for any thought that is passed on to the subconscious often enough and convincingly enough is finally accepted, and then translated into its physical equivalent by the most practical method available.

You remember the story of the king who felt that his child, if brought up in the court, would be spoiled by overmuch attention. So he put him in the family of an honest peasant, and had him raised as the peasant's own child. The boy had all the power, all the riches of the kingdom at his disposal—yet he knew it not. He was a great prince, yet because he knew nothing of it, he worked and lived as a lowly peasant.

Most of us are like that young prince, in that we are ignorant of our Divine parentage. We know nothing of the power that is ours, so we get no good from it. God is working through us, and there is nothing He cannot do, yet because we know nothing of Him, we are powerless.

There is no such thing as a human nobody. All have the Divine spark in them, all can kindle it into a glowing flame through faith. People let themselves be hypnotized by fear and anxiety, fear of poverty, of failure, of disease. They continually visualize these, and thus make them their dominant thought, using it as a magnet to draw these things to them.

Whatever form your thoughts and beliefs take, the Creative Force working through you uses as a mold in which to form your life and your surroundings. If you want to be strong, think of yourself as perfect. If you want to be prosperous, think not of debts and lacks, but of riches and opportunity. We go in the direction of our dominating thought. It strikes the keynote of our life song.

"The chief characteristic of the religion of the future," wrote Dr. Eliot, "will be man's inseparableness from the great Creative Force." We are in partnership with the Fountain Head of all good.

Emerson says that man is weak when he looks for help outside himself. It is only as he throws himself unhesitatingly upon the Creative Force within himself that he finds the springs of success, the power that can accomplish all things. It is only when he realizes that all outside help amounts to nothing compared with the tremendous forces working through him that he stands erect and begins to work miracles.

Nearly every man has a habit of looking back and saying—"If I had that period of my life to live over again, if I could go back and take advantage of the chance at fortune I had then, I'd be rich and successful today."

Yet a year from now, or five or ten years from now, most of you who read this will be saying the same thing of today.

Why? Because your future depends upon the foundations you are digging NOW. Yesterday is gone. There is no recalling it. And tomorrow has not come. The only time you have to work with is right now, and whether you will go up or down tomorrow, whether you will be rich or a failure, depends upon your thoughts today.

It took mankind thousands of years to learn how to control matter, how to provide comfort and safety and some degree of financial security. It has taken less than a generation to learn how to control one's own future. The knowledge is so new that most people are not yet aware of it. As David Seabury put it in his book—"They know that science and mechanics have made over the face of the earth. They do not know that psychology and its kindred sciences are making a like change in man's handling of his own nature."

Do you know why so few people succeed in life? Because it is so EASY that most people cannot believe in the methods that really make men successful. They prefer to look upon success as something arduous, something practically impossible for them to attain—and by looking upon it that way, make it so for themselves.

THE PERFECT PATTERN

YOU CAN HAVE WHAT YOU WANT—if you know how to plant the seeds of it in your thought. To know that is the most important thing that anyone can learn. It is not fate that bars your path. It is not lack of money or opportunity. It is yourself —your attitude towards life. Change it—and you change all.

Ask yourself this important question: Are you a victim of self-pity? Are you embittered at life and at those more successful than yourself? Do you think fortune has played you a scurvy trick? Or are you cheerfully, steadfastly, confidently working out ways of meeting and bettering the situations that life presents to you?

Most people will dodge that question. They are more concerned in defending their ego and putting the blame for their failures on something outside themselves than they are in getting ahead. Failure comes from the inside first. It cannot be forced upon a resolute, dauntless soul.

How about YOU? Will you give yourself an honest answer to this important question—"Are you a victim of self-pity?"

Think of the times when you have yearned for a future—when you have grown impatient with the barriers that seemed to hold you down—when you have heard of the success of some acquaintance whom you knew to be inwardly no more capable than yourself. Are you willing to keep on wishing and *envying* and looking to the future for your success? Or will you start that success in the only time that will ever be yours to work with—the everlasting NOW?

Remember what Emerson told us: "There is one Mind common to all individual men. Every man is an inlet to the same and to ALL of the same. He that is once admitted to the right of reason is a freeman of the whole estate. What Plato has thought, he may think; what a Saint has felt, he may feel; what has at any time befallen any man, he can understand. Who hath access to this Universal Mind is a party to all that is or can be done; for this is the only and sovereign agent—of this Universal Mind each individual is one more incarnation."

The Creative Force of the Universe is working through you. You can be as great an outlet for IT as anyone who has ever lived. You have only to provide the mold in which it is to take shape, and that mold is formed by your thoughts. What is your dominant desire? What do you want most? *Believe in it*—and you can have it. Make it your dominating thought, magnetize your mind with it, and you will draw to you everything you need for its accomplishment.

THE PERFECT PATTERN

"There is not a dream that may not come true," wrote Arthur Symons, "if we have the energy which makes or chooses our own fate. We can always in this world get what we want, if we *will* it intensely and persistently enough. So few people succeed because so few can conceive a great end and work towards it without deviating and without tiring. But we all know that the man who works for money day and night gets rich; and the man who works day and night for no matter what kind of material power, gets the power. It is only the dreams of those light sleepers who dream faintly that do not come true."

Knowing these things, can you ever again limit yourself, when you have such unlimited possibilities? Sure, there are times when you feel inferior. Everyone does. Just remember and realize that *you* are superior, one of the efficient few who take advantage of the Infinite Power inside them to carry you on to the heights of success.

Plato held, you remember, that in the Divine Mind are pure forms or Archetypes according to which all visible beings are made. And most of the great Mystery Schools of the older world held similar opinions. They taught growth by intent rather than by accident, a development from birth all through life towards the perfect image or Archetype of each of us that is held in Divine Mind. They visioned each of us growing into a destiny that had been imaged for him long before he was born.

Progress was movement in the direction of the perfect Archetype. Man became nobler as the interval between him and his perfect pattern grew less. To the Greeks, happiness meant peace between a man and his pattern, whereas if you lived in a manner inconsistent with your Archetype, you suffered from inharmonies of various kinds. They believed that it was not so much what you do that causes you to suffer, as it is the Inharmony between what you do and what you SHOULD DO to match your perfect pattern.

There is a perfect pattern for YOU in the Divine Mind, a perfect Archetype that you CAN match. It has perfect form, perfect intelligence, all power necessary to make your surroundings perfect. Why not make yourself like it?

You CAN! Just let your Archetype be your model. Fill your mind with thoughts of its perfection, make it your dominant thought, and you can draw to yourself whatever elements you need to manifest that perfect Image. And not merely the perfect image of yourself, but all that goes to make your surroundings and circumstances just as perfect. Remember, the only limit upon the Power working through you is the limit you impose.

THE PERFECT PATTERN

Bear these facts in mind:

1) Your subconscious mind is constantly amenable to control by the power of suggestion.

2) Its power to reason deductively from given premises to correct conclusions is practically perfect.

3) It is endowed with a perfect memory.

4) It is the seat of your emotions.

5) It has the power to communicate and receive intelligence through other than the recognized channels of the senses.

"Man contains all that is needful within himself," wrote Emerson. "He is made a law unto himself. All real good or evil that can befall him must be from himself. The purpose of life seems to be to acquaint a man with himself. The highest revelation is that God is in every man."

CHAPTER 7

TO HIM THAT HATH

THE LAW OF Increase states that: "To him that hath, shall be given." To him that is using his attractive powers, shall be given everything he needs for growth and fruition. "From him that hath not, shall be taken away even that which he hath." The penalty for not using your attractive powers is the loss of them. You are demagnetized.

Sounds simple, doesn't it, yet it is the basic law of all success, all riches, all power. It is the way the whole universe is run. You live by it, whether you like it or not, or you die by it.

To many, this law seems unfair, but in this, as in all things, Nature is logical, and when you understand exactly how the law works, you will agree that it is eminently just and right.

You see, everything consists primarily of electricity—of tiny protons and electrons revolving about each other. It is of these that your body is made, it is of these that all plant life is made, it is of these that all so-called inanimate life is made. Wherein, then, is the difference between all these forms of life? Largely in their RATE OF MOTION!

Remember this: Starting with the individual cell in your mother's womb, you attract to yourself only those elements that are identical in quality and character with yourself, and that are revolving at the same rate of speed. Your selective ability is such that you are able to pick such material as will preserve your quality and identity.

This is true of your body, of your circumstances, of your environment. Like attracts like. If you are not satisfied with yourself as you are, if you want a healthier body, more attractive friends, greater riches and success, you must start at the core—within YOURSELF!

TO HIM THAT HATH

And the first essential to putting yourself in harmony with the Infinite Good all about you is to relax, to take off the brakes. For what is worry or fear or discouragement but a brake on your thinking and on the proper functioning of your organs, a slowing down of your entire rate of activity?

"Get rid of your tensions!" says the modern psychologist. By which he means—think more about the agreeable things and less about the disagreeable ones. You know how martial music stirs your pulses, wakes even the tiredest man into action. Why? Because it tends to increase the rate of motion in every cell in your body. You know how good news has often cured sick people, how sudden excitement has enabled paralyzed people to leap from their beds. Why? Because good news makes you happy, speeds up your rate of motion, even as sudden excitement stirs up the whole organism. You know how fear, hatred, and discouragement slow you down. Why? Because those feelings put a definite clamp upon your rate of motion.

Remember this: Hatred, anger, fear, worry, discouragement—all the negative emotions—not only slow down your rate of motion, and thus bring on sickness and make you old before your time, but they definitely keep the good from you. Like attracts like, and the good things you desire have a different rate of motion from these negative ones.

Love, on the other hand, attracts and binds to you the things you love. As Drummond tells us—"To love abundantly is to live abundantly, and to love forever is to live forever." And Emerson expresses the same idea—"Love and you shall be loved. All love is mathematically just, as much as the two sides of an algebraic equation."

Whate'er thou lovest, man,

That, too, become thou must;
God, if thou lovest God,
Dust, if thou lovest dust."

And that, again, is strictly logical, strictly in accord with Nature's law that like attracts like. Whatever your rate of motion, the elements of like quality with that rate of emotion will be attracted to you.

Which brings us back to the law of increase: you will see that it is not mere money or possessions that attracts more money—it is the USE to which these are put. You can't bury your talent and expect increase. You must put it to good use. It is the rate of motion that attracts increase, what the modern merchant would call the "turn-over." The oftener he turns over his stock of goods, the more money he makes on his invested capital. But if he fails to turn it over, if his goods lie dormant on his shelves, they will gather dust or mold and presently be worthless.

We see the same thing happening every day. Statistics show that of all those who inherit money, only one in seventeen dies with money; of all those possessed of fortunes at the age of 35, only 17% have them when they reach 65.

The old adage used to be—"Three generations from shirtsleeves to shirtsleeves," but the modern tempo has speeded this up until now most fortunes hardly last out a single generation. Why is this? Because of the old law of the Rate of Motion. The man who makes the money has set in motion some idea of service that has attracted riches to him. More often than not, it is the idea or the service that is important in his mind. The money is incidental, and is attracted to him with other things of good because he has set in motion an idea that is bringing good to others.

But when he dies, what happens? Too often the business is carried on solely with the thought of how much money can be made out of it. Or the business is sold, and the money put out at interest, with the sole idea of hanging on to the money in hand. Naturally its rate of movement slows down. Naturally it begins to disintegrate and its parts are gradually drawn away by the stronger forces around it, until of that fortune there is nothing left.

You see exactly the same thing in Nature. Take any seed of plant life; take an acorn, for instance. You put it in the ground—plant it. What happens? It first gives of all the elements it has within itself to put forth a shoot, which in turn shall draw from the sun and the air the elements that they have to give; and at the same time, it puts out roots to draw from the earth the moisture and other elements it needs for growth. Its top reaches upward to the sun and air, its roots burrow deeply into the ground for moisture and nourishment. Always it is reaching out. Always it is creating a vacuum, using up all the materials it has on hand, drawing to itself from all about every element it needs for growth.

Time passes. The oak tree stops growing. What happens? In that moment, its attractive power ceases. Can it then live on the elements it has drawn to itself and made a part of itself through all those years? No, indeed! The moment growth stops, disintegration starts. Its component elements begin to feel the pull of the growing plants around them. First the moisture drains out of the tree. Then the leaves fall, the bark peels off—finally the great trunk crashes down, to decay and form soil to nourish the growing plants around. Soon of that noble oak, nothing is left but the enriched soil and the well-nourished plants that have sprung from it.

The Fundamental Law of the Universe is that you must integrate or disintegrate. You must grow—or feed others who are growing. There is no standing still. You are either attracting to yourself all the unused forces about you, or you are giving your own to help build some other man's success.

"To him that hath, shall be given." To him that is using his attractive powers, shall be given everything he needs for growth and fruition. "From him that hath not, shall be taken away even that which he hath." The penalty for not using your attractive powers is the loss of them. You are demagnetized. And like a dead magnet surrounded by live ones, you must be content to see everything you have drawn to yourself taken by them, until eventually even you are absorbed by their resistless force.

That is the first and fundamental Law of the Universe. But how are you to become an Attracter? How are you to make your start? In the same way that it has been done from the beginning of time.

Go back to the first law of life. Go back to the beginning of things. You will find Nature logical in all that she does. If you want to understand how she works, study her in her simplest, most elementary forms. The principles established there hold good throughout the universe. The methods there used are used by all created things, from the simplest to the most complicated.

How, for instance, did the earliest forms of cell life, either plant or animal, get their food? By absorbing it from the waters around them. How does every cell in your body, every cell in plant or tree or animal, get its food today? In exactly the same way—by absorbing it from the lymph or water surrounding it! Nature's methods do not change. She is logical in everything. She may build more complicated organisms, she may go in for immense size or strange combinations, but she uses the same principles throughout all of life.

Now, what is Nature's principle of Increase? From the beginning of Time, it has been—*Divide—and Grow!*

That principle, like every other fundamental Law of Nature, is the same in all of life. It has remained unchanged since the first single-celled organism floated on the surface of the primordial sea. It is the fundamental Law of Increase.

Take the lowest form of cell life. How does it grow? It DIVIDES—each part grows back to its original size—then they in turn divide and grow again.

Take the highest form of cell life—MAN. The same principle works in him in exactly the same way—in fact, it is the only principle of growth that Nature knows!

How does this apply to your circumstances, to the acquisition of riches, to the winning of success?

Look up any miracle of increase in the Bible, and what do you find? First division —then increase.

When Russell Conwell was building the famous Baptist Temple in Philadelphia, his congregation was poor and greatly in need of money. Through prayer and every other means known to him, Conwell was constantly trying to help his flock.

One Sunday it occurred to him that the old Jewish custom had been, when praying to God, to first make an offering of the finest lamb of the flock, or of some other much prized possession. Then, after freely giving to God, prayer was made for His good gifts.

So instead of first praying, and then taking up the collection, as was the custom, Conwell suggested that the collection be taken first and that all who had special favors to ask of the Creator should give freely as a "Thank Offering."

A few weeks afterwards, Conwell asked that those who had made offerings on this occasion should tell their experiences. The results sounded unbelievable. One woman who had an overdue mortgage on her home found it necessary to call in a plumber the following week to repair a leak. In tearing up the boards, he uncovered a hiding place where her late father had hidden all his money—enough to pay off the mortgage and leave plenty over!

One man got a much-needed job; a servant some dresses she badly needed; a student the chance to study for his chosen vocation, while literally dozens had their financial needs met. They had complied with the law. They had sown their seed—freely—and they reaped the harvest.

TO HIM THAT HATH

Many people will tell you—"I don't see why God does not send me riches, I have prayed for them, and promised that if I get them, I will use them to do good." God enters into no bargains with man. He gives you certain gifts to start, and upon the way you use these depends whether you get more. You've got to start with what you have.

And the place to start is pointed out in a little poem by Nina Stiles:

"The land of opportunity Is anywhere we chance to be,

Just any place where people live

And need the help that we can give."

The basis of all work, all business, all manufacturing, is SERVICE. Every idea of success must start with that. Every nucleus that is to gather to itself elements of good must have as its basis service to your fellow man. Carlyle defined wealth clearly when he said that "the wealth of a man is the number of things he loves and blesses, which he is loved and blessed by."

And that is the only kind of wealth that endures. Love and blessings speed up your rate of motion, keep your nucleus active, keep it drawing to you every element of good that you need for its complete and perfect expression. They are, in effect, a constant prayer—the kind of prayer Coleridge had in mind when he wrote—

"He prayeth well who loveth well.
Both man and bird and beast.
He prayeth best who loveth best
All things both great and small;
For the dear God who loveth us,
He made and loveth all."

Remember that the word often used in the Bible to signify "prayer" means, when literally translated—"To sing a song of joy and praise." In other words, to speed up your rate of motion with joy and thanksgiving. And you have only to read the Bible to know how often the great characters of the Bible had recourse to this method.

75

TO HIM THAT HATH

What do *you* want from life? Speed up your rate of motion and overtake it. Is it health you want? Then start by relaxing, by letting go of all your fears and worries. In a recent article, I read: "Dr. Loring Swaim, director of a famous clinic in Massachusetts, has under observation 270 cases of arthritis which were cured when they became free from worry, fear, and resentment. He has come to the conclusion after some years that no less than 60% of his cases are caused by moral conflict."

In the *Reader's Digest* some months ago, it was stated that, "Personal worry is one of the principal causes of physical ailments which send people to hospitals. It is literally possible to worry yourself sick; in fact, the chances are better than even that if you are ill, worry is causing the symptoms."

That is not a modern discovery, by any means. In Proverbs, you will find the statement—"A merry heart causeth good healing, but a broken spirit drieth up the bones." And Plato observed 19 centuries ago—"If the head and the body are to be well, you must begin by curing the soul."

So the first essential in curing yourself of any ailment would seem to be to let go of your resentments, your worries and fears. Make peace within yourself, within your thoughts. Laugh a little; sing a little. Dance a little, if you can. Exercise speeds up your rate of motion, but it should be joyous exercise. Do something you enjoy, something that speeds up your mind as well as your muscles. Dance, if you like dancing. Swim, ride horseback, play tennis—do something exhilarating to the spirit as well as the body. Mere routine exercises that soon become a chore do little good and often are harmful. Unless you can get mental as well as physical exhilaration out of your exercise, don't bother with it at all.

Do you want money, riches? Then use what you have, no matter how little it may be. Speed up your rate of turnover, as the merchant speeds the turnover of his stocks. Money is now your stock. Use it! Pay it out joyfully for any good purpose, and as you pay it, BLESS IT! Bless it in some such wise as this:

"I bless you...and be thou a blessing; May you enrich all who touch you. I thank God for you, but I thank Him even more that there is unlimited supply where you came from. I bless that Infinite Supply. I thank God for it, and I expand my consciousness to take in as much of it as I can use...As I release this money in my hand, I know that I am opening the gates of Infinite Supply to flow through my channels and through all that are open to receive it. The Spirit is making this money attract to itself everything it needs for growth and increase. All of God's channels are open and flowing freely for me. The best in myself for the world—the best in the world for me."

There is no quicker way of speeding up your rate of motion than by giving. Give of your time, of your money, of your services—whatever you have to give. Give of that you want to see increased, for your gift is your seed, and "everything increaseth AFTER ITS KIND!"

Solomon was the richest man of his day, and he gave us the key to his riches and success when he wrote:

"There is that scattereth, and increaseth yet more. And there is that witholdeth more than is meet. The liberal soul shall be made fat, and he that watereth, shall be watered himself."

Do you want power, ability, greater skill in what you are doing? Then use what you have, use it to the greatest extent of which you are capable. The *Sunshine Bulletin* had an excellent little piece along these lines:

"There is a task for today which can be done now better than at any other time. It is today's duty. And we are writing now a judgment upon our lives by our faithfulness or unfaithfulness at the present moment.

"This moment has its own priceless value, and if wasted, it can no more be recovered than jewels that are cast into the depths of the ocean.

"Each day has its share in the making of our tomorrow; and the future will be nobler or meaner by reason of what we now do or leave undone."

What is ambition but the inner urge that speeds up your rate of motion and makes you work harder and longer and more purposefully to the end that you may accomplish something worthwhile? What is perseverance but the will to carry on in spite of all difficulties and discouragements? Given that ambition and that perseverance, there is nothing you cannot accomplish, nothing with a rate of motion so high that you cannot overtake it.

TO HIM THAT HATH

"It is in loving, not in being loved, The heart is blessed.

It is in giving, not in seeking gifts, We find our quest.

"If thou art hungry, lacking heavenly bread, Give hope and cheer. If thou art sad and wouldst be comforted, Stay sorrow's tear.

*"Whatever be thy longing or thy need,
That do thou give. So shall thy soul be fed, and thou indeed Shalt truly live."*

—M. ELLA RUSSELL

CHAPTER 8

EVERYTHING HAS ITS PRICE

"Dear God, help me be wise enough to see That as I give so it is meted out to me! Help me to know that with my every thought The good or ill that's mine myself I've wrought!

Help me to place all blame of lack on me, Not on my fellow man, nor yet on Thee. Give me the courage, God, truly to know That as I'd reap in life thus must I sow!"

—VERAM. CRIDER

IN HIS ESSAY on Compensation, Emerson says:

"What will you have?" quoth God. "Pay for it, and take it!"

How can we buy the things we want at the counter of God? What pay can we offer?

Perhaps the answer lies in the ancient Law of Karma. Karma is Sanskrit, you know, and means "Comeback." It is one of the oldest laws known to man. It is the law of the boomerang.

In the parlance of today, it is—"Chickens come home to roost." Even in science we find it, as Newton's Third Law of Motion—"Action and reaction are equal to each other." Ella Wheeler Wilcox expressed the Law beautifully when she wrote—

"There are loyal hearts, there are spirits brave, There are souls that are pure

and true; Then give to the world the best you have, And the best will come back to you.

"Give love, and love to your heart will flow, A strength in your utmost need; Have faith, and a score of hearts will show Their faith in your word and deed.

"For life is the mirror of king and slave, Tis just what you are and do, Then give to the world the best you have And the best will come back to you."

One of the best illustrations of the working of the Law lies in the two seas of Palestine, the Sea of Galilee and the Dead Sea. The Sea of Galilee contains fresh water and is alive with fish. Green trees adorn its banks and farms and vineyards spread all around it. The River Jordan flows into it, and all the little rivulets from the hills around feed its sparkling waters.

The Dead Sea, on the other hand, knows no splash of fish, has no vegetation around it, no homes, no farms or vineyards. Travelers give it a wide berth, unless forced by urgent business to use its shores. The air hangs heavy, and neither man nor beast will drink of the waters.

What makes the difference? The River Jordan empties the same good waters into both seas. So it is not the river. And it is not the soil or the country round about.

The difference lies in the fact that the Sea of Galilee gives as it receives; for every drop of water that flows into it, another flows out. Whereas the Dead Sea holds on to all it receives. Water leaves it only through evaporation and seepage. It hoards all it gets, and the result is that the water stagnates, turns salt, and is good for naught.

In all of Nature, the only known law of increase is that you must give to get. If you want to reap a harvest, you must first plant your seed. If you want to increase your strength, you must first break up the muscle cells, and stimulate them to divide and grow.

Division and growth is the way that all of life increases. Watch a single cell at work in your body, in a plant, or in any form of life. What happens? It first divides, then each half grows until it reaches its normal size, when it divides and starts growing again. Without division, there is no growth—only atrophy and decay. You must divide to grow; you must give to get.

EVERYTHING HAS ITS PRICE

John Bunyan knew nothing of the law of cell growth, but he expressed it just as well when he wrote—

"A man there was and they called him mad; The more he gave, the more he had."

And Moffatt had the same thought in his couplet:

"One gives away, and still he grows the richer; Another keeps what he should give, and is the poorer."

Even the thoughts we send forth return to us laden with a harvest of their kind. That which we put into our thought comes back into our own lives, because for every thought there is a response, a return of the pendulum we have started swinging. It is the Einstein doctrine of the extended line, which must return to its source.

There is no use saying you have not enough money or abilities to be worth starting with. Start with what you have and plant your seed, no matter how small and unimportant it may seem. What you have to start with can hardly be smaller than a tiny seed. If it can grow into a tree, think what your seed may grow into.

"*Do the thing* and you shall have the power," says Emerson. "But they that do not the thing have not the power. Everything has its price, and if the price is not paid —not that thing but something else is obtained. And it is impossible to get anything without its price. For any benefit received, a tax is levied. In nature, nothing can be given—all things are sold. Power to him who power exerts.

"You are not higher than your lowest thought,
Or lower than the peak of your desire.
And all existence has no wonder wrought
To which ambition may not yet aspire.
Oh man! There is no planet, sun or star
Could hold you, if you but knew what you are."

EVERYTHING HAS ITS PRICE

The key to power lies in using what you have, for use releases more power, just as using your muscles builds them into greater muscles, and failing to use them makes them weak and useless. "The one condition coupled with the gift of truth," Emerson tells us, "is its USE! That man shall be learned who reduces his learning to practice."

And Goethe expressed it even more strongly when he wrote—

"Lose this day loitering, it will be the same story
Tomorrow, and the rest more dilatory;
Thus indecision brings its own delays
And days are lost tormenting over other days.
Are you in earnest? Seize this very minute;
What you can do, or dream you can, begin it;
Boldness has genius, power, and magic in it;
Only engage and then the mind grows heated;
Begin, and then the work will be completed."

CHAPTER 9

YESTERDAY ENDED LAST NIGHT

"I said to the man who stood at the gate of the year: 'Give me a light that I may tread safely into the unknown.' And he replied: 'Go out into the darkness and put your hand into the hand of God. That shall be to you better than a light and safer than a known way.'"

WHAT DO YOU WANT from life? Whatever it is, you can have it—and you have the word of no less an authority than God for that.

There was an article in *Unity* magazine recently that exemplified the idea so well that I quote it here:

"Let us say we are planning a business venture, or a social event, or a religious meeting, or the recovery of the sick. We are ready to pray over the situation. Now instead of futurizing our prayers and asking for something to take place tomorrow, let us imagine (imagination is an aid to the release of faith power) that everything has turned out just as we desired it. Let us write it all down as if it were all past history. Many of the Bible predictions are written in the past tense. Let us try listing our desires as if they had already been given us.

"Of course we shall want to write down a note of thanksgiving to God for all that He has given us. He has had it for us all the time or else we should not have received it. More than this, God has it for us or we could not even desire it now or picture it in our imagination.

What happens? After we have written down our desires in the past tense, read them over carefully, praised God for them, let us then put away our paper and go on about our business. It will not be long before we actually see the desired events taking place in ways so natural that we may even forget that God is answering our prayers.

"Imagination helps us to have faith, for it pictures the thing desired and helps make it real. After we have tried this experiment a few times we shall find that our imagination has increased our faith, and faith has turned to praise, and praise has opened our eyes to see what God has for us."

The habit of thanking God ahead of time for benefits about to be received has its firm basis in past experience. We can safely look upon it as a sure formula for successful prayer because the prophets used it. David always praised and thanked God when he was in trouble. Daniel was saved from the lions through the praise of God. And don't you, and everyone else, find satisfaction in being praised for a task well done?

Wrote William Law:

"If anyone could tell you the shortest, surest way to all happiness and all perfection, he must tell you to make it a rule yourself to thank and praise God for everything that happens to you. For it is certain that whatever seeming calamity happens to you, if you thank and praise God for it, you turn it into a blessing. Could you therefore work miracles, you could not do more for yourself than by this thankful spirit; for it...turns all that it touches into happiness."

And Charles Fillmore adds:

"Praise is closely related to prayer; it is one of the avenues through which spirituality expresses itself. Through an inherent law of mind, we increase whatever we praise. The whole creation responds to praise, and is glad. Animal trainers pet and reward their charges with delicacies for acts of obedience; children glow with joy and gladness when they are praised. Even vegetation grows better for those who love it. We can praise our own ability, and the very brain cells will expand and increase in capacity and intelligence, when we speak words of encouragement and appreciation to them."

So don't let anything that has happened in your life discourage you. Don't let poverty or lack of education or past failures hold you back. There is only one power—the I AM in you—and it can do anything. If in the past you have not used that power, that is too bad as far as the past is concerned, but it is not too late. You can start NOW. "Be still, and know that I AM God." What more are you waiting for? God can do for you only what you allow Him to do through you, but if you will do your part, He can use you as a channel for unlimited power and good.

The difference between failure and success is measured only by your patience and faith—sometimes by inches, sometimes by minutes, sometimes by the merest flash of time.

Take Lincoln. He went into the Black Hawk War a Captain—and came out a private. His store failed—and his surveyor's instruments, on which he depended to eke out a livelihood, were sold for part of the debts. He was defeated in his first try for the Legislature. Defeated in his first attempt for Congress. Defeated in his application for Commissioner of the General Land Office. Defeated for the Senate. Defeated for the nomination for the Vice Presidency in 1856. But did he let that long succession of defeats discourage him? Not he. He held the faith—and made perhaps the greatest President we have ever had.

Then there was Grant: He failed of advancement in the army. Failed as a farmer. Failed as a businessman. At 39, he was chopping and delivering cordwood to keep body and soul together. Nine years later he was President of the United States and had won a martial renown second in this country only to Washington's.

Search the pages of history. You will find them dotted with the names of men whom the world had given up as failures, but who held on to their faith, who kept themselves prepared—and when their chance came they were ready and seized it with both hands.

Napoleon, Cromwell, Patrick Henry, Paul Jones—these are only a few out of thousands.

When Caesar was sent to conquer Gaul, his friends found him one day in a fit of utter despondency. Asked what the matter was, he told them he had just been comparing his accomplishments with Alexander's. At his age, Alexander had conquered the entire known world—and what had Caesar done to compare with that? But he presently roused himself from his discouragement by resolving to make up as quickly as might be for his lost time. The result? He became the head of the Roman Empire.

The records of business are crowded with the names of middle-aged nobodies who lived to build great fortunes, vast institutions. No man has failed as long as he has faith in the Father, faith in the great scheme of things, faith in himself.

Yesterday Ended Last Night

When Robert Bruce faced the English at the battle of Bannockburn, he had behind him years of failure, years of fruitless efforts to drive the English out of Scotland, years of heart-breaking toil in trying to unite the warring elements among the Scotch themselves. True, at the moment a large part of Scotland was in his hands, but so had it been several times before, only to be wrested from him as soon as the English brought together a large enough army.

And now in front of him stood the greatest army England had ever gathered to her banners—hardy veterans from the French provinces, all the great English nobles with their armored followers, wild Irish, Welsh bowmen—troops from all the dominions of Edward II, over 100,000 men.

To conquer whom Bruce had been able to muster but 30,000 men, brave and hardy, it is true, but lacking the training and discipline of the English.

Was Bruce discouraged? Not he. What though the English had the better archers. What though they were better armed, better trained, better disciplined. He was fighting for freedom—and he believed in himself, he believed in his men, he believed in the God of battles.

And, as always, weight, numbers, armament, proved of no avail when confronted with determination and faith. The vast English host was completely defeated and dispersed. Bruce was firmly seated upon the throne of Scotland, and never more did an invading English army cross its borders.

It matters not how many defeats you have suffered in the past, how great the odds may be against you. Bulow put it well when he said—"It's not the size of the dog In the fight that counts, so much as the size of the fight in the dog." And the size of fight in you depends upon your faith—your faith in yourself, in the Creative Force working through you and in your cause. Just remember that yesterday ended last night, and yesterday's defeats with it.

YESTERDAY ENDED LAST NIGHT

Time after time throughout the Bible we are told that the battle is not ours—but the Lord's. But like all children, we know better than our Father how our affairs should be handled, so we insist upon running them ourselves.

Is it any wonder they get so tangled as to leave us in the depths of discouragement?

When the Black Prince with his little army was penned in by Philip of France, most men would have felt discouraged. For the hosts of France seemed as numerous as the leaves on the trees, while the English were few, and mostly archers. And archers, in that day, were believed to stand no chance against such armored knights as rode behind the banners of Philip,

The French came forward in a great mass, thinking to ride right over that little band of English. But did the Black Prince give way? Not he. He showed the world that a new force had come into warfare, a force that would soon make the armored knight as extinct as the dodo. That force was the common soldier—the archer.

Just as the Scotch spearmen overthrew the chivalry of England on the field of Bannockburn, just as infantry have overthrown both cavalry and artillery in many a later battle, so did the "common men" of England—the archers—decide the fate of the French at Crecy. From being despised and looked down upon by every young upstart with armor upon his back, the "common men"—the spearmen and archers—became the backbone of every successful army. And from what looked like certain annihilation, the Black Prince by his faith in himself and his men became one of the greatest conquerors of his day.

Troubles flocked to him, but he didn't recognize them as troubles—he thought them opportunities. And used them to raise himself and his soldiers to the pinnacle of success.

There are just as many prizes in business as in war—just as many opportunities to turn seeming troubles into blessings. But those prizes go to men like the Black Prince who don't know a trouble when they meet it—who welcome it, take it to their bosoms, and get from it their greatest blessings.

What is the use of holding on to life—unless at the same time you hold on to your faith? What is the use of going through the daily grind, the wearisome drudgery— if you have given up hoping for the rewards, and unseeing, let them pass you by?

YESTERDAY ENDED LAST NIGHT

Suppose business and industry did that? How far would they get? It is simply by holding on hopefully, believingly, watchfully—as Kipling put it: "Forcing heart and nerve and sinew to serve your turn long after they are gone, and so hold on when there is nothing in you except the will which says to them: 'Hold on'"—that many a businessman has worked out his salvation.

It is not enough to work. The horse and the ox do that. And when we work without thought, without hope, we are no better than they. It is not enough to merely hold on. The poorest creatures often do that mechanically, for lack of the courage to let go.

If you are to gain the reward of your labors, if you are to find relief from your drudgery, you must hold on hopefully, believingly, confidently—knowing that the answer is in the great heart of God, knowing that the Creative Force working through you will give it to you, the moment you have prepared yourself to receive it.

It is never the gifts that are lacking. It is never the Creative Force that is backward in fulfilling our desires. It is we who are unable to see, who fail to recognize the good, because our thoughts are of discouragement and lack.

So never let yesterday's failure discourage you. As T. C. Howard wrote in *Forbes* Magazine:

"Yesterday's gone—it was only a dream; Of the past there is naught but remembrance. Tomorrow's a vision thrown on Hope's screen, A will-o'-the-wisp, a mere semblance.

"Why mourn and grieve over yesterdays ills And paint memory's pictures with sorrow? Why worry and fret—for worrying kills—
Over things that won't happen tomorrow?

"Yesterday's gone—it has never returned—
Peace to its ashes, and calm;
Tomorrow no human has ever discerned,
Still hope, trust, and faith are its balm.

YESTERDAY ENDED LAST NIGHT

"This moment is all that I have as my own,
To use well, or waste, as I may; But I know that my future depends alone On the
way that I live today.

"This moment my past and my future I form;
I may make them whatever I choose
By the deeds and the acts that I now perform,
By the words and thoughts that I use.

"So I fear not the future nor mourn o'er the past
For I do all I'm able today,
Living each present moment as though 'twere my last; Perhaps it is! Who
knows! Who shall say?"

"Duty and today are ours," a great man once wrote. "Results and the future belong to God." And wise old Emerson echoed the same thought. "All that I have seen," he said, "teaches me to trust the Creator for all I have not seen." In short, a good daily prayer might be one I read in a magazine recently—"Lord, I will keep on rowing. YOU steer the boat!"

Easy enough to say, perhaps you are thinking, but you never knew such disaster as has befallen me. I am broken down with sickness, or crippled by accident, or ruined financially, or something else equally tragic. Shakespeare wrote the answer to your case when he told us—"When Fortune means to man most good, she looks upon him with a threatening eye."

In the town of Enterprise, Ala., there is a monument erected by its citizens for services done them. And you could never guess to whom it is dedicated. To the Boll Weevil!

In olden days, the planters living thereabouts raised only cotton. When cotton boomed, business boomed. When the cotton market was off—or the crop proved poor—business suffered correspondingly.

Then came the Boll Weevil. And instead of merely a poor crop, left no crop at all.

YESTERDAY ENDED LAST NIGHT

The Boll Weevil ruined everything. Debt and discouragement were all it left in its wake.

But the men of that town must have been lineal descendants of those hardy fighters who stuck to the bitter end in that long-drawn-out struggle between North and South. They got together and decided that what their town and their section needed was to stop putting all their eggs into one basket.

Instead of standing or falling by the cotton crop, diversify their products! Plant a dozen different kinds of crops. Even though one did fail, even though the market for two or three products happened to be off, the average would always be good.

Correct in theory, certainly. But, as one of their number pointed out, how were the planters to start? They were over their heads in debt already. It would take money for seeds and equipment, to say nothing of the fact that they had to live until the new crops came in.

So the townsfolk raised the money—at the Lord only knows what personal sacrifices—and financed the planters.

The result? Such increased prosperity that they erected a monument to the Boll Weevil, and on it they put this inscription:

"In profound appreciation of the Boll Weevil, this monument is erected by the citizens of Enterprise, Coffee Co., Ala."

Many a man can look back and see where some Boll Weevil—some catastrophe that seemed tragic at the time—was the basis of his whole success in life. Certainly that has been the case with one man I know.

When he was a tot of five, he fell into a fountain and all but drowned. A passing workman pulled him out as he was going down for the last time. The water in his lungs brought on asthma, which, as the years went on, kept growing worse and worse, until the doctors announced that death was only a matter of months. Meantime, he couldn't run, he couldn't play like other children; he couldn't even climb the stairs!

A sufficiently tragic outlook, one would say. Yet out of it came the key to fortune and success.

YESTERDAY ENDED LAST NIGHT

Since he could not play with the other children, he early developed a taste for reading. And as it seemed so certain that he could never do anything worthwhile for himself, what more natural than that he should long to read the deeds of men who had done great things. Starting with the usual boy heroes, he came to have a particular fondness for true stories of such men as Lincoln, Edison, Carnegie, Hill and Ford—men who started out as poor boys, without any special qualifications or advantages, and built up great names solely by their own energy and grit and determination.

Eventually he cured himself completely of his asthma—but that is another story. The part that is pertinent to this tale is that from the time he could first read until he was seventeen, he was dependent for amusement almost entirely upon books. And from his reading of the stories of men who had made successes, he acquired not only the ambition to make a like success of himself, but the basic principles on which to build it.

Today, as a monument to his Boll Weevil, there stands a constantly growing, successful business, worth millions, with a vast list of customers that swear by— not at—its founder. And he is still a comparatively young man, healthy, active, putting in eight or ten hours at work every day, an enthusiastic horseman, a lover of all sports.

"There is no handicap, either hereditary or environmental, which cannot be compensated, if you are not afraid to try." Thus wrote one of New York's greatest psychiatrists. "No situation in our heredity or in our environment can compel us to remain unhappy. No situation need discourage one or hold him back from finding a degree of happiness and success."

Age, poverty, ill-health—none of these things can hold back the really determined soul. To him they are merely steppingstones to success—spurs that urge him on to greater things. There is no limit upon you—except the one you put upon yourself.

"Ships sail east, and ships sail west, By the very same breezes that blow; It's the set of the sails, And not the gales, That determine where they go."

Men thought they had silenced John Bunyan when they threw him into prison. But he produced "Pilgrim's Progress" on twisted paper used as a cork for the milk jug.

Men thought that blind Milton was done. But he dictated "Paradise Lost."

YESTERDAY ENDED LAST NIGHT

Like the revolutionist of whom Tolstoy wrote—"You can imprison my body, but you cannot so much as approach my ideas."

You cannot build walls around a thought. You cannot imprison an idea. You cannot cage the energy, the enthusiasm, the enterprise of an ambitious spirit.

This it is that distinguishes us from the animals. This it is that makes us in very truth Sons of God.

"Waste no tears Upon the blotted record of lost years, But turn the leaf And smile, oh, smile to see The fair, white pages that remain for thee."

—ELLA WHEELER WILCOX

CHAPTER   10

THE UNDYING FIRE

"I want to do one kindly deed each day To help someone to find a better way. I want to lend a hand to one in need Or find some lonely stray that I may feed. I want to sing for someone a loved song To give them courage when the road is long. If just one smile of mine can lighten pain Then I shall feel I have not lived in vain."

—LENA STEARNSBOLTON

IN AN OLD NEWSPAPER CLIPPING, I read of a fire on the hearth of a farmhouse in Missouri that has not been out for a hundred years.

When the builder of that old homestead left Kentucky with his young bride a hundred years ago, he took with him some live coals from the home fireplace, swinging in an iron pot slung from the rear axle of his prairie schooner. Matches were unknown in those days, and the making of fire from flint and steel was too uncertain. So all through the long trek from Kentucky to Missouri, he kept that little fire alive, finally transferring it to his new log cabin home.

There his children grew and prospered. There he lived and there he died—by the light and warmth of that living fire. And so it must be with love—an undying fire.

The ancient Greeks had a legend that all things were created by love. In the beginning, all were happy. Love reigned supreme, and life was everywhere. Then one night while Love slept, Hate came—and everything became discordant, unhappy, dying.

Thereafter, when the sun of Love rose, life was renewed, happiness abounded. But when the night of Hate came, then came discord too, and sorrow and ashes. And truly without love, life would be dead...a thing of wormwood and death.

"I have seen tenderness and pity trace
A line of beauty on a homely face,
And dull and somewhat ordinary eyes
Made brilliant by a flash of glad surprise,
And lips relax and soften happily
At unexpected generosity.
But, oh, what strange, delightful mystery
Is there in love's breath-taking alchemy,
With power to take a drab, gray chrysalis
And form such radiant loveliness as this!"

—OPALW INSTEAD

The most fascinating women in history—Cleopatra, Helen of Troy, Catherine the Great, Queen Elizabeth, the Pompadour—none of them had beautiful features. Cleopatra's nose was much too big—but that didn't keep her from holding the ruler of the then-known world under her thumb for ten long years, and after his death, subjugating Anthony in his turn.

Of course, she had something else—as did all these famous women of history—something stronger, more subtle, more fascinating than beauty. She had charm—that enticing, bewildering thing called feminine charm; the same charm that is born in every daughter of Eve who has the brains to use it.

What is charm? Charm is something in the glance of the eyes, the turn of the head, the touch of the hand, that sends an electric thrill through every fiber of the one at whom it is directed, that speeds up his rate of motion. Charm is taking the gifts that God has given you and keeping them supernally young and fresh and alive. Charm is being so exquisitely buoyant and full of life, *keeping the magnet within you so surcharged with the joy of life*, that even poor features are lost sight of in the bewitching attraction of the whole.

Charm is keeping your loveliness all through life. It is holding on to your ability to stir the pulses and speed up the rate of motion of the one you love.

THE UNDYING FIRE

"For those we love, we venture many things,
The thought of them gives spirit flaming wings,
For those we love, we labor hard and long,
To dream of them stirs in the heart a song.
For those we love, no task can be too great,
We forge ahead, defying adverse fate.
For those we love, we seek Life's highest goal,
And find contentment deep within the soul."

"Though we travel the world over to find the beautiful," wrote Emerson, "we must carry it with us or we find it not." Charm is not to be bought in jars or bottles. Nor is beauty. Both must come from within. Both spring from that magnet of life which is the Creative Force within us.

There are women who seem to have been born tired—never exactly sick, never entirely well. They don't go out because they don't get any fun out of play. They are sallow, listless, having neither charm nor personality, because they have allowed the magnet of life within them to run down. To them I would say—renew your health first, renew your energy and vigor, renew your interest in those around you, speed up your own rate of motion—then begin to look for love. "For love," says Browning, "is energy of life."

"For life, with all it yields of joy or woe
And hope and fear,
Is just our chance of the prize of learning love—
How love might be, hath been indeed, and is."

How to inspire love in another? By first cultivating it in yourself. Love begets love, you know. Charge your mental magnet with thoughts of unselfish love and devotion, give to the loved one in your thoughts the admiration, the appreciation, the idealized service you would like to give in reality—and as you give, love will come back to you.

Love is giving. It cannot be jealous, for it seeks only the good of the one loved.

95

"Blessed is he that truly loves and seeketh not love in return," said St. Francis of Assisi. "Blessed is he that serves and desires not to be served. Blessed is he that doeth good unto others and seeketh not that others do good unto him."

Love such as that is never lost or wasted. It comes back as surely as the morrow's sun—oftentimes not from the one to whom you sent it, but it comes back, nevertheless, blessed and amplified. As Barrie says—"Those who bring happiness into the lives of others cannot keep it from themselves."

And Ella Wheeler Wilcox wrote—

> *"Who giveth love to all*
> *Pays kindness for unkindness, smiles for frowns*
> *And lends new courage to each fainting heart,*
> *And strengthens hope and scatters joy abroad."*

Why is it that many married women grow old quickly, lose their youthful lines and rounded cheeks, get sallow and wane while their husbands are still in their prime?

Bearing children? There are thousands of women with three and four and five children who still look as youthful as when they married.

Work? A reasonable amount of work is good for every woman. Then what is the reason?

STRAIN—unending, unceasing strain. There is not a servant in this country that you could hire to work every day and all day, without any period of freedom, any day of rest. Yet many men think nothing of making their wives do it.

When Taylor, the great efficiency engineer, was called in to re-organize the work of a certain foundry, he found a number of men with wheel-barrows engaged in carting pig iron from the pile in the yard to the cupola. They worked continuously, without rest except for lunch, and careful checking showed that each man carted from twelve to fifteen tons of pig iron a day. At the end of the day they were worn out.

Taylor took one of the men (an entirely average man), stood over him with a watch, and had him work exactly in accordance with his directions. He would have him load his barrow with pig iron, wheel it over to the cupola, dump it—then sit down and rest, utterly relaxing for a minute or more. When the minute was up, he would go through the same performance—and again rest.

It took two or three days to figure out the best periods of rest, but at the end of the week, Taylor's man was carting forty-five tons of pig iron every day, where before he had carted twelve to fifteen! And at the end of the day he was still fresh, where before he had been worn out.

If you have ever seen an army on the march, you know that no matter how great the hurry, the men are allowed to fall out for five minutes in every hour, and completely relax. Why? Because it has been found that this relaxation and rest enables them to march farther and faster.

There is not an organ in the body that does not require and take its period of rest, from the heart and lungs to the stomach and digestive tracts. Yet many a wife and mother goes all day and every day with never a moment of relaxation, never a minute when her nerves are not taut with strain. Is it any wonder they grow old years before their time? Is it any wonder they are nervous and irritable, unhappy themselves and making those around them depressed and unhappy?

To every such mother, I would say, first—relax. Sit down, lie down, every chance you get—*and just let go!* Don't listen for the baby—don't worry about dinner. Just blissfully relax—even if only for a minute or two at a time. If you can multiply those minutes by a dozen times a day, you will be surprised how much better you feel when night comes.

Give your inner magnet a chance to renew itself. Remember, the first essential toward speeding up your rate of motion is to relax, to get rid of your tensions, to LET the Creative Force work through you. Only then can you draw to you kindred elements of good.

> *"I pray the prayer the Easterns do,*
> *May the peace of God abide with you.*
> *Wherever you stop—wherever you go—*
> *May the beautiful palms of God grow;*
> *Thru days of love and nights of rest*
> *May the love of sweet God make you blest.*
> *I touch my heart as the Easterns do*
> *May the love of God abide with you."*

CHAPTER 11

PRAYER

"But the stars throng out in their glory,
And they sing of the God in man;
They sing of the mighty Master,
Of the loom His fingers span,
Where a star or a soul is part of the whole,
And weft in the wondrous plan."

—ROBERT SERVICE

IF YOU WOULD know the surest way of speeding up your rate of motion, and overtaking the things you desire, try PRAYER!

But when I say "prayer", I don't mean the begging kind. I don't mean a lot of vain repetitions, that seldom have the attention even of the one repeating them, much less of the Lord. Go to the Bible, and you will learn how to pray.

Out of 600,000 words in the Old Testament, only six, when literally translated, mean to "ask for" things in prayer, and each of these six is used but once.

Against that, the word "palal" is used hundreds of times to signify "to pray." And "palal" means— "To judge yourself to be a marvel of creation; to recognize amazing wonders deep within your soul."

Wouldn't that seem to indicate that prayer was meant to be a realization of the powers deep within you? Wouldn't you judge that all you need to do is to expand

98

your consciousness to take in whatever it is that you desire?

"What things soever you ask for when you pray, believe that ye receive them, and ye shall have them." You are not to think of your lacks and needs. You are to visualize the things you want! You are not to worry about this debt or that note, but mentally see the Infinite Supply all about you. "All that you need is near ye, God is complete supply. Trust, have faith, then hear ye, dare to assert the 'I'."

Remember this: If you pray to God, but keep your attention on your problem, you will still have your problem. You'll run into it and continue to run into it as long as you keep your attention focused upon it. What you must do is fix your attention upon God—upon His goodness, His love, His power to remedy any ill or adjust any untoward condition. Focus your attention upon these, and these are the conditions you will run into.

Prayer is expansion, and expansion of yourself into the God-self all around you. As Kahlil Gibran describes it in his great book "The Prophet"—"For what is prayer but the expansion of yourself into the living ether. When you pray, you rise to meet in the air those who are praying at that very hour, and whom save in prayer you may not meet. Therefore let your visit to the temple invisible be for naught save ecstasy and sweet communion. I cannot teach you to pray in words. God listens not to your words save when He Himself utters them through your lips."

Prayer is a realization of your Oneness with God, and of the infinite power this gives you. It is an acceptance of the fact that there is nothing on earth you cannot have—once you have mentally accepted the fact that you CAN have it. Nothing you cannot do—once your mind has grasped the fact that you CAN do it.

Prayer, in short, is thanksgiving for the infinite good God *has* given you. The word most often used for "prayer" in the Bible means—"To sing a song of joy and praise." And see how often you are adjured to "Praise the Lord and be thankful, that THEN shall the earth yield her increase." Probably no life chronicled in the Scriptures was more beset with trials and dangers than that of King David. And what was his remedy? What brought him through all tribulations to power and riches? Just read the Psalms of David and you will see.

PRAYER

"God reigneth; let the earth rejoice;
Let the multitude of isles be glad.
Bless God, O my soul;
And all that is within me, bless his His holy name...
Who forgiveth all thine iniquities;
Who healeth all thy diseases."

Throughout the Bible we are told—"In everything by prayer and supplication WITH THANKSGIVING let your requests be made known unto God." Again and again the root of inspiration and attainment is stressed: Rejoice, be glad, praise, give thanks! "Prove me now herewith, saith the Lord of Hosts, if I will not open you the window of Heaven and pour you out a blessing, that there shall not be room enough to receive it."

The most complete interpretation of prayer I have heard came from the man who wrote—"Once I used to say 'Please.' Now I say, 'Thank you.'" "Enter into His gates with thanksgiving," the Psalmist bade us, "and into His courts with praise. Be thankful unto Him and bless His name."

Someone has said that prayer is the spirit of God pronouncing His works good. "This is the day the Lord hath made. We will rejoice and be glad in it." It is sound psychology as well, as Prof. Wm. James of Harvard testified. "If you miss the joy," he wrote, "you miss all."

Complete, wholehearted reliance upon God—that is the prayer of faith. Not an imploring of God for some specific thing, but a clear, unquestioning recognition that the power to be and do and have the things you want is inherent in you, that you have only to recognize this power and put your trust in it to get anything of good you wish.

But perhaps you have prayed long and fervently for some particular thing, and it has not come? What then? Has it ever occurred to you that the answer was there, but you didn't receive it because you were not ready or willing to accept it?

God always answers prayer. Over and over He tells us this. The answer to your prayer is as sure as tomorrow's sunrise. YOU are the one who is not sure. You are not sure, and so you do not accept the answer.

PRAYER

If you accepted it, you would act on it, wouldn't you? Did you ever act upon the answer to those long and fervent prayers of yours? Yet that is the way it must be, if you are to pray for an answer— and GET it. If you pray for health, you must accept health. You must act as though you already had it. If you pray for other things, you must accept them at once and start doing—even on the smallest scale—the things you would do when the answer to your prayer became evident.

Dr. Alexis Carrel, the brilliant scientist who for many years headed the Rockefeller Institute, stated that, "prayer is the most powerful form of energy one can generate."

"The influence of prayer on the human mind and body," Dr. Carrel went on to say, "is as demonstrable as that of secreting glands. Its results can be measured in terms of increased physical buoyancy, greater intellectual vigor, moral stamina, and a deeper understanding of the realities underlying human relationships... Prayer is as real as terrestrial gravity. As a physician, I have seen men, after all other therapy had failed, lifted out of disease and melancholy by the serene effort of prayer. It is the only power in the world that seems to overcome the so-called 'laws of nature', the occasions on which prayer has dramatically done this have been termed 'miracles.' But a constant, quieter miracle takes place hourly in the hearts of men and women who have discovered that prayer supplies them with a steady flow of sustaining power in their daily lives."

An old peasant was kneeling alone in a village church, long after the services had ended. "What are you waiting for?" the priest asked him. "I am looking at Him," the peasant replied, "and He is looking at me." That is prayer, of the kind that Emerson said—"No man ever prayed without learning something."

"I never try to do my work by my own power alone.
When I begin I make my prayer before God's holy throne.
I ask that His Almighty power may work its will through me
And so each task is done with ease;
I'm charged with power, you see."

—HANNAH ORTH

PRAYER

It was said in the Vedas that if two people would unite their forces, they could conquer the world, though singly they might be powerless. And psychologists and metaphysicians everywhere agree that the power of two minds united in a single cause is not merely their individual powers added together, but multiplied manifold.

Perhaps this can best be explained in terms of electrical power. Take an ordinary magnet capable of lifting, let us say, 10 pounds of iron. Wrap this magnet with wire and charge it with the current from a small battery, it will lift—not merely ten pounds, but a hundred pounds or more!

That is what happens when one person prays and believes, and another adds his prayer and his faith. If you were stuck in a muddy road with a heavily loaded two-horse wagon, and I were stuck with another right behind you, what would be the quickest way out? To unhitch my horses, would it not, couple them on to your wagon tongue and let the two teams pull you out. They could then take my wagon in its turn and pull it onto solid ground. What neither team could accomplish alone, the two pulling together could easily do.

Have you ever noticed a locomotive pulling a long train of cars? To START such a train takes 90% of the locomotive's power. To keep it running on a smooth stretch takes less than 1%. So, a freight locomotive must have nearly a hundred times as much power as it needs for ordinary smooth running.

You are like a locomotive in that. To start you on the road to success requires every bit of energy you can muster. To keep you there, once you have reached the top, needs only a fraction of your abilities. The locomotive must carry its extra 99% of power as a reserve, to start it again when it stops for orders or water or to pick up or unload freight, or to carry it over a heavy grade. It can do nothing with all that extra energy at other times, except blow off steam.

But what about you? You need your full 100% to get started. Probably there are many times when you draw upon all of it to carry you through some grave difficulty, to push aside some obstacle that bars your way. But for the most part, you just carry that extra energy as reserve. What can you do with it? Find outlets for it.

PRAYER

All around you are men and women—earnest, hardworking men and women—who have put their hearts into their work, but lack some of the 100% energy that would start them on the road to success. They are like freight locomotives that are perfect engines, but not quite up to the task of starting as heavy a train as has been given them. Give them a push, help them to get started or over the hump of some obstacle or difficulty, and they will go far. But getting started is too much for them alone.

Why should you do this? Because only thus can you profit from that excess energy you have to carry for emergencies, but which you so seldom use. How do you profit? Through the additional reserve power it brings you. A stalled train is a useless thing. Worse than that, it is an encumbrance, in the way of everything else that uses the line. It may be generating all but 10% of the power required to move it, but without that 10%, the 90% is useless. So the 10% you furnish to get it started is of as much value to it as the 90% it furnishes, and is entitled to as great reward. When you help another in that way, you have in effect grub-staked him, and you share in the spiritual power that his success brings him. As Edwin Markham put it in his little poem—

"There is a destiny that mates us brothers; No man goes his way alone;

All that we send into the lives of others Comes back into our own."

So whenever you have some earnest purpose, or want to help a friend or loved one to accomplish some greatly cherished ambition, unite in prayer for a few minutes each day until you have brought about the answer to that desire.

And when praying alone, remember:

First, center your thoughts *on the thing that you want*—not on your need.

Second, read the 91st and the 23rd Psalms, just as a reminder of God's power and His readiness to help you in all your needs.

Third, *be thankful,* not merely for past favors, *but for granting of this favor you are now asking.* To be able to thank God for it sincerely, in advance of its actual material manifestation, is the finest evidence of belief.

PRAYER

Fourth, BELIEVE! Picture the thing that you want so clearly, see it in your imagination so vividly, that you can actually BELIEVE THAT YOU HAVE IT!

It is this sincere conviction, registered upon your subconscious mind that brings the answer to your prayers. Once convince your subconscious mind that you HAVE the thing that you want, and you can forget it and go on to your next problem. Mind will attend to the rest. So "sing and rejoice" that you HAVE the answer to your prayer. Literally shout for joy, as did the Sons of God in days of old.

Fifth, remember Emerson's advice—"Do the thing and you shall have the power."

Start doing— even on a small scale—whatever it is that you will do when the answer to your prayer is materially evident. In other words, ACCEPT the thing you have asked for! Accept it—and start using it.

> *"If you have faith in God, or man, or self,*
> *Say so; if not, push back upon the shelf*
> *Of silence all your thoughts till faith shall come.*
> *No one will grieve because your lips are dumb."*

> —ELLA WHEELER WILCOX

The Secret of
Gold

How to Get What You Want

Robert Collier

CONTENTS

FOREWORD: The Riddle of the Sphinx

"WHAT is it," asked the Sphinx, "that walks on four legs in the morning, on two legs at noon and on three legs in the evening?" And all who passed her way had to answer that question—*or be devoured!*

That was the Riddle of the Sphinx of olden days. But to modern man has come a far more difficult one—

"How can I earn more money? How can I make enough to get the necessities and the comforts of life to which my family and I are entitled?"

That is the eternal question which confronts you and will haunt you every day until you solve it. That is the present-day Riddle of the Sphinx that devours all who fail to answer it.

For lack is the greatest evil that mankind has to contend with.

Yet every man knows that in this old earth of ours are riches and abundance sufficient not merely for every soul now on this planet—but for all who ever will be! And in the very first chapter of the Bible, It is written that, "God gave man dominion over all the earth."

Not only that, but more than half the prophecies in the Scriptures refer to the time when man shall possess the earth. When tears and sorrow shall be unknown. When riches and abundance shall be yours for the taking.

That time is here—here and now for those who understand the power and the availability of that mysterious, half recognized Spirit within which so few people know, but which, fully understood, can do anything.

But in no book ever written is there any complete explanation of this Spirit within, any complete directions for availing one's-self of its infinite power and understanding. In no book, that is, but one!

And in the following pages I shall show you what that one Book is and

6

where to find the directions which tell you how to harness this truly illimitable power, how to make it bring to you anything of good you may desire. For—

"There hath not failed one word of all His good promises, which He promised by the hand of Moses, His servant."—I. KINGS, 8:56.

— ROBERT COLLIER

Chapter 1: The Genii of the Lamp

"Thou gavest also Thy Good Spirit to instruct them, and withheldest not thy manna from their mouth, and gavest them water for their thirst."—NEHEMIAH 9:20.

IN AN ancient town in far off Cathay, there once lived a poor young man named Aladdin. His father had been a tailor, but died before he could teach his profession to his son, and the boy and his widowed mother were frequently hard put to get enough to eat.

But despite his poverty, Aladdin was one of those cheerful souls who find life good. Many and often were the times that found him wandering joyfully in the mountains, when he should have been seeking the elusive yen in some odd job among his neighbors. And Fortune, looking down upon his cheery hopefulness, smiled—as has been the habit of Fortune since time began—for then, as now, she was a fickle jade, loving most those who worry least about her.

One day, wandering among the hills, Aladdin discovered a cave, its entrance closed by a great stone. Prying the stone away, he entered, and found therein a lamp burning upon a shelf. Thinking to use it at home, Aladdin stuck the lamp in his belt and, departing, took it with him.

Next morning, lacking the wherewithal for breakfast, he bethought him of this lamp, and since it looked old and tarnished, started to polish it in the hope of thus bringing for it a better price. What was his astonishment and terror to see immediately appear before him a Genii of gigantic proportions, who, however, made humble obeisance: "I am the slave of the lamp," quoth he, "ready to do the bidding of him who holds the lamp. What would you of me?"

Terrified though he was, Aladdin could understand that. So he took heart of grace, and decided to see if this great Genii really was as good as his word. "I am hungry," he therefore told him. "Bring me something to eat." The Genii disappeared. An instant later he was back again with a sumptuous repast!

Aladdin ate and was satisfied. And when next he hungered, summoned the Genii and ate again. Thereafter, to one so used to hunger, life was one grand song—just one endless succession of eating and sleeping, sleeping and eating again.

Until one day the Sultan's daughter passed that way. Her eyes had the mischievous sparkle in their depths that has drawn hermits from their cells. Her lips were twin rubies. Her teeth pearls.

So much Aladdin saw—and was enchanted. Life took on a new meaning. There was more to it than eating and sleeping after all. Here was something to live for, work for, hope for. Even though at the moment it never occurred to him that he might ever hope to win such loveliness, such divinity, for himself.

But then he bethought him of his Genii. If the Genii could bring him food, raiment, riches—why not position and power, too? Why not the Sultan's daughter? Why not, in fact, the Sultan's place? He decided to try.

First he astonished the Sultan with the magnificence of the gifts with which his good Genii furnished him. Then he built a palace more beautiful far than that of the Sultan himself. Finally he presented himself as suitor for the hand of the beautiful princess.

The Sultan laughed at the idea. But one cannot continue to laugh at a man whose raiment is more costly, whose retinue more splendid, whose palace more magnificent than one's own. One can only vie with him in splendour, and failing that—either fight him or take him into one's own camp.

The Sultan tried to vie with him. But princely riches could not compare with those of the Genii. He tried fighting. But who could hope to cope with the powers of the invisible world?

At last he decided to share that wealth, to benefit by that power. And so it came about that Aladdin won the lovely Princess of his dreams.

Fairy tales—you will say. And of course, they are. But back of them is more than mere childish fable. There is the Wisdom and the Mysticism of the East—so frequently hidden in parable or fable.

For those Wise Men of the East had grasped, thousands of years ago, the fundamental fact—so hard for our Western minds to realize—that deep down within ourselves, far under our outer layers of consciousness, is a Power that far transcends the power of any conscious mind.

"The Holy Spirit within us," deeply religious people term it. And, truly, its power is little short of Divine.

"Our Subconscious Mind," so the Scientists call it.
Call it what you will, it is there—all unknown to most of us—a sleeping Giant who, aroused, can carry us on to fame and fortune overnight; A Genii-of-the-Brain more powerful, more the servant of our every right wish, than was ever Aladdin's fabled Genii-of-the-Lamp of old.

Health and happiness, power and riches, lie ready to its hand. You have but to wake it, to command it, to get of it what you will. It is part of you—yet its power is limitless. It is Mind—Thought—Idea. It is an all-powerful mental magnet that can draw to you anything you may desire.

Just as electricity turns the inert electric bulb into a thing of light and life—just as the gasoline vapor turns your motor into a creature of speed and action—just as steam awakens the locomotive into an engine of power and usefulness—so this mental magnet can vitalize YOU into a Being capable of accomplishing ANY TASK YOU MAY SET, capable of rising to any height, capable of winning love, honor and riches.

You have seen hypnotists put subjects to sleep. You have seen men and women, while in this hypnotic trance, do marvelous feats of mind reading or of mental arithmetic. You have seen others show wonderful endurance or physical strength.

I remember one hypnotist who, after putting his subject in a trance, would assure him that he (the subject) was a bar of iron. Then the hypnotist would stretch him out between two chairs—his head on one, his feet on another—and pile weights upon him, or have several people stand upon him. A feat of strength that the subject could never have accomplished in his ordinary mind. Yet did it without strain or difficulty under the influence of the hypnotist.

How did he do it? Simply by removing the control of the conscious mind—by putting it to sleep—and leaving the Subconscious in sole charge. The power is in your body to do anything—only your conscious mind doesn't believe that it is. Remove these conscious inhibitions—place the Subconscious in entire charge—and there is nothing beyond your capacity to perform.

The hypnotist does his tricks by putting your conscious mind to sleep and then suggesting to your Subconscious the things he wants it to do. But it is in no wise necessary to deal with the Subconscious through some third party. It is no part of the Divine plan that you must first put yourself under some outside control. On the contrary, those who learn to use their own Subconscious Minds can accomplish far greater wonders with their bodies, with their brains, with their fortunes than could any hypnotist for them.

It is to show you how to properly use this Genii-of-your-Mind, how to summon it, how to control it, that this Course is written.

"But where shall wisdom be found? And where is the place of understanding?"—JOB
28:12.

"There is a Spirit in man; and the inspiration of the Almighty giveth him understanding."—JOB 32:8.

Chapter 2: The Spirit Within

YOU often hear a man spoken of as brainy. The idea being that he has more gray matter in his cranium than most of us. And for years the size of a man's head or the shape of his "bumps" was believed to indicate his mentality.

But science now shows that one man has just as good brains as another. Differences in weight or shape or size have nothing to do with it. Each of us has a perfect brain to start with. It is what we put *into* it and the way we *use* it that counts—not the size or weight!

Brains are merely the storehouse of the mind. They are not the mind itself. Each individual brain cell—and there are some nine billions of them—is like a phonograph record on which impressions are registered through the thousands of nerves from all over the body that center in the brain.

Once registered, that impression stays as long as the brain cell remains. When we have no occasion to use an impression for a long time, it is filed away in the nine-billion filing compartment—and apparently forgotten.

But it is never really forgotten. It can always be recalled by the proper suggestion to the subconscious mind. The only thing that can permanently destroy the impression is the removal of the brain cell itself. That is why injuries to the brain so frequently result in complete loss of memory as to many events in the individual's life.

But the registering of impressions is merely the first step. The animals have that. The next—and the step that puts man so far above all other creatures—is the reasoning mind. Mind uses the brain cells to recall any impression it may need. To compare them. To draw conclusions from them. In short, to reason!

Chapter 2: The Spirit Within

That is the most important province of mind. But it has another—the regulating, governing and directing of the growth and functions of the body. So complicated an affair that no conscious mind in the universe could ever grope with it.

Yet the subconscious mind does it with ease—does it for the youngest infant as well as for you or me—in fact, frequently does it better.

From the earliest moment of our birth, the subconscious mind takes control. It directs the beating of the heart, the breathing of the lungs, the complicated processes of digestion and assimilation. And the less it is interfered with, the better work it does.

Your body is the most wonderful and complicated chemical factory in the world. Made up of water, coal, iron, lime, sugar, phosphorus, salt, hydrogen and iodine, no man living could figure out the changes made necessary in its composition from minute to minute by heat, by cold, by pressure from without or by food taken within. No chemist in all the world could tell you how much water you should drink to neutralize the excess salt in salt fish. How much you lose through perspiration. How much water, how much salt, how much of each different element in your food should be absorbed into your blood each day to maintain perfect health.

Yet your subconscious mind knows. Knows without effort. Knows even when you are an infant. And furthermore, acts immediately upon that knowledge.

To quote the Rev. Wm. T. Walsh—"The subconscious mind directs all the vital processes of our body. You do not think consciously about breathing. Every time you take a breath you do not have to reason, decide, command. The SUBCONSCIOUS MIND sees to that. You have not been at all conscious that you have been breathing while you have been reading this page. So it is with the mind and the circulation of blood. The heart is a muscle like the muscle of your arm. It has no power to move itself or to direct its action. Only mind, only something that can think, can direct our muscles, including the heart. You are not conscious that you are commanding your heart to beat. The subconscious mind attends to that. And so it is with the assimilation of food, the building and repairing of the body. In fact, all the vital processes are looked after by the subconscious mind."

Whence comes all this wonderful knowledge? Whence comes the intelligence that enables day-old infants to figure out problems in chemistry that would confound the most learned professors? Whence but from the same Mind that regulates the planets in their courses, that puts into the acorn the image of the mighty oak it is to be, and then shows it how to draw from the sunlight, from the air, from the earth, from the water, the nutriment necessary to build that image into reality.

That Mind is God. And the subconscious in us is our part of Divinity. It is the Holy Spirit within.

The Bible teaches one Universal God, Father of all things, *the life of all things animate.*
And modern science shows us that all things are animate—even the rocks and the dirt beneath our feet. Even the supposedly dead piece of paper on which these words are printed. All are made up of tiny particles called atoms. And the atoms in turn consist of protons and electrons—bits of electrical energy, so minute as to be invisible to the naked eye, but very much alive and constantly moving, constantly changing.

In *The Secret of the Ages,* the consistency of matter is explained in detail. For those who have not read this explanation, suffice it here to quote from the *New York Herald-Tribune:*

"We used to believe that the universe was composed of an unknown number of different kinds of matter, one kind for each chemical element. The discovery of a new element had all the interest of the unexpected. It might turn out to be anything, to have any imaginable set of properties.

"That romantic prospect no longer exists. We know now that instead of many ultimate kinds of matter there are only two kinds. Both of these are really kinds of electricity. One is negative electricity, being, in fact, the tiny particle called the electron, familiar to radio fans as one of the particles vast swarms of which operate radio vacuum tubes. The other kind of electricity is positive electricity. Its ultimate particles are called protons. From these protons and electrons all of the chemical elements are built up. Iron and lead and oxygen and gold and all the others differ from one another merely in the number and arrangement of the electrons and protons which they contain. That is the modern idea of the nature of matter. *Matter is really nothing but electricity.*"

Everything has life in it. And life is God, Therefore, everything in this world, everything in the heavens above, in the earth beneath, or in the waters under the earth, is a manifestation of God.

God is life. He is the life in us. And the life in all created things. He is the "Father" in you. He is the life-force, the God-force, that flows through every atom of your being. Make yourself one with Him, and there is nothing you cannot do.

A great religious teacher once said that there are just two things in the Universe—God and His manifestations. Really there is just one —for God is in all His manifestations.

One of the Bible's greatest teachings is that ALL MEN ARE EQUALLY THE CHILDREN OF GOD!

Just think—if God is the Father of ALL men, then ALL are His children, equally entitled to the good things of life, equally dear to Him! This is the greatest message ever brought to any planet! That *man is the son of God.* That he inherits from the Father all of life, all of wisdom, all of riches, all of power.

God is the Parent. And man's every quality is derived from Him. Not only that, but *man inherits every quality of the Father!* He has only to grow up in knowledge, to learn the Father's ways, to lean trustfully upon the Father's help, in order to be supreme "amid the war of elements, the wreck of matter and the crush of worlds."

Apart from God, man is a weakling, the sport of circumstances, the victim of any force strong enough to overpower or brush him aside.

But let him ally himself with the Father, and he becomes, instead of the creature of law, the ruler through law. Instead of the sport of circumstance, he makes circumstances. Instead of the victim of fire or water or sickness or poverty, he masters the forces of nature, demands health and prosperity as his birthright.

The God that most of us were taught to believe in was a huge patriarchal Man-God, seated upon a throne high up in the skies. A King—stern, righteous and just— chastening His children mercilessly whenever He felt it was for their good. Holding an exact scale between the good they had done and the sins they had committed. And dispensing penances or rewards to balance the two.

Today, we are coming around to the idea of a loving Father-God. A God that is in each one of us, whose "good pleasure it is to give us the Kingdom", and to promise these same powers to us!

How, then, shall we take advantage of our son-ship? How use the infinite power it puts in our hands?

The purpose of this book is to develop the divinity that is in you. What is the first thing to do? Where shall you start? What shall you do?

Chapter 2: The Spirit Within

Reaching Into Infinity

The first essential is to find a point of contact with the Father. Benjamin Franklin sent a kite up into the clouds and brought down along its string a current of electricity. Through him, man has learned to harness this electricity for his daily servant. Franklin made his contact with the source of power.

Thousands of years before Franklin—centuries even before the common era—men began to send up kites (figuratively speaking) trying to contact with the source of life itself.

A few succeeded. A few great Prophets like Elisha, Elijah, Moses, contacted with the Source of all Power, and whenever and as long as they kept that contact, nothing could withstand them.

Franklin caught the source of electrical power, and by learning to understand and work with it, turned those terror-inspiring thunderbolts of destruction into man's greatest friend and servant. The electricity did not change. It is exactly the same now as afore time. It is merely man's conception of it that has changed.

Uncontrolled, lightning was a curse to mankind. Through understanding, man has harnessed it to serve his needs. Touch a button—and it lights your home. Touch another—and it brings to you news and instruction, entertainment and music from hundreds or thousands of miles away. The mere throwing of a switch releases the power of millions of horses. Pulling it out bridles them again. Was ever such a master servant?

Yet it is as nothing to the power latent in the Source of Life—the power of the Father of all things.

Even now, ignorant of this Power as most of us are, we occasionally contact with it, but we do it accidentally—*and we fail*

Chapter 2: The Spirit Within

to maintain the contact.

You know how often inspirational things have "come to you"—snatches of song, or speech, or verse such as man never wrote before. Visions of wonderful achievement. Echoes of great ideas. Glimpses of riches you could almost reach—the riches of the Spirit within.

If only you could tap that boundless Reservoir at will, what success would not be yours, how puny your present accomplishments would seem by comparison!

And you *can* tap it. You can make your contact with Infinity—if not at will—at least with frequency. All that is necessary is understanding and belief.

How to do it? How to go about it? Through the Holy Spirit within you. Through your part of Divinity. Through an understanding of what is commonly known as your Subconscious Mind.

We stumble upon His vast power occasionally—and call our resultant deeds superhuman! We contact now and then with Infinity —and regard the result as a miracle!

There is no such thing as a miracle. The occasional wonder-works that we do—the sudden healing from sickness, the miraculous escape, the answered prayer—are all divinely natural. The miracle is that it happens so seldom. We should be able to establish and keep that contact always! We should be able to contact with and use the power of the Spirit as readily as we now can use the power of electricity.

But just as Franklin had first to determine what the power was that made the lightning, so have you first to learn what is this Holy Spirit within you.

Chapter 2: The Spirit Within

To say that it is the subconscious mind is not enough. It is far more than that. The subconscious mind can be used either for good or for evil. Uncontrolled, it is as great a destructive force as the lightning. If you have read *The Secret of the Ages,* you know that you can suggest thoughts of health or of disease to your subconscious mind, of success or of failure—and whichever image you get across to the subconscious, it will proceed to work out. But the Holy Spirit can be used only for good.

What then is the Holy Spirit?

How do you acquire it? How contact with it?

Have you ever read any of the accounts you occasionally see of people who have been very sick—who have hovered for minutes or for hours right over the Valley of Death—and then come back? Remember their description of how they seemed to be looking down upon themselves, upon the whole scene, as one apart, as one having but a casual interest in what was going on? Remember how some little thing called them back and how frequently they went back with reluctance?

Stewart Edward White had a story in the May *American Magazine* that exactly illustrated the idea. It told of a man who, according to all scientific tests, had died— lay dead, in fact, for two hours. And here, in part, was his description of the experience:

"I was pretty ill before I died, and things about me got somewhat vague and unreal. I suppose I was half dozing, and partly delirious perhaps. I'd slip in and out of focus, as it were. Sometimes I'd see myself and the bed and the room and the people clearly enough; then again I'd sort of drop into an inner reverie inside myself. Not asleep exactly, nor yet awake. You'll get much the same thing sitting in front of a warm fire after a hearty dinner.

"Now, here's a funny one. I don't know if you'll get this: You know these pictures sent by radio? They are all made up of a lot of separate dots, you know. If you enlarged the thing enough, you'd almost lose the picture, wouldn't you? And you'd have a collection of dots with a lot of space between them. Well, that's how I seemed to myself.

"I could contract myself, bring all the dots close together, and there I'd be, solid as a brick church, lying in bed; and I could expand myself until the dots got separated so far that there were mostly spaces between them. And when I did that my body in the bed got very vague to me, because the dots were so far apart they didn't make a picture; and I—the consciousness of me—was somehow the thing in the spaces that held the dots together at all. I found it quite amusing contracting and expanding like that.

"Then I began to think about it. I began to wonder whether I held the dots together, or whether the dots held me together; and I got so interested that I thought I'd try to find out. You see, I wasn't the dots: I—the essence of me, the consciousness of me—was the spaces between the dots, holding them together. I thought to myself, 'I wonder if I can get away from these dots?' So I tried it; and I could. I must say I was a little scared. That body made of dots was a good, solid container. When I left its shelter, it occurred to me that I might evaporate into universal substance, like letting a gas out of a bottle. I didn't; but I certainly was worried for fear I'd burst out somewhere. I felt awfully thin-skinned!"

Remember how you have sometimes had similar experiences in dreams, when you seemed to be a disembodied spirit looking down on yourself from above?

That disembodied self is the soul of you—your subconscious mind. But it is something more, too. Imbue it with understanding of your oneness with the Father, confirm it with a realization of the God-life flowing so abundantly through you—and it becomes, in addition, *the Holy Spirit within you*—one with the Father, one with the Source of Life, of Power, of Abundance. In short, the Holy Spirit within you is your subconscious mind, vitalized through direct contact with the Father.

You have been told time and again how small a part of your real abilities you use when you confine your mental work to your conscious mind. Prof. Wm. James, the world-famous Psychologist, estimated that the average man used only 10 percent of his real abilities, while Dr. Mayo compares the mind to an iceberg—one-fourth above water (the conscious mind), and three-fourths submerged (the subconscious). Think, then, if the use of your subconscious mind adds so much to your abilities, how much your value will be increased if you add to that the infinite power of the Holy Spirit!

As the ordinary man uses it, the subconscious mind is largely a bundle of habits. You practice on the piano merely to set up a certain train of actions and reactions so that, after a time, your subconscious can take over the work from your conscious mind. The skilled pianist can play from memory the most difficult pieces and at the same time carry on a spirited conversation. Why? Because two entirely different provinces of the mind are carrying on their functions—the one through the fingers, the other through speech and hearing.

The same thing applies to every physical avocation. To become really skillful at anything, you must get it into the charge of your subconscious mind. As long as your conscious mind must take active control, you are tense, doubtful, hesitant—you blunder, become excited, fail. Let the action become automatic, however—in other words, let your subconscious have charge of it—and you relax naturally and do whatever is required of you without effort and will.

A man's responsiveness to subconscious reactions is usually the measure of his luck or ill luck in avoiding accidents. In the *New*

Chapter 2: The Spirit Within

York Herald-Tribune there was an editorial recently along this very line entitled—"Whom Ill Luck Pursues":

"The Industrial Fatigue Research Board has made an interesting report on the reasons for industrial accidents. It is already well known to thoughtful managers of factories that some men are persistently unlucky. If any one is to suffer a broken leg, it will be one of these individuals. When minor accidents are being dealt out by Fate these unfortunates never fail to receive more than their reasonable shares. No definite fault can be found with them. They are not noticeably careless or foolhardy. The poor things seem simply to possess an incurable propensity for being at hand when anything happens. Like the conventional innocent bystander, they are, almost by definition, the persons who get hurt.

"Armed with the modern magician's wand of careful record and exact statistical inquiry, two investigators for the research board have traced these instances of persistent ill luck to their cause. No demon of bad luck is concerned, although the uninstructed may well think so when they read that the cause's name is aesthetakinetic co-ordination. Translated into English, this means a lack of that instinct and exact correspondence between warning and action which some people possess and some do not. If a board in the floor is loose and happens to fly up when stepped on, some people will jump instantly and in the right direction. Others will move the wrong way or not at all. If a chair breaks some sitters will land on their feet, others on the floor. Under the conditions of modern civilization it is usually the latter who are being taken to the hospital."

The functions of your body—your heart, lungs, stomach, liver, the continual breaking down and rebuilding of all the cells—these, too, are the province of your subconscious mind. And as long as they are left to it in the full assurance that it knows its work and is tending faithfully to it, all will be well with them.

But let the conscious mind interfere, and as in playing the piano or doing any other difficult stunt, trouble will ensue.

Have you ever seen a football team whose classmates did nothing but "knock" it, tell it how rotten it was individually and collectively, how little chance it had of ever winning a game? You know how little chance that team would have of getting even a single goal.

But take that same team, put a real class spirit behind it, surround it with boosters and urge it on with a stirring college yell—and then watch it go!

So it is with your subconscious mind and your body. It knows perfectly how to rebuild your body—how to keep it well. But if you tell it, in effect, that you have no confidence in its ability to do this —if you are continually trying to take over the control through your doubts and fears and worries—you will soon have a mutinous or discouraged crew on your hands, that no longer believes in you or itself. And the result will be nervousness, apathy, failure.

As the Rev. W. John Murray put it— "Whatever order we issue to the subconscious mind, it promptly undertakes to carry out. Whatever state of existence you declare to be in being, the subconscious mind assumes exists and works within you accordingly. If a friend asks you: How do you feel today? And you reply: I am not well; I have a headache; I am all in; I don't feel up to the mark at all, you are unconsciously setting the subconscious mind to work to realize the state you declare yourself to be in. On the other hand if you say: I am well, happy and strong, the subconscious mind undertakes to realize this state for you.

"Hence you can see what a wonderful power is within your control for your happiness or unhappiness, your condition of body and mind, and how necessary it is for you to use this power always in a positive direction. *You are, in a word, what you think you are.* This is not a theory, a fancy or a fad. It is a law. And the reason why the world is filled with sin, disease, misery and misfortune is because it requires effort to think positive thoughts, while negative thinking is the result of inertia."

But it is not only in running the body-machine that the subconscious shows the power of the Spirit that is behind it. It has all knowledge of outside things as well. Contact with it, and you can learn what you will.

Some time ago there was an article in *The American* telling of the experiences of a convict, formerly the editor of a large newspaper.

Morphine had brought this man to prison. He had started taking it when, as a newspaper man, his body would be so worn out that he could no longer write. By "doping" the conscious mind into unconsciousness, he would bring the subconscious to the fore, with the result that the most wonderful articles flowed from his pen. In one case, without a clue to guide him, he traced a gang of criminals who were in hiding!

But his was not merely an impossible way to contact with the Holy Spirit—it was the wrong way to contact with the subconscious as well—and he paid a fearful price for it.

Take Theodore Roosevelt, on the other hand. When he entered Harvard in 1876, he was thin of chest, be-spectacled, nervous, weighing only 90 pounds. He was afraid to get on his feet and try to make a speech. Compare that with the man he became—the wonder of the world for efficiency, endurance, working power, and joyousness in life. He was a cowboy, a soldier, a lawyer, a statesman, a writer. And he did each of these things phenomenally well.

That is one example of what the right attitude towards the subconscious will do. Then there are those frequent cases you hear about like the one described in *Psychology Magazine.* Henry A.

Chapter 2: The Spirit Within

Wight never studied art—never knew he had any talent for painting. He went into the matter-of-fact-business of steel and coal, and was successful in it. Then when he was getting along in the thirties, he found himself with the desire to paint. So, to use his own laconic explanation, "he did it—that's all." And his monotypes have won the praise of the best critics.

I know a famous songwriter who never studied a note. Her music "just comes to her." I know a man—a successful businessman of nearly fifty—who suddenly started writing poems. Wonderful poems—that have been eagerly accepted by the best magazines. And he doesn't know a rule of prosedy! I know an eminent geologist who never consciously examines a stone. He just walks over his ground abstractedly and then tells—for a very high fee— what is underneath it.

Contacting with the Subconscious—contacting haphazardly, accidentally—yet getting marvelous results while the contact holds!

Whatever you want to know, whatever you wish to do—the knowledge and the power are there.

Ordinary contact with the subconscious is comparatively easy. The first essential is relaxation. To find a really comfortable easy chair or lounge or bed, where one can be quiet, undisturbed, unconscious of oneself and one's surroundings. To stretch luxuriously and then let every muscle relax. To review before your mind's eye every phase of the problem or the subject—not worriedly, not striving for the answer—but merely laying them before the spirit within in the way you would put them before some all-wise Solomon. To *know* that he *has* the answer—and will presently give it to you. To relax thankfully in this knowledge into slumber, with the contented feeling that you have got what you wanted. Do that—and your answer will come.

Chapter 2: The Spirit Within

Dr. W. Hanna Thomson, in "Brain and Personality," gives some instances of how this sometimes works out even when the person doing it has no knowledge of how to put his problem up to his subconscious mind. The first was told him by a fellow student at college. One night his roommate sat up late working at a difficult problem in mathematics. Failing to solve it, he rubbed his slate clean, put out the light and went to bed.

Later on that night the first student was awakened by the light shining in his eyes. Looking up, he saw his friend working away at his slate. The next morning he commented on it, only to have his roommate indignantly deny that he had been up at all during the night. To prove his assertion, the first student got the slate, and there on it was the problem that had puzzled his friend—*all worked out to the correct conclusion!*

The other case Thomson tells of was that of a British Consul in Syria. He had been studying Arabic diligently in an effort to better fit himself for his position, and one night tried to compose a letter to the Emir at Lebanon. After a couple of hours of fruitless effort, he finally lost all patience with the language and the job, and went to bed.

What was his astonishment to find on his desk in the morning a freshly written letter, in his own handwriting, couched in the purest Arabic, that the Slave-of-the-Lamp himself could not have improved upon!
The subconscious mind is your Slave of the Lamp. Use him, in the ways outlined above—and there is no problem he cannot work out for you.

But recognize your relation with God, your oneness with the Source of all life and Power—in short, contact with the Source of Power—and that subconscious mind becomes the Holy Spirit within you, to whom nothing is impossible!

Chapter 3: The Lode Star

THERE once lived in a town of Persia two brothers, one named Cassim, the other Ali Baba. Cassim had married a very rich wife, and become a wealthy but miserly and greedy money-lender. Ali Baba had married a woman as poor as himself, and lived by cutting wood, and bringing it upon his donkeys into the town to sell. But he had married for love and he worked cheerily, asking only of Allah that He watch over his little family and help him to teach his son to tread in the right path.

One day, when Ali Baba was in the forest cutting wood, he saw a great cloud of dust coming towards him from the distance. Observing it attentively, he soon distinguished a body of horsemen, and as honest people had little business that far from the haunts of men he suspected they might be robbers. Greatly frightened, he determined to leave his donkeys and save himself. Yet he was not so frightened as to lose all curiosity, so he climbed up a tree that grew on a high rock, whose branches, while thick enough to conceal him, yet enabled him to see all that passed beneath.

The troop, which numbered about forty, all well mounted and armed, came to the foot of the rock and dismounted. Each man unbridled his horse, tied him to some shrub, and hung about the animal's neck a bag of corn. Then each took off his saddle-bag, which from its weight seemed to Ali Baba to be full of gold and silver. One, whom he took to be their captain, came under the tree in which Ali Baba was concealed; and, making his way through some shrubs, pronounced these words—"Open, Sesame!" The moment the captain of the robbers had thus spoken, a door opened in the rock; and after he had made all his troop enter before him, he followed them, when the door shut again of itself.

The robbers stayed some time within the rock, during which Ali Baba, fearful of being caught, remained in the tree.

Chapter 3: The Lode Star

At last the door opened again, and as the captain went in last, so he came out first, and stood to see them all pass by him. Then Ali Baba heard him make the door close by pronouncing these words, "Shut, Sesame!" The robbers forthwith bridled their horses, and mounted, and when the captain saw them all ready, he put himself at their head, and they returned the way they had come.

Ali Baba followed them with his eyes as far as he could see, and afterward stayed a considerable time before he descended. Remembering the words the captain of the robbers had used to cause the door to open he was curious to see if his pronouncing them would have the same effect. Accordingly, he went among the shrubs, stood before it, and said, "Open, Sesame!" Instantly the door flew wide open.

Ali Baba, who expected a dark, dismal cavern, was surprised to see a well-lighted and spacious chamber, receiving its light from an opening at the top of the rock. Scattered around in profusion were all sorts of rich bales of silk stuff, brocade, and valuable carpeting, gold and silver ingots in great heaps, and money in bags The cave must have been occupied for ages by robbers, one succeeding another.

Ali Baba fell on his knees and thanked Allah, the Most High. "Here," thought he, "is the provision I have prayed for to keep us in our old age and to provide our son with a start in life."
So he went boldly into the cave, and collected as much of the gold coin, which was in bags, as he thought his three donkeys could carry. When he had loaded them with the bags, he laid wood over them in such a manner that they could not be seen. After he had passed in and out as often as he wished, he stood before the door, and pronounced the words, "Shut, Sesame!" and the door closed of itself.

Chapter 3: The Lode Star

When Ali Baba got home, he drove his asses into a little yard, shut the gates very carefully, threw off the wood that covered the panniers, carried the bags into the house, and ranged them in order before his wife. He emptied the bags before his astonished wife, raising such a great heap of gold as to dazzle her eyes. Then he told her the whole adventure from beginning to end, and, above all, recommended her to keep it secret.

The wife rejoiced greatly at their good-fortune, but woman-like, wanted to count the gold piece by piece. "Wife," replied Ali Baba, "never try to number the gifts of Allah. Take them—and be thankful. To number them is to limit them. As for this treasure, I will dig a hole and bury it. There is no time to be lost." "You are in the right, husband," replied she.

"But," she thought, as he departed into the garden with his spade, "it will do no harm to know, as nigh as possible, how much we have. I will borrow a small measure, and measure it."

Away she ran to her brother-in-law Cassim, who lived hard by, and begged his wife for the loan of a measure for a little while. Her sister-in-law asked her whether she would have a great or a small one. The other asked for a small one. She bade her stay a little, and she would readily fetch one.

The sister-in-law did so, but as she knew Ali Baba's poverty, she was curious to know what sort of grain his wife wanted to measure, and, artfully putting some suet at the bottom of the measure, brought it to her, with the excuse that she was sorry that she had made her stay so long, but that she could not find it sooner.

Ali Baba's wife went home, filled the measure with gold and emptied it in the corner. Again and again she repeated that, and when she had done, she was very well satisfied to find the number of measures amounted to so many as they did, and went to tell her husband, who had almost finished digging the hole. While Ali Baba was burying the gold, his wife, to show her exactness and diligence to her sister-in-law, carried the measure back again, but without taking notice that a piece of gold had stuck to the bottom. "Sister," said she, giving it to her again, "you see that I have not kept your measure long. I am obliged to you for it, and return it with thanks."

As soon as Ali Baba's wife was gone, Cassim's wife looked at the bottom of the measure, and was in inexpressible surprise to find a piece of gold sticking to it. Envy immediately possessed her breast. "What!" said she, "has Ali Baba gold so plentiful as to measure it? Whence has he all this wealth?"

Cassim, her husband, was at his counting-house. When he came home his wife said to him, "Cassim, I know you think yourself rich, but Ali Baba is infinitely richer than you. He does not count his money, but measures it." Cassim desired her to explain the riddle, which she did by telling him the stratagem she had used to make the discovery, and showed him the piece of money, which was so old that they could not tell in what prince's reign it was coined.
Cassim, after he had married the rich widow, had never treated Ali Baba as a brother, but scorned and neglected him; and now, instead of being pleased, he conceived a base envy at his brother's prosperity. He could not sleep all that night, and went to him in the morning before sunrise. "Ali Baba," said he, "I am surprised at you! You pretend to be miserably poor, and yet you measure gold. My wife found this at the bottom of the measure you borrowed yesterday."

By this discourse, Ali Baba perceived that Cassim and his wife, through his own wife's folly, knew what they had so much reason to conceal; but what was done could not be undone. Therefore, without showing the least surprise or chagrin, he told all, and offered his brother part of his treasure to keep the secret.

"I expect as much," replied the greedy Cassim haughtily; "but I must know exactly where this treasure is, and how I may visit it myself when I choose; otherwise, I will go and inform against you, and then you will not only get no more, but will lose all you have, and I shall have a share for my information."

Ali Baba told him all he asked, even to the very words he was to use to gain admission into the cave.

Cassim rose the next morning long before the sun, and set out for the forest with ten mules bearing great chests, which he designed to fill, and followed the road which Ali Baba had pointed out to him. It was not long before he reached the rock, and found out the place, by the tree and other marks which his brother had given him. Walking up to the entrance of the cavern, he pronounced the words, "Open, Sesame!" Immediately the door opened, and when he was in, closed upon him.

On examining the cave, his avaricious soul was in transports of delight to find much more riches than he had expected from Ali Baba's relation. Quickly he laid as many bags of gold as he could carry at the door of the cavern; but his thoughts were so full of the great riches he should possess, and how with them he should become the richest money-lender and usurer in the city, that he could not think of the necessary words to make the door open. Instead of "Sesame" he said, "Open, Barley!" and was much amazed to find that the door remained fast shut. He named several sorts of grain, but still the door would not open.

Cassim had never anticipated such a contingency as this, and was so frightened at the danger he was in, that the more he endeavored to remember the word "Sesame," the more his memory was confounded. He threw down the bags he had loaded himself with and walked distractedly up and down the cave, for the first time in his greedy life appreciating that to put your trust in money alone is to pin your faith to the most elusive thing in the world. Yet he had looked to it alone for so long a time that he knew now no other way to turn.

Chapter 3: The Lode Star

About noon the robbers visited their cave. At some distance they saw Cassim's mules straggling about the rock, with great chests on their backs. Alarmed at this, they galloped full speed to the cave, drove away the mules, which strayed through the forest so far that they were soon out of sight, and went directly, with their naked sabres in their hands, to the door, which on their captain pronouncing the proper words, immediately opened.

Cassim, who heard the noise of the horses' feet, at once guessed the arrival of the robbers, and resolved to make one effort for his life. He rushed to the door, and no sooner saw it open, than he ran out and threw the leader down, but could not escape the other robbers, who with their scimeters soon deprived him of life.

There is more to this old Eastern legend, but the meat of it lies here —that if you learn the Magic Secret, the "Open Sesame" of life, wealth and honor are yours for the taking.

But if you become like the greedy Cassim, and get so taken up with the riches that you can think of nothing else—you not only lose the Magic Secret, but you bring down speedy retribution on your head as well.

The "Open, Sesame!"

What is this "Open, Sesame" of life? What is the Philosopher's Stone which turns everything it touches into gold?

It is any controlling idea or desire so intense, so alive and real, that it carries utter faith with it and thus involuntarily establishes a contact with the Holy Spirit within, which attracts to itself everything it needs for its fulfillment.

It is, in short, the Lode Star—the Polar Magnet by means of which we may draw from the heavens above, from the earth beneath or from the waters under the earth anything that is necessary to our controlling idea or desire.

Ridiculous? Stop and think for just a moment.

Have you ever concentrated for days or weeks on the writing of an article or story, on the making of some device, on the discovery of some new formula—on anything that required the deepest thought and faith and concentration?

Remember how there seemed to pour in upon you all sorts of facts and information and material pertinent to the idea you had in mind? Remember how things came to you from the most unlikely and unexpected sources—from the chance words of associates or even strangers; from newspaper and magazine articles, picked up in the most casual way imaginable; from books you happened to see in the windows or in the hands of some friend; from *out of the air,* as it were, unsought, unbidden—except as they were sought out and brought to you by that Mental Magnet within.

The earnest desire for some definite thing, coupled with the sincere belief in your power to get it through the Spirit within, is the most powerful force in the world. As Marie Corelli says in "Life Everlasting":

"Nothing in the universe can resist the force of a steadfastly fixed resolve. What the spirit truly seeks must, by eternal law, be given to it, and what the body needs for the fulfillment of the spirit's demands will be bestowed. From the sunlight and the air and the hidden things of space strength shall be daily and hourly renewed. Everything in nature shall aid in bringing to the resolved soul that which it demands. There is nothing within the circle of creation that can resist its influence. Success, wealth, triumph upon triumph come to every human being who daily 'sets his house in order'— whom no derision can drive from his determined goal, whom no temptation can drag from his appointed course."

Chapter 3: The Lode Star

I know that when I first conceived the idea for this book and began to look for different works of reference to bear out the thought I had in mind, I was almost flooded with material—wonderful material that I had never even heard about, much less knew where to look for. Three of the best works on the subject I have ever seen, literally walked into my office—unsought, unbidden and without cost—and have been of more help to me than anything else I have found. And I am far from being alone in this experience.

In a recent issue of *Advertising and Selling,* Floyd W. Parsons tells how a piece of cheese tossed by one workman at another during the lunch hour missed its mark and dropped into the plating bath used in the production of copper disks from which wax phonograph records were stamped. Later the disks from that bath were found to be far superior to the others, and an investigation revealed that the casein in the cheese had done the trick. This disclosed a possible improvement worth several thousand dollars.

By inadvertently opening the wrong valve, a French scientist found the answer to the long search for liquid oxygen. Again an accident created an industry and gave us an explosive safer and mightier than dynamite.

A great corporation ordered its industrial chemists to produce a paint that could be applied quickly, would dry rapidly, and be tough, hard and resistant to the elements. It had to have some of the properties of glass and yet not crack, and it had to be proof against the action of oil, grease, and acid.

Everything went well up to the point of finding a way to keep the solution in a liquid condition so that it could be applied with a brush. All efforts to solve this problem failed until one day the machinery broke down and the material had to stand for days in the tank until the repairs were completed. When work started again, the chemists were amazed to find that the paint now retained its liquid form. The long-sought secret had finally been discovered, and an accident had again shaped the destiny of a business.

In short, when you have put all of your reasoning, all of your information into the cauldron of thought, there frequently flashes out an idea that is not the logical development of anything you have had before—but a direct inspiration from the Holy Spirit within.

"And thine ears shall hear a word behind thee, saying, This is the way, walk ye in it, when ye turn to the right hand, and when ye turn to the left."—ISAIAH 30:21.

"The key to successful methods," says Thos. A. Edison, "comes right out of the air. A real new thing like a general idea, a beautiful melody, is pulled out of space—a fact which is inexplicable."

Inexplicable? Not at all! It is simply that all knowledge already exists in Divine Mind—in the Father who fills all space and animates all things. There is nothing for us to discover—merely to *seek,* to *unfold.* Columbus did not discover America. It was here all the time. As the Englishman said after three days of traveling on a California-bound train—"How could he have missed it?" Columbus —and all of Europe—merely learned something that Divine Mind had known all the time.

Galileo did not discover that the earth was round; Copernicus did not discover the movement of the planets; Newton did not discover the law of gravitation; any more than your young son discovers the law of mathematics by which 2+2=4. He learns it—yes. He makes the information his own. And to him it partakes of discovery. But the law was known to Divine Mind since time began.

We are God's children, grasping a little at a time of the infinite knowledge He is constantly writing on the blackboard before us— and hailing each bit as a grand discovery of our own. Sir Isaac Newton, one of the greatest geniuses of all time, compared himself to a boy, gathering pebbles on the shore of the vast, unknown ocean of truth.

"God looked down from heaven," said David, "upon the children of men to see if there were any that did understand." —Psalms 14:2.

The great essential is to realize that the Father HAS all information —that the "vast ocean of truth" IS there—and that if we will do our best in the trustful knowledge that the Father *can* and very gladly *will* supply anything beyond our own powers to grasp, our faith and trust will be justified. When God is with us, the impossible becomes possible.

When any problem confronts you that seems beyond your ability to solve, just say to yourself—"I am one with the Infinite Intelligence of the Universe. And Infinite Intelligence HAS the correct answer to this problem. Therefore, I too have the answer, and at the right time and in the right way will manifest it."

There are no new gold deposits. No new diamond fields. All of them have been known to the Father for millions of years.

You don't need to discover anything. You don't need to create something new. All you need to do is to seek the riches and the methods that have been known to the Father for all time. And the place to seek them is not far afield—but in Mind.

A Radio with a Thousand Aerials

Our bodies are, in effect, radio stations powerful or otherwise, as our controlling ideas are strong or weak. The nerves that come to the surface all over our body act as thousands of aerials gathering in impressions from every source. And just as any station properly attuned and powerful enough to "get" it, can pick what it wants out of the air any minute of the day or night, so can you "get" anything you may want—be it riches or success, happiness or health—if your thought be properly keyed and powerful enough to receive it.

For our minds are vast magnets that can attract to us anything we may desire. The only requisite is—they have got to be *charged.* A demagnetized magnet won't draw to it or hold even the weight of a pin. Nor will a demagnetized man attract to himself a single idea or a single penny.

There are two ways of charging your mental magnet:

1. By occasional but heartfelt prayer—like the radio fan who lets his batteries run down until, when something special comes along that he particularly wants, he finds them so weak he can scarcely raise a sound, and forthwith takes himself to the battery man to have them recharged.

2. By praying without ceasing—to go back to the simile of the radio fan again, to attach your batteries to the electric light socket and keep them constantly charged to capacity, ready and able at all times to bring you anything you may wish.

Which method is yours? Old Mother Nature adopts the second. The flowers turn their faces to the sun not just once a day or once a week—but always. The waving grain, the shrubs, the trees, drink in the light and life of the sun every day and all day. They recharge themselves with life and fragrance whenever and as long as opportunity offers.

That is what you too must do. You must first charge the magnet of your mind with a compelling desire. Then keep it recharged with faith in the power and the willingness of the Father to give to you anything of good that may be necessary to the fruition of your prayer. Not only that, but you must realize your ability (through the Father) to draw to yourself anything of good. In short, you must realize your Sonship with God, and the consequent fact that all of good is already yours—that God has done his part—that it is up to you merely to manifest, to unfold, to SEE the good things that the Father has provided for you in such profusion.

When Hagar and Ishmael were wandering in the desert, and could find no water and seemed about to perish, then Hagar cried aloud to the Lord.

"And God heard the voice of the lad; and the angel of God called to Hagar out of heaven, and said unto her, What aileth thee, Hagar? Fear not; for God hath heard the voice of the lad where he is.
"And God opened her eyes, and she saw a well of water; and she went, and filled the bottle with water, and gave the lad drink."— Genesis 21:17, 19.

Again, when the three kings in the desert sought water for their men and horses, the Prophet Elisha told them: "Thus saith the Lord —Ye shall not see wind, neither shall ye see rain, yet make this valley full of ditches." — II Kings, 13:16-17.

And though it looked a hopeless task, the three kings set their men to work as directed, and after they had prepared the ditches, the rains came and filled them.
Wherever you are and whatever you need, supply is always there— for supply is in the Father, and the Father is everywhere. It is like the air we breathe—it is all around us, always available, always plentiful—unless we lock ourselves into the airtight houses of limitation.

The trouble is that we have for so long been taught that everything of good must be fought for, struggled for, taken away from someone else, that we can't believe when we are told that all we need do is to open up the windows of our souls and let in the Holy Spirit—open up the channels of supply and let riches flow freely to us. To quote Trench's beautiful poem

Chapter 3: The Lode Star

"Make channels for the stream of love,
Where they may broadly run,
For Love has overflowing streams
To fill them every one;

But if at any time we cease
Such channels to provide,
The very founts of Love for us,
Will soon be parched and dried;

For we must share if we would keep
Such blessings from above,
Ceasing to give, we cease to have,
Such is the law of Love."

We see others breathing deeply of the air about us, and we don't begrudge them it because we know there is plenty for all. We see others enjoying the sunlight; the clear water from the spring; and we rejoice with them in it. But let another make a lot of money, and immediately we become envious, for we think he has made it that much harder for us to get any.

The best things in life, the greatest essentials to life, are free. Air, sunshine, water— all are free, because the supply of them is inexhaustible.

What we fail to realize is that there is just as inexhaustible supply of the things that money will buy as there is of sunlight or water or air. And they can be drawn just as freely from the Father through the magic of faith and a compelling idea.

But you can't do it if you dam up the source of supply with doubts and fears. You must not limit supply as did the widow in the Scriptural story. Left destitute, her creditors were pressing her hard; and her sons, as was the law in that day, were to become bondsmen for the debt she owed. In her distress she came to the prophet Elisha, and he asked—"What have you in your house?" She replied —"I have nothing but a vessel of oil." He said—"Send out to your neighbors and borrow all the vessels you can; take them empty into a room, and pour into them the oil which you have." She did not question him but did as she was told; she poured the oil from the vessel which contained all that she possessed and filled all those which she had borrowed. Then she told her sons to get others, but they said—"We have no more." And as soon as they made that announcement, the oil stopped flowing—not one drop came after all the vessels were full—II Kings 4:2-6. Do you see who determined the quantity that should come to the widow? Was it God? I know your answer—"It was the woman herself." She received just the amount for which she had made preparation.

It's Not the Supply That Is Limited—It Is Ourselves!

Too many of us are like the little colored boy and the watermelon. An old gentleman, seeing the difficulty the boy was having in storing away so large a melon, stopped and asked, "Too much melon, isn't it, son?" "No, suh!" replied the youngster with conviction, "just not enough niggah."

Why does so large a part of humanity suffer hunger and want?

Certainly not from lack on the part of old Mother Earth. Ask the farmers and they will tell you their trouble is overproduction—not scarcity. Ask the scientists, and they will tell you that there is food in plenty in the very air. And not only food but power and riches. Ask the miners—whether of gold, or silver, or diamonds, or coal, or iron—and they will tell you that the supply exceeds the demand. Go to the manufacturer and ask him—and again your answer will be the same.

Evidently there is plenty to go around. Evidently the Father has not failed us, any more than he fails the birds of the air or the beasts of the field, in providing the supply. The problem is merely one of our ability to receive—to receive and digest and distribute and exchange.

There is plenty for all—of everything of good. The poor are hungry, the needy are in lack, not because there is not enough supply, but because their mental magnets have become so weak through discouragement, their channels so stopped up with fear and worry, that the stream of supply no longer reaches them.

If you cut your finger, what happens? You call upon your heart for an extra supply of blood to rebuild the damaged part. And the heart immediately responds.

If you have urgent need of money or other worldly goods, what should you do? Call upon the Heart of all things to send you an extra supply for your emergency—and He will just as promptly and cheerfully respond.

There's a little comedy on one of the Broadway stages that illustrates this idea clearly. A couple of young darkies are boxing— the first, an active, alert little fellow, on the go every minute—the second a tall, shambling, lazy sort, slow-moving, slow-thinking.

The big one is too lazy to really fight his active opponent. He contents himself with trying to guard himself. But every time he moves a hand, the little one gets in a punch.

Finally the big one catches hold of the little fellow by the shoulders, holds him off at arm's length and studies him for a minute. Then he puts one hand in the other's face and lets the little one jab at him, the while he holds him off at arm's length.

The little one swings and punches, but his arms are too short. He can't quite reach the big fellow. The lazy one throws back his head and laughs as he prepares to swing his good right arm at leisure.

"That's all I wanted to know," he says.

And all you need to know when that little devil of fear or worry or lack assails you and you want to hold him off for a while until you can swing your good right arm to put him out for the count, is that the answer to any trouble, the remedy for any lack, the antidote for any ill is just around the corner. Charge your mental magnet with earnest desire and faith—and the need does not exist which you cannot satisfy.

"The Lord's hand is not shortened, that it cannot save," promised the Prophet Isaiah
59:1. "Neither His ear heavy, that it cannot hear."

The principal reason there is so much truth in the Scriptural quotation—"To him that hath shall be given," is that the man who has a tidy sum safely put away loses all worry about supply. Like the darkey in the play, he feels that his money gives him that bit of extra reach with which he can easily fend off the attacks of want and fear and worry, while he is getting in his good licks elsewhere. True, he places his dependence upon money rather than upon the Spirit, but the belief that he has money enough not to have to worry emboldens him to demand more. He loses all sense of fear. He expects and demands only the *good* things of life—and consequently the good things of life come to him. To put it in the words of Solomon—"He that hath a bountiful eye shall be blessed"—Proverbs 22:9.

Remember the story of the merchant who saw ruin staring him in the face unless he could raise money immediately? He went to a wise friend, who gave him a great nugget of gold—on condition, however, that he was not to use it except as a last resource.

Knowing that he had the gold to use at need, the merchant went boldly about his business with a mind at ease—faced his creditors so confidently that they gladly trusted him further—with the result

43

that he never needed to use the gold.

But you don't need to go to the pages of fiction for such examples. Most of us have seen similar instances ourselves. There is the classic case of George Muller, of Bristol, England, who maintained orphanages which spent millions, through which hundreds of children were rescued from the slums and fitted for places of trust in the world—*all without any visible means of support!*

Like the oil from the widow's cruse, the money came through his perfect faith in the Giver of all good. Many and many a time utter penury stared him in the face, so that any man of less Job-like faith would have been discouraged. Once hundreds of hungry children sat waiting for their breakfasts—and there was not a mouthful to give them.

But always in time—though sometimes at the very last moment—his faith was justified and some generous donation would supply all their wants. Like Job, he might well have said—"I know that my Redeemer liveth."—Job 19:25. "Though He slay me, yet will I trust in Him."—Job 13:15.

Or with David—"Yea, though I walk through the valley of the shadow of Death I shall fear no evil, for Thou art with me."—Psalms 23:4.

For nothing stands between you and the dearest wish of your heart but doubt and fear. When you can pray without doubting, when you can believe as the Master bade us believe—"Whatsoever ye ask for when ye pray, believe that ye RECEIVE it and ye SHALL HAVE IT"—every desire of your heart will be instantly filled.

What, then, is the "Open, Sesame," of life? What is the Magic Secret that will bring to you everything of good you may wish?

It is simply a "Message to Garcia." There is within you a Holy

Spirit who is your part of Divinity—who knows all, sees all and can do all things. Give him a definite task, magnetize Him with your absolute belief in His ability and His readiness to accomplish it—charge Him with such absolute faith that you can actually SEE HIM DOING IT—and "as thy faith is, so it will be unto you." The Spirit within you can draw from the heavens or the earth or the waters under the earth whatever you may need for the consummation of your desires.

How do men talk 3,000 miles across the Atlantic—without wires, without cables? In the Marconi beam system, they do it by focusing the electric waves into one great beam, just as a searchlight focuses all the light waves into one powerful ray. Ordinary broadcasting stations let their waves radiate in all directions like the ripples a pebble makes in a pool of water. The Marconi beam system focuses them all into one powerful beam and then directs it straight across the Atlantic, with the result that they will carry your message wherever you wish it to go.

Focus your desires in the same way. Instead of frittering away your energy in a thousand directions, bring them all to bear in one powerful beam on one single desire at a time. Do that, and you can attract to yourself anything of good you may wish.

So what do you want?

Is it money? Then know that the Father is the source of all wealth. Go to Him—tell Him your need—ask Him for money in abundance to meet your needs. Bless the money you now have—know that the Father is in it even as he is in all good things— then see it, in your mind's eye, *multiplied.*

Send forth the Holy Spirit within you to the source of supply for as much as you need or can use to good advantage. Then SEE HIM DRAWING THAT SUPPLY! See a golden stream flowing to you in the sunlight, in the moonbeams!

Actually speak the word that sends your Spirit forth. Tell Him — "Holy Spirit, you know that the one Law of Supply is abundance —plenty for every right purpose, plenty for every right desire. You know that the Father has all of abundance, that there is unlimited money available for me right now, that as His son I am heir to it. Go you, therefore, bring to me of the infinite abundance that is mine, all that I may need for this purpose. If there is anything you wish *me* to do, give me a definite lead."

Speak the word, then cast your burden upon the Holy Spirit—and forget it! "My word shall not return unto me void, but shall accomplish that where unto it is sent."—Isaiah 55:11. Every doubt, every fear, every worry that you entertain is a shackle holding Him back. If you can release Him from all dominion of the conscious mind, if you can have the faith in Him that you have when you give a task to a trusted servant and thereafter look upon it as done—depend upon it, He will bring you what you ask for.

But it is so hard for us to let go. We are like a man on a desert isle, daily releasing our one carrier pigeon with a message for help, yet as often bringing him back to earth again by the string on his foot that we are too distrustful to untie.

Yet when at last in desperation we do cut off the shackles, our faithful messenger flies straight home with his message of need and brings succor to us immediately.

That is why so often our prayers are not answered until the eleventh hour. We won't turn loose the string. We won't trust entirely in the Spirit. We think He needs our help, too. When all that we need is a little trust.

It is the same no matter what you may want. Are you seeking a position? Know that in the Mind of the Father there is one right position for you—one position that in the present stage of your development is best fitted for you even as you are best fitted for it. You have a definite place in the great scheme of things. And there is one right position that marks the next step in your forward progress.

That position IS yours. You have only to *know* this and to realize it. Then send forth the Spirit within you to bring that position to you or you to it. *Speak the word.* Throw the burden upon Him, asking Him only, if there is anything you can do to forward the work, to give you a definite lead. Then rest content in the knowledge that the Spirit is doing the work.

"Prove me now herewith, saith the Lord of Hosts, if I will not open you the windows of heaven, and pour you out a blessing that there shall not be room enough to receive it."—Malachi 3:10.

What, then, is the answer? Is this a lazy-man's world, where all that one needs to do is to fast and pray?

By no means! It is a worker's world—and the only ones who ever get anything out of it that is worthwhile are the workers. Mere wishing never magnetized the Spirit within to bring anything of good.

Look at all of Nature—busy every moment, never idle—*but never worrying.* Model after her. Whatever it is you may want, remember that you must get it first in Mind. See yourself with it there—see yourself receiving it. Make it as real as you can. Be thankful for it!

Then set about manifesting that dream in the material world. Do anything you can think of that will help to bring it about. Concentrate your thought upon it in every conceivable way. But never worry as to the outcome. Know that after you have done all that is possible for you to do—if you are still lacking in some essential, you can sit back in the utter confidence that the Holy

Spirit within will supply that lack. Give of your best—and you need never fear for the outcome. Your best will come back to you—amplified a hundredfold.

"Ye know in all your hearts and in all your souls, that not one thing hath failed of all the good things which the Lord your God spake concerning you; all are come to pass unto you, and not one thing hath failed thereof."—Joshua 23:14.

Chapter 4: The Man of Brass

AWAY back in the 13th century, there lived a scientist so far ahead of his times that he had to record most of his discoveries in cypher —to keep from being burned at the stake.

Even as it was, he was thought by the ignorant to be a sorcerer, a magician, an apostate who had sold his soul to the devil. Only among the initiate was he known as "The Wonderful Doctor."

His name was Roger.

And wonderful he truly was. Many of the chemical formulas he discovered are in use today. He made gunpowder. He discovered the possibilities of the magnifying glass. He was a forerunner of Galileo and Copericus.

Innumerable legends grew up about him, some of which will be touched upon in the later volumes of this Course—notably his "Elixir of Life." But the most persistent of these legends deals with "The Man of Brass."

Roger, you must know, had mastered seven different languages in his efforts to wrest from every possible source the secrets of science that had been known to previous ages. Among these languages was the Arabic. And one day there was brought to him an old Arabic manuscript which some wandering knight had picked up in far-away Palestine.

Roger read the work and marveled. It told first how to fashion a man of brass. Then, by means of clockwork and wires leading to certain jars of chemicals (the first crude storage batteries), how the eyeballs could be made to glow, the tongue to move, smoke to issue from the nostrils, and noise from the mouth. But most important of all—how, by adhering to certain directions, the Man of Brass could be made to speak *and reveal a secret of the utmost importance to every Englishman.*

For seven years, Roger toiled over his Man of Brass. He is reputed to have spent a fortune in scientific experiments, and no small part of it must have gone into this brazen image. At last it was finished. Everything had been done with the greatest care, strictly in accordance with the directions given in the manuscript.

Then he sat down and waited. For more than a month, there was never a minute when Roger or his friend and confidante Friar Bungay was not sitting before the brazen image, listening for any sound it might utter. But neither friars nor philosophers can keep on without sleep.

One night, when Friar Bungay had gone home, Roger was nodding in his chair before the image. "If I can keep awake but a few hours longer," he muttered, "the wonderful voice will speak and the great secret will be known." But he could not keep awake. His eyes would close in spite of himself. Finally he called his servant, admonished him to wake him immediately if the image should speak and went off to snatch a bit of rest. The servant sat near the door, his eyes fastened in frightened fascination upon those of the image, his fingers gripped about the cudel in his hands.

Suddenly the eyes of the image glowed, its lips moved and in a whisper there issued from its mouth the words—
"TIME IS!"
The servant jumped to his feet and started to run, but as the brazen image seemed to remain rooted to the one spot, he paused on the threshold to see what more it might have to say.

Presently again the eyes lighted up, the lips moved, and a voice like the rattling of a kettle-drum shrilled out—

"TIME WAS!"

Chapter 4: The Man of Brass

This time the servant all but fled. But before he could get the door open, the eyes glowed once more and in a voice of thunder there issued the words—

"TIME IS PAST!"

And with that the image fell and smashed into a thousand pieces.

Roger is said to have been so bitterly disappointed at what he considered the wasting of all his seven years of labor that he burned his books, closed his study and spent the rest of his life in a monastery.

But had his work been wasted? Is there any secret of greater importance than the knowledge that—*"Time is NOW?* Most of us are so busy regretting the past or planning what we are going to be and do in some far distant day or state that we overlook the chances for happiness and success that are all around us now.

The past is gone and done with. No amount of regrets will bring it back. So let us forget it—except in so far as we may draw lessons from it. Let our motto be "Yesterday ended last night."

As for the future—it is still ahead of us, and no man may tell what it holds.

But the present is ours to do with as we will. So let us live it to the utmost. *"Time IS"*—not has been or will be. "Time *passes"*—you will never have one bit more of time than you have this minute.

So what do you want to do with it? What have you to ask of the Father of Life—not next year, or ten years from now, or in some indefinite future state— but NOW?

There's an old Eastern legend that the gates of Paradise are opened only once in each thousand years. And judging by most people's attitude toward life, that belief seems to have obtained credence among us, for most of us look forward to happiness and success as something in the far distant future. We pray—but look for the result of our prayers in some vague future state.

All of supply is already in existence. Why put off drawing upon it six months—or a year—or ten years? Why not charge the magnet of your mind to draw from Infinite Supply what you may want NOW?

"I cause those that love me to inherit substance, and I will fill their treasures."— Proverbs 8:21.

If you were to take a vote of the Christian peoples of the world, you would find them practically unanimous in believing that God intended to save their souls in the next world—but that in so far as their present existence is concerned, you've got to leave Him out of the reckoning!

Yet if you took from the Scriptures, all those parts that tell of His succoring those in trouble—not in some far-off future state, but in this life; if you left out all His promises of protection and reward here on earth to those that loved Him and kept His commandments —how much of the Bible would there be left?

"And the Lord shall guide thee continually, and satisfy thy soul in drought, and make fat thy bones; and thou shalt be like a watered garden, and like a spring of water whose waters fail not."—Isaiah 58:11.

If only all could realize that even in the heart of the humblest laborer, of the poorest scrubwoman, lies the key to riches inexhaustible, what a world of poverty and misery we might avoid.

Most of us find it easy enough to believe this when our pockets are full and all is going well with us. But let the wolf start scratching at the door and then watch us. Yet that is the very time when we most need faith! The fact is that we have more confidence in the weekly pay-envelope, uncertain as it is, than we have in the Almighty!

Consider the lilies of the field. Consider the birds; the denizens of the field; of the forest; of the air and the water; they don't lack for what they need. The big difference between them and you is that you have been given free will. You don't need to go to the Father unless you wish. You can struggle and toil on your own account. You can look upon this as a vale of tears—and find it so. Or you can do your best—and then rest in the arms of the Father while "He doeth the works."

"Yea, the Almighty shall be thy defence, and thou shall have plenty of silver,"—Job
22:25.

All that you need, all of good that you want, is right at your hand.

"The soul answers never by words," says Emerson, "but by the thing itself sought after."

Have you ever seen the Hopi Indians' Snake Dance—their prayer for rain? It is probably the oldest religious ceremony on this continent, and it is said that it never yet has failed to bring the rains.

"Speak to him thou, for he heareth
When Spirit with Spirit doth meet,
Closer is he than breathing,
And nearer than hand and feet."

Scientists may talk learnedly of atmospheric conditions and natural laws, but the fact remains—the Indians send up their heartfelt prayers to the Holy Spirit in simple faith—and so far as is known, the rains have never failed to promptly come!

Chapter 4: The Man of Brass

"Whither shall I go from thy Spirit?" cried the Psalmist of old, "Or whither shall I flee from Thy presence? If I ascend up into heaven Thou are there; if I make my bed in hell, behold Thou are there. If I take the wings of the morning and dwell in the uttermost parts of the sea; even there shall Thy hand lead me and Thy right hand shall hold me. If I say, Surely the darkness shall cover me; even the night shall be light about me."—Psalms 139:7-11.

There is in this universe a Power that hears the cry of the human heart. There is behind us a Father "whose good pleasure it is to give us the Kingdom." You don't have to beg Him for the good things of life any more than you have to beg the sun for its heat. You have only to draw near and take of the bountiful supply He is constantly holding out to you.

So what is it you want of the Father of Life? A house? A toy? A car? Success in this or that undertaking? Health? Love? Happiness?

Whatever it is, you can have it. Whatever of good you ask for with earnest desire and simple faith, the Father will gladly give.

So have no hesitancy in going to Him about little things. Don't you suppose He is as glad to see you clothed in a new suit or new dress as He is to see the birds preening their new feathers, the wild things of the forest in their shining new coat, the snake and his like in their new skins? Don't you suppose it gives Him as much pleasure to give you something you have been longing for as it gladdens the heart of an earthly father to give a much-desired toy to his little boy?

"Thou openest thy hand and satisfieth the desire of every living thing."

I have had people write me that prayer has brought to them such simple little things as flowers, as toys for the children, as an automobile. Last Christmas one reader wrote me that he had needed $500. That he had put his problem before the Father confidently, believingly. Then left it with Him. To use his own words, "The $500 came from so unexpected a source that if the President himself had sent it to him, he would not have been more surprised."

"No good things will He withhold from them that walketh uprightly."

The very fact that you have some earnest desire is the best evidence that the answer to that desire is in the great heart of God.

"Time is NOW!"

That earnest desire of yours is in the present. And the supply is just as much so. The Father is just as much present here and now as He will ever be. So why put off the realization of your desires to some vague and distant future? Why not realize them in the now?

What is it that you want?

Whatever it is, it already exists somewhere, in some form. And if your desire be strong enough, your faith great enough, you can attract it to you.

There are riches in abundance for you. They already exist. They are labeled YOURS in the mind of the Father. And until you get them, they will remain idle. You don't have to take them from someone else. You don't have to envy anyone else what hc has. All you have to KNOW is that somewhere all of richcs that you can ever desire are lying waiting for you.

Don't try to get them all at once.

If you had a million dollars on deposit in some bank, you wouldn't rush there and draw it out, to carry around with you or to hide about the house. No—as long as you had confidence in the integrity of the bank, you would leave your money on deposit there, drawing upon it merely as you needed it.

Have you less confidence in the Bank of the Father than in those of man? Must you ask It for all your heritage at once for fear the Bank will fail? Or can you ask each day for that day's needs—"Give us this day our daily bread"—in the simple faith that our every draft will be met promptly, fully, no matter what the size?

The man who has that simple faith will not try to pinch pennies. He won't "pass by on the other side" when a worthy need approaches him.

He will spend cheerfully—for any right purpose. He will bless the money he sends out, putting it to work in the confident knowledge that when used gainfully, it will come back increased and multiplied.

The same thing applies to your home, to your surroundings. There is a perfect home for you already built in the Father's mind. Know this—realize it—then, like Hagar in the wilderness, pray that your eyes may be opened that you may SEE this perfect home that is yours.

There is a perfect position for you. A perfect mate. A perfect work. A perfect idea of each cell and organism in your body. In later volumes of this set, I shall try to show you how through the promises of the Scriptures these may all be realized. Suffice it now to say that they all exist in the Father's mind. It is up to you merely to seek that you may find them.

You have the most powerful magnet on earth right within your own mind. Uncover it! Charge it with desire and faith. Speak the word that sends the Holy Spirit that is within you in quest of what you wish. Then cast the burden upon Him and thereafter look upon your

Chapter 4: The Man of Brass

desire as an accomplished fact.

"Whatsoever ye ask for when ye pray, believe that ye *receive* it and ye shall have it."

Prepare for the thing you have asked for, even though there be not the slightest sign of its coming. Act the part! Like the three Kings in the desert, dig your ditches to receive the water, even though there be not a cloud in the sky. And your ditches will be filled— even as were theirs.
"Be still—and know that I am God!" Wait calmly, confidently, in the full assurance that the Father has what you want and will gladly give it to you.

One's ships come in over a calm sea.

The Law of Karma

You have probably heard of the Law of Karma. It is Sanskrit, you know, for "Comeback." It is one of the oldest laws known to man— yet perhaps the least regarded.

It is the law of the boomerang. In the parlance of today, it is— "Chickens come home to roost." Even in science we find it, as Newton's Third Law of Motion—"Action and reaction are always equal to each other."

Wherein does this law affect us now? Only in that, if you wish riches, if you long for happiness, health, success, you must think abundance, you must charge your mind with happy thoughts, healthy thoughts, optimistic thoughts.

If you are seeking riches, you will never get them by stopping up all the avenues of outgo, and waiting for your vessel to fill up from the top. I remember one man who wrote me from down in West Virginia that when he received *The Secret of the Ages* he was a farmhand, working for $1 a day. Through the confidence and knowledge acquired through the books, he had landed a job at $6.20 a day of eight hours, where before he had labored for twelve hours on the farm. But, he wrote, "I've returned the books. You gave me time to get out of them what I wanted and return at your expense without buying them. I think now I can make a million. So I don't want to spend any money now. I want to make my million." That man was like a funnel—big at the receiving end, but little at the outgoing part. The Law of Karma will get him before he has gone far. You have got to cast your bread upon the waters, in the secure confidence that it will come back to you multiplied a hundredfold.

If you are longing for a beautiful home, you will never get it by thinking thoughts of poverty and lack. Forget the state of your pocketbook. Your supply is not there. All supply is in the Father, "with Whom is no variableness nor shadow of turning." So go to the Father with your desire. Try to picture in your mind's eye the perfect home that already is yours in Divine Mind. Make it complete in every detail. Realize that this perfect home is yours—that it already exists—in the mind of the Father. Then send forth the Holy Spirit to bring it to you or you to it.

Don't ask for some particular house. Ask, if you wish, for one like it. Don't try to take that which is another's. Know that the one perfect home for you already exists in Divine Mind, even though you may never have seen it. Then leave it to the Holy Spirit to manifest it.

Speak the word—then cast the burden upon the Holy Spirit within. The Father sends His gifts in His own way, even as earthly fathers frequently do. Make all preparations for them—dig your ditches—open up the windows of your soul. Be ready to receive.

Remember, in Genesis I: 1-2—"In the beginning, God created the heaven and the earth. And the earth was without form and void; and darkness was upon the face of the deep. *And the Spirit of God moved upon the face of the waters."*

That Spirit of God still moves upon the face of the waters. And upon the face of the land. That Spirit of God is the Holy Spirit within you. And just as He helped to form the earth from the void, so will He bring form to your dreams, your desires. If only you do your part. If only you have the faith. If only you can cast the burden upon Him—confidently, believingly!

"Oh Judah, fear not; but tomorrow go out against them, for the Lord will be with you. You shall not need to fight this battle; set yourselves, stand you still, *and see the salvation of the Lord with you."*
And the time to do it is NOW.

Chapter 5: Start Something!

A Spanish adventurer gets together a following of a couple of thousand out-at-elbows soldiers of fortune like himself—and with them conquers a nation! A disciplined, well-led warlike nation numbering millions! Defeats armies ten times the size of his little force, time after time! Captures a walled city garrisoned by a great army and protected by dykes and canals, and makes its emperor prisoner!

I refer to Hernando Cortez, conqueror of Mexico.

Another Spaniard, with a handful of followers, enslaves the whole of Peru, carries away the vast treasures of the Incas, and makes Spain the richest nation on the globe!

That was 400 years ago, but it is easy enough to find their counterparts today. A few years ago Persia had been almost dismembered by Russia and England. And Reza Khan was but a poor trooper in the Persian army. Today Persia has been restored to an independent state—and Reza Khan is its Ruler.

Before the war Mussolini was an unknown Socialist worker; during the war, a common soldier. Today he is head of a re-nationalized Italy.

Ebert, a saddle-maker before the war—becomes President of the new German Republic. Trotsky, a waiter in a cheap New York restaurant—is made War Minister of Soviet Russia. Mustapha Kemal, a good soldier—but until the war unknown—makes himself Ruler of Turkey. Every day brings its grist of new stars in the world firmament—new and comet-like rises to fame.

How do they do it? What is the secret behind such phenomenal successes?

Chapter 5: Start Something!

Not education—many of these men had no education to speak of. Not training—none of them was ever trained for real leadership. Then what is it?

Just one thing these men all had in common—the daring to *start something!*

If Cortez had been content to sit around in Cuba and wait for something to turn up, do you suppose we should ever have heard of him?

If Reza Khan had been content to do his mere duty as a Persian trooper; if Mussolini had sat down and rested on his laurels as a soldier; if Ebert had been satisfied to keep on making saddles; if Mustapha Kemal had merely obeyed whatever orders he received; do you suppose their countrymen would have started out on a still hunt for them, routed them out of their obscurity and put them at the head of their governments?
Not in a thousand years!

You may—and do—possess latent ability equal to any man on earth; you have ready to your call, through the Holy Spirit within you, not merely the wisdom of a Solomon but the Wisdom of God! Yet all of this will not get you anywhere—all of this will never result in the world calling upon you to lead it—*unless you use it to start something!*

"Bubbles"

You know the air castles a young fellow builds when he is planning his future with his Best Girl. You know what pictures of wonderful achievement he can paint for her. The wealth of the Indies is but a trifle compared with the fortune he is going to lay at her feet.

"Day dreams," we call them—and laugh good-naturedly at the

fondness of youth and love for believing in such bubbles, such figments of the imagination. But these dreams are very real and very dear to every boy—and girl. They embody all those things they hope some day soon to see materialize.

The only trouble with them is, that with most of us these bubbles are so soon pricked. We meet with discouragement. The fine point of our enthusiasm and ambition is blunted. Soon we lapse into a regular grind, and the man we hoped to be, the man we painted in such glowing terms to our Sweetheart—the man she really married —quietly passes out, leaving nothing but the husk of what might have been.

Is it any wonder there are so many unhappy marriages, when you compare the realities a man actually gives to the girl who marries him, with the "Bubbles" he promised her before?

The wonder is that so many girls shed only a few tears over their shattered dreams, forget their disillusionment, and knuckle down to the tiresome, dispiriting daily round of cooking and housework—of tending babies and being good wives to their plodding husbands.

The greatest waste in business today is the waste of the enthusiasm of all the fine young fellows that go into it. True—their enthusiasm is frequently misdirected—but that is *your* opportunity. Go look at Niagara Falls!

For uncounted years the Niagara River dashed over its rocky cliff, the power of millions of horses behind it—a beautiful sight for the occasional tourist —but nothing more!

Today that same Niagara turns the wheels of a hundred great industries—gives light and power to all of Western New York—is soon to become the basis of a giant superpower system for the entire Northeast.
What made the difference? The Niagara has not changed—it had

exactly the same power afore-time. 'Tis simply that man has learned how to *direct* that power, to use that energy for useful purposes.

"Give instruction to a wise man, and he will be yet wiser," says the Proverbs (9); "teach a just man, and he will increase in learning."

Remember the story of the young King of the Black Isles? He started out full of high ambitions. But the wicked enchantress (Lack of Initiative) turned him into black marble from the waist down. So he was condemned to sit in his palace and bemoan his fate until there came a new King to lift the spell, to inspire him for high emprise, to keep him from ever again lapsing into the state of half man and half statue.

"And Moses said unto the Lord, O my Lord, I am not eloquent, neither heretofore, nor since thou hast spoken unto thy servant: but I am slow of speech, and of a slow tongue.

"And the Lord said unto him, Who hath made man's mouth? Or who maketh the dumb, or deaf, or the seeing, or the blind? Have not I the Lord?

"Now therefore go, and I will be with thy mouth, and teach thee what thou shalt say."

The world's most tragic figure is the man who never starts anything. He is dead from the waist down. He sits and wishes and dreams; he goes through motions, doing routine things that a machine could do just as well, but he never gets anywhere.

How did Carnegie make his millions? By finding a new way to make steel—and then starting to *do* it! How did Woolworth, how did Penny, make their successes? By trying out new methods of merchandising—by starting something. How did Ford become the richest man in the world? By visioning the new transportation within the reach of everyone—and then starting to put it there!

You want to get out of the rut—to grow—to develop into something better. And there are unnumbered new methods in industry, new inventions, new ideas—waiting merely to be uncovered.

To whom will these prizes go? Nine times out of ten to the man who starts something—to the man who dreams great dreams, and then has the courage, the belief in himself, in his Spirit, in his Destiny, to make the start, to take the plunge, *to go!*

"And the Spirit of the Lord shall rest upon him, the spirit of wisdom and understanding, the spirit of counsel and might, the spirit of knowledge and of the fear of the Lord."—Isaiah II.

The Things That Can't Be Done

When John MacDonald first proposed to build the great New York subways, people laughed at him. He went to one "big" financier after another, and the answer of all was the same. "Dig a tunnel under all these streets and houses, with their maze of pipe lines and electric cables and gas mains and sewers? Impossible!"

But through it all he held to the one main idea. "You have a cellar under your house, haven't you?" he asked them. "And you dug it without much trouble, didn't you? Well, I'm not thinking of building a tunnel the length of this island. I'm planning to dig a string of cellars—*and then connect them together!*"

And he finally found a man big enough to see the idea—and to back it.

"Thou shalt make thy prayer unto Him, and He shall hear thee, and thou shalt pay thy vows.

Chapter 5: Start Something!

"Thou shalt also decree a thing, and it shall be established unto thee: and the light shall shine upon thy ways."—Job 22:27-28.

In this day of miracles, it would be a hardy spirit that would say that anything is impossible. The time is not far distant when men will harness the tides, get motive power and much of their food from the air and from the tropic seas, talk to anyone anywhere and see them while they talk. These and a thousand other inventions even more wonderful are in the very air. Why shouldn't you be the one to start some of them?

You don't need to be an engineer. You don't need to be an inventor. Pasteur was not a doctor, yet he did more for medical science than any doctor. Whitney was not a cotton planter. Not even a Southerner. He was a Connecticut schoolteacher. Yet he invented the cotton gin! Bell was a professor of elocution, and he once said that he invented the telephone because he knew nothing of electricity. He didn't know it couldn't be done! Morse, of telegraphic fame, was a portrait painter—not an electrician. Dunlop (maker of tires) was a veterinary surgeon. Gillette was a traveling salesman. Eastman a bank clerk. Ingersoll a mechanic. Harriman a broker. Gary a lawyer.

In fact, most of the great inventors and pioneers have been outsiders. Why? They don't know the things that can't be done—*so they go ahead and do them!*

"Opportunity," says Doc Lane, "is as scarce as oxygen; men fairly breathe it and do not know it."

It is not necessary to have a "pull" to succeed. In fact, a "pull" is more often than not just that—a pull backward. What we need is the "push" of necessity. For most of us are so constituted that, unless we have to put into the fight all our strength and energy, we just jog along in a slothful, ambitionless sort of way, getting nowhere.

Chapter 5: Start Something!

The saving event in many a man's life has been the blow that knocked the props out from under him and left him to look out for himself. As Emerson put it: "It is only as a man puts off all foreign support and stands alone that I see him firm and to prevail. He is weaker by every recruit to his banner."

So never envy the man with a "pull." Pity him. He has lost the greatest thing there is in business—the need for individual initiative.

You say you have to start at the bottom, while Bill Smith's father left him enough money to begin at the head of a real business? Never mind. Start something—even if it be only a peanut stand—and ten years from now you will have not only some very valuable experience, but a business that will be paying you dividends and give you an insurance for the future. Whereas the chances are that though Bill Smith may have the experience, that is all he will have. Most of the big businesses of today, you know, started on a shoestring.

"Thus saith the Lord; Refrain thy voice from weeping, and thine eyes from tears: for thy work shall be rewarded, saith the Lord."—Jeremiah 31.

Democracy is equality, not of place, but of opportunity. Just because you were born on Fifth Avenue doesn't mean that you are going to stay there. And just because you were born on the East Side doesn't mean that you have got to stay there. Al Smith is but one of thousands who have come up from humble surroundings to the topmost rung of the ladder of success.

"Always the real leaders of men," says Dr. Frank Crane, "the real kings, have come up from the common people. The finest flowers in the human flora grow in the woods pasture and not in the hothouse; no privileged class, no Royal house, no carefully selected stock produced a Leonardo or a Michelangelo in art, a Shakespeare or Burns in letters, a Galli Curci or Paderewski in music, a Socrates or Kant in philosophy, an Edison or Pasteur in science, a Wesley or a Knox in religion."

The Law of Compensation is constantly at work. When men grow to put too much dependence upon the fortune or the institution or the position that has been given them, these props are suddenly removed. When through grim necessity they have learned not to rely upon anything short of the Infinite, the channels of supply are reopened to them.

"Put not your trust in Princes," advised the Psalmist. Not because Princes are so much more unreliable than ordinary men, but because they are mere tributaries—even as you are—to the King of Kings.
Put not your trust in some other man or institution. Go direct to the Fount! Don't tap some other man's channel. Go direct to the main Source of Supply!

"By me kings reign, and princes decree justice.

"By me princes rule, and nobles, even all the judges of the earth.

"I love them that love me; and those that seek me early shall find me.

"Riches and honour are with me; durable riches and righteousness."
—Proverbs 8:15-19.

Be King in Your Own Thoughts

"Every man," says a mediaeval writer, "has within him the making of a great saint." And every one of us has in him the making of a great success.

Chapter 5: Start Something!

"Less than a year ago," reads a letter to me from W. Bruce Haughton, "I started in the automotive business in Jacksonville with $23.00 in my pocket. I bought $14.40 worth of tools and rented a two-car garage in the back yard of the house where I rented a room. I then went to several of the city professional men and told them what I could do for their cars. In thirty days I had a net return of $476.80 with an overhead of about $50.00.

"In June, 1926, I had to find bigger quarters to handle my business, for I then had 591 regular customers coming to my 'Back Yard' for service they could not buy elsewhere. Today I am negotiating with a concern for another corner in the best part of this city to handle my patrons who live in that section."

In the newspaper the other day, I read how Palmer C. Hayden, a Negro, 33 years old, was quitting his scrub bucket to study art in Europe. He had just won the $400 prize in art awarded by the Harmon Foundation. He had the courage to start something.

I know a young fellow who, while still in College, got the idea through a chance occurrence that there was an entirely virgin field among the undertakers for raincoats—black raincoats. He reasoned that there were so few undertakers in each city that no store could afford to carry a complete range of sizes for them, whereas one central store, selling to the whole country, could do so.

So he borrowed a few dollars and tried out his idea by mail. Today he is a millionaire—and it has all been the logical outcome of that one idea.

He started something.

If you could only realize that you have a definite place in a scheme so big that God has been working millions of years to bring it about; if you would only remember that every forward step you take has His approval and help; if you would look upon Him as a

Chapter 5: Start Something!

loving Father watching you, His little son, taking a few faltering steps, ready to catch you when you stumble, ready to help you over the difficult places, ready to strengthen and support you—how much of fear and worry you would avoid, how much more surely you would progress.

"If ye walk in my statutes, and keep my commandments, and do them;

"Then I will give you rain in due season, and the land shall yield her increase, and the trees of the field shall yield their fruit.

"And your threshing shall reach unto the vintage, and the vintage shall reach unto the sowing time: and ye shall eat your bread to the full, and dwell in your land safely.

"And I will give peace in the land, and ye shall lie down, and none shall make you afraid."—Leviticus 26:3-6.

But to progress, it is necessary that you learn to take a few steps for yourself. You can't remain tied to the Father's apron-strings if you are to become a man or woman worthy of the name.

You know how much these "Mother's darlings" are good for when they get out among other boys. You know how long these pampered children of the rich usually last, when they are thrown upon their own resources.

The Father above has the wisdom and the courage to do what very few earthly fathers can. He gives his children free will. He turns them loose, in a world full of pitfalls and dangers, to learn self-reliance, to become real men and women, worthy Sons of God.

Yet He is always just behind us. His arms ready to support us. His hand to guide us. His wisdom to counsel us—if only we will realize His presence. His solicitude, His Fatherly love and care.

Chapter 5: Start Something!

"He giveth power to the faint; and to them that have no might, he increaseth strength."—Isaiah 40:29.

He has given us free will, so He will not force Himself upon us. He has untied our apron-strings, so He won't *make* us take the great place He plans for us in the Divine scheme of things. But if we will learn to work with Him, if we will treat Him as a Father, run to Him with our joys as with our sorrows, have Him at the back of all our plans, know that we can rely upon His help in all our undertakings, what a difference it will make!

You need never hesitate, then, to start anything of good, because you will know that with Him behind you, it can not fail. You will never lack the faith, the enthusiasm, the power to carry through even the most difficult undertaking. Most of all, you will never lack the will to begin, for you will know that even the Father can not help you to accomplish until you yourself have taken the first step by STARTING SOMETHING!

"Since receiving your first books," writes M. D. C. of Capitola, California, "I have made, from insurance premiums in a new company which I was instrumental in forming, more than $100,000.00 in a little over six months' time. My previous income over a period of years has been approximately $7,500.00 per year."

He started something!

The Starting Point

Now, how about you—have *you* started anything? Do you want to? Then let's take stock of you for a moment:

1. The first thing to do is to list all of your successes, no matter how unimportant they may seem. Go back to your boyhood days. What was your favorite game? Was it one that required initiative, quick

thinking, prompt action? Were you a better "individual player" or "team-player"? In other words, were you a brilliant "star," or one of those who could sink his own individuality for the good of the team?

Did you ever captain any team successfully? Did your teammates like you, work with you enthusiastically? Could you inspire loyalty, cooperation, weld your team into a single unit with a common purpose?

Qualities such as these can be acquired, of course, but if you had them naturally as a boy, then you have them now, so by all means develop them to their fullest extent. They can be made your most valuable assets in business.

2. What sort of game do you prefer now? One that depends primarily upon yourself— or one that demands mostly teamwork? Games are wonderful indicators, you know, of your innate characteristics. I used to know a very shrewd old fellow who never formed a business friendship until after he had played poker with his prospective friend. How do you play bridge—with your partner or regardless of him? How do you play tennis—as two individual players, or as a team?

Don't misunderstand me—I am not decrying brilliant individual play. I am just trying to get you to analyze your innate characteristics. If you play best alone, by all means concentrate on the kind of work or the kind of business that is built up around one single figure. On the other hand, if your forte is teamwork, cooperation—go in for organized effort where your leadership and fairness and good-fellowship will have the greatest play.

3. List your characteristics frankly. Ability in particular lines, quickness in picking up new ideas, open-mindedness, versatility, honesty, sociability, interest in others, power to convince others, courage, aggressiveness, stick-to-it-iveness.

Chapter 5: Start Something!

In short, analyze yourself frankly—then from that analysis, from your past failures and successes, pick the work you have the greatest aptitude for—and go into it!

Don't go into it blindly. First study it. There are good books on every phase of business today. There are correspondence courses as good as any taught in colleges. Get them. Read them. Set your goal. Make your plans carefully. Start them in a small way first. Test each step before you put your weight upon it. But once sure of it, put your whole weight into it—your money and your ability and all your thought— *particularly all your thought.*

Don't scatter your energies. You can do it with the work of your hands but you can't do it with your thought. To make a great success, your thought has to be concentrated on your goal in the same way that the Marconi beam system concentrates all the power of its rays in the one direction. "No man can serve two masters"— with justice to either.

Choose your goal; then, like the searchlight, concentrate all your efforts, all your energies, all your thoughts in the one direction. Don't go running off after false gods. Don't fritter away your energies on inconsequential side issues. Focus them—focus them as you focus the rays of the sun through a magnifying glass. Do that —and you will speedily start something!

There is a definite place for you in the Divine plan. There is a work which you are to do, which no one else can do quite as well. Pray, therefore, to the Father that He may open your eyes to your right work, that He may open your ears to the promptings of His voice, that He may open your understanding of the right way.

"I will instruct thee and teach thee in the way which thou shall go: I will guide thee with mine eye."—Psalms 32;8.

Chapter 6: Rough Diamonds

OVER in the northwestern corner of Pennsylvania a few years ago, there lived a farmer who was interested in oil. His brother was in the oil business in Canada and had told him that fortunes were being made in it every day. So he sent for all kinds of books that told how and where to locate oil, took a course in geology, spent two years getting ready—and then sold his farm and went to Canada to work in the oil fields.

The man who bought the farm, walking over the place next morning, came to a little brook that ran through the middle of it. There was a heavy board across the brook to hold back the surface drift, and back of it for some yards the water was coated with a thick scum.

It seems that this scum had troubled the previous owner for a long time. The cattle wouldn't drink the water with it on it. So he had conceived the idea of the board to clear the scum from the surface and let the cattle drink from the water below.

To the new buyer, that "scum" looked and smelled and tasted suspiciously like oil! He sent for experts. They bored. And opened up one of the richest oil fields in Pennsylvania!

It is natural to think that the first step towards success is to go somewhere else or into some new business. The distant pastures always look greenest. But more often than not, our best opportunities lic right under our own nose.

When the original Pennsylvania oil wells seemed to be worked out, most of the oil men set off for fields and pastures new. But a few stayed. And those few found that the surface had merely been scratched! Instead of being worked out, scarcely 15 percent of the oil had been taken out of the ground. By the pressure system, or by boring deeper and striking new deposits, they found the other 85 percent!

And that is only one industry out of hundreds where fortunes have been made out of what other men had thrown away as worthless. No one has yet exhausted any line of thought. The inventions that mankind has already made are merely the introduction to bigger and greater things—the open door to opportunity. The most brilliant scientists are the first to tell you that their discoveries are but as a drop of water to the great ocean of achievement that lies beyond.

"For the earth shall be filled with the knowledge of the glory of the Lord, as the waters cover the sea."—Habakuk 2:14.

Nearly a century and a half ago, Malthus propounded his famous theory that population, when unchecked, tends to increase in geometrical proportion, whereas subsistence increases only in arithmetical proportion. In other words, that population increases many times as rapidly as the means of subsistence. And he visioned a time in the very near future when artificial checks would have to be put on population, or the world would starve.

Population has increased very near to the point he feared, but what has happened? We are farther away from the saturation point than in his day! The age of machinery came along; the age of scientific experiment; and these not only opened up new fields through better transportation, but greatly increased the yields in present fields. Now Prof. Albrecht Penck advances the belief that by the year 2227 there will be 8,000,000,000 people here on earth—and famine will be continuous, because the earth cannot support that many!

What little faith some of these economists have! They get so wrapped up in their own calculations that they can see nothing else. "By that time (2227 A. D.)," says the New York *Herald Tribune,* "man may be taking foodstuffs from the sunlight, from the air or from the power of the revolving earth! The only safe prediction about the future of man is that no limit dare be set to what he and Nature may cooperate to do."

"For I know the thoughts that I think towards you, saith the Lord, thoughts of peace and not of evil, to give you an expected end. Then, shall ye call upon me, and ye shall go and pray unto me and I will hearken unto you. And ye shall seek me, and find me, when ye shall search for me with all your heart."— Jeremiah 29:11-13.

For 5,000 years men have built houses of brick, and in all of that time there had been no change made, either in the tools used, or in the manner in which the work was done.

Along came Frank Gilbreth, studied the motions involved in laying brick, reduced them from eighteen to five, and increased the hourly output from 120 to 350 bricks!

Simple enough—but it took 5,000 years for someone to think up this simple solution. For 5,000 years mankind has been taught that some men are born with ability—some without—and that those without must serve those who have it.

No greater mistake was ever made. Every man is born with ability sufficient to carry him upward to the highest rung of success. "Ordinary ability, properly applied," said Theodore N. Vail, "is all that is necessary to reach the highest rung in the ladder of success."

Life's biggest blunder is to underestimate your own power to develop and accomplish. What if you are handicapped by lack of education, by poverty, by self-consciousness, by sickness, by some physical disability?

Thank God for it! A handicap is the greatest urge you can have towards success. Like the eagle which uses adverse winds to rise higher, you can mount to success on your handicap.

Chapter 6: Rough Diamonds

In an editorial some time ago, the *New York Globe* observed: "Nature is not democratic. She gives some women beauty and leaves others, of equal or greater merit, plain. She makes some persons intelligent and some stupid. In brief, we are not born free and equal nor do we become so. To some the Gods bring gifts and others they pass by. There are aristocracies of voices, of beauty and of intelligence. The best that democracy can ever do is to give every Caruso a chance to sing."

That is the general belief. That is the idea that prevails among most casual thinkers. But the man who thinks thus is overlooking the greatest force in life— the reserve force that lies so dormant in most of us—the power of the Spirit within to rise superior to any inequality, to overcome any seeming handicap or difficulty.

The greatest thing that can happen to any man is the discovery of this all-powerful Spirit within him. If it is necessary for him to undergo hunger, if it is necessary for him to suffer sickness or injury in order to make the discovery, let him suffer it cheerfully, gladly! No price is too high to pay to bring into your affairs the power of the Holy Spirit. For everything you have suffered, everything you have paid, will be made good to you a hundredfold. There is no maybe about this. I have seen it work out hundreds of times. I have learned it from very bitter experience. As in the case of Job of olden times:

"The Lord gave Job twice as much as he had before.

"So the Lord blessed the latter end of Job more than his beginning; for he had fourteen thousand sheep, and six thousand camels, and a thousand yoke of oxen and a thousand she asses.

"He had also seven sons and three daughters."—Job 42:10, 12, 13.

The Law of Compensation

Chapter 6: Rough Diamonds

What was it made Demosthenes the greatest orator of all time? NOT his natural gifts—but his natural handicaps! He was self-conscious. And he stuttered. Had he not been thus handicapped, he would probably have become a mediocre orator—and lived and died unknown to the world. But he had to study so hard to overcome his natural handicaps, he had to practice and work so long and so whole-heartedly, that when at last he was ready to appear before the public, his conscious efforts were backed by all the powers of the subconscious. He had so often called upon the Spirit within to help him in his practice that it came to his aid of Itself when the real need arose. It stood at his back to give him confidence, to lend him inspiration, to supply the power that moved his hearers as they had never been moved before.

In "Organ Inferiority and Its Psychic Compensation," Dr. Adler brings out the well-known scientific fact that any physical weakness or inferiority brings with it an extra urge to strive for superiority in some compensating way.

Napoleon, Caesar, Prince Eugene were little men, but the urge within them made them the biggest men of their day.

Whistler, the greater painter, had poor eyes. He was said to be colorblind. So he became a master in nuances. Edison was deaf—so he perfected the talking machine.

Beethoven, Mozart, Franz—all had defects in hearing. And worked so hard at their music that they became masters of technique, and musical geniuses.

The same principle applies to nations. Take Alaska and Switzerland as an instance. Alaska has enormous resources of gold and silver and copper and coal, vast virgin forests, 1,000,000 square miles suitable for agriculture, and the greatest fisheries in the world. Yet if Alaska were as densely populated as Switzerland it would be supporting 120,000,000 inhabitants!

The Swiss have few natural resources, so they are constrained to use their ingenuity instead. They take a ton of metal and put it together in such form as to make it worth a million dollars. They take cotton thread at 20 cents a pound, and convert it into lace worth $2,000 a pound. They take a block of wood worth 10 cents and convert it into a carving worth $100. And because as a nation they have learned the art of utilizing their talents, they have prospered abundantly.

Where is the moral? Simply this:

There is no lack, no handicap, *nothing,* that can defeat you. Obstacles are the greatest blessings God can give you. They bring out the soul of you. They bring the Holy Spirit to your help. And anything which acquaints you with the Spirit within you, anything that gives you an understanding of the infinite power within you, anything that brings the Holy Spirit into your daily affairs, is worthwhile no matter what its cost.

"And Jacob was left alone; and there wrestled a man with him until the breaking of the day.

"And when he saw that he prevailed not against him, he touched the hollow of his thigh; and the hollow of Jacob's thigh was out of joint, as he wrestled with him.

"And he said, Let me go, for the day breaketh. And he said, I will not let thee go, *except thou bless me.*

"And he said unto him, What is thy name? And he said, Jacob.

"And he said,, Thy name shall be called no more Jacob, but Israel: for as a prince hast thou power with God and with men, and hast prevailed.

Chapter 6: Rough Diamonds

"And Jacob asked him, and said, Tell me, I pray thee, thy name. And he said, Wherefore is it that thou dost ask after my name? *And he blessed him there.*"

That is what you, too, must do. Wrestle with every difficulty until you have learned something from it. Don't let go of any trouble until you have made it bless you.

Remember that back of you always is the power of the Holy Spirit and if the need arises, it can give you the strength—not merely of one man, but of ten! Like David going out to meet Goliath, realize that it is not you who is fighting the battle, but God. "Be not afraid, nor dismayed by reason of this great multitude; for the battle is not yours but God's."—II Chronicles 20:15. Knowing that, no obstacle need deter you, no experience terrify you. With God on your side, you are always in the majority. Struggles and trials are mere growing pains of your soul, to teach you that, though terrifying to you alone, they are as nothing to you when allied to the Father through the Holy Spirit.

Before you give up where you are and move to distant fields, before you seek your fortune afar, look around you! See if some of the riches in your own back yard won't bear cultivating.

There is a story told of an old Boer farmer living on a rocky bit of ground on the road between Kimberley and Pretoria. Scattered here and there over the ground, they often found dull looking pieces of crystal. The boys used them to throw at the sheep. Until one day a Cecil Rhodes engineer happened that way—*and discovered them to be diamonds!*

Many of us are just as literally walking on diamonds in the rough as were that farmer's boys. Only most of us never know it until someone comes along and points them out to us.

Chapter 6: Rough Diamonds

Let us resolve to do some of this discovering for our own selves. Let us look at every job with the question—how can this be done easier, quicker, better? Let us devote part of our thoughts to finding new outlets, new methods, new needs. Let us get a fixed objective —and then work towards it. Some great thinker once said that we should be a world of successes if the idea of a fixed objective and a set goal possessed us.

A fixed objective—it serves much the same as the controlling idea outlined in Chapter 3, magnetizing your thoughts and your work and yourself with the one intense desire. Add to that a sublime faith that shall bring the Holy Spirit within into cooperation with you— and your objective is assured.

"First have something good," said Horace Greeley, "then advertise!" First have your fixed objective, then call upon the Holy Spirit to help you, and there is no goal you cannot win.

"For the vision is yet for an appointed time, but at the end it shall speak, and not lie; though it tarry, wait for it; because it will surely come; it will not tarry."— Habakkuk2:3.

I know a man who had a $2,500 job. He had just been offered another paying $500 more. And he went to a friend of mine to ask his advice about changing. The first question my friend asked was what he had to offer these new people. He told him, the usual round of routine knowledge.

"That isn't worth much," my friend informed him. "These people are in the same line of business that you have been working at for years. If in all those years you haven't thought out ways in which that work could be vastly improved, if you haven't been perfecting in your own mind short cuts, money-saving ways, practical ideas— then hold on to your $2,500 job until you do. You're not worth a cent more.

Chapter 6: Rough Diamonds

"My advice to you is to go home and write down on paper what you have to offer this new firm. What new methods you can show them that any other $2,500 man can't. What new ideas you have that will make money for them.

"When you get them all down, center your attention on the best of them, and work it out. Then go to these people and tell them you will give them your idea and your services—NOT for $3,000, but for $6,000!"

That talk woke this man up. He did some really serious thinking for the first time in his business life. With the result that he refused the $3,000 offer then, but kept the position open for a few weeks until he could get his big idea ready.

Then he not only landed his $6,000 but made good on his idea so completely that within six months that $6,000 was increased to $7,200.

"There is guidance for each one of us," says Emerson, "and by lowly listening we shall hear the right word." Give of your best—not merely in manual labor but in ideas—and you can safely leave the rest to the guidance of the Holy Spirit within.

As pointed out in *The Secret of the Ages,* the basic principles of all business are the same, be they as big as the Steel Trust or as small as the corner newsstand. The whole practice of commerce is founded upon them. Summed up, and boiled down to the fewest possible words, they are two:

I—Give to get.

2—This one thing I do.

1—You can get away with dishonest values, with poor service, for a little while. You can take two dollars worth of value for every one you give. But the Law of Karma will get you soon or late. If you intend to stay in business, it pays to make it a rule to try to give a little more of value or of service than you are paid for.

2—Remember that each task, no matter how great, is but a group of little tasks, any one of which you can easily do. Like the great New York subways, it is but a succession of cellars connected together. Find a place to start. Take the first step. The rest will follow easily.

So many are afraid of giving too much for the amount that is paid them. And so many wives get inflated ideas of their husband's value to or work in a business, and urge them not to give so much unless the business pays them more for it.

Poor things—they mean well. But no man ever has to be urged not to work too hard at his business. He can work too hard at worrying about it—yes. But every bit of honest work he puts into his business will pay him an honest return. He is not working merely for some man or some institution. He is doing God's work. And God is the most generous Paymaster there is. He doesn't label His paychecks. He doesn't say—"This is in payment of such-and-such invoices." But the pay comes—just as surely as the day follows night.

"I cause those that love me to inherit substance; and I will fill their treasures."— Proverbs 8:21.

There is a place for you in the Divine plan—a place that no one but you can fill. There is a work for you in the great scheme of things —a work that no one can do as well as you.

So, if you have been drifting, if your work has been joyless, your business profitless, look around you for the right niche that was made for you to fill. Don't mind how humble it may seem. To do even the most humble thing supremely well is artistry—and will bring its reward. Let your daily prayer to the Spirit within you be that He manifest the Divine design in your life—that He bring you to your proper work, your right place.

Say to Him each day, as F. S. Shinn suggests in *The Game of Life and How to Play It*—"Infinite Spirit, open the way for the Divine design in my life to manifest. Let the genius within me now be released. Let me see clearly the perfect plan."

And then, if you like, ask Him to give you a lead, an indication of the next step for you to take.

"Call upon the Almighty," says the old Eastern Sage. "He will help thee. Thou needst not perplex thyself about anything else. Shut thy eyes and while thou art asleep, God will change thy bad fortune into good."

"Blessed is the man that trusteth in the Lord, and whose hope the Lord is. For he shall be as a tree planted by the waters, and that spreadeth out her roots by the river, and shall not see when heat cometh, but her leaf shall be green; and shall not be careful in the year of drought, neither shall cease from yielding fruit."—JEREMIAH 17:7-8.

Chapter 7: Ich Dien—I Serve

YOU want riches. You want five talents, ten talents, a thousand—a million. But what have you to offer in return? Has it never occurred to you that you must make an accounting of them?

If someone were to offer you a million right now, what would you do with it? Buy a yacht—an automobile—have a good time! But what sort of an accounting would that make for the Master? And why should He put Himself out to place riches in hands no better prepared to use them to good purpose than that?

Suppose you went to a banker for money—a banker who knew you well—and asked him to lend you $100,000. What is the first question he would ask of you? "What are you going to do with it?"

If you could give him no better answer than—"Buy a yacht, an automobile, have a good time"—how much do you suppose he would lend you? Not a red cent! No more will the Father which is in Heaven.

You have got to have an idea first before you can borrow money from a bank. And if the banker is wise, he will make you prove your idea in a small way before he will advance you any great sum to spend upon it.

And when you approach the Father for ten talents or a thousand, you must first have an idea that will be of some benefit to mankind.

Henry Ford is worth a billion dollars. He is probably the richest man in the world. How did he get it?

He started out with an idea—an idea that the automobile should be put within reach of everyone. That idea was of definite benefit to mankind. It opened up remote districts. It brought light and life into

84

the lives of millions of farm dwellers. He was entitled to a generous reward.

Woolworth accumulated a fortune of millions. He performed a definite service. So did Penny. So has many another merchant on a smaller scale. And the supply flows to him in proportion. But before reward, must come the idea. You must give to get.

The United States has become the richest of all peoples. Half the world's gold is in our possession. In 75 years the wealth of the country has increased fifty times over. All the world has become richer, but in no other country has the wealth increased to anything like that extent. Why?

Some will say because of our great natural resources. But Mexico has great natural resources. So has Russia. And China. Yet all these countries are backward.

What then is the answer?

The fact that in America manufacturers have learned to share with the workers the fruits of industry. America began to forge ahead of the rest of the world the moment its manufacturers learned that every worker was entitled to a share of the good things of life.

Automobile manufacturers saw every workman as a potential automobile owner. And then proceeded to make that ideal feasible. Telephone companies, gas companies, electric light and equipment companies, radio manufacturers, saw every home as a user of their products—and proceeded to put them within the reach of all.

Never since life first appeared upon this planet has there been so much of comfort, happiness and contentment among all the people as there is in these United States. And the reason? Free education. Equal opportunity. And the realization on the part of manufacturers that their best market and their biggest one is right among the workers—that the more they share with the workers, the more will come back to them.

You must give to get.

Russia has enormous resources of land and minerals and oil. So has China. And Mexico.
Why then are they so poor?

Because the ruling classes have tried to keep all these riches for themselves. They wanted to take all—and give nothing. That may work for a little while, but always there is an accounting.

"For they have sown the wind, and they shall reap the whirlwind: it hath no stalk: the bud shall yield no meal: if so be it yield, the strangers shall swallow it up."—Hosea 8:7.

You must give to get.

There is a story by Samuel Butler that describes the idea exactly:

"In Erehwon," he says, "he who makes a colossal fortune in the hosiery trade and by his energy has succeeded in reducing the price of woolen goods by the thousandeth part of a penny in a pound, this man is worth ten professional philanthropists. So strongly are the Erehwonians impressed with this that if a man has made a fortune of over £20,000 a year they exempt him from all taxation, considering him as a work of art and too precious to be meddled with. They say, 'How much he must have done for society before society could be prevailed upon to give him so much money!' "

Unfortunately, we have not yet reached the ideal state visioned by Butler, where every millionaire earned his money through unusual service to the community. Too many are still robber captains or greedy moneylenders like Cassim.

86

The Law of Karma is steadily at work. Give it time. There is always an accounting. Meantime, thank God for the Fords and the Edisons and the Burbanks and the thousands of others of their kind who are not only making this the richest country on earth, but are helping to spread those riches around and make it also the happiest.

The Bank of God

The true purpose of every worthy business is to help in the distribution of God's gifts among men.

Judge your work, your ideas, by that standard. If you want money, if you seek riches, ask yourself—"Could I go to God and tell Him as my banker that the purpose for which I want this money is anything but a selfish one? Could I honestly assure Him that my primary idea is service—giving to people a little better value, a little more of service, a little greater comfort or convenience or happiness than they are now getting?"

Don't misunderstand me. You are entitled to money to meet your daily needs. You have a right to ask for all those things necessary to your happiness, as long as they do not infringe upon the happiness of others. You even have a right to demand just as much more than that as you can use to advantage. But you have got to account for it!

Given a right idea, given a controlling thought, dollars will seek you, even as iron filings seek the magnet. You can claim all that you can use to good advantage.

So get your thought right first. Make sure that you have something the world needs. Then draw on the Great Banker for all the money you need, never fearing, never doubting that He will honor your draft.

"For the Lord God is a sun and shield. The Lord will give grace and glory. No good thing will he withhold from them that walk uprightly."—Psalms 84:11.

After all the proofs of God's power to supply them with food and water; after He had brought them safely through every conceivable danger; when another crucial time came, the children of Israel fearfully called out—"Can God furnish us a table in the wilderness?"— Psalms 78:19.

Of course He can!

"Hast thou not known? Hast thou not heard? That the everlasting God, the Lord, the Creator of the ends of the earth, fainteth not, neither is weary?"—Isaiah 40:28.

Draw on Him as you need. Don't wait to start until you have all the money in hand. How many businesses—big and successful today— do you suppose would have been started if their founders had waited until they had all the money in hand they were going to need? Use the talent you have. Your credit is good for just as much more as you can use to advantage. More than that is a weight around your neck.

If you had a business proposition, and knew that your banker would extend you credit to the extent of a million dollars to develop it, you wouldn't think of drawing that million all at once. No—you would ask for credit as you needed it. You would draw upon it only as your business required it. You wouldn't burden yourself with one cent more of interest than was necessary.

Do likewise with the Lord. If your banker promised you the money as you needed it, you would go ahead with your plans, secure in the knowledge that his word was just as good as the actual money in the bank. Do you rate the promises of the Father any lower than those of man?

Chapter 7: Ich Dien—I Serve

"Be glad then, ye children of Zion, and rejoice in the Lord your God: for he hath given you the former rain moderately, and he will cause to come down for you the rain, the former rain, and the latter rain in the first month.

"And the floors shall be full of wheat, and the vats shall overflow with wine and oil.

"And ye shall eat in plenty, and be satisfied, and praise the name of the Lord your God, that hath dealt wondrously with you: and my people shall never be ashamed.

"And ye shall know that I am in the midst of Israel, and that I am the Lord your God, and none else: and my people shall never be ashamed."—JOEL 2:21, 23, 24, 26, 27.

What is it you want money for? Get your idea clearly in mind. Satisfy yourself that it is for a worthy purpose. And when you are thoroughly satisfied of that, then go right ahead with your plans.

How much do you need for this stage of them? How much would you draw on the bank for, this moment, if you had unlimited credit there? $100? $1,000? $10,000? Explain your need to the Father just as you would to a very wise and sympathetic banker. Then tell Him you are drawing upon Him for that amount. Actually write out a draft and mail it—anywhere—to me if you like. Then go about your plans as confidently, as believingly, as though the Father's Bank were just around the corner.

But don't try to fool yourself. Above all, don't try to deceive the Father. Don't camouflage merely selfish desires in some high and mighty guise as benefits to mankind.

Remember the old Spanish Conquistadores? Freebooters they were —neither more nor less—searching for booty, and caring not how they came by it. They robbed the Indians, they massacred thousands, they enslaved whole nations—all for lust of gold.

But that wasn't their tale about it. They put it all upon the high and mighty plane of spreading Christianity, of saving the souls of the heathen.

It worked for the Spaniards for a little while. But they became so puffed up that they thought to use the same ideas upon the heretics of England, of the Netherlands, upon the entire world. Then came the disastrous Armada, followed by swift and certain decline.

It was only 300 years ago that Spain was the richest nation in the world, her power pre-eminent in Europe, her sovereignty extending over most of America. Now look at her—even the Riffians laughed at her until France came to her aid.

We reap what we sow. A grain of corn planted reproduces only corn. A grain of wheat brings forth wheat. And the seed of the deadly nightshade brings forth poisonous flowers.

God cannot be mocked. We reap in kind exactly as we sow.

What then shall you do to succeed? What is the modern law of business? The same as two commandments given to us thousands of years ago:

"Thou shalt love the Lord thy God with all thy heart and with all thy soul and with all thy mind." And, "Thou shalt love thy neighbor as thyself."

"Thou shalt love the Lord thy God." Thou shalt use the talents He has given thee. Thou shalt use them to benefit thy neighbor, to benefit all of mankind, and in so doing thou shalt benefit thyself. Do that, and thy Lord will say unto thee: "Well done, thou good and faithful servant; thou hast been faithful over a few things, I will make thee ruler over many things: enter thou into the joy of thy Lord."

But to those who fail to use, or who abuse their talent, the Lord says even as he did of the unprofitable servant: "Take therefore the talent from him and cast him into outer darkness: there shall be weeping and gnashing of teeth."

Chapter 8: The Coming of the Spirit

THERE was a certain Sultan of the Indies that had three sons, the eldest called Houssain, the second Ali, the third Ahmed.

He had also a niece, remarkable for her wit and beauty, named Nouronnihar, whom all three Princes loved and desired to wed.

Their father remonstrated with them, pointed out the troubles that would ensue if they persisted in their attachment, and did all he could to persuade them to abide by his choice of which of them should wed her.

Failing that, he sent for them one day and suggested that the three Princes should depart on a three-months' journey, each to a different country. Upon their return, whichever one should bring to him the most extraordinary rarity as a gift, should receive the Princess in marriage.

The three Princes cheerfully consented to this, each flattering himself that fortune would prove favorable to him. The Sultan gave them money, and early next morning they all went out at the same gate of the city, each dressed like a merchant, attended by a trusty officer habited as a slave, and all well mounted and equipped. The first day's journey they proceeded together; and at night, when they were at supper, they agreed to meet again in three months at the khan where they were stopping; and that the first who came should wait for the rest; so that as they had all three taken leave together of the Sultan, they might return in company. The next morning, after they had embraced and wished each other success, they mounted their horses, and took each a different road.

Prince Houssain, the eldest brother, had heard of the riches and splendor of the kingdom of Bisnagar and bent his course toward it.

Chapter 8: The Coming of the Spirit

Arriving there, he betook himself to the quarters of the traders, where a merchant, seeing him go by much fatigued, invited him to sit down in front of his shop. He had not been seated long before a crier appeared, with a small piece of carpeting on his arm, for which he asked forty purses. The Prince told him that he could not understand how so small a piece of carpeting could be set at so high a price, unless it had something very extraordinary about it which failed to show in its appearance.

You have guessed right, sir," I replied the crier; "whoever sits on this piece of carpeting may be carried in an instant wherever he desires." "If that is so," said the Prince, "I shall not think forty purses too much." "Sir," replied the crier, "I have told you the truth. Let us go into the back warehouse, where I will spread the carpet. When we have both sat down, form the wish to be transported into your apartment at the khan, and if we are not conveyed there at once, it shall be no bargain."

On the Prince agreeing to this, they went into the merchant's back shop, where they both sat down on the carpet; and as soon as the Prince had expressed his wish to be carried to his apartment at the khan, he in an instant found himself and the crier there. After this convincing proof of the virtue of the carpet, he paid over to the crier forty purses of gold, together with an extra purse for himself.

Prince Houssain was overjoyed at his good fortune, never doubting that this rare carpet would gain him the possession of the beautiful Nouronnihar.

After seeing all the wonders of Bisnagar, Prince Houssain wished to be nearer his dear Princess, so he took and spread the carpet, and with the officer whom he had brought with him, commanded the carpet to transport them to the caravansery at which he and his brothers were to meet, where he passed for a merchant till their arrival.

Chapter 8: The Coming of the Spirit

Prince Ali, the second brother, designed to travel into Persia, so, after parting with his brothers, joined a caravan, and soon arrived at Shiraz, the capital of that empire.

Walking through the quarters of the jewelers, he was not a little surprised to see one who held in his hand an ivory tube, about a foot in length, and about an inch thick, which he priced at fifty purses. At first he thought the man mad, and asked him what he meant by asking fifty purses for a tube which seemed scarcely worth one. The jeweler replied, "Sir, you shall judge yourself whether I am mad or not, when I have told you the property of this tube. By looking through it, you can see whatever object you wish to behold."

The jeweler presented the tube to the Prince, and he looked through it, wishing at the same time to see the Sultan his father. Immediately he saw before him the image of his father, sitting on his throne, in the midst of his council. Next, he wished to see the Princess Nouronnihar; and instantly beheld her laughing and talking with the women about her.

Prince Ali needed no other proof to persuade him that this tube was the most valuable of gifts in all the world, and taking the crier to the khan where he lodged, paid him his fifty purses and received the tube.

Prince Ali was overjoyed at his purchase, for he felt fully assured that his brothers would not be able to meet with anything so rare and admirable, and the Princess Nouronnihar would be his. His only thought now was to get back to the rendezvous as speedily as might be, so without waiting to visit any of the wonders of Shiraz, he joined a party of merchants and arrived without accident at the place appointed, where he found Prince Houssain, and both waited for Prince Ahmed.

Prince Ahmed had taken the road to Samarcand, and the day after his arrival went, as his brothers had done, into the merchants quarters, where he had not walked long before he heard a crier, with an artificial apple in his hand, offer it at five-and-forty purses. "Let me see your apple," he said to the man, "and tell me what extraordinary property it possesses, to be valued at so high a rate." "Sir," replied the crier, giving the apple into his hand, "if you look at the mere outside of this apple it is not very remarkable; but if you consider its miraculous properties, you will say it is invaluable. It cures sick people of every manner of disease. Even if a person is dying, it will cure him instantly, and this merely by his smelling of the apple."

"If that be true," replied Prince Ahmed, "this apple is indeed invaluable; but how am I to know that it is true?'" "Sir," replied the crier, "the truth is attested by the whole city of Samarcand; ask any of these merchants here. Several of them will tell you they had not been alive today had it not been for this excellent remedy."

Many people had gathered round while they talked, and now confirmed what the crier had declared. One among them said he had a friend dangerously ill, whose life was despaired of; so they could now see for themselves the truth of all that was said. Upon this Prince Ahmed told the crier he would give him forty-five purses for the apple if it cured the sick person by smelling it.

"Come, sir," said the crier to Prince Ahmed, "let us go and do it, and the apple shall be yours."

The sick man smelled of the apple, and was cured; and the prince, after he had paid the forty-five purses, received the apple. He then joined himself to the first caravan that set out for the Indies, and arrived in perfect health at the caravansery, where the Princes Houssain and Ali waited for him.

The brothers embraced with tenderness, and felicitated each other on their safe journeys.

Chapter 8: The Coming of the Spirit

They then fell to comparing gifts. Houssain showed the carpet and told how it had brought him thither. Ali brought out the ivory tube, and nothing would do but they must at once look through it at their beloved. But—alas and alack! For the sight that met their eyes. The Princess Nouronnihar lay stretched on her bed, seemingly at the point of death.

When Prince Ahmed had seen this, he turned to his two brothers. "Make haste," he adjured them, "lose no time; we may save her life. This apple which I hold here has this wonderful property—its smell will restore to life a sick person. I have tried it and will show you its wonderful effect on the Princess, if you will but hasten to her."

"If haste be all," answered Houssain, "we cannot do better than transport ourselves instantly into her chamber on my magic carpet. Come, lose no time, sit down, it is large enough to hold us all."

The order was no sooner given than they found themselves carried into the Princess Nouronnihar's chamber.

Prince Ahmed rose off the carpet, and went to her bedside, where he put the apple to her nostrils. Immediately the Princess opened her eyes, expressed her joy at seeing them, and thanked them all for their efforts in her behalf.

While she was dressing, the Princes went to present themselves to the Sultan, their father. The Sultan received them with joy. The Princes presented each the rarity which he had brought, and begged of him to pronounce their fate.

The Sultan of the Indies considered what answer he should make. At last he said, "I would that I could declare for one of you, my sons, but I cannot do it with justice. It is true, Ahmed, that the Princess owes her cure to your artificial apple; but let me ask you, could you have cured her if you had not known of the danger she was in through Ali's tube, and if Houssain's carpet had not brought you to her so quickly? Your tube, Ali, discovered to you and your brothers the illness of your cousin; but the knowledge of her illness would have been of no service without the artificial apple and the carpet. And as for you, Houssain, your carpet was an essential instrument in effecting her cure. But it would have been of little use, if you had not known of her illness through All's tube, or if Ahmed had not been there with his artificial apple. Therefore, as I see it, the carpet, the ivory tube, and the artificial apple have no preference over each other, on the contrary, each had an equal share in her cure."

The story goes on to tell how the Sultan, after repeated trials, finally did choose a husband for the Princess. How Prince Ali wed her. How Prince Ahmed wandered away, disconsolate. How he met the Fairy Princess Banou. And how through her he finally won the greatest prize of all—contact with the Spirit within that knows all, sees all and can do all things.

In *The Secret of the Ages,* I endeavored to show how your subconscious mind can be made to serve as the Ivory Tube, giving you the answer to any problem you may put up to it in the right way.

In later volumes of this set, I shall try to prove to you how the Spirit within can and gladly will serve you better than Magic Carpet or Curative Apple. Length of days is in His right hand, freedom from fear, protection from harm, health, happiness and prosperity.

Do I promise too much? Just listen:

"But be ye glad and rejoice for ever in that which I create: for, behold, I create Jerusalem a rejoicing, and her people a joy.

"And I will rejoice in Jerusalem, and joy in my people: and the voice of weeping shall be no more heard in her, nor the voice of crying.

"There shall be no more thence an infant of days, nor an old man that hath not filled his days:

"And they shall build houses, and inhabit them; and they shall plant vineyards, and eat the fruit of them.

"They shall not build, and another inhabit; they shall not plant, and another eat: for as the days of a tree are the days of my people, and mine elect shall long enjoy the work of their hands.

"They shall not labour in vain, nor bring forth for trouble; for they are the seed of the blessed of the Lord, and their offspring with them.

"And it shall come to pass, that before they call, I will answer; and while they are yet speaking, I will hear."—ISAIAH 65:18-24.

But how to find this Kingdom? How shall we bring the Holy Spirit into our lives?

By going into the quiet, into thought. By concentrating all thoughts on communing with the Father above, without outside distractions. By praying. And if we will pray rightly, the heaven will open to us and God will come upon us.

But He will never do it for the mere repetition of lip prayers that we have learned by rote.

The Soul's Sincere Desire

Do you know what prayer is? Just an earnest desire that we take to God—to Universal Mind—for fulfillment. As Montgomery puts it —"Prayer is the soul's sincere desire, uttered or unexpressed." It is our Heart's Desire. At least, the only prayer that is worth anything is the prayer that asks for our real desires. That kind of prayer is heard. That kind of prayer is answered. (From *The Secret of the Ages.)*

Mere lip prayers get you nowhere. It doesn't matter what your lips may say. The thing that counts is what your heart desires, what your mind images on your subconscious thought, and through it on Divine Mind.

Go where you can be alone, where you can concentrate your thoughts on your one innermost sincere desire, where you can impress that desire upon the Spirit within, and so reach the Father.

But even sincere desire is not enough by itself. There must be BELIEF, too. "What things soever ye desire, when ye pray, believe that ye *receive* them and ye shall *have* them." You must realize God's ability to give you every good thing. You must believe in His readiness to do it. Model your thoughts after the Psalmists of old. They first asked for that which they wanted, then killed all doubts and fears by affirming God's power and His willingness to grant their prayers.

What is it you want most right now? Ask yourself frankly—Is it good that I should receive this? Is it right? Will it work no injustice to anyone else? Then have no hesitancy in asking it of the Father— secure in the knowledge that anything of good He will gladly give to you. Here is His promise. Read it, and see if you can still doubt:

"I will say of the Lord, He is my refuge and my fortress: my God; in Him will I trust.

"Surely He shall deliver thee from the snare of the fowler, and from the noisome pestilence.

"He shall cover thee with His feathers, and under His wings shalt thou trust: His truth shall be thy shield and buckler.

Chapter 8: The Coming of the Spirit

"Thou shalt not be afraid for the terror by night; nor for the arrow that flieth by day.

"Nor for the pestilence that walketh in darkness; nor for the destruction that wasteth at noonday.

"A thousand shall fall at thy side, and ten thousand at thy right hand; but it shall not
come nigh thee.

"Because thou Hast made the Lord, which is my refuge, even the most High, thy habitation.

"There shall no evil befall thee, neither shall any plague come nigh thy dwelling.

"For He shall give His angels charge over thee, to keep thee in all thy ways.

"They shall bear thee up in their hands, lest thou dash thy foot against a stone.

"Thou shalt tread upon the lion and adder: the young lion and the dragon shalt thou
trample under foot.

"Because he hath set his love upon me, therefore will I deliver him: I will set him on high, because he hath known my name.

"He shall call upon me, and I will answer him: I will be with him in trouble; I will
deliver him, and honor him.

"With long life will I satisfy him, and show him my salvation."—
PSALMS 91:6.

Chapter 8: The Coming of the Spirit

"Surely goodness and mercy shall follow me all the days of my life. And I will dwell in the house of the Lord forever." —PSALMS 23:6.

The Bible prepares us to do God's work, guiding us how to use our spiritual powers, offering detailed instructions to follow and practice.

Don't you suppose that you can follow them quite easily—can practice them successfully?

Let's try! In the volumes to come, I am going to do my humble best to continue to show the way.

WE HAVE BOOK RECOMMENDATIONS FOR YOU

**The Power of Your Subconscious Mind by Joseph Murphy
ABRIDGED - (Audio CD)**

**The Power of Your Subconscious Mind by Joseph Murphy
MP3 [UNABRIDGED] (Audio CD)**

**Think and Grow Rich [MP3 AUDIO] [UNABRIDGED]
by Napoleon Hill, Jason McCoy (Narrator) (Audio CD)**

**As a Man Thinketh [UNABRIDGED]
by James Allen, Jason McCoy (Narrator) (Audio CD)**

**Your Invisible Power: How to Attain Your Desires by Letting
Your Subconscious Mind Work for You [MP3 AUDIO]
[UNABRIDGED]
by Genevieve Behrend, Jason McCoy (Narrator) (Audio CD)**

Thought Vibration or the Law of Attraction in the Thought World [MP3 AUDIO] [UNABRIDGED]
by William Walker Atkinson, Jason McCoy (Narrator)
(Audio CD)

www.bnpublishing.com

Lightning Source UK Ltd.
Milton Keynes UK
UKOW022035130113

204812UK00004B/260/P